German Disarmament after World War I

This book examines the difficult challenge that disarming Germany posed to the Allied enforcement of the Treaty of Versailles.

The destructive legacy of war convinced the victorious nations, especially Britain and France, of the importance in minimizing German military strength. French post-war security concerns, however, were often faced with the unwillingness of Britain to enforce the totality of the military articles of the treaty while German obstruction also influenced Allied disarmament policies.

The book examines three major areas of the international disarmament of Germany from 1920–1931: the role and experience of international arms inspectors working amidst an embittered German populace, the ramifications of the divergent disarmament priorities of Britain and France, and the effectiveness of united allied policies backed by sanctions. Despite strained Allied relations and German violations of the military clauses of the treaty, the author demonstrates that arms inspections crippled Germany's ability to pose a military threat to European security.

This book will be of great interest to students of military history, modern European history and security studies.

Richard J. Shuster is a historian for the Defense Intelligence Agency (DIA) in Washington, DC. His research interests include inter-war diplomatic and modern military history.

Cass series: strategy and history
Series editors: Colin Gray and Williamson Murray
ISSN: 1473-6403

This new series will focus on the theory and practice of strategy. Following
Clausewitz, strategy has been understood to mean the use made of force,
and the threat of the use of force, for the ends of policy. This series is as
interested in ideas as in historical cases of grand strategy and military
strategy in action. All historical periods, near and past, and even future,
are of interest. In addition to original monographs, the series will from
time to time publish edited reprints of neglected classics as well as collec-
tions of essays.

German Disarmament after World War I

The diplomacy of international arms inspection 1920–1931

Richard J. Shuster

Routledge
Taylor & Francis Group

LONDON AND NEW YORK

First published 2006
by Routledge
2 Park Square, Milton Park, Abingdon, Oxon OX14 4RN

Simultaneously published in the USA and Canada
by Routledge
270 Madison Ave, New York, NY 10016

Routledge is an imprint of the Taylor & Francis Group

© 2006 Richard J. Shuster

Typeset in Sabon by Wearset Ltd, Boldon, Tyne and Wear
Printed and bound in Great Britain by Biddles Ltd, King's Lynn, Norfolk

British Library Cataloguing in Publication Data
A catalogue record for this book is available from the British Library

Library of Congress Cataloging in Publication Data
A catalog record for this book has been requested.

ISBN 0–415–35808–6

Contents

To my family

1 Introduction

When the guns in Europe fell silent on 11 November 1918, the victorious Allied and Associated Powers, as well as the defeated Central Powers and their allies, opened their eyes to a Europe changed forever by the brutality of war. Over eight million soldiers had died, roughly equal to the amount killed in the previous eight centuries of warfare in Europe.[1] The rapid advance of technology had outpaced the strategic and tactical doctrines of the great European General Staffs and had helped lead to the sustained and costly casualty rate. Geopolitical ambition, diplomatic ineptitude, arrogance, willpower, obsolete planning, together with the twentieth-century arsenal of heavy artillery, machine-guns, tanks, poison gas, submarines and airplanes, had destroyed a generation. Hence, the leaders of the victorious powers vowed never to allow the repetition of such a catastrophic event. Britain and France held the fate of the powerful German military in their hands, and the diplomatic path upon which the two nations embarked would leave an indelible mark upon the entire post-war decade.

Spawned by strategic concerns and the moral outrage left as a legacy of World War I, the Allies initiated their decision to disarm Germany in broad terms in the Armistice in November 1918 and then much more comprehensively as an entire section of the Treaty of Versailles in June 1919.[2] The disarmament of a defeated enemy was not a novel concept in 1918 but the scale involved in disarming Germany was unprecedented. The most recent instances of European disarmament concerning great powers occurred in the Napoleonic era. Prussia in 1808, Austria in 1809, and France itself in 1815 had experienced various disarmament measures.[3] The scale, however, was simply not comparable to the disarmament of a great twentieth-century power. With the introduction of highly lethal weapons, organized General Staffs and industrial proficiency, the modern arsenal of the great powers far surpassed the military capacity of the previous century. To make matters more difficult, the men and material of the German army at the end of the war were quantitatively and qualitatively among the world's elite. Britain, France and the United States stood victorious over a military force of over 400,000 soldiers, tens of thousands of artillery pieces and trench mortars, approximately 100,000 machine-guns, countless rounds of ammunition, and various types of equipment that constituted a superior modern army. In addition, the German industrial base that produced massive amounts of war materials remained intact. The German military, defeated and demoralized at the end of the war, faced the indictment of the victorious democracies, and the subsequent development and implementation of Allied disarmament strategies and efforts toward Germany became a crucial element of European post-war diplomatic and military affairs.

With the defeat of Germany, Britain and France emerged from World War I as the dominant European powers and quickly established authority over the development and enforcement of the Treaty of Versailles. Although Britain, France and the United States were responsible for drafting the treaty, the diplomatic and political withdrawal of America from Europe after the final rejection of the treaty in 1920 resulted in Anglo–French control over the peace settlement toward Germany. Although Belgium, Italy and Japan participated in Allied disarmament operations in Germany, they generally supported either the policies of Britain or France with little initiative of their own. Thus, the disarmament of the German military remained essentially an Anglo–French affair for its duration from 1920 to 1931. Although British and French losses in the war justified Anglo–French control of the disarmament process, the strained relationship raised questions about the efficacy of disarmament operations in Germany. In fact, British and French differences over disarmament priorities augmented the instability of the post-war period and created difficulties in enforcing the military clauses upon a bitter Germany. As a result, Britain and France attempted to assert themselves and rise above the dissolution of the entente in an attempt to control the course of German disarmament.

Great Britain and France emerged from World War I with bipolar outlooks concerning European affairs, and their foreign policies reflected this disparity. Britain, with an insular location essentially safe from military aggression, focused upon the restoration of the balance of power and stability on the Continent.[4] France, on the other hand, was exclusively concerned with security against the threat of renewed German aggression. Allied in the intense struggle to defeat Germany in World War I, at war's end the common factor that united the two nations was gone, and the unified effort to bring an everlasting peace to Europe would soon become entangled in conflicting strategies toward the enforcement of the economic, territorial and military aspects of the Treaty of Versailles. Although the British and French eventually reached an accord toward German disarmament at the Paris Peace Conference, differences would remain throughout disarmament operations.

When the war came to a close, Britain found itself in a more advantageous and stable position than France. As a major imperialist rival before the war, Germany had threatened Britain's security, trade routes, and colonial empire with its navy. Once a primary concern to British interests, German naval competition disappeared with Germany's defeat and the subsequent scuttling of the Imperial Navy, interned in Scapa Flow, in 1919. During the war Britain had abandoned its traditional foreign and military policy by becoming heavily involved with ground forces on the Continent. With its security re-established in 1918, however, Britain sought to restore the balance of power and stability on the Continent by preventing French domination of Germany. This strategy was present throughout the discussions and negotiations at the Paris Peace Conference, and continued to influence British decisions concerning Allied disarmament operations.

In comparison to the relative safety of Great Britain, French political and military authorities considered their security threatened by Germany's larger population and dominant military-industrial potential. The French had lost Alsace-Lorraine to Germany in the Franco–Prussian War, and World War I left France with almost one and half million dead and many important industrial areas destroyed. The terrible losses in the war thus rendered France obsessed with security, and victory allowed the French to attempt to bolster their position vis-à-vis Germany. Germany's industrial and military potential was superior to every nation in Europe, and most French leaders, despite emerging victorious from the war, believed that German military-industrial power would inevitably dominate the Continent once again. As a result, at the Paris Peace Conference and throughout the 1920s, France attempted to weaken Germany to ensure French security and leadership on the Continent. Britain, in seeking to maintain a stable balance of power in Europe, feared French hegemony and attempted to thwart French schemes for political and territorial aggrandizement. The result was a mix of treaty enforcement, lengthy negotiations, conferences, modifications and appeasement.

The disarmament of Germany was a contentious issue in post-war international affairs that ultimately proved to be an area of Allied success. As one of the main sections of the Treaty of Versailles, German disarmament emerged in the war's aftermath as an enormous challenge to the Allied quest for European security. British and French leaders viewed the disarmament of Germany as a focal point of the peace settlement, pushing it to the forefront of issues that the victorious powers addressed in Paris. Although the Treaty of Versailles sought to secure European peace through territorial revision, reparations, occupation, and disarmament, only the latter represented the most concrete means to remove the possibility of German aggression. The Allies agreed unanimously that they had to place severe restrictions upon the German military, and disarmament became an instant and enduring test of Allied treaty enforcement. Despite philosophical differences and German obstruction to their efforts, the Allies stuck to the task for the entire post-war decade. The issue of

German disarmament remained a priority in the development and enforcement of the peace and had lasting effects upon the Allied coalition by fostering international cooperation through a system of diplomatic conferences, military operations, and the creation and maintenance of Allied civilian and military organizations.

Disarmament operations in Germany allowed British and French troops, along with their Belgian, Italian and Japanese allies, to work in concert on German soil. The British, French and Belgian soldiers that evaluated the extent of German disarmament eventually outlasted their compatriots stationed at the Rhine bridgeheads in Cologne, Mainz and Coblenz. At the center of the issue of disarmament was the system of international arms inspection that the Allies implemented from 1920 to 1927. The presence of "boots on the ground" in international disarmament operations in Germany should not be underestimated as inspections guaranteed direct oversight of German military installations and industry. Disarmament operations also allowed the inspectors to observe and report on military and political conditions inside Germany. Allied soldiers working to disarm Germany provided critical analysis in evaluating the capability and intentions of the German military for over a decade.

The Allied disarmament of Germany from 1920 to 1931 is relevant to contemporary questions and lends insight into the understanding and application of foreign policy at the start of the twenty-first century. Although the geopolitical situation of the 1920s differs dramatically from that of the 1990s and early 2000s, the Allied disarmament of Germany does provide certain lessons that could be applied to current events. Some similarities between the Allied attempt to disarm Germany and the efforts of the United Nations in the disarmament of Iraq in the 1990s have been particularly illuminating. For instance, illegal chemical weapons production, clandestine caches of war material, and denial of access to inspectors to sensitive sites are just some of the issues that confronted international inspection efforts in Germany and Iraq. In both cases, inspectors were able to overcome many of the difficulties they faced. Although a continuing controversial subject, evidence suggests that international disarmament operations in Iraq in the 1990s successfully eradicated stockpiles of weapons of mass destruction while the second round of inspections in 2002 to 2003 seemed to verify this success. A robust inspection process, especially when supported by an international coalition that imposes sanctions to punish noncompliance with disarmament demands, can prove to be an effective means of enforcement. Disarmament efforts continue to be a focal point of international affairs in the twenty-first century, and the international community can benefit from the knowledge of Allied strategies and successes in efforts to disarm a modern power of the twentieth century.

The historiography of European inter-war diplomacy is plentiful and diverse, yet the Allied disarmament of Germany has not received the attention it deserves. As Philip Towle argues in *Enforced Disarmament: From the Napoleonic Campaigns to the Gulf War*, military historians have focused on wartime strategy rather than peacemaking, while diplomatic historians have examined the political questions of peace conferences at the expense of their military aspects.[5] Despite numerous studies concerning the multitude of issues arising from the Treaty of Versailles, there has been no specific work that encompasses multinational efforts to disarm Germany after World War I. Reparations, occupation, territorial questions and illicit German rearmament have received copious amounts of attention yet historians have largely neglected the question of disarmament. The scholarship has consisted of either general studies or has examined only the German side of the issue. David Williamson, in *The British in Germany, 1918–1930: The Reluctant Occupiers*, examines British occupation forces in Europe after World War I and surveys Allied disarmament efforts in Germany in the 1920s. In referring to disarmament, Williamson outlines general British policy and concerns, including initial insight into British differences of opinion in assessing the level of fulfillment of the disarmament clauses of the treaty, but points out that there has been no comprehensive analysis of British efforts toward the disarmament of Germany.[6] Aside from the publication of memoirs of Allied officers involved in the disarmament of Germany, such as General Nollet's *Une Expérience de Désarmement* and Paul Roques's *Le Contrôle Militaire Interallié en Allemagne*, the French perspective in disarming Germany has been equally neglected.

On the other hand, in *Entwaffnung und Militärkontrolle in Deutschland, 1919–1927*, Michael Salewski focuses on German strategy and reaction to Allied disarmament and bases his book exclusively upon German archival sources. He argues that the IAMCC exaggerated German violations and asserts that Allied disarmament efforts injured German honor and sovereignty.[7] Salewski does not, however, provide an analysis of Allied disarmament policies and concludes his study in 1927, four years before the final elements of Allied disarmament disappeared. Francis Ludwig Carsten has explored the political role of the German army after World War I in *The Reichswehr and Politics, 1918–1933*, where he briefly discusses German violations of the military clauses of the Versailles Treaty.[8] Within the context of the emergence of the *Reichswehr* as a political force in Weimar Germany, Carsten's analysis of German disarmament focuses on some of the German military evasions and strategies under General Hans von Seeckt without an examination of the Allied perspective on German disarmament. One additional study, *Covert German Disarmament 1919–1939* by Barton Whaley, also focuses upon German disarmament violations of the Treaty of Versailles but precludes an examination of Allied roles in the enforcement of the military clauses of the treaty.[9]

Secondary sources on inter-war Anglo–French relations and the enforcement of the Treaty of Versailles are voluminous. Classic studies such as

Arnold Wolfers' *Britain and France Between Two Wars* and Robert Jordan's *Great Britain, France, and the German Problem, 1918–1939* provide historians with the nuts and bolts of inter-war European diplomacy.[10] Current historians have not shied away entirely from additional studies of this particular period of history, nor has the Treaty of Versailles been collecting dust in the current historiography; but the Allied enforcement of disarmament has not yet received due attention. William Kleine-Ahlbrandt in *The Burden of Victory: France, Britain, and the Enforcement of the Versailles Peace 1919–1925* surveys Allied conference diplomacy from Versailles to Locarno but ignores disarmament.[11] Similarly, Sara Moore, in *Peace Without Victory for the Allies 1918–1932*, concentrates exclusively on economic issues in Anglo–French relations.[12] Astonishingly, the most comprehensive analysis of the Treaty of Versailles to date, *The Treaty of Versailles: A Reassessment After 75 Years*, examines reparations, territorial questions, war guilt, and British, French, and American policies toward the drafting and enforcement of the treaty but entirely neglects the issue of German disarmament.[13]

In assessing Allied disarmament operations in Germany from 1920 to 1931, this study examines three major areas of interest: the ramifications of the divergent disarmament priorities of Britain and France, British dominance in controlling the direction of Allied disarmament policy toward Germany, and the Allied success in destroying German military strength, most effectively through a united policy backed by military sanctions. The three focal points of the study are interrelated, and in order to clarify Allied motivations behind the disarmament of Germany, they necessarily overlap at various times throughout the period of Allied operations. In addition, the general foreign policy strategies of Britain and France in the post-war period, the balance of power versus security, respectively, will serve as a backdrop to the study.

From the outset of Allied disarmament operations in Germany, Britain and France held dichotomous opinions toward the most efficient means of degrading the strength of the German military. Whereas British political and military authorities advocated the destruction of German armaments as the most effective means to disarm Germany, the French stressed the reduction of the German army and police and the eradication of all paramilitary organizations. Although the French supported and initially demanded the enforcement of every clause of the Versailles Treaty, their focus on the question of German armed military personnel led to a distinct difference of opinion with the British in the development and implementation of Allied disarmament strategies and operations. The most pressing ramification of the Anglo–French variance in disarmament priorities was the centrifugal force it applied to a common disarmament policy. The Allied promises of 1918 to enforce a peace settlement in its entirety would not survive the post-war divergence of British and French disarmament priorities, but Allied disarmament operations in Germany would last beyond all expectations.

Within the post-war Anglo–French relationship, British leadership in the development and implementation of Allied disarmament operations was an influential factor in the outcome of German disarmament. Although German disarmament was largely an Anglo–French undertaking, British political and military leadership asserted itself as a forceful presence from the Paris Peace Conference in 1919 to the withdrawal of the last vestiges of Allied military control in 1931. After the political and military withdrawal of the United States from Europe, the Anglo–French relationship was the key to the maintenance of peaceful European relations in the post-war period. The Allied enforcement of the Treaty of Versailles was the initial means to achieve such lofty ends, but changes in British attitudes toward enforcement throughout the 1920s impacted upon overall German fulfilment, albeit in a relatively trivial amount. French security depended upon the strict enforcement of the treaty but the clash of British and French strategies toward treaty enforcement and the disarmament of Germany necessitated a change in French policy. The dominant British presence and the reciprocal French acquiescence in the Allied disarmament of Germany was a microcosm of Anglo–French relations toward Germany in the inter-war period. The periodically antagonistic Anglo–French relationship of the 1920s would have lasting effects until the outbreak of World War II.

An examination of the use of Allied sanctions to ensure fulfilment of the military clauses of the Versailles Treaty is crucial to assessing the effectiveness of Anglo–French disarmament efforts in Germany and sheds light upon a subject that will continue to influence modern foreign and military relations. The Treaty of Versailles reflected Allied desires in 1919 to punish Germany for her aggressive role in the outbreak of the war, address nationalistic ambitions and the cries for self-determination of peoples, and prevent another world war. It was an ambitious attempt to address Europe's grievances but contained a serious flaw. Although the treaty comprised 440 articles, an oversight that would affect the enforcement of the disarmament clauses and the execution of the treaty in general was the absence of any effective schemes to address German non-compliance or violations other than the prolongation of the Rhineland occupation. As a result, Britain and France had to develop *ad hoc* policies of enforcement.

Despite violations of the military clauses of the treaty, the Allies experienced much success in disarming Germany, especially when enforcing common disarmament strategies with the threat of military sanctions. The development and implementation of Allied sanctions to enforce the disarmament clauses of the Treaty of Versailles illustrated the importance Britain and France placed upon the demilitarization of Germany. With no legal recourse to apply sanctions in case of German non-fulfilment of its treaty obligations, except to extend the duration of the Rhineland occupation under Article 429, the Allies eventually established their authority in the enforcement of the military clauses of the treaty by applying the threat of occupation. The use of the threat of military sanctions by Britain and France in July 1920, May 1921 and January 1925 would have considerable and immediate effects upon German disarmament.

The Allied disarmament of Germany after World War I was a complex mosaic of diplomatic strategies, political and military policies, technical and logistic endeavors, and individual ambitions within the context of the enforcement of the Treaty of Versailles. The different Anglo–French political and military policies and priorities, the physical execution of the disarmament clauses of the treaty, and the various personalities involved in a joint effort to disarm Germany during the tumultuous period of the 1920s comprised a massive undertaking rife with difficulties. The Allies did not realize the complexity of the military aspects of the treaty when they drafted the disarmament clauses in Paris. Britain, France, and Germany would all interpret the language of the treaty in a way that best suited their own interests. As a result, the victorious Allied powers, recently united against a common foe, soon clashed with one another and with Germany in the attempt to carry out the military clauses of the Treaty of Versailles. The Allied disarmament of Germany, however, survived the entire postwar decade and eliminated the threat of German military aggression.

The development and implementation of Allied disarmament operations in Germany was a monumental endeavor on a scale never experienced before in history. The sudden collapse and surrender of German forces in November 1918 caught the victors by surprise. Despite the fact that the defeat of Germany had been possible only through a coalition of the world's powers, Britain and France were unprepared for the profuse number of tasks that lay ahead. Similar to the effort taken to defeat the Central Powers on the field of battle, an Allied undertaking was needed to enforce the peace and disarm Germany. After the American withdrawal from European diplomatic and military affairs soon after the war, the victorious powers of Britain and France, and to a much lesser extent Italy, Belgium and Japan, were left to enforce the Treaty of Versailles and cripple Germany's military capacity. The colossal scope of disarmament, the divergence of foreign policies towards Europe, and the lack of foresight of the Allies in 1918 set the stage for Anglo–French friction in disarming Germany in the 1920s. The unprecedented forceful pacification of an embittered modern power was to be replete with tense negotiations, momentous decisions and international conflict – all basic ingredients of disarmament and the diplomacy of arms inspection.

Part I
Allied disarmament (1919)

2 Allied demands at the Paris Peace Conference

After more than four years of unsurpassed violence, intensity and magnitude, the fighting of World War I came to an end on 11 November 1918, five hours after Allied and German military and political officials signed an armistice in a railroad car nestled in the peaceful woods of Compiègne, France. The war dragged on beyond the initial hopes of the combatants yet the collapse of the German army had come suddenly. Only months before, the Germans had threatened to capture Paris and divide the British and French armies. However, the final German push to drive a wedge between the Allies, Ludendorff's spring offensive, had failed. As the Allied and American forces pushed the reeling German troops back toward their own frontier, the German military and political leadership sued for peace. The termination of hostilities caught the Allied leaders by surprise. In fact, in the fall of 1918, the Allied military leadership considered the possibility of the war carrying on into 1919, even 1920.[1] The Allied and Associated powers had been essentially concerned with military victory. As a result, the post-war aims of Britain and the United States encompassed vague principles while the French dreamed of more concrete aims.

During the war the Allied and Associated powers had discussed the disarmament of Germany, which would soon comprise a significant element of the Treaty of Versailles, in rather nebulous terms.[2] Although the German army had rapidly disintegrated and suffered severe casualties and loss of morale in the final Allied offensives, the German military still constituted a considerable fighting force. In addition, the Armistice ended the hostilities but a state of war still existed with Germany. Thus the Allies were left with momentous questions. How could the German armed forces be rendered ineffective? Would Allied disarmament demands lead to a German refusal to sign the Armistice? Most importantly, what was to be done with the German army?

In order to understand the motives behind Allied policy-making toward Germany from November 1918 to June 1919, the period must be seen in the context of the horrendous destruction, both in men and material, caused by the war. The effects of modern warfare transformed both the demography and the industrial and agricultural productivity of the combatants, particularly France. Manpower losses had been terrible.[3] Over eight million combatants died from 1914 to 1918, with Germany, Russia, France and Britain suffering the highest casualties. The number of disabled and wounded soldiers exceeded this figure fourfold. Material destruction was concentrated in northeast France and Belgium, the areas of the Western Front that experienced the heaviest fighting. In France alone, 600,000 industrial structures had been damaged or demolished, 6,000 kilometers of rail lines destroyed, and 1,000,000 horses, 2,500,000 cows and 7,000,000 sheep killed.[4] Fresh from the victorious rout of German forces in the previous three months of fighting, the Allies hoped to prevent a reoccurrence of such a terrible conflict, and sought both reparation and revenge through the emasculation of German military, industrial, financial and territorial strength.

The swiftness of the collapse of German forces and the termination of hostilities in November 1918 caused the Allies to formulate much of the Armistice on an *ad hoc* basis. This type of Allied policy-making, generally reactive, would continue throughout the disarmament of Germany from 1920 to 1931. Not until the beginning of October 1918, when President Wilson of the United States and officials of the German government attempted to work out rudimentary armistice conditions, did the Allies start to draw up concrete proposals concerning the military terms of the impending armistice. Initially, Allied military representatives of the Supreme War Council, including senior officers from the British, French, American, Italian and Japanese armies, considered the disarmament of the German army to be the highest priority.[5] French Marshal Ferdinand Foch, the hero of 1918, however, used his position to dictate Allied military terms to the Germans. As the Commander-in-Chief of the Allied armies, Foch was the most powerful military leader in the world at the end of the war. He would continue to play a crucial role in the disarmament of Germany as an Allied expert on military matters until his death in 1929.

The Allied armies took steps to disarm Germany before the end of the war but these initial actions affected the German army far less than the Armistice or the Treaty of Versailles. On 8 October 1918, with the approval of French Premier Georges Clemenceau, Foch demanded that the German army retreat to a line ten kilometers east of the Rhine River within fifteen days of the signing of an armistice.[6] All war material that the German army could not keep would be surrendered to the Allies. Foch's proposal, which focused upon the strategic importance of Allied control of the Rhine, was actually less stringent than the proposals of the military representatives of the Supreme War Council.[7] More concerned with Allied occupation and control of the Rhine and its strategic bridgeheads, Foch neglected to make the disarmament and demobilization of the German army a primary concern. Major General Tasker Bliss, the American military representative of the Supreme War Council, later pointed out that the crucial error of the Allies at the war's end was waiting to disarm Germany in 1920, and not in 1918.[8]

Marshal Foch heavily influenced the final Armistice terms.[9] Consequently, British, Belgian, American and French troops occupied three bridgeheads of the Rhine at Cologne, Coblenz and Mainz. The Armistice forced Germany to retreat to the east of the Rhine and surrender 2,500 heavy guns, 2,500 field guns, 25,000 machine guns, 3,000 trench mortars, 1,700 airplanes, 5,000 locomotives, 5,000 trucks and 150,000 railroad cars.[10] Difficulties arose immediately when the Germans complained about their ability to surrender armaments and tried to include obsolete artillery in the overall amounts.[11] Yet the disarmament of Germany had only just begun. At the Paris Peace Conference, when Allied leaders had time for reflection and where national interests played such an important role, the Allies would produce much more rigorous demands upon the German military. Britain, France, Belgium, Italy, the United States and Japan attempted to transform the basic tenets of the military terms of the Armistice into a comprehensive settlement. Germany would eventually surrender thousands of guns, machine-guns, trench mortars, and various pieces of military equipment in excess of the amounts demanded in 1918. In addition, in Paris the Allies demanded the transformation of Germany's factories to commercial production, reduction in the size of the German army and the destruction of German fortifications. The major difference between the disarmament clauses of the Armistice and the Treaty of Versailles was that the former demanded the surrender of a definite amount of war material and ignored demobilization of the German army, while the latter restricted the Germans to precise numbers of weapons, munitions, equipment and troops.

The Paris Peace Conference

When the Allied and Associated powers met in Paris to formulate a postwar settlement in the winter and spring of 1919, they viewed the disarmament of Germany as a crucial issue among many. Territorial questions involving the Rhineland, Upper Silesia and the Polish Corridor, along with the issue of reparations, were important factors in the future peace of Europe. The territorial settlements led to protracted and often bitter negotiations among the British, French and American delegations. The reparations issue was not settled until 1921, and then was subject to further negotiations and modifications throughout the 1920s. While territorial and reparations questions took months, even years to settle, the Allied and Associated powers worked quickly to draft German disarmament clauses into the final peace settlement. Even though the Allies had few conceptions regarding disarmament policy toward Germany entering the Peace Conference, and subsequently experienced a divergence of opinion when initially drafting such policies, the establishment of future disarmament operations in Germany would essentially be settled within two months of the start of discussions in Paris.

The traditional foreign policies and national self-interests of Britain, France and the United States influenced the Allied ability to ensure and enforce a comprehensive peace settlement after the war. The priority of Britain throughout the war, fully immersed in the destructive fighting in France and Belgium from 1914 to 1918, had been to end the war in victory, thereby allowing for the withdrawal of its forces from the Continent. Britain's traditional policy of non-interference with continental affairs and its hope in strengthening imperialist ties, as well as lack of fear toward a defeated Germany, precluded the disarmament of Germany as a war aim.[12] In terms of substantive post-war schemes, therefore, Britain initially lacked any detailed policies regarding the disarmament of Germany. Lloyd George, who often ignored the advice of his political, economic and military experts, was unquestionably the dominant force behind British policy-making at the Paris Peace Conference.[13] Free from the burden of war and motivated by public opinion and campaign promises, Lloyd George wished to see a hasty end to compulsory service in Britain.[14] The nation had experienced two years of war before the horrendous losses on the Western Front led to the implementation of conscription. Compulsory service in Britain was anathema both to politicians and the public.[15] Lloyd George sought early negotiations in Paris concerning the disarmament of Germany and threatened to maintain compulsory military service in Britain unless Germany reduced its military forces. The Allies would soon address this issue in Paris.

French policy toward the German question at the Conference placed the greatest emphasis upon security, with Georges Clemenceau, the French Premier, and Marshal Ferdinand Foch, the Commander-in-Chief of the Allied armies, its major advocates. While encouraging the eradication of German military strength, the importance of ensuring French influence in the Rhineland transcended disarmament in importance. Foch especially was skeptical of the practicability and judiciousness of controlling Germany's military might. Since the end of the war, he advocated "physical guarantees" of French security through the maintenance of French influence in the Rhineland and a powerful force of Allied troops in Germany.[16] Clemenceau shared Foch's view of the importance of French influence in the Rhineland and, during both of the discussions concerning the Armistice and the Versailles Treaty, Clemenceau and Foch regarded control of the Rhine as a greater priority to French security than the disarmament of Germany.[17] On the other hand, at the Paris Peace Conference, Clemenceau and many French government and military officials were aware that the war left Germany with a large number of trained officers and men.[18] In addition to establishing an Allied presence on the Rhine, the French would pursue the disarmament of Germany with great zeal.

Woodrow Wilson and his closest adviser, Colonel Edward House, formulated American policies toward Germany at the Paris Peace Conference. Similar to the decision-making powers of Lloyd George and Clemenceau, both of whom never lacked self-confidence, egotism and great leadership abilities, Wilson ignored Secretary of State Robert Lansing and developed policies on his own initiative.[19] Wilson's priority at the Conference was the creation of the League of Nations, which symbolized his grand vision of the establishment of an international organization to prevent war and foster worldwide cooperation. Yet Wilson's influence upon Allied discussions regarding German disarmament was relatively minor and he often expressed his disarmament proposals in general principles. For example, in his Fourteen Points address of January 1918, Wilson vaguely demanded the reduction of national armaments "to the lowest point consistent with national safety" and later in the Covenant of the League of Nations the President suggested that German disarmament should be the antecedent to general disarmament. Wilson instead gave authority in military matters to General Tasker Bliss, the American military representative on the Allied Supreme War Council. The American general was a staunch supporter of the League of Nations and believed that modern war was a threat not just to Europe, but to the existence of civilization.[20] Bliss had advocated an extensive disarmament of Germany in the Armistice discussions as a preliminary step in the reduction of armaments for the future security of the world.[21] Yet in the Paris Peace Conference discussions, Bliss had a moderating influence upon Allied demands toward the disarmament of Germany.

British, French and American fears either of the explosion of Bolshevism in Germany or the spread of Bolshevism from the east influenced their decisions in Paris. The fear of a Bolshevist *coup d'etat* appeared during the hectic days of January 1919 when an uprising by the German radical left-wing party, the Spartacists, erupted in bloody street battles in Berlin. Bolshevism also made short-term inroads into Bavaria (Kurt Eisner) and Hungary (Bela Kun) in early 1919. Yet Allied perception of a widespread political victory of Bolshevism often surpassed any real threat of Bolshevik success. Furthermore, the Allies and Germany promoted national self-interests by using the fear of Bolshevism as a political weapon.[22] At the end of March 1919, Lloyd George, in his Fontainebleau Memorandum, attempted to modify French demands by claiming that a harsh peace settlement could lead to the overthrow of the German Republic by a Bolshevik regime.[23] British General Henry Wilson claimed that the danger of Bolshevism even exceeded any possible threat posed by the German army.[24] Marshal Foch entertained ideas of invading Russia with Allied, Polish and Czech forces, although Bolshevism did not influence his ideas concerning German disarmament.[25] President Wilson insinuated that a reduction in the size of the German army in early 1919 could increase the chances of a Bolshevik *coup d'etat* in Germany.[26] In addition, the German government played upon Allied fears and claimed that a reduction of its military forces would facilitate a Bolshevik takeover in Germany. The German government used this tactic during the Armistice and the Paris Peace Conference, and would espouse this line of attack throughout the first few years of Allied disarmament operations.[27]

The British, French and American delegations at the Paris Peace Conference first expressed their viewpoints concerning the disarmament of Germany at a meeting of the Supreme War Council one week after the opening of the Conference. In this meeting on 24 January 1919, the Allies met for the first time to discuss treaty terms to disarm Germany and to modify the various disarmament schemes of the Armistice. From the beginning of the disarmament discussions, Lloyd George and Marshal Foch displayed the disparity between the British and French viewpoints. Given his success as Minister of Munitions in Britain during the war, Lloyd George held a rather haughty view of his own expertise in the issue of disarmament. While lacking technical knowledge, Lloyd George had witnessed the effect of heavy artillery during the war and had significantly increased the production and delivery of British armaments and munitions to the Front. His ministry had also been responsible for the organization of resources, factories, and labor.[28] The British Prime Minister believed the key to disarming Germany was to dismantle and destroy Germany's ability to produce and manufacture weapons of mass destruction.[29] He opened the disarmament discussion therefore by proposing that Germany deliver arms and machinery used in armament production to the Allies.[30] The Prime Minister also suggested that the German army reduce its number of troops "to the minimum necessary for the maintenance of internal order."[31]

The Americans and French had mixed feelings toward Lloyd George's proposals. General Bliss fully supported the Prime Minister's ideas. On the other hand, Foch questioned the dubious effectiveness of military control and favored a much more direct approach in ensuring Germany's continued military prostration – the maintenance of strong Allied military forces in Europe. Foch believed that the control of factories, surrender of war material and reduction in the size of the German army would be impossible to enforce.[32] Foch's pessimistic outlook, however, would not preclude him from becoming a major force in disarming Germany in the 1920s; after all, disarmament was intended to weaken Germany at France's benefit. Lacking agreement, the Supreme Council decided to establish a committee to formulate the final terms of the disarmament of Germany.[33]

The second important stage in developing Allied disarmament policies toward Germany, soon to be established as the military clauses of the Treaty of Versailles, occurred in February 1919. So far, Allied proposals had been steeped in rhetoric and lacked both substance and precision. But in February the discussions increased in intensity when Allied representatives presented diverse and detailed plans. Influenced by Lloyd George's predilection of stressing the destruction of Germany's industrial capacity for the production of munitions and armaments, the Supreme Council, on 1 February, attempted first to define what constituted war material, a problem that would continue to plague Allied disarmament operations for years. The Council decided that excess war material included any finished products in the possession of the German army, located in parks, depots and factories, or in the process of production. All such material was to be handed over to Allied officers at selected points.[34] The Supreme Council estimated initially that it would take eight months to demilitarize German factories and proposed setting up subcommittees responsible for sending Allied officers to conduct inspections of factories in the major industrial areas of Germany. If the German government refused to comply, Allied troops would occupy Duisburg, an important coal area at the edge of the Ruhr. It was obvious that the Allies feared the German industrial capacity to produce massive amounts of armaments and munitions, since there was still no discussion of the future organization and size of the German army.

The British General Staff agreed wholeheartedly with Lloyd George's emphasis on the control of German industrial production of war material. On 5 February, they drew up a plan for the disarmament of Germany that included controlling German factories and destroying machinery that produced war materials. Their proposal supported Lloyd George, who wanted simply to destroy German machinery and who viewed the inspection and control of German armaments as a "temporary substitute."[35] In addition, the British General Staff believed that the surrender of all excess war materials to Allied control officers would significantly reduce German war-making capacity. Unlike Foch, who did not trust German acquiescence in disarmament demands, the British General Staff proposed that the German government actually promise not to produce war materials. In case such a promise did not sufficiently ensure compliance with their disarmament demands, they suggested that the Allies consider occupying Duisburg and Essen, important industrial centers in Germany.[36] Although the British General Staff would have an influence upon future German disarmament, Lloyd George essentially ignored their contributions and recommendations in Paris.

The disarmament terms of the Treaty of Versailles neared completion on 7 February 1919, when the Loucheur Committee presented its report to the Supreme War Council. The Committee, made up of delegates from Britain, France, Italy and the United States, proposed an Allied organization of 200 officers to control German armaments and munitions, restrict the German army to thirty divisions, and set limits for German war material.[37] The Loucheur Committee also aimed to ensure German disarmament and prevent industrial production of war material through a military occupation of the entire Westphalian Basin.[38] The idea of such a huge occupation would later emerge in 1923, when the French and Belgians marched into the Ruhr and took over the heart of German industry.

Allied political and military leaders reacted to the Loucheur Report with little enthusiasm. Lloyd George merely repeated his obsession that German militarism could be crippled only through the surrender of artillery. Foch remained skeptical about the control of German armaments and adamantly claimed that only war, occupation, blockade and the restriction of supplies into Germany could guarantee German fulfilment of the military terms. Foch's pessimism led him to claim that "it would be impossible to prevent a country like Germany from doing what she wished at home."[39] President Wilson called the Loucheur report a "panic program" and claimed that significant changes to the Armistice were not "sportsmanlike."[40] The following day, another Allied committee (Committee for the Reduction of German Armaments) proposed that Germany surrender all excess war materials by 17 March 1919.[41] Lacking agreement, the Allies suspended discussions of disarming Germany until 12 February, when the Supreme War Council appointed a Military Commission under Marshal Foch to draft military terms for the peace treaty. Foch subsequently instructed the French, British, American, Italian and Japanese members of his commission to draft individual plans.[42]

The plans of the representatives of Foch's Military Commission, each representing the policies of their own governments, revealed important Allied differences toward German disarmament. The issues of the size of the German army and the length of time for enlistment illustrated essential variations. The French military experts favored a small German army of 190,000 men with a one-year enlistment period.[43] The Italians proposed similar conditions, limiting the German army to 210,000 men, with approximately half of the troops enlisted for one-year service periods. On the other hand, the British experts proposed a German army with a maximum strength of 450,000 troops with a long-term voluntary enlistment period of twelve years, while the Americans proposed the same size but wanted to leave the issue of the enlistment of the German army exclusively to German authorities. The Japanese plan lacked details other than limiting the German army to thirty-five regiments. The military experts threshed out their differences however, and on 21 February they agreed to limit the German army to 200,000 troops. Although British General Wilson reluctantly accepted the French short-term enlistment proposal to avoid confrontation over the issue, the enlistment period of the German army remained a contentious issue for the Allied heads of state during subsequent discussions over disarmament policies in Paris.[44]

In March, the specter of Bolshevism returned to haunt Allied leaders when a German communist general strike led to the outbreak of more violence in the streets of Berlin. This Red Scare had an impact upon Allied perceptions of a Bolshevik victory and influenced Allied discussions over the military terms of the treaty. At the end of the month, Lloyd George and his closest advisers produced a memorandum at Fontainebleau outlining British fears that a harsh treaty, including the reduction of the German military to a mere police force, would lead to political instability and make Germany ripe for Bolshevism. In effect, the British delegation exploited Allied fears of Bolshevism to modify the clauses of the Treaty of Versailles and restrain French aspirations, but the fear of Bolshevism also genuinely influenced Allied policies toward disarmament. For instance, Marshal Foch devised a French plan to reduce the strength of the regular German army to 110,000 soldiers with a temporary additional force of 90,000 troops with the sole purpose of protecting Germany from Bolshevism.[45] President Wilson claimed that "all we need contemplate was the amount of armed force required by Germany to maintain internal order and to keep down Bolshevism."[46] General Bliss also held this sentiment. In fact, when the Allies first agreed upon the figure of 200,000 men for the German army, Bliss commented that he agreed "to what seemed a reasonable force that would enable a stable government to maintain order against the incipient Spartacist or Bolshevist movement."[47] Although the fear of Bolshevism influenced the development and negotiations of Allied policy toward the disarmament of Germany, it would ultimately have little effect upon the comprehensiveness of the final terms of the treaty.

Anglo–French divergence of opinion over German disarmament became readily apparent in March, when the Allies drafted the final plans for the disarmament and control of German military industry. The crux of Anglo–French disparity over the disarmament of Germany lay in the proposed terms for the enlistment period of the German army. On 3 March, Foch's Military Commission officially proposed to the Supreme War Council a reduction in the German army to 200,000 troops, with enlistment periods of twenty-five years for officers and fifteen years for NCOs (non-commissioned officers), and the establishment of a Committee of Control for the reduction of the German army and armaments. However, the proposal stipulated that enlisted men would have one-year service periods. While Foch explained that the report was an Allied effort, he also noted that the British delegation in his committee opposed the short-term service enlistment period proposed for the bulk of the German army.[48] British Foreign Secretary Balfour responded despondently that Foch's proposal could result in the eternal military control of Germany. Without the presence of Lloyd George at the meeting, Balfour insisted that the Supreme War Council await the arrival of the Prime Minister to discuss the proposal for German disarmament.[49]

When Lloyd George returned to the Paris Peace Conference on 6 March, he revealed a fundamental difference of opinion with Foch. The Prime Minister argued that Foch's plan would allow Germany to train 200,000 men every year and that Germany would be able to amass a sizable trained army within ten years. When the Marshal claimed that his system prevented the creation of cadres (which drove the "flocks of sheep"), Lloyd George countered Foch's argument by pointing out that Britain's conscripted troops in the war lacked long-term training and performed successfully.[50] The Prime Minister also dismissed Foch's plans by claiming that conscription was not a matter for "technical delegates."[51] Lloyd George therefore brushed aside the committee he had helped create. By dismissing the proposal of the military experts, Lloyd George ensured that the disarmament of Germany would be left to the political leadership of the major powers.

Lloyd George's arguments the following day, 7 March, marked a turning point in the disarmament discussions in Paris. He proposed a volunteer German army (similar to Foch) with a maximum size of 200,000 men but with a twelve-year enlistment period for all soldiers.[52] Lloyd George believed that long-term military service, a fundamental change from previous Allied proposals, would prevent any reinstitution of the historic Krümper system.[53] He shared some of Foch's pessimism as to the effectiveness of military control when he claimed that permanent disarmament was an illusion, and that Germany would be able to produce war materials clandestinely. Yet it was Clemenceau who quickly settled any differences when he accepted Lloyd George's demands and dismissed the proposed military terms of Foch's committee by declaring that such matters did not concern military experts.[54] The French Premier, like Lloyd George, insisted that ultimate policy decisions rested with the heads of government and that political power transcended military authority.[55] Clemenceau's support of Lloyd George in Paris was an integral factor in Britain's success in shaping Allied policy toward the disarmament of Germany. The French Premier openly distrusted military authority and refused to risk disintegrating the Entente over the details of the military terms for Germany. As a result, the Allied leaders asked Foch's committee to draw up a final plan based upon Lloyd George's suggestions.

The Allies had substantially completed the drafting of the military terms of the treaty when the French delegation officially accepted Lloyd George's plan on 10 March. The French, however, demanded a reduction in German troop strength to 100,000 men. Using rather convoluted logic, Foch had come to the conclusion that the German army must be reduced to 100,000 men, which, including the police, forest guards and customs officers, would still amount to a force greater than 140,000.[56] Clemenceau, in an attempt to justify the severity of the reduction, stated that Foch's Commission had recently decreased the number of German effectives to 140,000 and rationalized the additional decrease to 100,000 by stating that a short-term enlisted army had a proportion of soldiers in training that lacked military value; however, a long-term enlisted army negated this effect.[57] General Bliss complained that this additional reduction of the German army would render it unable to maintain order, but Lloyd George, obviously pleased that he could now abolish conscription in Britain, supported the French proposals. When the American Secretary of State Robert Lansing (filling in for the absent Wilson) proclaimed his support for the new proposals, the meeting adjourned in agreement. With Allied policy regarding the disarmament of Germany now essentially united, only the task of drawing up the final military terms of the treaty remained.

The drafting of the final military clauses of the Treaty of Versailles by Foch's Inter-Allied Military Committee and the ultimate acceptance of the terms by the Supreme War Council marked the concluding steps in Allied negotiations concerning the disarmament of Germany. The Supreme War Council received the final proposals, based upon the previous recommendations of Lloyd George and further modifications by Clemenceau and Foch, on 17 March. After a month of discussions, debate and critical discourse, Allied political leaders and military experts approved the plans of Foch's Military Committee with only minor revisions in the phrasing of the clauses.

The military clauses of the Treaty of Versailles intended to weaken the German army so as to prevent any possible military threat in the future. Only a firm coalition of the world's powers ensured victory against Germany and the Central Powers in World War I; the German army was therefore considered to be one of the elite armies of the world, with excellent officers, training and equipment. The military clauses, Part V, Section I of the Versailles Treaty, intended to eliminate Germany's effective capacity to conduct offensive actions by limiting the number of troops, amount of war material and number of fortifications of the German army. Article 160 limited the German army to 100,000 troops (including 4,000 officers), imposed strict organizational terms for seven infantry and three cavalry divisions, and prohibited the existence of the Great General Staff. Furthermore, the treaty limited the German police to its pre-war size (Article 162), abolished conscription (Article 173) and replaced it with a twelve-year enlistment period for NCOs (non-commissioned officers) and soldiers (Article 175), while officers had to serve for twenty-five years (Article 175). The Allies allowed Germany only three military schools (Article 177) and forbade the existence of paramilitary associations (Article 177), mobilization (Article 178) and sending military missions abroad (Article 179).

In addition, the treaty restricted Germany's armaments and munitions (Articles 164–167), limited war material production to authorized factories (Article 168), and forbade the importation and exportation of war material (Article 170), as well as the manufacture and use of poison gas and tanks (Article 171). The Allies set deadlines by demanding that Germany reduce the size of its army and amount of armaments by 31 March 1920 (Articles 163 and 166, respectively). Finally, the Allies demanded the destruction of German fortifications in the Rhineland zone but allowed those in the south and east of Germany to be maintained in their existing state (Article 180); no alterations could be made to the forts located along Germany's coasts (Article 196). The Allies initially set up the Military Commission of Control to supervise the control of the surrender and destruction of excess German war material but left the details of the organization of the control commissions to future interpretation and discussions.[58] Consequentially, the organization of the commissions was not concluded until July, after the signing of the Treaty of Versailles.

While much of the discussions of 17 March pertained to minor revisions of the actual terms of the military clauses of the Treaty of Versailles, one of the modifications made to the proposals of Foch's committee had a significant effect upon the future of disarmament. When President Wilson raised the point of the duration of the Military Control Commission, he opened a debate that would affect the duties of the IAMCC throughout the 1920s. He declared that the military clauses did not contain any time limit for the duration of the control commissions and feared the unlimited continuation of Allied and American armies in Germany. Wilson suggested that the control commissions remain in Germany for a period of only three months but Balfour claimed that the duration of control should be an "indefinite, but not an eternal period."[59] Foch simply wanted to tie the duration of the commissions to German fulfillment of the military clauses. Most importantly, the lack of a time limit for the control commissions led to a modification of the original proposals. As a result of Wilson's and Balfour's fears of an extended presence of Allied troops in Germany, the Supreme War Council stipulated that only the military clauses which had a specific time limit had to be fulfilled under the authority of the control commissions.[60] The Allies placed all the military clauses under the jurisdiction of these commissions, and the ambiguity of a number of the military clauses left the important decision as to what constituted fulfilment to future interpretation.[61] Undoubtedly, the lack of precise language helped subsequently to extend the duration of the Inter-Allied Military Control Commission's operations in Germany.

Although the Allies had essentially drafted the disarmament clauses in March, they added one other element to the final military settlement with Germany. In discussions regarding the Covenant of the League of Nations at the end of April, President Wilson suggested that Germany would be more amenable to the military terms of the Treaty of Versailles if they "were presented as preparing the way for a general limitation of armaments for all nations."[62] Therefore, the Council of Four decided to add to the Covenant of the League of Nations a rather nebulous phrase that German disarmament was to be a prelude to the *general* disarmament of the League members. In addition, the Allies sent a note to the German government on 16 June 1919 which stated that German responsibility for the outbreak of the war in 1914 justified the demand that Germany disarm first.[63] Part of Wilson's visionary plan to ensure post-war international security, this supplementary stipulation would be used in the future by the German government to justify the rejection of the military clauses of the Versailles Treaty. In addition, it later helped embitter Allied–German relations in the Disarmament Conference in 1933.[64]

The debates between Lloyd George, Clemenceau, Foch and the military experts in Paris culminated with the Supreme War Council's acceptance of the final military terms of the Treaty of Versailles on 17 March. French acquiescence to Lloyd George's demands over the enlistment period of the German army, a key component in the future organization of the *Reichswehr*, would have a significant impact upon the work of the Inter-Allied Military Control Commission and reflects Britain's often decisive influence regarding German disarmament in Anglo–French relations. Considering the importance which the French placed on German military personnel issues, compared to the British priority in controlling armaments and munitions, the French concession over enlistment illustrated Britain's key role and policy-making power concerning German disarmament. While Clemenceau and Foch had convinced Allied leaders in Paris to limit the German army to 100,000 troops, this demand also played into the hands of Lloyd George by providing justification to reduce British military strength to pre-war standards. The drafting of the armaments clauses caused little Allied dissension because Britain placed a priority upon them and France supported everything that weakened Germany.

Considering France's obsession with security and Britain's rather lack-adaisical attitude toward German military strength, the fact that Britain played such a crucial role in Anglo–French relations toward Germany reflected Britain's ability to enforce its political will and manipulate French fears of acting independently. Although Clemenceau attempted to ensure French security through a number of demands, British policies, and in particular, Lloyd George, had a significant restrictive influence upon French continental ambitions. Consequently, the British lessened French ambitions to increase national power through the emasculation of German territorial and economic strength. For instance, Britain and the United States prevented the French from either acquiring or separating the Rhineland from Germany, one of France's priorities at the Peace Conference. As a result, Clemenceau had reluctantly traded exclusive French control of the Rhineland, which Foch had so vociferously demanded, for the Treaties of Mutual Guarantee with Britain and the United States. The Supreme Council's acceptance of the crux of Lloyd George's military proposal signaled a diplomatic victory for the British, and was a harbinger of continued British success and French acquiescence in future Allied policies toward German disarmament. A microcosm of the post-war Anglo–French relationship, British policies at the Paris Peace Conference toward German disarmament exemplified their modifying influence on French schemes for achieving continental dominance as well as the French fear of losing British support. While the occupation of the Ruhr in 1923 would mark the last time the French initiated major action against Germany without British support during the period of disarmament operations, French fears of independent action appeared as early as 1919. Faced with conflicting policies and the threat of the weakening or disintegration of the Anglo–French entente, the French often hesitated to act independently and bowed to British policy-making decisions.

3 The organization and hierarchy of Allied disarmament and military control

World War I left an indelible mark upon the course of European history as it transformed international relations, political and social institutions, as well as the national boundaries of Europe. These metamorphoses, accelerated by the brutal consequences of war, resulted in widespread uncertainty, disillusionment and chaos. In evaluating the events of the immediate post-war era, the turbulent atmosphere of Europe must serve as a backdrop to the peacemaking in Paris and the enforcement of the Treaty of Versailles. Although victorious, the Allies certainly felt the effects of modern warfare. Britain had forsaken its traditional wartime policy of limiting the preponderance of continental involvement to naval and economic warfare and had sent hundreds of thousands of soldiers into the trenches in Belgium and northern France. The extraordinary number of casualties helped quicken the return of the traditional British policy of limiting political and military involvement on the Continent. French losses in men, industry and territory led to an overwhelming conservative victory in France in the elections of 1919, and to an obsessive drive for guaranteeing French security at Germany's expense. After helping save Britain and France from German dominance, the United States began to immerse itself once again in political isolation. The last member of the great alliance, Russia, was an enigma. After suffering total defeat in the war, Russia had been torn apart by revolution and was in the midst of a bloody civil war when the peacemakers gathered in Paris.

The political and economic situation in Germany also added significantly to the chaotic post-war atmosphere of Europe. Revolution had transformed Germany's traditional political institution of an elitist-dominated empire in the waning days of the war into a socialist-led republic. Frequent outbreaks of violence characterized the political instability of the immediate post-war years. The socialist Ebert government initiated a tacit alliance with the right-wing-dominated army and used paramilitary groups (*Freikorps*) to crush leftist uprisings in 1919. Political opponents fought bloody battles in the streets of Berlin. Inflation began to increase as defeat had foiled the plans of the military regime of Ludendorff and Hindenburg to pay for the war through the spoils of victory. The German public had been led to believe throughout the entire war that Germany was on the cusp of victory; thus the Treaty of Versailles would become the symbol of Allied cruelty and Weimar defeatism. The perceived threat of Bolshevism, originating from within Germany or spreading from the Bolshevik armies in the east, also threatened traditional political institutions throughout Europe. Thrown into the cauldron of European instability, set to boil by the exigencies of war, the Allies thus inherited the task of drafting a peace settlement that would put an end to all wars.

The Treaty of Versailles was signed on 28 June 1919, thereby allowing the Allies to breathe a sigh of relief and cast aside their contingency plans for the military invasion of Germany. Consisting of 440 articles, the treaty comprised a comprehensive peace settlement that placed stringent territorial, economic and military obligations upon Germany. The most significant territorial demands upon Germany included the loss of a sizable tract of territory in Upper Silesia and Prussia to Poland, the return of Alsace-Lorraine to France, the cession of Eupen and Malmedy to Belgium, the loss of the Saar for fifteen years, and the Allied occupation of the Rhineland. Economically, Germany was later obligated to pay a reparations amount of thirty-three billion dollars to the Allies. In addition, the war guilt clause, an Allied attempt to justify reparations legally by making Germany responsible for the outbreak of war, and the preclusion of German participation in the Paris negotiations, aside from submitting written modifications to the treaty, exacerbated international tensions and escalated German hostility and bitterness toward the Allies and the Treaty of Versailles. Allied motivations in the imposition of the terms of the treaty upon Germany amounted to a complex conglomeration of issues: an intense fear of a future and more destructive war, revenge for Allied losses in men and territory, Germany's decisive role in the outbreak of war, and the response to the cries of national self-determination. As difficult as the Paris negotiations had been, in the summer of 1919 the Allies faced the Herculean task of enforcing the Treaty of Versailles upon an antagonistic and disintegrating Germany.

In conjunction with the numerous restrictions placed upon the German army, which were no less resolute than the economic and territorial demands of the treaty, the Allies established the Military, Naval and Aeronautical Control Commissions to supervise the execution of the military, naval and air clauses, respectively. With the bulk of the German navy scuttled at Scapa Flow and the size of the German air force relatively insignificant, the most difficult and extensive mission fell to the Inter-Allied Military Control Commission. The crucial task of this commission was to oversee the surrender and destruction of all excess German war material and fortifications, and the reduction of German armed forces. The treaty also bound the German government to cooperate with the IAMCC in the execution of its duties.

The military clauses of the Treaty of Versailles, however, contained a number of ambiguities, especially concerning the definition of war material and the length of disarmament operations.[1] For instance, some military equipment had civilian uses, such as clothing and tools, and the definition of war material became a prolonged and contentious issue between the German and Allied governments. The duration of IAMCC operations depended upon German fulfillment of only certain treaty articles and, even then, evaluating fulfillment was not always precise. Most important was the fact that the Allies had not established any treaty stipulations, other than the prolongation of the Rhineland occupation, concerning the possibility of German non-compliance with the military terms. This negligence would lead to *ad hoc* reactive Allied policies throughout disarmament operations. Left to Allied and German interpretations, these important issues created continuous points of friction between the former combatants and allies. However, if the military clauses were fulfilled to the letter, the Treaty of Versailles would indeed cripple German war-making capacity. But therein lay the problem that the Allies were about to encounter. How would the Allies know when Germany was disarmed and just how were the military clauses to be enforced? What would the Allies do in case Germany flouted the disarmament and military control of their once vast military industrial institution?

The Inter-Allied Military Control Commission (IAMCC)

From the early stages of the Paris Peace Conference to the day the Treaty of Versailles went into effect, the Allies established three administrative bodies involved in the disarmament and military control of Germany: the Inter-Allied Military Control Commission, the Conference of Ambassadors, and the Allied Military Committee of Versailles. In mid-March 1919, British, French, American, Italian, and Japanese leaders, convening in Paris to draft the clauses for the treaty of peace with Germany, concluded their negotiations concerning German disarmament. They addressed major issues such as the size and enlistment period of the German army, the limitations of German armaments and the destruction of any excess material, and the creation of control commissions to oversee the execution of the military clauses. The organization of Allied authority to oversee the enforcement of the military clauses of the treaty, however, remained incomplete. In addition, the treaty contained no stipulations regarding the detailed organization of the Inter-Allied Military Control Commission. While everyone understood the overall duty of the IAMCC, matters such as the personnel, bureaucratic organization and operating procedures of the commission had yet to be determined.

The drawing up of organizational details of the IAMCC moved closer to completion on 26 June, when the Council of Four agreed that the military experts of the Supreme War Council and Marshal Foch should draft detailed plans for the organization, administration and work of the control commissions.[2] On 9 July, the military representatives of the Supreme War Council subsequently delivered a report to the Allied Heads of Delegations, which approved the final details of the organization and duties of the IAMCC.[3] The Allies delegated each of the three control commissions established by the Treaty of Versailles – Military, Naval and Aeronautical – a president representing the two major Allied powers. They approved a French general for the presidency of the IAMCC and entrusted a British admiral and brigadier-general with supervising the Inter-Allied Naval Control Commission and the Inter-Allied Aeronautical Control Commission, respectively.[4] The German government would be responsible for the expenses of the control commissions, including salaries and officers' accommodations. The Allies also established initial salaries and allowances for the officers and men of the control commissions in August.[5] In the following years, when the value of the mark plummeted in the midst of drastic inflation, the payment of the control commissions experienced constant revisions and disputes with German authorities.

The Inter-Allied Military Control Commission, responsible for supervising the disarmament, destruction and control of one of the largest and most powerful military forces in the world, was the largest of the three commissions.[6] The Allies placed the IAMCC in charge of supervising the execution of the military clauses of the Versailles Treaty and expected Germany to fulfill the terms. The IAMCC consisted of three sub-commissions – Armaments, Effectives and Fortifications. The Allies placed the Armaments Sub-commission under the presidency of a British general with an Allied staff of thirty officers and charged it with overseeing the execution by Germany of treaty Articles 162–72, 180, 195 and 196. These clauses contained a number of crucial issues in disarming Germany, including the surrender and destruction of excess German war material and the control of German industrial production. The Allies placed the Effectives Sub-commission under the presidency of a French general with an Allied officer staff of approximately thirty officers. They charged it with the execution of Articles 159–63 and 173–8, which included the reduction of the German army, limiting the size of the police, and the abolition of conscription and paramilitary associations. Finally, the Allies placed the Fortifications Sub-commission under the presidency of an American general with a staff of approximately fifteen Allied officers to supervise the execution of Articles 180, 195 and 196, the maintenance of authorized forts in their present state, and the dismantling of the remainder of fortifications and fortified works. In addition, the Allied governments established the proportions of officers in the IAMCC as follows: 25 percent French, 20 percent British, 20 percent Italian, 15 percent American, 10 percent Belgian, and 10 percent Japanese.[7]

The fact that the Allies agreed to place the presidencies of the Armaments and Effectives Sub-commissions under British and French leadership, respectively, represented the importance the duties of each of these sub-commissions had to these nations. The negotiations of the Paris Peace Conference clearly exemplified this point. Lloyd George had been a constant and vociferous advocate of the dismantling and control of German industrial production of war material and believed this was the most effective means of disarmament. The extent of the military clauses of the Versailles Treaty that pertain to this subject demonstrated the success that Lloyd George had in convincing Allied leaders of their importance. The French had experienced higher losses in manpower, in proportion to their population, than any other major nation in World War I.[8] In addition, France was adjacent to a bitter enemy with a substantially larger population. As a result, Clemenceau and Foch concerned themselves most with the question of the size, recruitment, and enlistment of the German army. Although they had allowed Lloyd George to infringe upon one of their priorities of demanding a short-term enlisted German army, French political and military leaders expressed relief that the German army would be forced to maintain its strength far below the size of the French peacetime army. General Charles Nollet, the IAMCC's first President, believed that the Armaments Sub-commission's duties were the immediate priority of the IAMCC but that the Effectives Sub-commission was responsible for the most important issues in the future. Nollet considered the task of the Fortifications Sub-commission to be the least important, considering that many German forts were located in the occupied territory of the Rhineland. The French General also addressed the question of the size of the IAMCC, and on 8 August the Allied governments accepted his proposal for a staff of 1,300 men, comprising 350 officers, 800 men, and 150 interpreters.[9]

The Allies finalized the IAMCC's organization by the late summer of 1919. After establishing the ratio of officers and nationality of the presidents of the control commissions, the Allies next appointed the key personnel of the IAMCC. Marshal Foch, with the support of the coalition, chose General Charles Nollet as President of the Inter-Allied Military Control Commission.[10] Nollet was a true professional soldier and had served in the French army as a Corps commander during the war.[11] With an astute mind, he was able to comprehend all the details involved in the disarmament and military control of Germany.[12] General Nollet, along with Marshal Foch, attempted to enforce the military terms of the Versailles Treaty in the strictest sense possible. Never intimidated by German opposition and rarely influenced by the British, Nollet was a perfect vehicle for post-war French policy toward Germany. Under the presidency of Nollet, the Allies appointed British General Francis Bingham and French General Barthélemy as presidents of the Armaments and Effectives Sub-commissions, respectively.[13] Furthermore, the subsequent rejection of the Treaty of Versailles by the United States directly affected the organization and personnel of the IAMCC. As a result, the Allies replaced the proposed American president of the Fortifications Sub-commission with French General Raymond Bizouard and changed the ratios of Allied offi-

cers in the commission. Consequently, the final percentages of Allied officers of the IAMCC when it began work in January 1920 were 45 percent
French, 32 percent British, 14 percent Belgian, 6 percent Italian, and 3 percent Japanese, illustrating the preponderance of Franco-British control
over the IAMCC.[14]

The administrative organization of the IAMCC allowed for the participation of all Allied officers but gave numerical supremacy to the French.
The Allies established a Council of the IAMCC, made up of the heads of
each delegation and senior officers, as the executive body of the commission. The Council was composed of four French officers, two British officers, and one officer each from the Belgian, Italian and Japanese armies.[15]
Council decisions were originally taken by majority vote. The Allies set up
twenty-two district committees under the sub-commissions throughout
Germany, delegating eleven of them for Armaments, eight for Effectives
and three for Fortifications.[16] Initially, the personnel of the IAMCC
included 311 officers, 117 interpreters, 897 troops; and 203 automobiles,
but these numbers often fluctuated. In October, for instance, the Allies
decided to reduce personnel by about 25 percent, with the percentages of
French and British officers fixed at 35 percent and 27 percent respectively.[17] The complex inter-allied machinery for the disarmament and military control of the German army, however, still existed only on paper, and
the IAMCC would not begin its work until all the signatories ratified the
Treaty of Versailles. The debate in the United States between President
Wilson and the Republican-led Senate delayed the ratification of the
Treaty of Versailles, thereby prolonging the date the treaty was due to go
into effect. Since the Paris Peace Conference would soon come to a close,
the Allies also needed a political organization to oversee the IAMCC as
well as the other commissions created in Paris.

The IAMCC vanguard

The work of the IAMCC to disarm the German military could not start
until the major powers ratified the Treaty of Versailles but the German
government itself assuaged Allied restlessness to implement their disarmament schemes. On 11 August, Baron Kurt von Lersner, President of the
German delegation at Versailles, requested from Clemenceau that the
Allies send a commission to Berlin to "negotiate" the multitude of
complex military questions concerning the disarmament and military
control of Germany.[18] The German government's offer had two major
facets of rationale: to prevent the possibility that the Allies could attempt
an even stricter application and interpretation of the military clauses, and
to attempt to ease the severe restrictions that the Treaty of Versailles
demanded of the German military. There had been no verbal discussions
regarding any clauses at the Paris Peace Conference.

The British and French political and military leadership reacted quickly to the German request. They absolutely refused all negotiations over any of the terms of the Versailles Treaty but they did agree to send an advance delegation to Germany. Within six days of the German government's request, French General Weygand sent a letter to Clemenceau outlining Foch's position that the advance commission would be composed of senior Allied officers but its purpose would be to discuss, not negotiate, means to carry out the execution of military terms of the treaty.[19] On 31 August, Foch announced the official creation of an advanced delegation of the IAMCC to the German government. General Nollet formed the vanguard with sixty officers, seventy-seven troops, twelve interpreters and thirteen automobiles taken from all of the Allied delegations.[20] When the Germans learned of the size of the vanguard, they claimed that such a large force would create difficulties with the bitter, and somewhat hostile, German population.[21] Using the threat of a hostile public as a pretext to prevent Allied disarmament operations was a harbinger of future problems. In reality, the German government realized that the Allies, far from being willing to negotiate the military clauses of the Versailles Treaty, intended to initiate disarmament. German hopes of modifying the treaty's military clauses appeared dead. With the support of General Nollet, who pointed out that the Allies had no legal right to send the IAMCC vanguard if the Germans opposed it, the Allied Heads of Delegations decided to drop the whole idea.[22] Yet the uncertainty of German expectations of Allied disarmament operations led the German government to overcome its resistance to the size of the Allied force, and Clemenceau announced that the IAMCC vanguard would leave for Berlin on 11 September.[23]

In what would amount to the first of many complaints made by German authorities about the activities and presence of the IAMCC, on 13 October Baron von Lersner objected to the fact that members of the Allied advance delegation dressed in their military uniforms. The Allied Heads of Delegation, however, rejected his request that IAMCC members wear civilian clothes after the comment by Eyre Crowe, the British Under-Secretary of State for Foreign Affairs: "Whoever knew Germans knew that a man in uniform is far more respected than a civilian." [24] While trying to crush the spirit of Prussian militarism in Germany, the members of the IAMCC, all of whom served in the military of their respective nations, would remain symbols of Allied military supremacy. As the tension of the war subsided and the work of supervising the disarmament and military control of Germany proceeded, many IAMCC officers would later wear civilian garb.

The task of the advance delegation of the IAMCC was to reduce any problems concerning the execution of the military clauses of Versailles and to make the transition to the implementation of the treaty as efficient as possible. Most importantly, the work of the IAMCC vanguard was a necessary step towards establishing the authority and presence of Allied disarmament operations in Germany. On 12 September 1919, the vanguard left for Berlin. Alternatively, the German government was responsible for housing the members of this delegation, providing transportation and office space for them, and paying their allowances.[25] The first meeting between members of the IAMCC and German military authorities was a fiasco, as each delegation hoped to gain an authoritative position. The Germans attempted to preside over the conference by seating themselves before the Allies but Nollet refused to be beaten at this high-level game of protocol and walked out. Eventually they reached a compromise in which each delegation would enter the room simultaneously![26] This rather amusing incident illustrated the desperation of the German authorities in attempting to influence the execution of the military clauses of the Treaty of Versailles as well as the Allied resolve to maintain their authoritative supremacy. It also symbolized the strained IAMCC–German relationship that characterized Allied disarmament operations in Germany. Furthermore, the Germans hoped to keep their former adversaries contained (and controlled) in Berlin and objected to the fact that the Allies were planning to send inspectors into districts throughout Germany.[27]

Since the Allies relied initially upon intelligence estimates of the total amount of German war materials, Nollet ordered the sub-commission presidents in the advance delegation to draft questionnaires for the German military authorities. The premise of the questionnaires was to ascertain the amount of existing German war material, thereby calculating the extent of destruction the IAMCC would have to supervise.[28] Obtaining genuine statistics of German war strength and production remained a difficult challenge. To make matters worse, while the Allies waited to begin disarmament operations, the Germans continued to import, export, and manufacture war material.[29] Nonetheless, the IAMCC vanguard had broken the ice in IAMCC–German relations and remained in Germany until the final ratification of the Versailles Treaty.

While the German government had invited the advance delegation of the IAMCC to Germany with the hope of favorably influencing the execution of the military clauses of the Treaty of Versailles, the *Reichswehr* Ministry (*Reichswehrministerium*) created Army, Navy, and Air Peace Commissions in September, reciprocal organizations to the Allied control commissions, as well as a liaison office (*Verbindungstelle*) that acted as the headquarters to the Peace Commissions.[30] Officially set up to work with Allied inspectors to oversee the execution of the military clauses and justified by the fact that the Treaty of Versailles had actually stipulated that Germany supply representatives to work with Allied control officers, the Peace Commissions acted as a counterweight to the IAMCC.

The Germans modeled the Army Peace Commission (*Heeresfriedenskommission*) after the IAMCC and established three sub-commissions within it.[31] Initially under General August von Cramon, the Army Peace Commission would often clash with Allied government and military officials.[32] For instance, in the last meeting between the IAMCC vanguard and German military officials on 14 November 1919, the Germans complained about the presence of Allied officers in German districts other than Berlin, arguing that the Allies could supervise the demobilization but not the *creation* of new *Reichswehr* units. The Germans also claimed that the Allies had no immediate right to supervise military control in Germany, since the Treaty of Versailles gave Germany three months to reduce its army to 200,000 troops.[33] Nollet rejected these demands, and the IAMCC did not meet again with German military officials until disarmament operations started in earnest in January 1920. While deriding the treaty as an Allied *diktat* that would destroy the political, economic, and social fabric of Germany, whenever German political and military authorities found that specific treaty clauses could be interpreted favorably, they were quick to use the Treaty of Versailles as a pretext to further national aims.[34]

The Conference of Ambassadors

In order to supervise the implementation and execution of all of the clauses of the Treaty of Versailles, the Allies decided in July 1919 to create an Allied political organization that would ultimately replace the Supreme Council. Such an organization was necessary to coordinate the interpretation and execution of Allied policy in the Versailles era. Since the IAMCC was purely a military organization, composed entirely of Allied army officers and men with the task of supervising the execution of only the military clauses of the treaty, the peacemakers needed a more extensive commission to supervise the execution of the multitude of treaty clauses. No official Allied organization existed to supervise the control commissions. In a Supreme Council meeting on 1 July, Clemenceau advocated the creation of an Allied commission that would "superintend the work of all Commissions dealing with the details of the provisions of the Treaty."[35]

At the end of July, the Supreme Council agreed to set up a commission in Paris to coordinate the interpretation and execution of the entire treaty. Each of the principal Allied belligerent nations would be represented on the commission, which eventually became known as the Conference of Ambassadors. In terms of the administration and organization of the enforcement of the military terms of the treaty, the Conference of Ambassadors now had supervisory power over the IAMCC. In fact, the Allies ordered all the control commissions to address the Conference of Ambassadors with regular reports of the status of the execution of the military clauses of the treaty. Eventually, under British pressure, the Allies entrusted the Ambassadors' Conference with the authority over all three control commissions, as well as the numerous commissions created at Versailles, and charged it with the authority to settle all Allied disagreements over disarmament.[36]

At the Paris Peace Conference, Britain played a key role in restricting French post-war ambitions and now feared that the Conference of Ambassadors could become a tool of French policy. Britain's initial reticence as to the creation of the Conference of Ambassadors was due to the fear that this new political body might be used to enforce the Treaty of Versailles all too comprehensively. Foch's ambitions and policies toward Germany especially concerned British political and military circles.[37] British policymakers, however, realized that the Conference of Ambassadors could be used to prevent "French centralization" of political and diplomatic power, and that it could work as a "clearing-house" between the IAMCC and the Allied governments.[38] Henceforth, Britain supported the creation and work of the Ambassadors' Conference.[39] With a prophetic view toward the future, British diplomats realized that this new Allied body could be used to settle the inevitable differences with the French in the post-war period.

By November, the Allied governments had made their appointments to the Conference of Ambassadors.[40] Under Belgian pressure, France requested the addition of its smaller northern neighbor as a member of the Conference.[41] The Allies soon agreed to allow a Belgian representative to participate with the Allied body when they discussed Belgian issues.[42] Aside from the fact that Belgium had been part of the Allied coalition that had defeated Germany in the war, Britain and France agreed that Belgium qualified for membership in the Ambassadors' Conference since it bordered Germany and was part of the occupation force in the Rhineland. Although Britain, France, the United States, Italy, and Japan were the principal nations of the Conference of Ambassadors, the American representative on the Conference remained only as an observer with no official responsibility after the United States rejected the Treaty of Versailles.[43] Finally, the Allies decided to allow political figures such as foreign ministers and heads of state to sit in the Conference of Ambassadors as a substitute for any nation's appointed ambassador.[44] As a result, a number of different representatives from all member nations would ultimately participate in important negotiations and decisions.

The final duties of the Conference of Ambassadors were quite extensive, and eventually included interpreting and executing questions from *all* the post-war treaties. Therefore, any contentious issues arising from the treaties of Versailles, St, Germain, Trianon, Neuilly, and Sèvres fell under the jurisdiction of the Conference of Ambassadors. The amount of work was staggering, and the disparate political agendas of Britain and France led to a number of bitter disputes within the Conference of Ambassadors. Although deeply involved in the disarmament of Germany, its representatives examined a plethora of questions such as the Marienwerder and Allenstein plebiscites, the Upper Silesian dispute, and the military control of Austria, Bulgaria and Hungary. With regard to the military clauses of the Treaty of Versailles, this Allied "clearing-house" would ultimately address all major policy changes.

The Allied Military Committee of Versailles (AMCV)

Although Marshal Foch served the Allied cause in the war with distinction, the end of the war raised questions concerning his role in post-war Allied military affairs. With the threat of renewed hostilities all but evaporating with the signing of the Treaty of Versailles in June 1919, Foch's position became uncertain. Shunned at the Paris Peace Conference after demanding the separation of the Rhineland and the creation of a long-term enlisted German army, Foch had no intention of losing influence and control over Allied policies toward the future course of the German military. Despite the fact that Foch's role in international affairs had declined since the end of the war, the marshal soon played a particularly important role in the creation of the third organizational Allied body involved in the disarmament and military control of Germany: the Allied Military Committee of Versailles.

On 15 October, Foch addressed a letter to Clemenceau asking to be relieved of duty as Supreme Commander of Allied forces. Foch, however, also explained that the execution of the military clauses of the treaty could be carried out only by "an Interallied Military organ operating under a single head" which would have command over Allied control commissions, occupation forces, and general military questions.[45] Thus, the marshal wanted to give up nominal command of Allied military forces to play both a military and political role in the execution of the military clauses of the Versailles Treaty. In the discussion of Foch's letter in a meeting of the Heads of Delegations on 18 October, British delegate Eyre Crowe pointed out that the control commissions were already set up to supervise the execution of the treaty. However, Clemenceau justified Foch's requests by explaining that a central Allied body would obviate potential confusion over Allied command structure. For instance, instead of requesting instruction from each delegation's national government, the control commissions could work with a single organization. Revealing French pride toward the former Commander-in-Chief, Clemenceau added that "it would never do for the Germans to think that they were finally rid of him."[46]

In December, the Allied decision to create an international organization to supervise the execution of the Versailles Treaty and furnish advice to Allied governments concerning military matters moved a step closer to completion. There was general Allied consensus that Foch would head such an organization. Even British General Henry Wilson claimed that there was "no bigger gun than Marshal Foch."[47] Lloyd George agreed with Clemenceau that Foch's organization would not have executive powers but that it would serve as an advisory body to the Allied governments.[48] Both Lloyd George and Clemenceau were careful once again not to invest any military authority or organization with executive power. Allied policy-making decisions remained in civilian hands while military authorities retained only technical and supervisory powers.

The official creation of the Allied Military Committee of Versailles occurred on 10 January 1920, the same day the Treaty of Versailles went into effect. Despite an earlier objection by Italy that the committee should not be headed by such a prestigious military leader as Marshal Foch, the political Allied leadership appointed Foch to lead the AMCV.[49] They established the AMCV as an advisory body to the Allied governments concerning military matters pertaining to the post-war settlements and gave it the power to carry out Allied orders regarding the control commissions and occupation forces.[50] The AMCV's duties included interpreting the military clauses of the treaties, assessing the general military situation in Europe, and formulating some of the military clauses for the treaties with Turkey and Hungary.[51] In addition, Lloyd George insisted that the committee's advisory powers included general military matters and specifically mentioned the military troubles in Russia. The AMCV was composed of Allied officers from the French, British, Italian, Belgian and Japanese armies, while an American representative served occasionally in an advisory role.

The political and administrative organizations that the Allies created in 1919 and early 1920 to oversee the disarmament and military control of Germany thus consisted of three inter-allied bodies: the Inter-Allied Military Control Commission, the Conference of Ambassadors, and the Allied Military Committee of Versailles. This organizational machinery had important ramifications in the enforcement of the military clauses of the Treaty of Versailles. When the United States dropped out of European diplomatic affairs in 1920, the implementation of disarmament became an Anglo-French affair. After having made terrible sacrifices in the war, Britain and France, as Europe's powers, positioned themselves to administer the peace settlement with Germany by ensuring control of all three Allied disarmament bodies. For instance, France (with four members) and Britain (with two members) dominated the executive body within the IAMCC, the Council. Initial majority Council decisions favored the French but the initiative would later pass to the British in early 1922 when the Allies diminished French membership on the Council and decided to make decisions only by unanimous vote.

While the task of the Inter-Allied Military Control Commission dealt specifically with supervising the execution of the military clauses of the Treaty of Versailles, the authority and tasks of the Conference of Ambassadors and Allied Military Committee of Versailles were more pervasive and ambiguous. Within this hierarchical triumvirate, the Conference of Ambassadors was the superior body with executive control. Both the German government and the IAMCC would refer problems, especially concerning the interpretation or execution of the military clauses of Versailles, to the Conference of Ambassadors, which would then force the IAMCC to comply with its decisions. Despite initial British reticence toward its creation, the Conference of Ambassadors, as a clearing-house for Allied problems, would eventually become a political platform for the British to thwart French disarmament plans. British insistence in early 1921 to refer all political decisions to the Conference of Ambassadors later increased the authority of the executive body and allowed the British to veto French demands.

The Allies created the Conference of Ambassadors as a purely civil administrative body without technical expertise in military matters. Despite the existence of the IAMCC, an international body composed of professional military officers and men, the Allied governments agreed to allow the AMCV to act as the Conference's technical adviser on military matters. This decision would ultimately influence the enforcement of the military terms of the treaty by undermining the authority and ability of the IAMCC to supervise disarmament operations. The German government would later exploit the Allied organizational structure of disarmament and military control by simply bypassing the authority of the IAMCC through endless complaints to the Conference of Ambassadors. This strategy helped prolong Allied disarmament operations well beyond the initial hopes of both Allied and German governments.

Part II

Germany disarmed
(1920–1922)

4   Armaments

The Allied offensive on war material

The costly experiences of World War I illustrated vividly to the Allies the devastating effectiveness of twentieth-century weaponry. On the Western Front, the horrendous toll inflicted by machine-guns and artillery had indeed shown the Allies and Germany the power and destructive capacity of a modern military power. Disarming Germany therefore seemed an obvious step toward preventing another world catastrophe and a way to punish Germany for its leading role in the outbreak of war. At the Paris Peace Conference, Allied leaders decided to place severe restrictions upon German ownership of armaments and munitions. Consequently, Articles 164–6 of the Treaty of Versailles fixed the maximum number of armaments for a German army made up of 100,000 men and designated a specific number of rounds for each weapon.[1] The treaty prohibited the heavy artillery, poison gas, tanks (Article 171) and submarines that had terrorized Allied forces. In addition, under Article 170, the victorious powers forbade Germany to import or export war material. Although they sanctioned the disarmament of the German armed forces as a prelude to world disarmament, the Allies wanted to make sure that they prostrated the German army before they agreed to consider similar actions.[2]

Under the treaty's terms, the Allies allowed Germany two months after the effective date of the Treaty of Versailles to surrender all war material in excess of the specified amounts and to store all authorized war material in points communicated to the Allies.[3] Therefore, the Allies would know that any war material found outside of the specified areas would be a violation of the treaty. In addition, the Allies sought not simply to contain German ownership and use of armaments and munitions but to severely restrict, even eradicate, Germany's massive industrial capacity to manufacture war material. Under Article 168, the Allies thus specified a number of German factories that subsequently would be allowed to produce war material. Any other German factory that participated in the "manufacture, preparation, storage or design of arms, munitions, or any war material whatever" would be in breach of the treaty and subject to closure.[4]

The era of disarmament in Germany began on 10 January 1920, when the Inter-Allied Military Control Commission officially started its work. The Allies set up the IAMCC's headquarters in Berlin and billeted the officers and men in a number of hotels in the city.[5] The commission set up its own postal and medical services, as well as telegraph and telephone communications to Marshal Foch and other important military headquarters throughout Germany. After having tested the waters in the fall of 1919 while awaiting the ratification of the Treaty of Versailles, the IAMCC was ready to proceed with the disarmament of Germany's military and industrial establishments.

The Armaments Sub-commission of the IAMCC, with approximately 150 Allied officers, was the largest of the three sub-commissions.[6] Under the leadership of British Major-General Francis Bingham, the Armaments Sub-commission had its headquarters in Berlin. Bingham, a senior artillery officer, had played a vital role at the Ministry of Munitions during the war by helping place British industry on a war footing.[7] Hence, Bingham's career and wartime experiences shaped his post-war outlook. He was a consistent advocate of the destruction of German armaments, Britain's main line of disarmament policy from the Paris Peace Conference until the end of disarmament operations. He believed that the destruction of armaments and munitions was the most effective manner of disarming Germany and considered the destruction of German artillery "a matter of urgency."[8] Bingham and his adjutant, Lieutenant-Colonel Stewart Roddie, also placed much greater trust in German intentions than did their French counterparts.[9] The French and Bingham's second-in-command, Brigadier-General J.H. Morgan, considered Bingham's subsequent inclination to believe German reports of fulfilment to be naive. As a result, the underlying tension in the command of the IAMCC led to a number of clashes.

Under Bingham's command, the Allies set up eleven armament district committees, authorized to conduct local control of armaments. The British and French had been sure to locate the district committees strategically throughout Germany.[10] The mission of the Armaments Sub-commission was twofold. First, the Armaments Sub-commission had the responsibility of overseeing the surrender and destruction of all armaments and munitions, in excess of the limits prescribed by the Treaty of Versailles, that were under German possession. Second, but no less important to the IAMCC, the Armaments Sub-commission could close all non-authorized arms-producing establishments in Germany and oversee the production of authorized plants. Members of the sub-commission had the explicit authority to conduct inspections of German facilities to verify compliance with the treaty.

War material: definition and ownership

The restriction and destruction of German war material produced a number of difficulties for the Armaments Sub-commission. The ambiguous nature of the definition of war material led to serious problems of interpretation and enforcement. Consequently, the IMACC, AMCV and Conference of Ambassadors had to debate the question of two main issues: the definition and ownership as well as the surrender and destruction of war material. The definition of war materials presented immediate problems to the Allies. For instance, should the Allies restrict or destroy the trucks, ambulances, and uniforms that the German army possessed? The problem of defining war materials would plague early Allied disarmament efforts and test the Allied relationship with German political and military authorities.

Under the terms of the treaty, the Allies expected Germany to surrender all excess stocks of war material, including captured foreign armaments, as well as the machines used for war production.[11] Without a precise definition of war material, however, questions abounded over what was dangerous to Allied security.[12] Thus, the IAMCC, working in conjunction with the AMCV and Conference of Ambassadors, drafted a list of war material that the Germans would be forced to surrender. The outcome of this project was a lengthy (thirty-three chapters) and detailed list known as the Blue Book.[13] In addition to artillery pieces, armored cars, rifles, grenades, flamethrowers, shells, fuses, and detonators, the IAMCC listed less obvious equipment such as gas masks, optical instruments, signalling equipment, uniforms, field ambulances and telephones. The Blue Book even contained the number of blank cartridges the German army used in training.[14] Although involving a relatively small number of individuals, the Allied disarmament and control of the German military establishment was to be pervasive, ubiquitous and demanding.

The dual-use nature of some military equipment challenged the Allied definition of war material. On 20 April 1920, the German government criticized the size and scope of the Allied definition of war materials, arguing that the inclusion of items such as cooking utensils, and more importantly transportation, would not only hurt the German economy but would hinder reparations deliveries to the Allies and make German political conditions conducive to Bolshevism.[15] The Allies changed their definition of war material, and soon the IAMCC acquired the responsibility of distinguishing between war material as a security threat (which had to be destroyed or rendered useless) and war material that had peaceful uses (which was sold). The control commissions therefore possessed "full discretionary powers" in determining whether to destroy or sell war materials.[16] Non-fighting material, such as clothing, was sold within Germany only (the export of all war material was forbidden) and dispersed throughout the country to eliminate any possible military utility. Nollet drew up a list of non-military items that included motor vehicles, railway material, harness, barbed wire, spades, picks and various tools. Henceforth, the Allies sold non-military war material and credited Germany's reparations account with the proceeds.[17]

The issue of distinguishing between war material for combat purposes or peaceful means continued to have a deleterious effect upon German relations with the Armaments Sub-commission of the IAMCC. In January 1921, the Fehrenbach government asked the IAMCC to revise the non-combat war material list, but the IAMCC upheld its decision on the illegality of items such as gas masks and field ambulances.[18] Despite continued German objections, in August 1921 the Allies demanded the surrender of all German uniforms, jackets, pants, backpacks and tents (subsequently sold) and the destruction of helmets.[19]

Another disagreement between the Allies and Germany arose over the ownership of surrendered or destroyed war material. The treaty obligated Germany to surrender all excess war material to the Allies. Yet nowhere did the treaty stipulate what action to take regarding the ownership of the remaining product, which could still have utility as well as monetary value. Foch had responded to Nollet's appeal of 31 January on the issue of the ownership of such material by advising that the Allies should retain ownership of all surrendered war material. The Conference of Ambassadors subsequently adopted Foch's proposal on 10 February 1920.[20] The Allied governments had already given authority to the Reparation Commission to liquidate surrendered or destroyed war material.[21] The AMCV now reiterated that the Reparation Commission already had the responsibility to conduct the sale of destroyed war material and to credit all proceeds to Germany's reparations account.

In May the question of ownership of destroyed war material resurfaced as the German government simply refused to conform to the 10 February decision of the Conference of Ambassadors.[22] Once again, the Conference of Ambassadors stated that the term "surrender" (*livrer*) was equivalent to the transfer of ownership and upheld its previous decision.[23] Lord D'Abernon, the British Ambassador in Berlin from 1920 to 1926, as well as Bingham, thought that Allied efforts regarding strict adherence over ownership of scrap from destroyed war material were simply unnecessary.[24] Nevertheless, in June the Allied governments reaffirmed the responsibility of the Reparation Commission, which set up the Bureau of Liquidation for War Material, for the sale of surrendered or destroyed German war material.[25] These sales would later influence Allied decisions concerning the export of any German military products.

War material: surrender and destruction

The Treaty of Versailles stipulated that the IAMCC was responsible for the *supervision* of the surrender and destruction of German war material. Moreover, since the IAMCC was simply not large enough to carry out the destruction of all excess German armaments, munitions and equipment, the treaty entrusted the German government with a significant amount of responsibility for the destruction of its own military prowess. Placing such responsibility and trust in a defeated and bitter nation led to constant violations and delays. One glaring example occurred when the Allies asked the German government to hand over production registers of armaments factories so as to ascertain the amount of prohibited German war material. While the Allies later found many of the registers in a basement of a factory in Spandau, the Germans reneged on their promise to hand them over and never placed then in the possession of the Allies.[26] Consequently, some Allied officers expressed doubt about the exact state of German disarmament throughout the reign of the IAMCC.

In order to carry out its duties of collecting and destroying surrendered war material the German government had set up a civilian organization in August 1919, the *Reichstreuhandgesellschaft* (War Disposals Board).[27] This German office established depots of surrendered material, safeguarded these stocks, and carried out the destruction of war material under IAMCC surveillance.[28] Overall, the IAMCC had to oversee the work of approximately 200 centers of destruction and 300 depots of war material.[29] Destruction methods varied, depending upon the material in question. German laborers cut barrels of weapons and gun carriages into pieces with oxyacetylene blowtorches and often had to crush larger guns in industrial presses. They rendered rifles and machine-guns inoperable before melting them down into raw material, burned gunpowder, and destroyed shells by cutting through the shell casings with a machine saw.[30] In the Krupp factories, workers filled the shrinking pits used in the production of heavy artillery with cement and destroyed the heavy plant, such as furnaces and oil-tanks, with dynamite.[31] They also cut the massive guns of the mighty arms producers of Germany into small sections and stacked them in towering yet harmless piles of scrap.

After two months of inaction, the IAMCC effectively began to supervise war material destruction in March 1920.[32] Prior to 10 March, the deadline for the delivery of all surplus German war material, the IAMCC actually witnessed few accomplishments.[33] Although obligated to produce lists of war material in excess of the stipulated treaty amounts, German military authorities delivered such lists, often containing inaccurate figures, well past Allied deadlines. Foch warned that Germany still possessed about 18,000 artillery pieces and therefore posed a dangerous military threat to the Allies. The British and French political and military authorities were also skeptical about the claims of the German government concerning the German destruction of war material from the period of the Armistice up until 10 March, when German authorities finally supplied the Allies with lists of surrendered and destroyed material. Unfortunately, the IAMCC had no means of verifying this alleged destruction. Foch actually complained that premature destruction of war material by Germany violated the Treaty of Versailles since the treaty obligated Germany to surrender all excess material to Allied authorities.[34] Furthermore, Foch set the tone for French policy regarding the enforcement of the Treaty of Versailles on

20 March by delivering a dire warning to the Conference of Ambassadors: "Beware! It is not an advantageous peace that you have but a dangerous war that is threatening you, and I, General-in-Chief of the Allied Armies, will not take the responsibility of your tranquility if you do not disarm these people as stipulated."[35] This adamant French insistence upon the absolute enforcement of the Treaty of Versailles soon came into conflict with British policy regarding German disarmament and set the stage for Franco–British hostility in the ensuing years.

In addition to the debate over the surrender of German war criminals and the instability created by the Kapp *putsch*, German opposition to the Treaty of Versailles' stipulations for the size of the *Reichswehr* delayed the surrender and destruction of German armaments. Since the treaty restricted armaments to an army of 100,000 men, Germany was slow to surrender and destroy its war material in the hopes that the Allies might still allow an increase in the size of the *Reichswehr*.[36] German military and political authorities also hesitated to return Allied armaments question- naires and provided false statements regarding the amount of excess war material.[37] By mid-1921, the numbers of destroyed weapons had easily surpassed the German figures. Modification of the effectives clauses of the treaty, a major element of German strategy, would soon play a role in the negotiations of the Spa Conference.

The British and French governments met in Paris in the latter half of May to discuss German fulfilment of the military clauses of the Treaty of Versailles. In essence, the amount of war material simply overwhelmed the embryonic destruction efforts. The British and French demanded that Germany surrender excess war material and recognize war material allowances and the number of factories authorized to produce it.[38] These demands followed in the wake of the German claim that the consumption of ammunition was a domestic matter and therefore outside Allied juris- diction.[39] The Allies allowed new deadlines for the surrender of police and fortification armaments (31 May) and *Reichswehr* and civilian arms (10 June), the surrender of all excess war material (30 June), and the passage of legislation forbidding the import and export of war material (30 June). Thus, after a delay of a few months, the Allies had already modified the original deadlines set by the Treaty of Versailles. At this stage of disarma- ment, the Allies did not consider reinforcing the modified dates with the threat of military sanctions, but what would they do if Germany did not meet these new deadlines?

Despite the initial delay in Allied efforts to disarm Germany, by June 1920 the Armaments Sub-commission reported significant progress in the surrender and destruction of German armaments. Allied officers verified the destruction of thousands of rifles, heavy guns, optical instruments, sighting pieces, fuses, shells, bombs, grenades, small arms ammunition, and cartridges in the last weeks of spring. While these amounts disap- pointed the French, the British General Staff pointed out that Allied

district committees had destroyed "most of the material in their possession."[40] In addition to compiling detailed records of all material
surrendered and destroyed under its supervision, the Armaments Sub-
commission had been able to verify some of the war material destroyed by
Germany before January 1920 and to determine the nationality and
amount of surrendered non-German war material.[41]

The Spa Conference

In the immediate post-war years, Britain and France held a number of conferences to settle outstanding issues, especially German disarmament and
reparations, from the peace settlements of 1919. Allied conferences of San
Remo and Hythe in April and May 1920, respectively, led to rather vague
discussions of disarmament but reaffirmed the Anglo–French desire to
discuss the enforcement of the Treaty of Versailles and produced an Allied
agreement to meet with a German delegation in Spa, Belgium.[42] At conferences in Boulogne and Spa, the Allies attempted to determine the extent of
German fulfilment of the military clauses of Versailles and to set time
limits for their execution. Despite the progress of the IAMCC, the treaty's
disarmament deadlines had long since passed. Therefore, at the Boulogne
Conference in June 1920, the British and French governments expressed
their disappointment in German fulfilment of the military clauses of the
Versailles Treaty and demanded that the German government meet its disarmament obligations.[43] The Allies also conceded important modifications
to the size of Germany's police forces. If Germany produced no positive
results, the Allied governments threatened "to study the means required to
ensure the complete execution of the terms of the Treaty."[44] The idea of an
occupation of German territory, first seen in the discussions in the Paris
Peace Conference, remained a possible course of action. Yet the importance of the Boulogne Conference was the fact that the British and French
had united their policies towards German disarmament and the enforcement of the Treaty of Versailles, at least for the time being. The French, in
particular, expressed delight with Lloyd George's emphasis upon the
speedy disarmament of Germany.[45]

At the Spa Conference in July, the British and French governments
again tackled the subject of German compliance with the military terms of
the treaty and produced a stringent plan of action to ensure German
progress towards disarmament. The Spa Conference, which had the distinction of being the first post-war conference between the Allies and
Germany, was held from 5 July to 16 July 1920. Representatives at the
conference included Lloyd George, French premier Alexandre Millerand,
and German Chancellor Konstantin Fehrenbach, a moderate conservative
of the Center Party. The German delegation used the disarmament negotiations at Spa as a forum for the modification of the Treaty of Versailles'
military clauses, and the major thrust of the German argument focused on

justifying the maintenance of an army twice the size prescribed by the treaty. Time and again the German delegates argued that political stability in Germany depended upon the maintenance of a German army where "at least 200,000 men were necessary to ensure public order and tranquility."[46] Chancellor Fehrenbach also played the Red card and stressed the danger in the rise of Bolshevism if Germany were not allowed to keep a sufficient military force. However, Lloyd George, while fearful both of the rise of left-wing and right-wing political extremists, kept the negotiations at Spa focused upon the precise fulfilment of the military clauses of the treaty and demanded a detailed report on German surrender and destruction of war material.

Disarmament discussions at Spa entered a new stage on 7 July, when General Hans von Seeckt reported on the status of German armaments, including rifles, machine-guns, trench mortars, and artillery. As head of the *Reichswehr*, General von Seeckt would later attempt to circumvent a number of military clauses of the Treaty of Versailles.[47] Out of a total of just over six million rifles, Seeckt claimed that Germany lost close to 1.5 million in the 1918 retreat and subsequently surrendered 1.8 million to the *Reichstreuhandgesellschaft*. He reported that Germany had surrendered 55,800 machine-guns, 6,400 trench mortars and 11,000 artillery pieces, and that only about 3,400 machine-guns, 4,000 trench mortars, and 346 heavy guns remained. Seeckt also requested a gradual reduction of the German army in stages, in which the level of 100,000 would not be reached until 10 October 1921.[48]

Lloyd George responded critically to the vast amount of armaments that remained in German possession and claimed that General von Seeckt had seriously underestimated the number of machine-guns that Germany possessed. The fact that the Allies did not contest the small number of heavy guns that Seeckt claimed remained in German possession illustrated Allied confidence in the destruction of Germany's heavy armaments. Under instructions from Lloyd George and Millerand, Marshal Foch subsequently outlined a plan for German fulfillment of five Allied demands. Aside from the surrender of all excess war material, the Allies demanded that Germany disarm the *Einwohnerwehr* (civil defense forces) and the *Sicherheitspolizei* (heavily armed security police) immediately, publish a public demand for German civilians to surrender all arms, take measures to abolish compulsory service and reorganize the *Reichswehr*, and fulfil the naval and air clauses of the Treaty of Versailles. They also decided to allow Germany a gradual reduction of the *Reichswehr*, but not along the lines of Seeckt's proposal. Most importantly, if Germany did not pass legislation to abolish conscription by 1 September 1920, reduce the *Reichswehr* to 160,000 by 1 October 1920 and to 100,000 by 1 January 1921, or fulfill the other demands, the Allies agreed to occupy German territory, possibly the Ruhr region, until they verified absolute compliance.[49] This latter stipulation marked the first time that the Allies used the threat of occupation in enforcing disarmament, and the subsequent results assured that it would not be the last.

The reaction of German political and military authorities to the Spa Protocol varied. German Foreign Minister Walter Simons supported the modification of the reduction of the German army but criticized the new threat of Allied occupation.[50] But Allied unity and the threat of sanctions backed Germany against a wall. Although Simons disliked Spa's ramifications he agreed that the treaty bound Germany to the fulfilment of its obligations.[51] While the right-wing press blasted the failure of Fehrenbach to obtain serious modifications to the Treaty of Versailles, General von Seeckt, no advocate of the Weimar Republic, supported disarming the public in order to eradicate the threat of armed workers.[52] The Allies, however, refused to allow any other treaty modifications, and the German delegation signed the protocol on 9 July.

While fear of political instability resulted in Allied modification to the effective clauses of Versailles, Lloyd George remained adamant in demanding the surrender and destruction of German armaments. Similar to the negotiations concerning the military clauses at the Paris Peace Conference, Lloyd George had once again successfully pushed for the destruction of German armaments. Allied policy toward armaments remained uncompromising despite the modifications to Allied policy toward German effectives. At the Spa negotiations, Millerand had opposed the extension of the period of Germany's reduction of the *Reichswehr* but succumbed to Lloyd George's wishes. France was simply not willing to risk losing British support in disarming Germany. Thus, Lloyd George's concession towards the reduction of the German army mildly appeased the German government, eased his fear of Bolshevism, and sacrificed French policy to British interests.

The Allied occupation ultimatum of the Spa Protocol produced immediate results, and Britain and France quickly learned the benefit of military sanctions. After the Spa Conference, the disarmament of Germany's arsenal increased in intensity. In fact, by the first week of August, General Bingham believed that Germany had surrendered as many guns as it possessed at the end of the war.[53] Thus, the head of the British delegation of the IAMCC believed the destruction of Germany's heavy guns to be near completion. In terms of surrendered and destroyed war material, the British War Office considered the remaining number of rifles and machine-guns in the hands of German civilians to be a primary concern. French policy toward German disarmament remained tied to the larger issue of the complete enforcement of the Treaty of Versailles. In August, French Army Headquarters in Paris warned that disarmament was still far from complete despite the recent progress.[54] This line of policy remained entrenched in French political and military circles throughout disarmament operations in Germany. The policy of occupation as a weapon of Allied enforcement, however, had a successful debut and it would continue to have a significant impact upon future disarmament operations in Germany.

At the Spa Conference, the Allies had determined that the German civilian population possessed a large number of rifles and other small arms. The Spa Protocol forced the German government to take steps to disarm the population by posting notices throughout Germany to surrender arms. On 7 August, Germany enforced a law to disarm the civil population and by the end of the month published proclamations regarding fines for those who did not surrender arms.[55] Actual surrender of war material by civilians began in mid-September. The German Commissioner for Disarmament, Dr. Peters, even offered monetary compensation to individuals who surrendered weapons and informed the authorities of hidden arms.[56] Civilians could hand over armaments for reimbursement up until 21 October and could avoid legal action if they surrendered weapons by November.[57] The Germans set up destruction centers where German civilians turned in a variety of weapons for payment, including rifles, machine-guns, trench mortars and flamethrowers. Initial results of civil disarmament fell below Allied expectations, especially in northern and eastern Germany. By the end of September the Armaments Sub-commission still considered the civil population to be in possession of a significant amount of arms.[58] In October the IAMCC ordered that all destruction of civilian arms be conducted exclusively in destruction centers of the Control Commission.[59]

In addition to the ownership of illegal weapons by German civilians, the Armaments Sub-commission faced the problem of accounting for non-German armaments, most notably Russian arms in the possession of the *Reichswehr*. As stipulated by the Treaty of Versailles, Germany had to surrender and destroy any war material in excess of the limits of the treaty, regardless of its origin. In fact, the Conference of Ambassadors ordered the IAMCC to destroy all Russian armaments in Germany and the Reparation Commission to sell the scrap material, with the proceeds of these sales delivered to the states of pre-war Russia.[60] Most military experts considered the overall quality of Russian armaments to be inferior to German weapons, but nevertheless, the IAMCC destroyed thousands of Russian rifles, bayonets, and shells, as well as dozens of artillery pieces.[61]

The IAMCC experienced considerable progress supervising the destruction of German war material in the first year of disarmament operations. In mid-October, Nollet admitted that aside from optical and signaling equipment, harness and armored cars, the demilitarization of German war material was proceeding well.[62] Bingham reported that a mere 373 guns remained in Germany's possession, though his second-in-command, Brigadier-General Morgan, contested this figure.[63] By the end of November, the IAMCC believed that the diminishing numbers of surrendered and destroyed German guns was simply due to the fact that few remained.[64] The number of guns, trench mortars, machine-guns, rifles, and shells destroyed under IAMCC auspices in 1920 was impressive. By 13 January 1921, the Germans had surrendered to the IAMCC almost 30,000 guns and barrels, 10,300 trench mortars, 70,300 machine-guns, 2.9 million rifles, thirty-three million shells, 412 million rounds of small arms ammunition, as well as parts of various armaments.[65] This amounted to about 90 percent of the artillery, 87 percent of the trench mortars, and 72 percent of the machine-guns that Germany would ultimately surrender.[66] Consequently, the British General Staff considered the surrender of artillery significant enough to prevent German aggression and believed such disarmament efforts would be complete by mid-March 1921. Despite this success, the German army did not yet conform to the military clauses of the Treaty of Versailles.

At the end of the first year of Allied operations, German opposition to the strict fulfillment of the military terms of the Treaty of Versailles increased. As a result, the French government proposed that the AMCV draft a general report on the state of execution of the military and air clauses of the treaty. The subsequent report became the basis for the Paris Note of 29 January and the London Ultimatum of 5 May 1921. Three major points concerning the armaments obligations of Germany remained: excess war material from the reduction of the *Reichswehr* to 100,000 men, excess war material maintained by the German government for training purposes and for replacement of worn-out material, and the existence of civilian arms. In the final days of December, the AMCV agreed that while "the surrender and destruction of German war material has already attained very considerable figures, it is nonetheless true that the disarmament of Germany is still far from complete."[67]

From 24 to 29 January 1921, the Allies met in Paris to discuss the execution of the Treaty of Versailles, focusing upon disarmament and reparations. French Prime Minister Aristide Briand, who also held the office of Foreign Minister, considered the question of German disarmament "a matter of life and death to France," and Foch still believed Germany "capable of undertaking very serious military operations."[68] However, British policy-makers began to distance themselves from the French insistence on total enforcement. Lloyd George's closest adviser, Philip Kerr, had recently warned his Prime Minister that the public could reject the disarmament of Germany, and that France must be made to understand that Britain could not support the strict application of the Treaty of Versailles.[69] At the Paris Conference, Lloyd George claimed he supported enforcement of the Versailles Treaty but thought "conditions of the moment" should affect the treaty's strict enforcement. Thus, the British Prime Minister did not rule out possible treaty modification. These Anglo–French differences would soon threaten the future of Allied disarmament enforcement but for now the British and French continued to work effectively in concert.

On 29 January, the Allies backed up demands that Germany pass a new military law and surrender excess war material by 15 March, reorganize the *Reichswehr* by 15 April, and disband all military associations by 30 June 1921, with the threat to enforce economic and military sanctions and occupy more territory in the Rhineland.[70] However, the new deadlines passed without significant progress. In fact, these Allied disarmament decisions would not be accepted by the Germans until the Wirth government pledged Germany to a policy of fulfilment in May 1921.[71] In the meantime, the Allies rejected a German request for an independent tribunal to settle the outstanding issues. Consequently, the lack of German compliance in the fulfilment of disarmament and reparations obligations led to the enforcement of the Paris sanctions. On 8 March, French, British, and Belgian forces occupied the cities of Duisburg, Ruhrort, and Düsseldorf as Allied leaders applied economic sanctions; these troops remained until 25 August 1925.[72] Although the occupation failed ultimately to elicit German treaty compliance, it clearly pointed out that the Allies were not loath to use force in the enforcement of either economic or military demands upon Germany. The Allied policy of military sanctions, however, would soon bear fruit and become a diplomatic tool in the quest for enforcement.

In the spring of 1921, as the modified deadlines of the military clauses of Versailles expired, French doubts about a timely conclusion of German disarmament increased. General Nollet believed that true fulfilment of the military clauses of the Treaty of Versailles was not yet near completion. The French General blamed the German government for the delay and obstruction faced by Allied officers of the IAMCC. The Armaments Sub-commission, encouraged by the surrender and destruction of rifles, expressed dismay about excess pistols, machine-guns, trench mortars, harness, vehicles, optical and bridging equipment, and flamethrowers.[73] By the first week in April, Nollet reported that he had not witnessed any new progress towards the surrender and destruction of German armaments, and that Germany continued to default on a number of the treaty's clauses.[74] Most importantly, the German government now declared that it could not surrender all excess war material until 30 April at the earliest.

On 5 May 1921, Britain and France once again attempted to enforce the articles of the Treaty of Versailles through the threat of military sanctions. The Allies decided to allow the German government new deadlines to surrender war material but threatened to occupy the Ruhr Valley if Germany did not fulfil its disarmament and reparations obligations.[75] This demand was a repetition of the recent Paris strategy in January, subsequently emphasized by the marching of Allied troops into the Rhineland in March. The renewed threat of an Allied occupation forced the hand of the German government. Consequently, Fehrenbach resigned and Joseph Wirth, a member of the Center Party and an advocate of fulfillment, replaced him. Although the crux of the ultimatum concerned the payment of reparations, Wirth's acceptance of the Allied note also obligated the

German government to complete the execution of the modified military articles of the Treaty of Versailles.[76] The German rationale behind acceptance of the London ultimatum, aside from wanting to prevent an Allied occupation, was to eliminate any pretext for the maintenance of Allied disarmament operations.[77]

The entire issue of the disarmament of Germany reached an important crossroads by the early summer of 1921 as the British first broached the question of future disarmament operations. At this point, the execution of the military clauses remained incomplete but much work had been carried out. In fact, the British Foreign Office believed that only the surrender of some excess arms, equipment, and signaling materials, as well as the disarmament of various coastal fortresses, remained. As a result of Allied enforcement efforts backed by the threat of military sanctions in the May ultimatum, in June British military intelligence reported that disarmament was once again proceeding well and that only the district of Königsberg had recently experienced a dilatory response in the surrender of excess war material.[78] By July 1921, Britain's attitude toward German disarmament started to change perceptibly. The amount of destroyed war material dramatically influenced British perceptions of the state of German disarmament. Increasingly, British political and military authorities rejected previously held assumptions of German intransigence for the belief that German fulfillment of the military clauses of Versailles approached completion.

Although there were some exceptions to the change of British policy, most notably Brigadier-General Morgan, both the Foreign Office and the War Office considered the surrender of German armaments negligent only in certain surplus weapons. Two Central Department members of the Foreign Office, Sydney Waterlow and Ralph Wigram, believed that Germany had "substantially executed" the military clauses of the treaty and that only the surrender of excess German war material such as signaling equipment and the disarmament of some coastal fortifications remained incomplete.[79] The progress of the Armaments Sub-commission's disarmament results also pleased Major-General Bingham.[80] On the other hand, General Nollet's often hostile attitude ebbed and flowed. At times he vociferously demanded the complete fulfilment of the military clauses of the treaty. Nollet's bi-weekly reports to Foch in the spring of June 1921 emphasized Nollet's impatience with German disarmament violations and obstruction to Allied efforts. Nollet focused his anger, justified by the French demand for the complete fulfilment of all the military clauses of the treaty, primarily at Germany but also at the glowing British attitude toward the destruction of a single aspect of disarmament. Yet in July, even Nollet could not deny the success of the May ultimatum and reported that the surrender and destruction of German war material was proceeding well; he admitted that regarding illicit war material, Germany essentially only had to surrender optical instruments, signaling equipment, and harness.[81]

The Armaments Sub-commission faced a number of difficulties in supervising the surrender and destruction of German war material. One problem that plagued the efforts of the Armaments Sub-commission was the surplus of German war material in *Reichswehr* depots that the German government regarded as training equipment. Certain German authorities gave inaccurate war material figures to the Allies to omit various amounts of spare parts and practice weapons.[82] Consequently, the IAMCC refused any consideration of training weapons as non-war material. In addition, the Armaments Sub-commission faced the unauthorized transportation of war material by German authorities. At times, the Germans would move war material from depot to depot, thereby altering the amounts under supervision.[83] This ploy hindered the work of the Armaments Sub-commission in determining the amount of destruction that remained, and the IAMCC decided to force the Germans to obtain a special permit for the transport of any war material within Germany.[84] Previously, in October 1920, the IAMCC had declared that all transport of German war material within Germany be authorized through notification of the local IAMCC district.[85] Altogether, the great number of difficulties that the Armaments Sub-commission experienced in the early days of disarming Germany would strain Allied–German relations, hinder progress towards the completion of the IAMCC's duties in Germany, and prolong Allied disarmament operations in Germany.

The AMCV also criticized the level of German disarmament. In August, Foch claimed that without the lists of war material that Germany possessed in 1918, the Allies could not verify German disarmament to the levels of the Treaty of Versailles. Foch's belief hinted at permanent control. Furthermore, the AMCV demanded the completion of every detail of German disarmament, including the surrender of wagons, bridging equipment, and field bakeries.[86] Therefore, even though Germany had already surrendered and destroyed a vast amount of armaments under the IAMCC's supervision, Allied disarmament organizations lacked a consensus of opinion toward Germany's fulfilment of disarmament. As a result, even amid discussions of diminishing the extent of military control in Germany, the IAMCC continued full operations. By the end of 1921, the discovery of a number of illegal war caches by inspectors of the Armaments Sub-commission raised doubts about the extent of German disarmament.[87] While discussions in the British Foreign Office raised the possibility of modifying the system of military control, which General Bingham supported, the British section of the AMCV believed that German disarmament was still not complete.[88]

The crucial difference between British and French perceptions toward German fulfilment of the military clauses of the Treaty of Versailles would remain until the disarmament of Germany finally came to an end in 1931. By the spring of 1921, both the British and the French involved in disarming Germany experienced the surrender and destruction of vast amounts of

German armaments. This was not the contentious issue, though the French were more willing to believe that Germany still possessed a substantial amount of armaments. The difference in thinking was that the British, in light of the fact that German heavy armaments had been destroyed, essentially viewed the remainder of the surrender and destruction of remaining German war material as negligible and the remaining points of disarmament as less important than the armaments question. The French continued to insist upon the enforcement of the Treaty of Versailles down to the last field kitchen. Since the British believed the destruction of armaments essentially disarmed Germany, a hint of complacency began to filter through British disarmament efforts. The Allied enforcement of disarmament through the threat of military sanctions had produced results that satisfied the Allies. Certainly the majority of both British and French IAMCC members did not believe that Germany was capable of offensive action. A tough enforcement policy now softened the British stance on German disarmament while the French remained intransigent to any alteration in treaty enforcement. This divergence of opinion continued to affect Anglo–French relations and policies toward German disarmament, and would later increase dramatically after the Franco-Belgian occupation of the Ruhr in January 1923.

British and French evaluations of German disarmament fluctuated in the second year of operations. In February, the IAMCC reported that the disarmament of Germany would take at least another three months to complete and began to reduce the overall number of centers of surrender and destruction.[89] By April, however, General Nollet reported minimal disarmament progress while Friedrich Sthamer, the German Ambassador to London, regarded Allied complaints as petty.[90] The Conference of Ambassadors once again set new deadlines for the fulfillment of the military clauses of the treaty, expecting Germany to surrender all excess war material by 15 July and to transform its factories by 1 October 1922.[91] Without specific measures to enforce compliance other than verbal warnings, Allied demands did nothing to compel the German government to meet these deadlines.

In July, Nollet claimed that the destruction of German war material had slowed down.[92] The French General pointed out that Germany still had to surrender clothing, gas masks, and both signaling and bridging equipment. While the Treaty of Versailles outlawed these items, they were hardly a threat to Allied security. Nonetheless, the French insisted on the surrender of all remaining war material, regardless of its inherent combative or administrative nature. The French feared that any further modification to the treaty would lessen the importance and possibly undermine the enforcement of other clauses of the treaty. Alternatively, British policy toward German disarmament was becoming less compatible with French demands. In a June memo, the War Office emphasized the military clauses that concerned German armaments. The War Office essentially agreed with the German position that the amount of illegal war material found in clandestine caches paled in comparison to the amount of war material that had already been surrendered and destroyed.[93]

In the summer of 1922, Anglo–French differences regarding the disarmament of Germany approached boiling-point. Lloyd George and the French Prime Minister, Raymond Poincaré, revealed the fundamental divergence of policy between the British and French attitude toward enforcement of the military clauses, and in reality the entire treaty. Dominating the discussions, Lloyd George declared that Germany was not capable of equipping an army that could threaten Europe, even if the IAMCC had determined that Germany still possessed a number of illegal guns. Furthermore, the Prime Minister stated that "Germany could not equip an army strong enough to stand up to Czechoslovakia, let alone France, and she could not manufacture in two years, even with the knowledge and consent of the Allies, the quantity of munitions equivalent to what she had given up to the Disarmament Commission (*sic*). Germany as a military Power was broken, prostrate, and in the dust."[94] On the other hand, Poincaré insisted that German obstruction to Allied disarmament efforts continued to increase and that Lloyd George was being too optimistic. The French President remained intransigent to anything but the complete execution of the Treaty of Versailles.

By the autumn of 1922, the surrender and destruction of German armaments had been considerable. Consequently, throughout the spring and summer the Allies, especially Britain, discussed the possibility of withdrawing the IAMCC and replacing it with a smaller Allied supervisory organization. Eventually, in what would prove to have serious ramifications upon the future course of Allied disarmament of Germany, the Conference of Ambassadors drafted a note on 26 August that outlined five major points Germany had to fulfill in order for the Allies to consider withdrawing the IAMCC and replacing it with a smaller and less ubiquitous organization. This note, sent to the German government on 29 September 1922, stipulated that Germany must complete the transformation of factories, surrender all excess war material, turn over the 1918 inventories of war material in existence or production, reorganize its police forces along the lines of the Treaty of Versailles, and pass legislative measures to prohibit both the import and export of war material and any illegal recruiting for the German army.[95] If Germany fulfilled these measures, the Allies agreed to replace the IAMCC with a smaller "Committee of Guarantee." Shortly after the delivery of this Allied proposal, however, Germany unleashed a stream of complaints to the Conference of Ambassadors, especially criticizing Allied proposals for the organization of the German police, and a number of IAMCC officers experienced violent attacks in conducting their duties in Stettin, Passau and Ingolstadt. The eventual response of the German government on 27 October to the Allied note of 29 September did not even address the issue of the Committee of Guarantee, and the question remained in suspense at the end of the year.[96]

At no other time in the history of Allied military control in the post-war period was the disarmament of Germany carried out so extensively as in the period from 1920 through 1922. The Allied threat at the Spa Conference in July 1920 and in the London ultimatum of May 1921 to occupy German territory helped induce the surrender and destruction of hundreds of heavy guns, thousands of machine-guns and trench mortars, and millions of rifles and shells. While below the lofty expectations of the Treaty of Versailles, the impressive amount of destroyed war material had rendered Germany a second-rate military power by 1922.[97] The Allies had learned that disarmament deadlines without any serious threat of sanctions to enforce them were not conducive to success. While the British became mostly satisfied with the level of disarmament, the French adamantly insisted upon overseeing the complete fulfilment of the military clauses of the treaty.

By 1922, the unity in British and French policy toward German disarmament experienced a reciprocal relationship to results: as the numbers of destroyed German weapons mounted, Allied unity diminished. The British political and military leadership had considered Germany disarmed as early as 1921 and their efforts to begin discussions on the future of military control revealed their confidence that the IAMCC would soon be withdrawn from Germany. The British viewed the remainder of the military clauses that Germany had to fulfill as superfluous. The real work had been done. The Allies had destroyed Germany's heavy guns and, with them, the serious threat of German military aggression or defiance. On the other hand, French political and military authorities continued to view Germany as an armed nation since the Treaty of Versailles had not been carried out to the letter. No clause or surplus weapon was insignificant to the French. With the British generally satisfied with the amount of German disarmament and the French insistent upon continued extensive military control, Anglo–French relations began to bend under the strain. Anglo–French discord in German disarmament, together with German intransigence to fulfil the military clauses in their entirety, would soon boil over as a result of the Franco-Belgian occupation of the Ruhr in 1923. Allied disarmament operations, however, would survive.

5 Armaments

The Allied offensive on war production

The import and export of war material

While there were significant inroads into the surrender and destruction of excess German war material from the summer of 1920 to the autumn of 1922, the illegal importation and exportation of war material into and out of Germany remained a constant source of friction for the Allies during this period. In order to maintain German armaments at a fixed level and to prevent clandestine rearmament, Article 170 of the Treaty of Versailles strictly forbade the importation and exportation of "arms, munitions, and war material of every kind."[1] The importation of war material, in actuality, was more a question of maintaining the restricted state of German disarmament than any serious threat to Allied security. Where importation did play a role was in the sphere of strict German compliance with the treaty since the Allies demanded that Germany pass administrative and legislative measures to prohibit both the importation and exportation of war material.[2] Although the importation of war material was insignificant, the Allies always feared that it could enhance German war-making capacity.

The substantial exportation of German war material during this period, however, presented a difficult challenge. Germany often exported arms, machines, gauges and other types of war material to prevent its destruction.[3] Furthermore, the exportation of German war material to neutral nations complicated Allied enforcement efforts. With determination to enforce the treaty, the IAMCC, AMCV and the Conference of Ambassadors warned Germany repeatedly of this illegal activity and took a number of steps to eradicate it. The Allies responded initially with hesitation, however, and the illegal export of war material would continue to plague efforts to enforce the treaty for years.

At the heart of the problem of the illegal import and export of war material was the fact that neutral nations participated, and the Allies simply did not want to threaten relations with most of those involved. A significant number of neutral countries imported German war material but none, with the possible exception of Russia, participated as frequently as the Netherlands.[4] Germany and the Netherlands had maintained close economic relations throughout the war and this relationship continued into the post-war period. The position of the Netherlands regarding the exiled Kaiser had already strained relations with Britain and France, and the Allies had been unable to convince the Netherlands to release Wilhelm for trial. However, the position of the Netherlands regarding German war material constituted a blatant disregard of the Treaty of Versailles. The French had been aware of shipments of German war material to the Netherlands as early as November 1919, when 25,000 machine-guns arrived in Amsterdam.[5] The amount and type of exported war material soon increased. In mid-March 1920, Marshal Foch reported that Germany was exporting heavy artillery, trench mortars, machine-guns, rifles, grenades, machinery, gun molds, even airplanes and submarine parts, to the Netherlands.[6]

By March 1920, the British and French considered that the extent of German war material exported to the Netherlands had reached "dangerous proportions."[7] Whereas a Royal Decree of 1919 prohibited the importation of arms and munitions without government consent, the Dutch government had authorized some sales of German armaments and had a difference of opinion with the Allies as to what constituted war material.[8] The Dutch Foreign Minister, Herman van Karnebeek, pointed out that his government was unaware of the details of the Treaty of Versailles and that the French had exaggerated many of the reports of war material.[9] Yet even when the Allies apprised the Dutch government of the details of the treaty, the traffic in military materials continued.

The initial indecision of the Conference of Ambassadors over the export of German war material prolonged the transport of contraband. The Allies merely informed the Dutch government that all war material traffic with Germany constituted a breach of the Treaty of Versailles.[10] In April, the British government authorized Lord Derby, the British representative on the Conference of Ambassadors, to warn the Netherlands, Switzerland and all Scandinavian governments that they were accomplices in the violation of the treaty.[11] The Allied governments rejected the more forceful AMCV measure to charge Germany with reparations payments for the amount of war material exported from Germany.[12]

In June 1920 the Conference of Ambassadors officially placed General Nollet in charge of all information regarding war material traffic between Germany and neutrals and asked the French General to convey the "unfriendly character" of the problem to those who were involved.[13] Nollet first raised the question of the commercial nature of some of the war material exported from Germany. Should Germany be allowed to export goods and equipment that formerly had some type of military value? This issue soon became a source of conflict between the Reparation Commission and Marshal Foch, who quickly imposed his authority over Nollet. The Reparation Commission thought that the sale of non-combat material outside of Germany would facilitate Germany's reparations debt and therefore benefit the Allies.[14] On the other hand, Foch thought that any alterations to the Treaty of Versailles would open a floodgate of modifications. In short, Foch's viewpoint represented the core French policy of enforcing the entire treaty. Modifying a single clause of the treaty to the benefit of Germany would be analogous to extracting a stone from the foundation of a wall; the whole structure might collapse. Nevertheless, the Ambassadors' Conference resolved the issue in July when it reiterated its earlier decision to prohibit all war material, regardless of potential non-military value, from entering or leaving Germany.[15]

In an abrupt turnaround at the end of November, the Conference of Ambassadors decided to allow the Reparation Commission to conduct sales of exported German war material that did not have a direct military nature. British influence had decisively shifted the Conference's opinion but Foch's anger was mitigated somewhat when he insisted that the war material must be dispersed to negate potential military value.[16] For instance, sales of army boots could not be conducted in mass numbers with any single business or locale in order to prevent any possibility of military use. In addition, the Allies decided to make the change in policy subject to General Nollet's approval. Yet when Nollet refused to back down and continued to oppose the sale of all German war material, the Conference of Ambassadors supported Foch and the AMCV, thereby ignoring Nollet and the IAMCC.[17] Despite the stellar efforts of the IAMCC, the Conference of Ambassadors regarded Foch as the unparalleled expert on military affairs.

The fact that Germany had dumped a substantial amount of arms and equipment in the Netherlands during the 1918 retreat hindered Allied disarmament efforts. Subsequent German actions in exporting war material to the Netherlands in 1920 illustrated a conscious effort to stockpile war material in the hope of retaining it or at least acquiring some type of compensation for it in the future. The crux of the problem was obvious. How could German war material, stored outside of German territory, be subject to the Treaty of Versailles when the treaty itself did not stipulate what action to take over violations and only forbade the export of such material after 10 January 1920? German motivations were also obvious. Since it appeared that the German army would be unable to use this equipment, Germany could at least make a profit from the sales, thereby circumventing the authority of the IAMCC in supervising the collection and destruction of all excess war material and the Reparation Commission in the sale of the material.

The continuation of the illegal war material trade led to the Allied creation of frontier stations on the German border in the hope of uncovering attempts to transport armaments, equipment, and spare parts. Together with Allied intelligence, these stations succeeded in discovering illegal activities, but they could do nothing to acquire the German war material stockpiled on Dutch soil. In May, the Conference of Ambassadors asked the Dutch government to hand over all German war material to IAMCC officers at the frontier stations.[18] Once again, the Netherlands refused to comply, and the German war material remained in its possession.

In October, the Conference of Ambassadors took another step to resolve the problem when it asked the Dutch government again to stop importing German war material and demanded that Germany turn over all its war material in the Netherlands.[19] In response, the German government claimed that the Treaty of Versailles' armaments clauses referred exclusively to war material in Germany, thereby using the diktat as a pretext to promote self-interests. Furthermore, with the value of the material placed at fifteen million marks, Germany hoped to make a six-million mark profit from the sale of the material.[20] This reaction placed the Allies in a difficult position because they did not want to appear weak in their resolve to enforce the treaty. Yet they could not coerce a neutral country into compliance for fear of alienating themselves from international opinion and threatening to increase sympathetic support for Germany. Thus, the Allies ruled out the possibility of destroying the German war material that had been surrendered to the Netherlands in 1918.[21]

Acting tentatively, the Conference of Ambassadors ordered the AMCV to draft instructions for Allied military attachés in The Hague to supervise the sale of German war material in the Netherlands and to ask Germany to whom they intended to sell the material.[22] The Dutch government agreed to protect the war material in its possession and to sell it under the auspices of Allied military attachés.[23] The Allies had now implemented Germany's initial idea of selling the stockpiled material for profit, a step previously rejected outright by the Conference of Ambassadors. The persistence of the German government in avoiding the surrender of this material to the Allies benefited Germany and certainly influenced German perceptions of methods to delay and obstruct the enforcement of the military clauses of the treaty. The Conference acted more decisively in October 1922 when it ruled that the liquidation of German war material in the Netherlands had to be completed by mid-November and that any material not sold by that date would have to be transported to Germany and destroyed by the IAMCC.[24] In reality, the Allies could do little other than attempt to persuade the Dutch government to comply with Allied wishes regarding the enforcement of the Treaty of Versailles. As a neutral nation and a non-signatory of the treaty, the Netherlands was free to act in accordance with its own wishes. Similar to its protection of the ex-Kaiser in the face of British and French demands, the Netherlands again chose to retain its special relationship with Germany, thereby helping to undermine Allied disarmament operations.

In addition to the illegal transfer of German war material to the Netherlands, budding German relations with Bolshevik Russia led to a number of violations of the military clauses of the Treaty of Versailles. Initial contacts between German and Bolshevik officials started as early as 1919 and increased in intensity throughout the 1920s. Military discussions began in 1921, and Germany formed a special section of the *Reichswehr* Ministry under General Hans von Seeckt, *Sondergruppe R*, to collaborate with the Red Army. In an effort to circumvent the restrictions of the Treaty of Versailles upon German production of war material, in 1922 Germany began to send military and technical aid to the Soviets and to manufacture airplane engines, poison gas, and Krupp armaments on Soviet soil.[25] The German government also set up a special department, "Gefu," under the *Reichswehr* Ministry to conduct military transactions with the Bolsheviks.[26] The Treaty of Rapallo, signed in April 1922, increased Soviet-German economic and diplomatic cooperation, thereby forging closer military relations between the two nations. By 1924, Germany had set up training schools for tanks and airplanes in the Soviet Union, both of which were banned by Versailles. Other than stopping the passage of German war material at border areas and ports, the IAMCC could do little. Unaware of the true extent of German–Soviet military relations, the Allies lacked the diplomatic, military, and political means to prevent the production of German armaments in the Soviet Union.

Initial Allied suspicions of German–Soviet military cooperation were well founded, and by the summer of 1920 the Allies were cognizant of German military and industrial transactions with Russia. A Polish military attaché informed the British government in July 1920 that a ship, which contained a cargo of 400,000 rifles and 200 million cartridges bought by Bolsheviks in Germany, was about to sail from Lubeck or Hamburg to Reval.[27] The following month, French military intelligence reported that 89,000 German workers from factories in Upper Silesia and Essen, including specialists from Krupp, had emigrated to Kolomna, an industrial city southeast of Moscow.[28] Over the next two years, Germany continued to attempt to sell arms, munitions, ammunition, medical supplies, and planes to Bolshevik forces.[29]

In the years immediately following the signature of the Treaty of Versailles, neutral nations continuously attempted to purchase war material from Germany. The Conference of Ambassadors spent much time and effort in developing policies to prevent such violations of the treaty. The AMCV and the IAMCC played lesser roles except for insisting that Germany pass legislation to prohibit the importation and exportation of war material. From a neutral nation's perspective, the decision to import war material from Germany could be justified under the pretext that it had not signed the Treaty of Versailles (and was therefore not bound or even aware of its stipulations). Neutrals hoped to make a profit from a desperate Germany, which itself attempted to unload its vast quantities of war material in lieu of surrendering it to the victors.

War material transactions between Germany and non-signatories of the Treaty of Versailles are too voluminous to list in their entirety but, in order to illustrate the problem the Allies faced in disarming Germany, it is necessary to outline some of the major deals that Allied military intelligence and disarmament operations uncovered. For instance, in February 1920 the Conference of Ambassadors refused to allow Poland to purchase 300,000 rifles from Germany and then rejected Foch's proposal to allow Czechoslovakia to import German machine-gun and rifle cartridges.[30] In a clear example of political interests, the French government supported sales of war material to its allies while Britain insisted upon enforcement of the treaty.[31] British and French actions demonstrated the influence of self-interests upon Allied decisions: the Czech example reveals France's postwar diplomatic efforts to ally itself with its eastern allies and British attempts to thwart French gains on the Continent.

After the first year of treaty enforcement, the illegal export of German war material continued but to a lesser degree. In the summer and fall of 1921, the Conference of Ambassadors rejected attempts by neutral nations such as Sweden, Finland, and even the United States to purchase war material from Germany.[32] By 1922, Allied disarmament efforts had significantly diminished the amount of war material in Germany's possession, and the illegal export of war material out of Germany slowed to a trickle. A few incidents still attracted the attention of the Conference of Ambassadors, such as a proposed sale of German helmets to the Finnish government in February 1922, but overall numbers had become negligible.[33]

Prohibiting the import and export of war material across German borders, the enforcement of Article 170 of the Treaty of Versailles presented a difficult proposition to Allied disarmament operations. The Allies had demanded that Germany pass legislation to enforce Article 170, yet the German government hesitated to do so. A major source of irritation to Allied efforts, the delay in passage of an adequate German law appeared interminable, and the problem continued to beleaguer the IAMCC until its withdrawal in 1927. The possibility of the violation of the Treaty of Versailles in importing or exporting war material in the future was as important to the Allies as an actual violation. In 1920 the IAMCC objected to two attempts by the German government to issue a law prohibiting the import and export of war material because the German definition of war material was not adequately extensive.[34] Therefore, nothing had been done on the federal level to prohibit transactions of arms, machines and equipment that matched the Allied definition of war material. This fundamental problem led to another IAMCC demand in April 1921 that the German government pass such a law by the end of June.[35] The deadline passed without action.

The third year of Allied disarmament operations gave no respite to British or French concerns over passage of a German law prohibiting the import and export of war material. With the British considering the war material question a priority and the French simply content to push for

German compliance with all the disarmament clauses, the issue of enforcing the legal prohibition of the import and export of war material in Germany was one area of Anglo–French unity. This issue, however, would never be resolved to the liking of the IAMCC, and in January 1923 it joined a number of disarmament obligations that would be delayed for over a year.

Like many other facets of Allied disarmament, by 1923 the question of importing and exporting war material remained in perpetual suspension. Overall, Allied efforts to stop war material traffic emanating from Germany had mixed results. The IAMCC slowed but did not stop German sales of war material to neutral nations. Allied indecision and lack of enforcement measures allowed Germany to violate the treaty's prohibition of importing and exporting war material without fear of retribution. Yet IAMCC inspectors and Allied military intelligence uncovered much of the illegal traffic, which decreased significantly over time as destruction efforts succeeded in destroying surplus material. The success of Allied disarmament regarding this issue also depended upon others. Similar to the need for German compliance in the surrender and destruction of war material, prevention of the exportation of war material out of Germany relied upon the cooperation of non-signatories of the Treaty of Versailles. A number of neutral nations profited from Germany's disarmament violations. Thus, the enforcement of the treaty was by no means exclusively in the hands of the Allies. While it is easy to blame Britain and France for ineffectively enforcing the Treaty of Versailles, neutral nations also helped widen the cracks in the treaty's foundation.

The demilitarization of German industry

From the unification of Germany in 1871 to the signing of the Treaty of Versailles in 1919, Germany had become the leading industrial nation in Europe.[36] During the war, German industrial and technological leadership in Europe had been crucial to the massive production of armaments and munitions for the German war effort. As a result, throughout the Paris Peace Conference the Allies and especially Britain stressed the need to limit Germany's ability to produce war material. Lloyd George had been a staunch advocate of the dismantling of German industrial production of war material and believed it was the most effective means to control Germany's military capacity. Winston Churchill, as Secretary of State for War, wholeheartedly supported the destruction of German factories and machines that manufactured war material.[37] The French obsession with security following the war was due in large part to the fact that Germany not only had a larger population but a stronger industrial base. The British and French both feared the current capacity and future potential of German military production.

The war, which transformed large tracts of French industrial territory into a quagmire, left intact Germany's enormous industrial capacity to manufacture war material. While the Allied blockade and the manpower drain of the Western Front hindered German productive output during the war, the victorious Allies realized that Germany still retained her potential for industrial supremacy in Europe in the post-war period. Consequently, Britain and France hoped to eradicate Germany's powerful military industrial base by transforming a vast number of German factories from the production of war material to the manufacture of products that precluded military utility. The complex task of transforming or closing down all German establishments that produced war material (upwards of 7,500), other than those authorized by the Allies for the needs of the restricted *Reichswehr*, fell to the Armaments Sub-commission of the IAMCC.

In order to diminish Germany's industrial capacity to produce war material, the Treaty of Versailles gave the Allies the right to control Germany's military production. Specifically, Article 168 stipulated that the Allies could authorize the number of German factories allowed to produce war material and that all other establishments that manufactured armaments after three months of the effective date of the treaty would be closed down. Article 169 stipulated that Germany must surrender to the Allies all industrial plant used to produce war material in excess of prescribed amounts. All excess plant was to be destroyed. Finally, Article 172 demanded that the German government give the Allies information regarding the "nature and mode of manufacture" of armaments and chemicals used in warfare.[38] Thus, the treaty gave the IAMCC sweeping powers concerning the transformation and destruction of Germany's war industries. These powers would soon lead to bitter disputes between the German government and workers on one side and the Conference of Ambassadors and the IAMCC on the other.

The interpretation of the French version of the treaty, which used the rather vague term "*supprimer*" (suppress) in dealing with German factories that produced war material, led to disputes within the IAMCC itself, and the Ambassadors' Conference stepped in on 10 February 1920 to settle the issue. Pushed by General Bingham, the Conference ruled that "*supprimer*" was to be interpreted as the prevention of German factories from manufacturing war material by the destruction of their installations, machinery, dies and equipment.[39] The Germans could reopen a factory after converting it to commercial production. Furthermore, the treaty made Germany responsible for the destruction of war-producing facilities, equipment, and machinery, and prohibited the sale of such machinery. The German workers and industrialists who had reaped the benefits of war production from 1914 to 1918 would soon feel the impact of the treaty.

The tasks of the Armaments Sub-commission of the IAMCC relating to German war production amounted to a variety of difficult undertakings. First, the IAMCC had to authorize a specific and limited number of German factories to produce the amount of war material stipulated by the

Treaty of Versailles for the 100,000-man *Reichswehr*. This question would remain in dispute and would be subject to modification in the upcoming months. Initially, on 26 February 1920, the Conference of Ambassadors authorized only six German factories to produce war material.[40] The Allies deliberately chose moderately sized factories with the exception of Krupp, which could produce a limited number of guns. This decision led to German complaints of economic inefficiency but the Conference of Ambassadors rejected a subsequent German request to allow Krupp to produce more armaments.[41] After Germany requested upwards of seventy-nine war production facilities, the IAMCC eventually compromised and allowed fourteen German factories to produce war material, though they authorized each relatively small firm to produce only a certain type of weapon.[42]

The Armaments Sub-commission was also responsible for the seizure and destruction of the plant, machinery and munitions of a vast number of diverse German factories.[43] These were no simple tasks. Despite false information supplied by the German government, British and French IAMCC officers discovered that over 7,000 factories in Germany had to be inspected.[44] The daunting task left the Armaments Sub-commission hard pressed to carry out its numerous duties, and only Allied inspections could accurately determine whether a factory was in compliance with IAMCC stipulations. For instance, after an inspection, if IAMCC officers considered the machinery of a German factory to be destroyed, transformed, or dispersed, they could release the factory in question from Allied control.[45] The IAMCC treated machines in a similar fashion to the way it dealt with war material. It destroyed special machines that produced only war material, while either dispersing throughout Germany or leaving intact those machines that produced commercial goods. Allied officers carried out numerous inspections of the same factories over the years of disarmament operations.[46]

The district committees of the IAMCC conducted inspections of barracks, military establishments and factories. They also drafted a program for visits and contacted the appropriate German liaison office (*Verbindungstelle*) to accompany the inspectors.[47] The Armaments Sub-commission also carried out surprise inspections. These often led to trouble with the German authorities, especially after Allied operations resumed following the Ruhr crisis, but were the best method in determining compliance with the treaty.[48] The German government tried to make all inspections contingent upon the accompaniment of a German liaison officer but the Conference of Ambassadors declared on 4 March 1920 that the IAMCC had the authority to conduct surprise inspections of German establishments.[49] Factory directors often disputed the right of the IAMCC to destroy machinery, and the German government appealed to the Conference of Ambassadors on numerous occasions to put an end to factory closings and machinery destruction.[50] German efforts in this regard frequently delayed the work of the Armaments Sub-commission.

Initially, the IAMCC made a key distinction between state and private firms by insisting on the destruction of machinery that could produce war material in state firms but only on the dispersal of such machinery in private firms. The Allies believed that state firms were more dangerous, since they could carry out armaments orders according to national policies where private firms would simply fulfill contracts for profit. But the political atmosphere in Germany led the IAMCC to ameliorate conditions for German workers, especially concerning the Deutsche Werke, the former state conglomeration responsible for war production. The Allies feared that increased unemployment would give rise to Bolshevism while the workers of the Deutsche Werke went so far as to swear to General Nollet that they would not manufacture war material. On 10 February 1920, the Conference of Ambassadors, in agreement with both the AMCV and IAMCC, ruled that the Allies would leave open state factories that had a "non-military purpose" (thus keeping a number of German workers employed) but would restrict the production of commercial arms and munitions (for example, sporting rifles).[51]

The fact that German machines and industrial products had a multitude of uses created problems for the Armaments Sub-commission. Machines that produced war material could also be used to produce commercial products, and many industrial products could be used for both military and peaceful purposes. For instance, steel and other metals included in its production were major components of armaments yet also had a number of commercial uses. Similarly, while German chemical factories produced munitions, many of these chemicals had a variety of uses. In addition, some German factories produced only single parts of weapons that were harmless in their unassembled state. Consequently, in April, an argument arose in the IAMCC Council over the risk that dual-purpose machinery posed to Allied security. While French General Senechal claimed that leaving machines grouped in plants was potentially dangerous, General Bingham stated that Germany must be allowed to maintain her means of production in order to render reparations payments to the Allies.[52] Lacking agreement, they passed the problem along to the Conference of Ambassadors.

The Allies resolved the question of dual-purpose machinery on 26 May 1920. Based upon a proposal of the AMCV, the Conference of Ambassadors decided that machines currently used for general purposes, regardless of prior production, were *not* to be destroyed, and the IAMCC had to distinguish between "machinery for general use and machinery especially intended for the manufacture of war material."[53] Hence, the Armaments Sub-commission classified machines into three categories: A category machines produced war material exclusively and would be destroyed; B category machines capable of producing both war and non-war material would be dispersed or left intact; and C category machines used primarily for commercial purposes would also be left intact.[54] The issue continued to embitter Allied–German relations. When Germany complained that the presence of Allied officers in their factories was illegal, the AMCV pointed out that the Treaty of Versailles gave IAMCC members the right to visit "any factory or any establishment whatsoever."[55] Nollet pointed out that the IAMCC had weighed the economic needs of private German industry against the clauses of the treaty. Consequently, German complaints did nothing to change Nollet's mind, and the Conference of Ambassadors stuck to its decisions of 10 February and 26 May 1920.

The Armaments Sub-commission, which numbered only about 400 Allied soldiers at its peak, faced the extensive task of inspecting thousands of German factories capable of producing war material. Inspections of factories began in April 1920 and increased in scope the following month. As President of the Armaments Sub-commission, General Bingham was keenly interested in the disarmament of Germany's industrial base. Armaments officers delivered questionnaires to German factories to fill out with information regarding their size, number of employees, machinery, tools and production.[56] In April, Bingham reported that the initial inspections of German factories showed that the Germans were steadfastly transforming their factories from military into commercial production.[57] By June 1920, the suppression of German factories experienced a great deal of progress. Altogether, the IAMCC inspected a total of 887 private factories and destroyed 300 machines, thirty tons of dies and small machinery, 12,000 accessories and 225,000 gauges.[58] When the Armaments Sub-commission found that a German factory had met IAMCC's demands for "destruction, dispersion, or conversion of plant and machinery," it released the factory from Allied control and gave it a clearance certificate (*Quitus*).[59] As a result of these inspections, 577 German factories received their certificates from the IAMCC.

While the IAMCC had difficulties ensuring that German heavy industry did not produce war material, it faced a particularly complex problem in transforming the German chemical industry into peaceful endeavours. Similar to war material and machinery, chemicals could also be used both for commercial and military purposes. For instance, the plant needed for the manufacture of cellulose for commercial sale was similar to the plant necessary for the production of nitroglycerine.[60] Even the German fertilizer industry would be affected by the restrictions on chemical production. The fact that Germany had one of the largest chemical industries in the world, approximately 3,400 chemical factories located throughout Germany, compounded the problem. By inspecting German factories that produced chemicals used in the manufacture of explosives or poison gas, such as nitric acid, sulfuric acid, glycerin, chlorine, ammonia, and the more dangerous nitrocellulose and nitroglycerine powders, the IAMCC aimed to reduce the German chemical industry to its pre-war level.[61] By August 1920, inspections had significantly reduced chemical production.[62]

The Allied policy of closing German factories, instead of destroying or dispersing their machinery, troubled many German politicians and soured German labor relations with the IAMCC. At times, German workers simply refused to surrender or destroy their machinery.[63] According to Bingham, the destruction and dispersal of machinery did not result in the discharge of German workers or have any negative effect upon the German economy.[64] Allied records, however, indicate that the IAMCC closed down a substantial percentage of German factories that they inspected. The hasty transformation to commercial production of the German factories that the IAMCC allowed to remain open, especially at a time when Germany faced increasing inflation, reparations payments, and the unemployment of a number of veterans, placed a severe burden upon German workers.[65] By the end of the first year of disarmament operations, the Allies had inspected about half of all German factories. After Allied inspectors had destroyed, dispersed, or left the factories' machinery intact, the IAMCC either gave the factories a clearance certificate and freed them from Allied activity, or they closed them down. Overall the Allies inspected 3,200 of over 6,000 known factories, closing more than 2,600 of these in the first year of operations.[66] Attempts by the German government in appealing many of the closings went unheeded. With unified determination, the British and French refused to grant the German military industry any reprieve.

After a relatively successful debut in transforming German industry into commercial production and dismantling German war industries, the Armaments Sub-commission experienced a much less sanguine start to the second year of disarmament operations. At the beginning of 1921, problems between the IAMCC and the German government and industries increased. In March, Nollet reported that the IAMCC had made little progress in switching any more German factories to commercial production.[67] In fact, inspectors discovered that some factories continued to manufacture automatic pistols and cartridges, items strictly forbidden by the Treaty of Versailles and the Conference of Ambassadors. The German government also had not yet accepted the number of factories that the Allies had authorized to produce war material for the German army.[68] In addition, German resistance to the transformation, closing down and destruction of factories increased.

The Allied response to the decreased productivity in disarming German industry varied. Bingham, despite the premium that the British placed upon dismantling German war production capacity, summarily dismissed reports of German non-compliance. In July 1921, he pointed out that the discoveries of the illegal manufacture and hidden caches of war material were minor problems in light of the fact that the Allies had supervised the destruction of Krupp's shrinking pits, special machinery, plant, and gauges.[69] Bingham's attitude, similar to the future course of British policy concerning the enforcement of the military clauses of the Treaty of Versailles, sheds important light upon Allied attitudes in the second year of operations. Even after only a year of operating in Germany, the IAMCC had significantly disarmed Germany relative to pre-war German military strength and to an even greater degree when considering Allied military strength at the start of 1921. Relative to the enforcement of all the military clauses of the Treaty of Versailles, however, the Allies still had quite a lot of work to accomplish. Increasingly when evaluating German disarmament, British political leaders and IAMCC officers, with the visible exception of Morgan, would point to the past results of the IAMCC. This attitude was distinctively different from the French political and military authorities, especially Foch and Nollet, who pointed instead to the future tasks that the IAMCC must yet complete.

Krupp

Allied attempts to control German war production often focused upon the two major industrial firms in Germany that produced war material: Krupp and the Deutsche Werke (German Works). To disarm Germany effectively, the Allies had to inspect these immense industrial conglomerates and decide whether to destroy or transform their ability to produce war material. The question of the future of Krupp had been an Allied priority since the closing of hostilities. Krupp, centered in Essen but with branches in Bottrop, Kiel, Magdeburg, and Munich, had a historic tradition in central Europe that rose to fame with the Industrial Revolution.[70] Krupp's production of steel and armaments began in the early nineteenth century and culminated in the massive output of armaments during World War I, when Krupp's production of war material was superior to all other European industries. The IAMCC realized that successful disarmament depended upon controlling the Krupp factories, which quickly became a British priority and an important component of French security policy.

Officers of the IAMCC, armed with the Treaty of Versailles, had the responsibility of supervising the destruction and transformation of the Krupp works. They allowed Krupp to produce only a handful of guns per year and would later reject German attempts to increase Krupp production of artillery.[71] Altogether, the IAMCC demanded that Krupp destroy approximately 160 experimental guns, 380 installations, 9,300 machines, 800,000 tools and appliances, and almost 160,000 cubic feet of concrete installations.[72] Inspections of the Krupp factories commenced in May 1920. As early as March, however, Allied inspectors reported that Krupp continued to manufacture heavy artillery and ammunition wagons and consequently demanded an end to these illegal activities.[73] From mid-May onward, Allied officers of the IAMCC, mostly British, actually lived in the Krupp plant in Essen for six years.[74] Under the supervision of British Colonel Leverett, workers on the payroll of Krupp had the task of destroying all the war-producing plant.[75] Born to a destructive purpose, the machinery, plant and tools met a violent end as the workers smashed thousands of machines, leveled dozens of buildings and dismantled tons of equipment.

Although the historic Krupp factories produced howitzers, fuses and shells, the IAMCC focused its attention on the production of heavy artillery. Giant blast furnaces, shrinking pits and gun lathes filled a crucial need in Krupp's production of the massive artillery pieces turned out for the war. Altogether, Krupp had seventy-eight colossal gun lathes, crucial to the production of heavy artillery, eleven of which the Inter-Allied Naval Control Commission allowed the Germans to maintain (the Treaty of Versailles allowed Germany pocket battleships, and Krupp manufactured the guns and armor plate for them). When Germany argued for possession of all their gun lathes for commercial purposes, Bingham eventually compromised and allowed Krupp possession of thirty-six of them.[76] In fact, as soon as the war was over, Krupp had shrewdly attempted to change its persona under the slogan "*Wir machen alles*" (We make everything) and started to produce everything from locomotives to cash registers, typewriters, and sprinklers.[77] The IAMCC never resolved the question of the number of gun lathes it allowed Krupp to maintain, and eventually Germany merely promised to destroy the excess lathes. Nonetheless, while Krupp would continue to design armaments for the future and retool for arms production in the 1930s, by the end of 1922 the IAMCC had effectively eradicated Krupp's productive armaments capacity.

Deutsche Werke

Deutsche Werke was the other great industrial establishment in Germany, and the Allies immediately focused their disarmament efforts on it following the war. At the end of 1919 and in January 1920, the German government transformed a number of state arsenals into a single private corporation, known as Deutsche Werke. These factories had manufactured everything from heavy artillery and gunpowder to small arms and ammunition during the war. Masquerading as a private firm, Deutsche Werke's true nature was discovered when the Allies proved that the German government owned a significant amount of stock in the German conglomerate.[78] The ownership of a German factory had particular significance since the Treaty of Versailles stipulated that Germany had to dismantle all its state arsenals and discharge their personnel three months after the treaty went into effect. The Ambassadors' Conference decision of 10 February 1920, however, allowed state factories that manufactured products other than war material to be left open. Thus, a German factory that proved it was dedicated to peaceful endeavors could remain productive, albeit in a new capacity.

By the closing months of 1921, the Allies were still not satisfied with the amount of transformation of Deutsche Werke into commercial production. The fact that Deutsche Werke had recently produced huge numbers of sporting rifles only added to the hostility of the Allies.[79] Angry at this lack of transformation into commercial manufacturing, the IAMCC ordered reductions in Deutsche Werke's personnel and production.[80] This decision led to the closing down and dismantling of a number of plants of the conglomerate and created great resentment of German workers, industrialists and government officials toward Allied disarmament efforts. Many of the targeted plants were in Bavaria (Dachau, Ingolstadt, and Amberg in particular), and a storm of protest emanated from the large southern German state. Workers became hostile to IAMCC efforts to destroy machinery both in the Deutsche Werke and Krupp plants.[81] In addition to the cries of the workers, the Bavarian Prime Minister, Count Lerchenfeld, cried foul and claimed that the plants only conducted peaceful production, such as the manufacture of agricultural machinery.[82] Moreover, he insisted that the closing down of the Deutsche Werke plants would create severe economic strains. In the hope of dividing Allied policy toward German factories, the German government complained to the Reparation Commission that the closings would hinder Germany's ability to pay reparations.[83] Other government officials claimed that the IAMCC's policies damaged economic development in Germany, pushed the nation toward political instability, and not only interfered with the administration of Deutsche Werke's plants but also prohibited the construction of new facilities.[84]

Since effective disarmament depended upon German cooperation, the British and French could not always disregard German protests. In addition, Bavaria was already a hotbed of anti-IAMCC activity, especially in the arming and training of a significant number of paramilitary units, and the IAMCC could not risk inflaming Bavarian hostility toward Allied disarmament efforts. Thus, at the end of 1921, the IAMCC instituted an important policy change regarding the transformation of Deutsche Werke. In order to appease the German workers, industrialists, and politicians, the IAMCC Council modified the deadline for Deutsche Werke to complete transformation *after* the termination of Allied operations and agreed to safeguard the interests of German workers amid the current transformation of the plants.[85] Nonetheless, Allied disarmament policy had severe ramifications. By the end of disarmament operations Deutsche Werke had disappeared, forcing 22,000 employees out of a total workforce of 37,000 out of work as a result of its switch to commercial production.[86]

By the third year of Allied disarmament efforts, Allied teams had successfully dismantled German war production after inspecting approximately 7,500 German factories. While the progress in transforming German factories had been substantial, a number of problems continued to worry the Allies. The IAMCC had already increased the number of German factories it allowed to produce war material from six to fourteen. Although the Armaments Sub-commission had completed operations in the smaller factories, it still needed to inspect and transform some of the more substantial plants. In addition, the IAMCC still had to disperse 15,000 machines of Krupp and Deutsche Werke and to destroy countless buildings, machines, and gauges of other factories.[87] Nollet and Bingham estimated that this work would take up to six months to complete.

For the remainder of the year, Allied operations to transform German industry continued to make slow progress against determined German opposition. In August, Leopold von Hoesch, the German ambassador in Paris, protested vehemently against the destruction of German machinery and claimed that the IAMCC was attempting to destroy machines intended for commercial purposes. Furthermore, in an argument intended to play upon Keynesian sentiments in Britain, he argued that since the German fertilizer industry would be severely affected by the destruction of its machinery, the German economy, and hence the world economy, would face fatal consequences.[88] The Allies refused to be swayed by such sweeping arguments and in September, the IAMCC sent a note to the German government listing five major issues that remained to be fulfilled, including the complete transformation of factories to peace production.[89] The Allied memorandum contained no threat of inducement but did try to convince the German government that if the demands were met then the IAMCC would be quickly withdrawn and replaced by a much less extensive organization. Soon afterward, the German government bombarded the IAMCC with an abundance of appeals to modify disarmament operations, and public violence against Allied inspectors threatened the security of inspection teams. With no renewed German effort to fulfil Allied wishes, the future of the entire disarmament question remained up in the air at the beginning of the fateful year of 1923. The Ruhr Crisis would soon put an end to any pretense of fulfilment.

6 Effectives
The reduction of German military forces

The accomplishments of the German army in World War I exemplified Germany's status as the foremost military power in the world and deeply affected Allied post-war disarmament policies. The second largest army in Europe next to Russia, yet the best trained and equipped, the German army had gained combat experience on the Western Front, Italy, Russia, the Balkans, the Middle East, and Africa.[1] Despite fighting in these numerous campaigns, the Germans had been poised for victory in the spring of 1918. Only the combined efforts of a great coalition of powers had been able to force their final collapse. Consequently, the Allies decided to dissolve and transform the German army proportionally into the smallest army in Europe. Yet the Treaty of Versailles also went beyond the immediate reduction of the regular army by forbidding attempts by Germany to mobilize any portion of its manpower. Thus the Allies sought to reduce and reorganize the German police force and dissolve the numerous paramilitary organizations in Germany. These difficult tasks fell to the officers and men of the Effectives Sub-commission of the IAMCC.

French and British leadership of disarmament operations dominated the Allied coalition's efforts to eradicate the German army as an effective fighting force. French policy in the disarmament of Germany supported the enforcement of the Treaty of Versailles in its entirety but within this context, the French focused on demilitarizing all of Germany's sources of armed manpower. In fact, the French quickly became the driving force behind the reduction and dissolution of German effectives. The French delegation at the Paris Peace Conference had focused upon restricting the size of the German army, and now Nollet and Foch would insist upon restricting the size and organization of the German army and police, and disbanding any civilian military associations. Germany's larger population convinced the French of the necessity of minimizing the quantity of German armed forces.

Nollet, whose reports to Foch often focused on effectives questions, firmly believed that disarming the German population was the key to the entire issue of disarmament.[2] He advocated the idea of "moral disarmament," where the German people themselves would have to reject militarism for Germany to be truly disarmed.[3] In essence, Nollet believed that the smaller the proportion of the German population that received military training and the longer the society remained disarmed, the greater the chance for European peace. Yet the notion of moral disarmament through treaty enforcement was inherently contradictory, and the French military could not understand why "Germany gives in to force for the surrender of its war material but it does not disarm morally."[4] The use of military force and occupation succeeded in only physically disarming Germany, and Nollet initially blamed the German government for failing to "lead the German people in peaceful ways" and allowing them "to develop tendencies entirely contradictory to the spirit of the Treaty."[5] In 1922, Nollet finally understood that the prolongation of Allied disarmament efforts in Germany hindered the moral disarmament of the nation.[6] However, by continuing to embrace the strict enforcement of the Treaty of Versailles, Nollet guaranteed the failure of moral disarmament. German obstruction and rejection of Versailles throughout the 1920s was a testament to that failure.

The Effectives Sub-commission of the IAMCC had its headquarters in Berlin, where it was billeted in the Hotel Adlon.[7] It was the second largest of the three sub-commissions, with approximately seventy Allied officers.[8] The President of the Effectives Sub-commission was General Edouard Barthélemy, who had recently worked in the French War Office. The IAMCC set up eight district committees throughout Germany and placed them under Barthélemy's command.[9] They were responsible for the local control of German military forces. The head of the British delegation of the Effectives Sub-commission was Brigadier-General John Hartman Morgan, who would play a major role in revealing German attempts to circumvent the military clauses of the Treaty of Versailles. Barthélemy's pragmatism, Morgan's tenacity, and Nollet's stubbornness would soon force the Germans to bend under relentless Allied pressure. The Effectives Sub-commission witnessed an initial period of great success, emerging as a forceful tool of Allied disarmament operations in Germany.

As Britain's senior officer in the Effectives Sub-commission, Morgan worked diligently to enforce the military articles of the Treaty of Versailles. A professor of constitutional law at University College in London, Morgan's star rose quickly as a result of the war. He began the war as a staff captain but was promoted to Brigadier-General in 1918 so as to have proper authority as a member of the British delegation at the Paris Peace Conference.[10] However, Morgan's prior appointment in 1915 as Vice-Chairman of the Committee of Inquiry into Breaches of the Laws of War deeply influenced his work on the IAMCC. After interrogating British and German officers, as well as Belgian civilians, Morgan developed an anti-German bias and began to see all Germans culpable for wartime atrocities. He believed Germans were all afflicted with "moral distemper" and were "rotten to the core."[11] Morgan's experiences investigating German breaches of the laws of war had forged his *Weltanschauung*. As the head of the British delegation of the Effectives Sub-commission and second only to Bingham as a member of the British section of the IAMCC, Morgan soon established himself as a zealous supporter of the enforcement of the Treaty of Versailles, revealing a number of German schemes to violate the effectives clauses of the treaty. While his tenacity, foresight, and thoroughness often led to problems with General Bingham and the British Foreign Office, Morgan's stance on strict disarmament and anti-German bias made him a favorite of Marshal Foch and General Nollet.

The Articles of the Treaty of Versailles regarding the reduction of the *Reichswehr* were both comprehensive and complex. Formulated to restrict the German army so that Germany would not be capable of conducting any offensive actions, the effectives clauses set strict limits upon the size, organization and classification of all military personnel in Germany. Every aspect of the German military would be subject to Allied limitations and control. Article 160 set the standard as it limited the German army to 100,000 men, made up of seven infantry and three cavalry divisions, for the "maintenance of order within the territory and to the control of the frontiers." The Great German General Staff was to be eradicated and the German officer corps could not exceed 4,000 men. The Allies placed exact restrictions upon German headquarters, divisions, administrative services and individual units. In addition, Article 173 prohibited conscription while Article 175 stipulated twelve- and twenty-five-year enlistment periods for soldiers and officers, respectively.

The ultimate responsibility of the fulfilment of the military clauses of the treaty fell to the German government, while the IAMCC took on the role of caretaker, charged with supervising and evaluating compliance with the size, organization, and classification of German military forces. The time limits placed upon the fulfilment of these clauses, however, were inherently contradictory due to the long delay in the treaty's ratification. For instance, Article 163 stipulated that the German army be no greater than 100,000 men by 31 March 1920 yet allowed Germany three months after the effective date of the treaty to reduce the army to a transitory 200,000 before the final reduction.[12] This contradiction in the treaty terms gave Germany a possible loophole, which it would attempt to exploit at the Spa Conference in July 1920.

The reduction of the *Reichswehr*

The reduction of the German army to the level stipulated by the Treaty of Versailles – 100,000 men – was a crucial, yet controversial issue in the first months of Allied inspections. The Allies estimated the size of the German army on the eve of treaty enforcement to be 400,000 troops.[13] Therefore, they agreed that immediate steps be taken to eradicate the effective fighting capacity of the German army. The Germans and even some members of the Allied coalition soon raised questions, however, as to the practicality of such a decrease in strength stipulated by the treaty. Although the Allies had agreed in Paris upon the restricted size of the German army, and Germany had obligated itself to the clauses of the treaty through its signature, the unstable political atmosphere in Germany in the embryonic days of treaty enforcement led to a re-examination of the *Reichswehr* question in both the Allied and German camps. The British War Office began to question the political rationale of diminishing the *Reichswehr* when Bolshevism appeared to be increasing in strength in Germany. In fact, in light of the political instability in the early months of 1920 and the fear of a *coup d'état*, the War Office proposed that Germany be allowed to retain a *Reichswehr* of 150,000 to 200,000 troops.[14]

German political and military leaders decried the vast reduction of its symbol of stability at a time when street fighting in Berlin was a common occurrence. Furthermore, they attempted to play on Allied fears of Bolshevism by claiming that the *Reichswehr* would soon be little more than a police force, incapable of guarding its borders while simultaneously combating internal chaos and unrest. On the other hand, French political and military leaders wholeheartedly supported the complete reduction of German military might and sought to enforce the Treaty of Versailles in its entirety. In order to enforce operational effectiveness and maintain unity, the Allies worked quickly to resolve differences of opinion over the reduction of the *Reichswehr*, an issue crucial to the successful disarmament of Germany. Indeed, before the Spa Conference in July, British and French leadership agreed to enforce the reduction of the *Reichswehr* to treaty limitations, leaving the hopes of German government and military officials for a 200,000-man army in the wake of Allied unity.

Due to the unexpected delayed ratification of the Treaty of Versailles, and the American rejection, the Allies had to take steps to alter the time limits placed upon the German government's obligations to reduce the *Reichswehr*. In early February 1920, General Nollet pointed out contradictions in the treaty when he explained that Article 160 demanded a 100,000-man German army by the last day of March while Article 163 stipulated a reduction to 200,000 by 10 April (three months after the effective date of the treaty). To clarify the situation, he proposed a reduction in stages: the *Reichswehr* had to be reduced to 200,000 troops by 10 April and to the prescribed 100,000 by July 10.[15] The Allied governments subsequently accepted Nollet's proposal on 18 February.[16]

Whereas the British War Office worried about the political situation in Germany in the early months of 1920 and advocated important modifications to the military clauses of the Treaty of Versailles, Foch and Nollet focused upon strict Allied enforcement and German fulfilment. In March, the Marshal claimed that the "dispositions of the Treaty, concerning the disarmament of Germany or the reduction of its effectives have up to now remained a dead letter."[17] General Nollet reported in April that the strength of the German army was 290,000, nearly three times the final amount allotted by the Allies.[18] Although this estimate included the *Freikorps* units that the German government used to combat leftist uprisings, the Germans had at least begun to dissolve them. For instance, within a month the notorious Erhardt Brigade, instrumental in the violence associated with the Kapp *putsch*, disappeared.[19]

Disillusioned by the thoroughness of the Treaty of Versailles, the German government attempted to modify the military clauses of the treaty in the first few months of enforcement and again at the Spa Conference in July. On 18 February, Nollet rejected the German government's proposal to increase its troop strength.[20] Ten days after the initial April reduction deadline, the Bauer government asked to maintain the army at a level of 200,000 troops along with heavy artillery and airplanes. The German government justified its request by claiming that the maintenance of order and frontier defense necessitated an increase in troop strength and armaments above the restrictions of Versailles.[21] At this point, Brigadier-General Morgan estimated the *Reichswehr* to include at least 250,000 troops, as well as 40,000 *Freikorps* and 50,000 security police (*Sicherheitspolizei*) forces.[22] Foch and the AMCV, however, refused to budge and demanded the reduction of the German army to 100,000 men. They agreed only to the modification of the size of the German police force. While the Germans had dissolved many of the *Freikorps* units by the summer of 1920, as well as a number of other volunteer units (*Zeitfreiwillige*), the German army still remained twice the size prescribed by the treaty. Although the Allies raised the possibility of extending the time limit for reduction, the Conference of Ambassadors eventually demanded the final reduction of the *Reichswehr* by 10 July.[23] Other issues such as the existence of excessive infantry, cavalry, and engineer units, and additional units involved in the liquidation and pension bureaus in the German army, would have to be addressed as well.[24]

Allied conference diplomacy, prevalent in the spring and summer of 1920, was a crucial factor in building the foundation of a common policy toward German disarmament in the first year of operations. During the months of April, May, and June, the Allies met in the conferences of San Remo, Hythe, and Boulogne to discuss a number of post-war problems. Throughout these discussions, they viewed the disarmament of Germany as a priority and an "indispensable" factor in preserving the peace of Europe.[25] When the German government tested the fragile entente with a request in April for the maintenance of 200,000 troops, the Allies held firm by rejecting any augmentation of the *Reichswehr*.[26] Furthermore, on the eve of the Spa Conference in Boulogne, the Allied governments adamantly voiced their displeasure at the lack of German fulfilment of the military clauses of the treaty. In a declaration that did not mince words, the Allies declared that they had "unanimously decided to adhere completely to the clauses of the treaty signed by Germany."[27] Thus, the Allies entered the Spa Conference as a multinational coalition united in its determination to enforce the Treaty of Versailles; but how long would such unity last?

At the Spa Conference in the summer of 1920, Allied–German discussions centred on the issues of disarmament and reparations; however, a priority of the discussions at Spa concerned the future organization of the German army. The German delegation at Spa focused upon the issue of the size of the *Reichswehr* and the German government, intent on maintaining at least a 200,000-man army, urged the Allied governments to acquiesce to their demands. Chancellor Konstantin Fehrenbach and Otto Gessler, Minister of Defense, feared that discharging 100,000 men from the army would exacerbate the current political instability in Germany and hinder efforts to prevent the rise of Bolshevism.[28] General Hans von Seeckt proposed a gradual reduction in the *Reichswehr* to October 1921.[29] Reacting angrily, Lloyd George emphasized his displeasure with German delays and claimed that the dilatory German response to the military clauses was without justification.[30] The Allies therefore rejected German proposals but agreed to modifications of the time limits placed upon the reduction of the German army.

Under the terms of the Spa Protocol of 8 July, the Allies gave Germany until 1 October 1920 to reduce the *Reichswehr* to 160,000 and until 1 January 1921 to reduce it to the final 100,000 men.[31] The Allies also demanded the reorganization of the *Reichswehr* to the terms of the Treaty of Versailles as well as the abolition of compulsory service in Germany. More importantly, the Allies added teeth to their proposal. As an incentive for compliance, they threatened to occupy German territory if their demands went unheeded. When disarmament discussions concluded, it was obvious that the specter of Bolshevism had frightened the Allied governments into modifying the effectives clauses. The threat to occupy German territory would have to offset the lack of strict enforcement.

Although Allied demands at Spa marked the second major alteration of the effectives clauses of the Treaty of Versailles, the German government reacted bitterly. Foreign Minister Walter Simons pointed out that the new deadlines to reduce the *Reichswehr* were favorable to Germany, but he decried Allied insistence on reducing Germany's volunteer defense forces and the threat of Allied occupation over German non-fulfilment of the treaty's clauses.[32] Gessler pointed out that Spa shattered any German hopes for a modified treaty.[33] He also struck a particularly sensitive nerve by bringing the Bolshevik specter to life. Nonetheless, the threat of an occupation left the Germans with little choice but to comply, and in August the German government implemented a law to abolish compulsory service. The *Reichswehr*, though not organized along the strict guidelines of Article 160, continued to shrink in size.[34]

The threat of occupation in the Spa Protocol pushed German

compliance and by the end of November, Allied inspectors reported that the *Reichswehr* numbered 100,000 troops. Nollet reported that "the reduction of strength, the suppression or the merging of units is being carried on without interruption."[35] The German army had put an end to short-term enlistments and had increased discharges. The IAMCC was cognizant of the fact that the German army in its transitional state included an excess of officers in divisional commands as well as senior officers in regimental units. However, they expected an initial surplus of officers and claimed they would resolve the issue in the future. In addition, the Allies still awaited the passage of the modified *Wehrgesetz*, which they hoped would settle the issues of compulsory conscription, formation of separate armies under state laws, surplus units, and the 5 percent discharge rate of *Reichswehr* soldiers.[36] The discovery by British military intelligence that the German army budget for 1921 was twenty times the per capita amount for 1914 caused a stir in IAMCC headquarters.[37] The Allied coalition feared that Germany was preparing an offensive army for the future, so the IAMCC continued to scrutinize German army budget expenditures.

Despite the delays, violations, and fears, the British assessed the reduction of the *Reichswehr* in the first year of disarmament operations as positive.[38] Believing that Germany had "ceased to be a military danger to the Allies for a considerable period of time," the British War Office pointed out that Germany had reduced the *Reichswehr* accordingly and that only official Allied verification remained.[39] Lord Kilmarnock, former head of the Military Mission in Berlin in 1920, believed that the Allies had essentially disarmed Germany and reported that the German army had been "duly reduced" to the 100,000 level by 1 January.[40] Nollet assessed the Allied reduction of the *Reichswehr* in a far more negative light than his British counterparts. The French General criticized German officials for the number of officers and administrative units in the German army that exceeded the stipulations of Article 160.[41] Nollet's anxiety would not be eased until the German government passed the *Wehrgesetz*, which he hoped would bring the *Reichswehr* unconditionally into line with the Treaty of Versailles.

By the start of 1921, the *Reichswehr* had been reduced to the 100,000 troop level with various extenuating circumstances. Inspections determined that while Germany had carried out reductions of its army, various problems remained. For instance, surplus officers, as well as excess administrative, pioneer, bridging, and bicycle units still existed.[42] Thus, aside from the major questions of the police and self-defense organizations, only the detailed organization of the *Reichswehr* required resolution. When the Reichstag finally passed the *Wehrgesetz* on 18 March 1921, the IAMCC had high hopes that it could soon settle the remaining problems concerning effectives questions. Significant progress in the terms of the law, however, did not satisfy the Allies. They pointed out that the new law referred ambiguously to the absolute number of officers in the German army and could allow for an officer to replace a discharged enlisted man.[43]

In May 1921, the Allies threatened Germany with military sanctions for the second time. In the London ultimatum, they warned Germany that they would occupy sections of the Ruhr Valley if Germany did not acquiesce to Allied demands to organize the *Reichswehr* along the lines of the Treaty of Versailles, reorganize the police, and abolish the self-defense organizations. German promises to comply with the ultimatum bore fruit for Allied disarmament efforts and, by the summer of 1921, matters concerning the reduction of the *Reichswehr* appeared all but settled. In one of his more positive reports concerning German disarmament, Foch stated that Germany had reduced the army to the prescribed level of 100,000 troops, abolished conscription, and maintained military schools at the proper level.[44] Military sanctions had produced the desired effect.

In the midst of generally positive British reports of German compliance with the military articles that concerned the demilitarization of the *Reichswehr*, a solitary voice stood out. Brigadier-General Morgan, British head of the Effectives Sub-commission and second-in-command in the British delegation of the IAMCC, had previously sent three lengthy reports in 1920 to the War Office outlining his belief that the German army had violated the military articles of the Treaty of Versailles in every serious regard.[45] Morgan was convinced that Germany was attempting to violate the application of the treaty in maintaining conscription, short-term service, excess staff, officers, regiments, and even the Great General Staff. He vociferously proposed that the Germans were preparing for a future war. Similarly, in June 1921, Morgan claimed that the *Reichswehr* was "nothing but a cadre for expansion and the evidence all points to a design to expand it by passing a large number of men through its ranks for short periods of training."[46] While admitting that the German army numbered 100,000 men, he believed that few German troops engaged for the full twelve years but only volunteered for short periods of time. Morgan feared a rebirth of the Krümper system, a strategy devised by Prussia to circumvent Napoleon's disarmament demands in the Treaty of Tilsit in 1807. As evidence, Morgan cited the *Wehrgesetz*, in which the German government tried initially to allow unlimited discharges from the army, and he pointed to the fact that Germany maintained 800,000 uniforms, along with the unit names and numbers of the Imperial army. In addition, Morgan pointed out that the Germans were keeping their old army registers, which would facilitate a mobilization that could call upward of one million troops to the colors. While he saw the handwriting on the wall that pointed to the withdrawal or at least a reduction in the size of the IAMCC, Morgan asserted that only some form of continued inspections could prevent such serious violations from leading to the possibility of aggression.

By the third year of operations, Allied inspectors had helped significantly to diminish the strength of the German army. Whereas the IAMCC still needed to address the organization of the German General Staff and the final disappearance of a small number of administrative staff attached

to the *Reichswehr*, even General Nollet admitted that disarmament was
"at hand."[47] The German army numbered 100,000 troops, only four military schools remained to train new volunteers, mobilization records no
longer existed, and conscription had disappeared. Yet important differences highlighted French and British approaches to German disarmament.
Unlike their British colleagues, the French insisted upon their desire to see
the organization and recruitment of the *Reichswehr* in exact accord with
the Treaty of Versailles.[48] Fearing the revival of German militarism, and
especially the superior manpower that Germany possessed, French military
and political authorities pushed for the prohibition of all illegal recruitment of soldiers in Germany, the expelling of all surplus troops, and the
organizational conformity (especially fewer officers and NCOs) of the
Reichswehr to the stipulations of the treaty. The reconstitution of the Great
General Staff, discovered by the IAMCC, soon became another major
concern of the Allies.[49] Without strict German compliance with these
demands, the French would not consider terminating Allied inspections.

To the delight of Nollet and Foch, Morgan also reappeared in the lime-
light in the summer of 1922 by reasserting that Germany was secretly
preparing for a future war. Morgan was now sending his reports directly
to the Foreign Office, operating behind the back of his commanding
officer, Major-General Bingham. Although Foreign Office officials believed
Morgan's arguments had credibility, they held rather demeaning opinions
of Morgan and considered him to be more a lawyer than a soldier.
However, Morgan's reports helped sway the Foreign Office's opinion of
Bingham. Eyre Crowe admitted that he "lacked confidence in the judgment
and strength of character of General Bingham ... who sees everything rosy
and through intensely pro-German spectacles," while Hardinge added that
Bingham was "disposed to pigeon-hole unpalatable reports."[50] But
Bingham was a career officer, Morgan a lawyer in uniform, and the
Foreign Office respected protocol. British policy toward German disarmament now embraced partial fulfillment of the Treaty of Versailles as plans
were already well underway in the summer of 1922 to replace the IAMCC
with a much smaller control organization. Although both the Foreign and
War Offices read Morgan's reports of German violations, they ignored
them and took no action.[51]

In 1922, the Allies drafted two detailed notes regarding the fulfillment
of the military clauses of the Treaty of Versailles. In April, the AMCV outlined the remaining clauses Germany needed to fulfill before the Allies
would consider replacing the IAMCC with a less obtrusive organization.
The AMCV demanded that Germany conform strictly to the stipulations
of Versailles concerning the organization of the German army and police,
including the abolition of surplus administrative units, by 1 October
1922.[52] The second note of 1922 was a laundry list of all the remaining
steps toward disarmament that the Allies wished to see carried out. The
Allied coalition had accomplished much in reducing and reorganizing the

German army although details still remained. However, before the German government could reply, a number of violent attacks upon IAMCC members refocused the attention of the Allied governments on necessary retribution.[53] The subsequent Franco-Belgian occupation of the Ruhr brought Allied–German tensions to boiling-point, and inspections came to an abrupt halt.

The police question

In addition to limiting the German army to 100,000 troops, the Allies sought to truncate another armed force of manpower in Germany – the police. The creators of Versailles insisted on preventing the police from becoming a surplus reserve of armed and trained manpower for the German military. Article 162 of the treaty stipulated that the German police could not exceed its pre-war size of 1913 in its various districts, except in proportion to regional increases in the German population. The territorial losses inflicted by the treaty on Germany therefore could not be used to increase proportionally the police forces in the new boundaries of the nation. Overall, the treaty limited the German police to a strength of 92,000, not including an independent force of 20,000 in the Rhineland. The Allies not only placed a ceiling upon the size of the German police force but also prohibited all members from receiving any military training and forbade military organization, which amounted to centralization of control, and mobilization measures. In a glaring omission, however, the treaty failed to prescribe any terms of enlistment for the German police. In theory, the Germans could pass a large number of men through the ranks of the police over time, thereby establishing a sizable force of men with at least small arms training. Hence, Allied efforts in enforcing the military clauses of the treaty regarding the German police focused upon preventing any military or central organization of the police forces as well as precluding their use of military arms.

The various types of police under the responsibility of the Effectives Sub-commission illustrated the complexity of the police question in disarming Germany. Before the war, the German police force comprised two major groups: the *Gendarmerie* and the *Ordnungspolizei*. The former, which numbered 11,000 in 1914, were the armed rural constabulary. Armaments of the *Gendarmerie* varied but generally each member carried a rifle, pistol, saber, and bayonet and, at times, would be mounted. On the other hand, the *Ordnungspolizei*, made up of state, local, criminal, and administrative police, were under the control of the individual states of Germany. This force numbered 80,000 in 1914 and armed themselves with pistols and sabers, and occasionally had access to rifles.[54] Thus, the lightly armed *Ordnungspolizei* comprised the bulk of the German police but the Allies did not consider them to be a military threat. Altogether, the Versailles Treaty allowed Germany to maintain 12,000 *Gendarmerie* and

80,000 *Ordnungspolizei*.[55] The Allies authorized specific factories to produce arms for the German police forces.[56]

After the war, the German police force changed perceptibly. The Allies focused their attention on the emergence of a new, centrally organized police force in 1919, the *Sicherheitspolizei* (security police or *Sipo*). This police force was of a purely military nature, lived in barracks, and trained to use heavy armaments such as rifles, machine-guns, flamethrowers, trench mortars, tanks, and even airplanes.[57] The IAMCC argued that the *Sipo*, which comprised an elite force of specially picked men that numbered 60,000, formed a reserve for the *Reichswehr*. The *Sipo* wore gray-green uniforms similar to the *Reichswehr*, enlisted for short periods of time, and were recruited from officers and NCOs of the German army.[58] In fact, the AMCV asserted that they were recruited, armed, trained, and organized like the *Reichswehr*.[59] Even before the Treaty of Versailles went into effect, the Allies tried to persuade the German government to dissolve the *Sipo*.[60]

The Allies and Germany frequently discussed the size of German armed manpower throughout the first year of Allied disarmament operations. Immediately following the effective date of the treaty, the German government attempted to increase personnel strength to 92,000 *Ordnungspolizei* and 60,000 *Sicherheitspolizei*. In addition, the German army was already transferring men into the *Sipo* to keep them employed and to fulfill a military role.[61] The Allies demanded the completion of the reorganization of the police by 15 July.[62] But the German government's cries for modifying the terms of the Versailles Treaty soon came to fruition. Amidst the continued political turmoil in Germany in May and June, the AMCV, while opposing any increase in the size of the *Reichswehr* above its treaty limit, argued that Germany be allowed a police force larger than that prescribed by the treaty to maintain order.[63] Surprisingly, the AMCV thus supported Germany's request for an augmentation of police strength to 150,000 but ruled that regional administration and only light armaments could be maintained for the entire force. The Versailles Committee advocated an increase in the *Gendarmerie* to 17,000 but insisted upon the dissolution of the *Sipo*.[64]

At the Boulogne Conference in June 1920, the Allied governments officially sanctioned the plan of the AMCV and authorized modifications to the size of the German police forces prescribed by the Versailles Treaty. In what amounted to significant concessions to the German government, the Allies allowed Germany an increase of its police to 150,000 and the *Gendarmerie* to 17,000. However, they also imposed conditions: Germany had to organize its police under local administration and control, arm all police under IAMCC guidelines, and dissolve the *Sipo* by 22 September.[65] The police forces in the occupied and demilitarized Rhineland had been the responsibility of the Rhineland High Commission and therefore were not included in the 92,000 limit of Versailles. The Allies, however, tempered the increase in German police strength by including the 20,000 police in the demilitarized and occupied Rhineland zone in the overall number of 150,000.

The Allies soon reiterated their demand for the discontinuation of the *Sipo* at the Spa Conference but by August the Germans had still not fulfilled Allied expectations. The fact that Allied demands at Spa were inconsistent with their Boulogne demands made matters worse; at Boulogne the Allies allowed Germany three months to dissolve the *Sipo* but at Spa the Allies demanded immediate dissolution. The continuation of the *Sipo* at a size of up to 120,000 particularly vexed the French military leadership. The French considered the *Sipo*, armed to the teeth and located mainly in the frontier regions of Germany, "the principal reserve of cadres of the German army."[66] In his memoir of his time as President of the IAMCC, General Nollet referred to the German police as the equivalent of a second army.[67] The police question never concerned British authorities, with the exception of Morgan, to the same degree as their French colleagues.

In October 1920, the German government established a unified police force. Eight of the sixteen German states, including Prussia, had already issued decrees dissolving the *Sipo*, and by January 1921 the *Sipo* had all but disappeared.[68] The Germans, however, forged a new police force, the *Schutzpolizei* (or *Schupo*), from former *Sipo* members, and armed them with rifles, pistols, sabers, bayonets, automatic pistols, armored cars, and machine-guns.[69] The IAMCC supported the establishment of a fourteen-year enlistment period for the new police force but ultimately rejected the creation of the *Schupo*, regarding it as a slight variation of the *Sipo*, and demanded the dissolution of its centralized command structure.[70] The Allies sought to prevent the establishment of a second national army. The *Schupo* numbered 12,000; Germany intended to increase its total to over 17,000 men (out of a Prussian total of 85,000) although there was no direct connection between the new police force and the German army.[71] Allied demands to dissolve the *Schupo* embittered the Germans, who considered this police force a necessary measure to provide political stability. The Germans also tried to bend the will of the Allies by claiming that the *Schupo*'s dissolution "would imperil the power of industry to make reparations."[72]

A number of less important problems exacerbated the difficulties in disarming German armed personnel. One such complication arose from the fact that Germany organized the police forces under a federal system, without a national police force (except for the illegal *Sipo*); thus each state was responsible for its own police. This system made matters difficult for the IAMCC since police organization in the various German states had not been uniform prior to Allied disarmament demands. The IAMCC considered Prussia, with the largest police force in Germany, a priority, and Prussia soon fell into line with Allied demands before all other German states. The Effectives Commission also kept a watchful eye on Germany's armed civil servants, and allowed Germany to retain and arm a force of 21,794 foresters, gamekeepers, and water guards.[73]

In the Boulogne decree of June 1920, the Allied governments attempted to reorganize the German police by establishing three categories of police – uniformed, criminal, and administrative. They increased the size of the uniformed police to 150,000 and increased the plain-clothes police by percentages depending upon the state.[74] However, by the end of the year, the Allies insisted that the German police forces had not been reorganized along the policies established at Boulogne and Spa. The German government rejected Allied criticism and insisted that the new police force was under local control.[75] Germany accused the Allies, especially the French, of illuminating minor non-fulfillment as a pretext to occupy the Ruhr.[76]

Allied dissatisfaction with the police question continued into the next two years but was never as demonstrative as it had been in the first year of operations. In the spring and summer of 1921, the Allies continued to complain that the Germans had still not reduced the police force to the levels stipulated by the agreement at Boulogne.[77] The police question, however, made no more measurable progress for the remainder of the year. Although reorganized significantly, the state of the German police did not quite meet Allied demands. The British evaluation of the police, more favorable than that of the French, estimated the size of the German police force at 150,000 men and 17,000 *Gendarmerie*. Out of the total number of 150,000, they estimated the size of the *Schutzpolizei* (armed according to IAMCC demands) to be 90,000 and the criminal, administrative, and local police to be 60,000.[78] Nollet, however, pointed out that the police were still twice the size of the German army and their training, equipment, quarters, and staffs were under central control.[79] He was also concerned that the German police forces included 5,000 former *Reichswehr* officers. The IAMCC therefore demanded that Germany fulfill all Allied police demands by 15 March.[80] But negotiations and demands over the same issues (eradication of military or central control and all surplus units) dragged on for months. Without the threat of economic or military sanctions, the Germans merely ignored Allied demands. The police question was far from settled when the Allies suspended disarmament operations in early 1923.

The dissolution of the paramilitary groups

The numerous paramilitary organizations that sprouted in Germany immediately after the war represented another major source of manpower that posed a potential threat to the Allies.[81] Formed from overzealous, patriotic volunteers, paramilitary organizations emerged in Germany in the chaotic days of post-war political turmoil. Most of these self-defense forces (*Selbstschutz*) formed as volunteer organizations in 1919 to combat Bolshevism, augment the German army in Berlin or the Ruhr, or to crush popular unrest. Thousands of civilians and former soldiers rallied to the political and military demand for volunteers. Many of the paramilitary organizations in Germany in the early Weimar era served as an outlet for anti-republicanism and a number of them formed under governmental guidance in early 1919 to combat Bolshevism.[82] At the Paris Peace Conference, Allied leaders knew of the existence of these militant associations and sought to restrict all sources of German military aggression. As a result, Article 177 of the Treaty of Versailles forbade any civilian associations from taking part in "military matters" and the instruction of civilians in the use of arms. In addition to supervising the reduction and reorganization of the *Reichswehr* and police, the Effectives Sub-commission intended to eradicate all paramilitary organizations in Germany.

As early as December 1919, the Allied Supreme Council ordered all German paramilitary forces to be dissolved by 10 January 1920, the effective date of the Treaty of Versailles.[83] The Allies, particularly the French, saw German paramilitary organizations as a threat to the peace of Europe. Similar to their fear of a large *Reichswehr* and a strong police force, French political and military leaders regarded armed civilian organizations as a reserve army intent on destroying the peace that had taken millions of lives to forge. Once again, the French yearning to bridge the manpower gap led them to work diligently to oversee the eradication of these German forces. The British, too, feared the possibility of a military threat from the German paramilitary groups but wavered at times in their opposition to them. With their ranks filled with monarchists and reactionaries, British political and military authorities considered German paramilitary organizations to be a shield against Bolshevism. By the spring of 1920, however, the British began to fear the possibility of a right-wing *coup d'état*.[84] The French and British generally worked together in overseeing the dissolution of the paramilitary groups. Of all the questions concerning the Effectives Sub-commission, the maintenance of these German self-defense forces remained the most time-consuming and bothersome of all.

The Germans established three major types of paramilitary organizations: the Free Corps (*Freikorps*), short-term volunteers (*Zeitfreiwillige*), and the Civic Guard (*Einwohnerwehr*).[85] The Effectives Commission of the IAMCC had the task of overseeing the disarmament and dissolution of all of these organizations. In addition, there were a number of smaller organizations in Germany, such as the *Technische Nothilfe, Jungdeutscher Orden, Grenzwehren*, and even armed sports clubs, but their size, organization, and armaments made them less of a concern to the IAMCC. On the other hand, the *Freikorps*, formed in December 1918 from soldiers and students, numbered in the tens of thousands in the spring of 1919.[86] The German government had taken no steps to see to their dissolution.[87] For two years, the *Freikorps* fought intermittently against various leftists, revolutionaries, and foreigners in Germany, Upper Silesia, Poland, and the Baltic states. After the spring of 1920 the *Freikorps* began to diminish in strength, and on 24 May 1921 the German government finally published a decree that outlawed the organization of any *Freikorps* units.[88] This decree had an immediate effect upon a number of these combat-experienced volunteer formations, and an additional government order in November 1921 essentially dissolved them. Although the *Freikorps* faded away, a number of members simply joined the ranks of other paramilitary groups in Germany.

The *Zeitfreiwillige* formed under the auspices of the German army in January 1919 to preserve order, establish a military reserve, and augment the *Freikorps* in Berlin.[89] The German government, which armed these forces with rifles and the occasional machine-gun, generally called them to service only in times of crisis. Like the *Freikorps*, the *Zeitfreiwillige* received training from German military units. These volunteers consisted mostly of young, educated, bourgeois members of German society.[90] The British War Office estimated their strength at almost 200,000.[91] The *Zeitfreiwillige*, while an initial threat to Allied disarmament policies, were short-lived. Moreover, even Morgan assessed the military value of the *Zeitfreiwillige* as practically negligible.[92] They were officially dissolved by government order on 31 March 1920 and by June, the Allies considered both the *Zeitfreiwillige* and the *Freikorps* to be dissolved.[93] With the overlapping tendencies of the German paramilitary organizations, all of which shared a common purpose, a number of the *Zeitfreiwillige* undoubtedly joined the ranks of the *Einwohnerwehr*.

The *Einwohnerwehr* constituted the largest of the paramilitary organizations in Germany. Formed in 1919 as protection against political unrest and Bolshevism, the dissolution of such a vast patriotic and militant organization posed a most difficult task for the Allies. Aside from virulent anti-communism, this paramilitary association advocated a rightist political line in trumpeting a German revival through the revision of the Treaty of Versailles.[94] The German states, which controlled the *Einwohnerwehr*, generally armed them with rifles and a few machine-guns.[95] While the state government of Bavaria helped subsidize the *Einwohnerwehr*, the German government helped provide them with rifles.[96] The IAMCC estimated the strength of the Bavarian *Einwohnerwehr* alone to be over 300,000 men.[97]

The question of disbanding the self-defense organizations in Germany challenged Allied disarmament efforts in 1920. The political stance of Bavaria, a hotbed of IAMCC opposition, exacerbated the difficult nature of dispersing armed civilian groups. Conservatives dominated the southeastern German state, and members of right-wing political parties provided most of the members for the *Einwohnerwehr*.[98] After the short-term Bolshevik coup in 1919, the determination of so many Bavarians to prevent any repetition of a Bolshevik victory made the dissolution of the Bavarian *Einwohnerwehr* a particularly arduous undertaking. The IAMCC sent many notes to the German government demanding the dissolution of the *Einwohnerwehr* throughout Germany by 10 April 1920.[99] Consequently, on 8 April, the German government ordered the dissolution of the *Einwohnerwehr* but the law fell short of IAMCC expectations.

Although it forbade military exercises and modified armaments, the law essentially delegated the question to the German states.[100]

Although Prussia, Saxony, and some smaller German states had disbanded their paramilitary forces, the *Einwohnerwehr* was a thorn in the side of Allied disarmament efforts in East Prussia and Bavaria. In these latter states, the *Einwohnerwehr* remained armed and well organized.[101] In the Paris meetings in May 1920, the Allies requested that the German government hand over a list of organizations and demanded the dissolution of all paramilitary forces in Germany by 20 June.[102] German representatives from Baden, Württemberg, and Bavaria met to pressure the German government to enter negotiations with the Allies to maintain the *Einwohnerwehr*.[103] In reaction to Allied demands to dissolve the *Einwohnerwehr*, the German government claimed that the organization existed merely to protect "the life and property of the peaceful population."[104] In the summer of 1920, Bavaria still made no efforts to do away with its illegal military formations while a number of other German states had taken legal measures to do so. In fact, the IAMCC reported that all German states, with the exception of Bavaria and Bremen, had either disarmed or abolished the *Einwohnerwehr*.[105] Unfortunately for the Allies, the Bavarian *Einwohnerwehr* was the largest of all the paramilitary organizations in Germany. French military intelligence estimated the total strength of the *Einwohnerwehr* to be two million men.[106] Consequently, Nollet repeatedly called for the dissolution of the *Einwohnerwehr* in the late summer and early autumn months.[107]

The establishment of a paramilitary administrative body, the *Organization Escherich* (*Orgesch*), augmented the complexity of the paramilitary question. Georg Escherich, leader of the Bavarian *Einwohnerwehr*, founded the *Orgesch* in Bavaria, which also had headquarters in Munich, Berlin, Hanover, and Marburg. It was administered by the Ministry of Labor, received state funding in emergencies, and maintained a close liaison with the *Reichswehr*.[108] Escherich, a member of the Bavarian forestry department who owned a farm outside of Munich, claimed that the *Orgesch* was a self-defense organization that demanded only the ouster of Bolshevism from Germany; he estimated the strength of his organization at around 300,000 men in the autumn of 1920.[109] The platform of this bastion of conservatism demanded the protection of the constitution and personal property, and the maintenance of public order and the Reich. But the *Orgesch* also had a grand plan for all the bourgeois and conservative paramilitary groups in Germany as it tried to consolidate all the self-defense associations.[110] In essence, the *Orgesch* acted as the central body of all the self-defense forces in Germany. In August, Prussian Minister of the Interior Wilhelm Severing forbade the presence of the *Orgesch* in Prussia, and the governments of Saxony and Württemberg took similar measures, but Bavaria refused to bend under Allied pressure.

Overall, the IAMCC had made significant strides toward the dissolution of paramilitary organizations in Germany with the exception of Bavaria. In fact, Nollet expressed optimism that all of northern Germany had disbanded the *Einwohnerwehr*.[111] On the other hand, a direct meeting with Ritter von Kahr, the Bavarian Prime Minister from 1920 to 1921, convinced Nollet that Bavaria had little intention of disarming or disbanding its paramilitary forces.[112] Nollet asserted that the *Einwohnerwehr* was directly involved with the *Reichswehr* as the IAMCC had ascertained that officers of the German army worked as liaisons with the paramilitary organization.[113] Nollet believed that the time for any Bolshevik take-overs had long since passed, and in December he reiterated his demands for the dissolution of all paramilitary organizations.

Nollet's position on the paramilitary question was incompatible with British interests. The British War Office did not consider the *Einwohnerwehr* to be a military threat, and together with the Foreign Office and Lord D'Abernon, proposed a compromise of the gradual reduction of the paramilitary organization.[114] In fact, the War Office regarded the membership of the *Einwohnerwehr* as consisting of "all the law abiding and best elements in the Bavarian population" while D'Abernon considered any Allied attempts to abolish the *Einwohnerwehr* as "insane."[115] The ambassador's *Germanophile* tendencies and virulent anti-communism would continue to run counter to Nollet and the IAMCC. The threat of Bolshevism, still the British bugbear, had not yet run its course, and continued to influence British policies toward German disarmament and the enforcement of the Treaty of Versailles.

The *Einwohnerwehr* issue at the end of 1920 symbolized relations between Britain, France, and Germany in the enforcement of disarmament. In short, Britain advocated leniency, France remained intransigent, and Germany denied everything. The attitude of the War Office, as well as D'Abernon, illustrated the changing diplomatic policies of Britain toward Germany in the post-war era and reveals the crucial difference between French and British viewpoints. The British were at least willing to modify the demands that had been made in the Paris Peace Conference while the French believed their national existence was predicated upon those very demands. While the British War Office correctly assessed the relevant military value of the *Einwohnerwehr* (and the *Reichswehr*) as less than a threat against the combined arms of Britain and France, the modification of either the treaty or the subsequent Allied demands worked as a centrifugal force toward the fragmentation of the unofficial Franco–British entente. Treaty modification was the fatal chink in the French armor of Versailles. In the paramilitary question, and in upcoming discussions, Britain would be more willing than France to meet present exigencies than to honor demands of the past. German policy often widened this Anglo–French disparity by continuing to reinforce delay, with the hope that Allied disarmament operations would simply disappear.

At the beginning of 1921, the British and French governments met in

Paris where they discussed crucial German disarmament questions and threatened occupation of the Rhineland unless Germany complied with their demands. One important step taken by the Allies was the demand for the termination of the *Einwohnerwehr*.[116] As a result, Foreign Minister Simons pressured the Bavarian government to comply with orders to dissolve the paramilitary forces in the southern German state.[117] The Bavarian government, under Ritter von Kahr, remained intransigent to Allied and German demands until the Allied ultimatum of 5 May. The policy of sanctions, with the threat to occupy the Ruhr, finally broke von Kahr.[118] By mid-June 1921, Germany had surrendered to the IAMCC two-thirds of all small arms in the possession of its self-defense forces.[119] At the end of the month, the German government took another step to disband the self-defense forces that appeared free from federal control. It published a decree on 24 June that dissolved the *Einwohnerwehr* and *Orgesch* throughout Germany, although it focused upon Bavaria and East Prussia.[120] The Allied ultimatum had broken the back of the paramilitary movement as the state governments finally bent to Allied and federal pressure by supporting the dissolution of the self-defense forces. Progress in this matter appeared to increase substantially. In fact, D'Abernon was sufficiently convinced in July that Germany had entirely dissolved all of the paramilitary organizations.[121] In light of the crackdown against the paramilitary organizations in Germany, the *Einwohnerwehr* went into hiding and partially reconstituted itself a year later as another politically motivated paramilitary force in Bavaria.[122] The AMCV continued to warn that the self-defense organizations constituted a strong military reserve.[123]

While paramilitary forces continued to exist in Germany throughout the life of the IAMCC, they never again posed a serious threat to Allied disarmament efforts. In the spring of 1922, the IAMCC continued to press the Germans to fulfill their obligations toward the self-defense organizations that remained in Germany. In April, the Conference of Ambassadors, which played a rather minor role in the paramilitary question, agreed that Germany disband all military associations before the Allies would consider terminating inspections.[124] By mid-1922, the IAMCC expressed much less anxiety about the presence of German paramilitary forces. Nollet merely reported that the German government had ordered their dissolution and was in the process of carrying out this policy.[125] Yet the deal remained: either Germany terminated all paramilitary associations throughout the nation or Allied troops would remain billeted in the heart of Germany.

7 Fortifications
The destruction of German defenses

The third major element of Allied disarmament operations involved the destruction of Germany's system of fortifications, which represented an integral part of German military strength. Made up of dozens of heavily armed forts and coastal batteries, hundreds of concrete dugouts, and hundreds of kilometers of telephone cables, trenches, railroad tracks, and canals, Germany's fortified works presented a formidable line of defense. The Allies therefore sought to cripple this extensive defensive network. The Germans had built the heart of their fortresses in the Rhineland, and a number of forts stood along the coastal waters of the Baltic and North Seas as well the eastern and southern border areas of Germany.[1] Constructed for defensive purposes, Germany's forts did not play a major role in World War I. In light of the fact that the Allies placed such emphasis on the reduction of German armaments and armed manpower, the Allies did not consider the dismantling and destruction of German fortifications to be a priority in the disarmament of Germany. Unlike armaments and troops, forts were fixed structures and could not be easily concealed from Allied inspections. Because British, French, Belgian, and American troops occupied the Rhineland, the Allies could dismantle the key German fortresses with impunity. Nonetheless, Allied inspectors expended great effort in enforcing the treaty articles regarding German fortifications and focused on the armaments that the forts contained.

The ambiguous nature of the clauses of the Treaty of Versailles that dealt with the dismantling and destruction of German fortifications and defense systems allowed for a rather loose interpretation of the original intent of the treaty's creators in Paris. Allied inspectors divided their work into two areas: Articles 180, 195, and 196 of the Versailles Treaty charged the Allies with destroying the German forts located in the demilitarized and occupied Rhineland, as well as the area surrounding and including Kiel. On the other hand, the treaty allowed German forts in the south, east, and within fifty kilometers of the North and Baltic Seas, to be kept in their existing state. Strategically, these forts did not concern the disarmament coalition but the extent of their armament was a focal point of the work of Allied inspectors. Some of the eastern and southern German forts were simply obsolete, positioned to defend Germany from past enemies, while others helped to defend the eastern reaches from the emerging Bolshevik threat.

On Germany's western frontier, the treaty's precise wording left no doubt: Article 180 demanded that Germany disarm and dismantle all fortifications west of a line drawn fifty kilometers east of the Rhine. The Rhineland had great strategic importance to the security of France. As part of the Allied strategy to demilitarize the Rhineland, the treaty forbade Germany from having any defensive works in this zone. The Allies gave Germany two months to disarm all fortifications outside of the Allied occupation in the west and a period of four months to dismantle them. With a coalition of troops occupying the Rhineland, the Allies put off any decisions regarding deadlines to dismantle and destroy the German forts that lay within the boundary of the occupation. The troop presence in the Rhineland could be used to ensure and maintain treaty compliance, but the fortifications system in the Rhineland was a formidable array of defenses and would take the longest to dismantle and destroy. The peacemakers in Paris also restricted the number of rounds within all German forts and forbade any modifications or enhancements to any defensive structure after 10 January 1920.[2] One final treaty stipulation which increased tension between the Allies and Germany was the demand that the German government furnish a detailed inventory of all forts.

Germany's eastern and southern defenses were another matter altogether. While the Versailles Treaty designated the forts in the west for destruction, thereby facilitating France's quest for security, the Allies allowed Germany to maintain its eastern and southern forts. Germany had fourteen forts located in the east and south but the Allies did not consider them to be strategically important. A single sentence of Article 180 of the treaty, however, was culpable for the polarized interpretations and disagreement that followed: "The system of fortified works of the southern and eastern frontiers of Germany shall be maintained in its existing state." The central concern was the ambiguity of the phrase "existing state." The Allies intended that Germany could not modify the condition and armaments of any fort located in the east and south of the nation after 10 January 1920, but the German government had other plans. Grasping at anything to weaken the military clauses of the hated treaty, the Germans attempted subsequently to retain and rearm a series of archaic forts. In addition, to assess the "existing state" of Germany's southern and eastern forts, the IAMCC planned a series of inspections. Germany opposed these inspections as an illegal affront to its sovereignty, and disagreement between the Allies and the Germans over this particular issue would last throughout the first year of disarmament operations.

The Allies treated Germany's coastal forts like those in the east and south. Germany had to maintain all forts within fifty miles of the coast or on coastal islands in their existing state of January 1920. Thus, the

Germans would have to make do with the quantity, quality, and caliber of guns that were in place in the forts when the treaty went into effect. The Allies also forbade any new defensive construction in these locations. More importantly, the treaty targeted the massive fortifications located in and around Kiel for destruction. Allied inspectors allowed Germany only three months to destroy the masonry of the Kiel fortifications and six months to dismantle the entire system.[3] The determination of the armaments of the other German coastal forts, including the massive forts in Königsberg, took months to settle. Yet in terms of the fulfillment of the military clauses of the Versailles Treaty, the dismantling and destruction of German fortifications was the most efficient and successful area of Allied disarmament operations in Germany.

The politics of fortifications

The Fortifications Sub-commission, with approximately thirty Allied officers, was the smallest of the three sub-commissions of the IAMCC. The British and French, similar to their leadership of the two larger sub-commissions, dominated its command. Despite the Fortifications Sub-commission's diminutive size, French president General Raymond Bizouard and his British colleague Colonel Gruble led its inspectors to great success.[4] The Allies established three district committees in Cologne, Kiel, and Stuttgart.[5] After a series of delays and complaints, the work of the Fortifications Sub-commission proceeded in a fairly straightforward fashion. Essentially, the Sub-commission had a search-and-destroy mission. The IAMCC gave its inspectors the responsibility of supervising the dismantling and destruction of dozens of forts and gun batteries, hundreds of dugouts and trench systems, as well as the means of logistical support. After a few months of fruitless discussions with their German counterparts, the Allies eventually conducted a series of inventory inspections of all of Germany's forts. These inspections allowed Allied disarmament officers to take stock of German defenses and formulate a precise plan on how to dismantle them.

The most pressing task for the fortifications inspectors was evaluating the military capability of the German forts in the east and south, and on the German coasts. The Treaty of Versailles forbade any modifications to the forts after 10 January 1920. Regarding the idea of the "existing state" of fortifications, the treaty focused upon the number and size of guns that lurked within the German defensive systems. Quite simply, the Allies would allow Germany to keep the exact number and caliber of guns that the forts held in place in January 1920. However, in order to determine the existing state of German forts, the Allies either had to rely on German inventory reports or visit the forts and make their own inventories. The subsequent issue of inspections therefore became another sticking point in the disarmament of Germany's fortifications.

In order to make the best of a difficult situation, the Germans naturally interpreted the fortifications articles to coincide with their own interests. In January 1920, the Germans presented the Allies with a list of armaments that the Germans intended to maintain in a number of fortresses. German political and military officers showed great initiative between the time of the Armistice and the effective date of the Treaty of Versailles by stockpiling about 4,000 heavy and field guns, as well as various other armaments, in twelve forts located throughout the eastern and southern districts of Germany.[6] These amounts included over 2,000 heavy guns with 871 replacement barrels, almost 1,500 pieces of field artillery, and over 500 anti-aircraft guns. The German government also notified the Allies that their coastal forts had about 400 heavy guns, 200 field guns, and almost 500 anti-aircraft guns.[7] In presenting the forts as heavily armed in January, the Germans obviously hoped to force the Allies to allow them to keep a large number of guns and other assorted armaments. This strategy did not dupe the British, French, Belgian, Italian, and Japanese officers responsible for disarming Germany. Reacting forcefully to the figures that Germany inflated beyond the normal capacity of the forts in question, the Allies gave no quarter and worked to put an end to German pretensions of maintaining a formidable artillery reserve.

Differences between the Allies and Germany over the interpretation of the Treaty of Versailles' fortifications articles continued through the winter, thereby delaying the work of the inspectors. The major sticking point was the right of inspections. Although the treaty demanded that Germany turn over detailed lists of inventories of all fortifications, the German government undertook no effort to produce them. Eager to fix the amount of artillery in each fort and suspecting that Germany had exaggerated its claims, the Allies hoped to verify German fortifications through their own inventory inspections. Consequently, General Nollet demanded the right to inspect the German forts and to take inventories to determine their actual state at the time the treaty went into effect.[8] In his distrust of German intentions, fueled by German armament demands for the eastern and southern forts, the French general claimed that the IAMCC had the right to verify German armaments claims for the forts. General von Cramon, adamantly opposed to all forms of disarmament, vehemently protested any Allied visits of German fortifications.[9] At the end of February, Nollet reported to the Allied leaders of the Conference of Ambassadors that the German government had contested the right of the IAMCC to verify, and therefore inspect, the current state of German fortifications. After Marshal Foch and the AMCV upheld the right of Allied inspections, the Ambassadors' Conference ruled on 11 March that the IAMCC had the right to visit, inventory, and verify the coastal forts as well as the forts located in the east and south of Germany.[10] With the issue settled, full-scale Allied inspections of German fortifications began late in the spring.

The Allies also made decisions regarding the forts into which Germany had transported a significant arsenal of artillery. In order to prevent Germany from attempting to establish an artillery reserve, the IAMCC demanded in March that Germany could only retain the number of guns corresponding to the number of gun emplacements in each fort. Allied officers of the IAMCC interpreted the phrase of Article 196 concerning fortification guns, "those in position," as guns that were permanently fixed to the forts in emplacements. Thus, the Allies would not allow any mobile artillery, and Germany would have to surrender the stockpiles to the Allies. Most importantly, the IAMCC rejected German proposals to maintain (and arm) a number of these ancient forts.[11] On 13 March, and again on 5 May, the IAMCC demanded a reduction of over 4,000 guns that the Germans had hastily assembled in the towns in which the forts were located. On 28 May, the IAMCC notified the German government that only the forts of Königsberg, Pillau, Swinemünde, Küstrin, and Ulm could be maintained, whereas the question of their armaments remained up in the air. On the other hand, the IAMCC decided that the defense systems in Breslau, Marienburg, Ingolstadt, and Königstein could not be considered to be or maintained as fortresses.[12]

The issue of obtaining detailed inventories of the German fortifications remained a pressing concern to Allied disarmament authorities. In June, the Germans had still not given the Allies any inventories of their fortifications.[13] This negligence was not lost on Marshal Foch, and the AMCV demanded the completion of the dismantling of forts in the Rhineland by 10 July. On the other hand, the Allies allowed a delay in the dismantling of the coastal forts until 10 December.[14] Aside from the lack of inventories, the problems over the legal interpretation of recording the number of German guns in the forts in the east and south and dismantling other German forts effectively prevented the Fortifications Sub-commission from accomplishing its major tasks.[15] The surplus of shells the Germans retained for their fortifications' artillery was a crucial Allied concern.

The matter of the quality and quantity of the armaments used in the eastern and southern German forts continued to concern the Fortifications Sub-commission, and only the completion of inventories could ease the IAMCC's worries. In fact, Nollet sent General Bingham to the forts of Königsberg, Pillau, and Küstrin to examine their armaments. After a personal inspection, Bingham believed the Allies should treat Königsberg differently than Pillau and Küstrin, but still proposed a significant reduction in the German demand for Königsberg's armaments.[16] Other Allied inspections revealed that the Germans had collected and stored armaments in many of the forts in question. In the face of constant Allied pressure, in July the Germans finally turned over detailed plans of their forts to the Allies, who in turn fixed the armaments restrictions for all the forts except for Königsberg. Consequently, the IAMCC allowed Pillau five batteries of heavy guns and ten anti-aircraft guns on the north coast, and restricted the fortress at Swinemünde to twenty-eight heavy guns and four anti-aircraft guns.[17] But the IAMCC disallowed any armaments for Ulm and Küstrin and continued to study the question of Königsberg's armaments.[18] Based on the reports of the inspectors, the Allies refused to sanction spare gun tubes for any of the forts and forbade any surplus personnel weapons within the forts. In addition, the IAMCC would not allow any attempt to improve the conditions of the forts. As a result, the Germans eventually reduced the guns in the forts in question to a mere 106, and Germany eventually surrendered excess weapons *in toto* by May 1921.[19] The persistence and tenacity of the IAMCC in enforcing and interpreting the fortifications articles of the Treaty of Versailles, facilitated by the accord reached within the disarmament coalition (especially the British and French), was primarily responsible for this Allied success.

As a result of numerous inspections of Germany's eastern, southern, and coastal forts, the Allies thwarted German designs of increasing its military strength through the circumvention of Allied disarmament intentions and policies. Allied inspection teams discovered that many German demands for heavy armaments in the forts were indeed specious in intention and devious in scope. The southern German forts of Neisse, Ulm, Glatz, Königstein, and Ingolstadt were simply obsolete, with some of them dating back as far as the eighteenth century.[20] These forts could barely withstand a barrage of modern artillery, and lacked command posts, communications, and gun emplacements. The IAMCC would not allow the obsolete, decaying, and neglected relics to be used as mere storehouses for German artillery. Inspections of the eastern forts of Küstrin, Glogau, and Breslau revealed the same conditions. In addition, inspectors discovered illegal weapons caches that amounted to 250,000 rifles, 2,300 machineguns, and 2,000 trench mortars.[21] By October, the Allies completed all of their inventory inspections of German forts, saving the older forts of Neisse, Glatz, and Königstein for last.[22] The inspectors only had to complete their detailed dossiers of these fortifications to complete their tasks.[23] The extent of mobile artillery the Allies found in each defensive structure concerned the IAMCC, and once they discovered the true nature of these stockpiles, the state of German fortifications became a secondary issue of disarmament.

Despite rapid progress on all fronts, the IAMCC considered the attempt of Germany to retain a mobile heavy artillery reserve in the coastal forts to be of crucial importance.[24] On 8 November 1920, the Conference of Ambassadors demanded that the German government surrender surplus artillery from the forts of Küstrin, Lotzen-Boyen, and Königsberg. The Germans refused to comply. Furthermore, in January 1921, the German government demanded the right to protect Germany's eastern and southern forts with 2,600 machine-guns (more than the allotment for the entire 100,000 man army!), refused to surrender coastal fort artillery, and demanded to keep over twice the 420 guns that the IAMCC authorized. As a result, the Allies toughened their stance, and at the Paris meetings in

January 1921, the British and French governments notified the Germans that they had refused to allow any guns for Küstrin and Lotzen-Boyen. The Allies also decided to allow only twenty-two heavy guns for Königsberg.[25] In addition, German pleas to keep rifles, machine-guns, and mortars within the walls of the forts fell on deaf ears. In allowing German coastal forts only 420 guns, the Allied governments had implemented the proposals of their arms inspectors as well as the Conference of Ambassadors.

Although the Allies gave Germany until 28 February 1921 to comply, they did not resort to any economic or military sanctions to strengthen their demands. Once again the deadlines expired without action, and non-compliance merely led to new deadlines. At the Paris meeting, the Allies also demanded that Germany surrender its surplus land fortification armaments by the end of May and its surplus coastal fort armaments by 10 June. The threat of a Ruhr occupation in the May ultimatum, coming on the heels of the Allied occupation of Düsseldorf in the spring, was too much for Germany, which surrendered all surplus guns in its eastern and southern fortifications to the Allies for destruction.[26] Only the armaments of the forts of Küstrin and Königsberg remained in question. The Allied use of physical sanctions to force German compliance proved to be the most successfully strategy in all three areas of disarmament: armaments, effectives, and fortifications.

The mechanics of fortification dismantling and destruction

Although the Germans contested Allied actions regarding the maintenance of a number of old fortresses, the Fortifications Sub-commission experienced remarkable progress. In essence, of all the questions facing the IAMCC, the destruction of German forts was the most straightforward task. The IAMCC refused to back down in the face of German opposition, and the work soon progressed with alacrity. The Allies knew the locations of the forts and the IAMCC merely had to verify their dismantling and destruction. At times, the French demanded more extensive demolition than their British counterparts. While the British focused upon the destruction of all gun emplacements, platforms, and masonry, the French even demanded the complete leveling of earthworks surrounding some forts.[27] Nonetheless, the work of the Fortifications Sub-commission was a true Allied effort, with little of the squabbling that occurred over armaments and effectives issues.

The dismantling and destruction of German forts began in earnest in the summer of 1920. Similar to all disarmament efforts, Allied enforcement and German acquiescence determined the amount of progress. Inspectors of the Fortifications Sub-commission acted in a supervisory role while German workers produced the manual labor. The Allies contracted private German demolition companies to carry out the destruction of the fortifications, which involved the supervision of hundreds of German laborers. The German government had the responsibility of drafting detailed plans of demolition while the inspectors evaluated these plans and then directed their execution.[28]

The type of work varied at different sites but it always involved the demolition of fortresses and fortified works with high explosives. The fortresses comprised a defensive network of concrete emplacements and shelters, armored batteries, and massive earthworks, linked together by a complex web of phone cables and railroad tracks. The Germans had built most of the defensive works to withstand artillery barrages, but the forts succumbed easily to the efforts of the skilled demolition teams. In destroying a fort, teams of experts exploded charges in the concrete and earthen defenses, thereby crippling the overall strength of the defenses. Once established, a breach facilitated further demolition and would be quickly enlarged. The actual demolition of German forts began in the early summer, and by June the inspectors witnessed the destruction of the underground gun emplacements and concrete shelters in Wesel. Seven different contractors started demolishing the numerous artillery emplacements, infantry shelters, and observation posts in Istein, hoping to complete the work by the end of July. Kiel was a much more massive endeavor and the Allies surmised that the destruction of the gun emplacements, munitions shelters, ranging stations, blockhouses, and observation posts would not be completed until the end of the year.[29] By the end of the summer, inspectors reported progress in the leveling of the escarpment at Wesel and the destruction of the majority of Istein's concrete shelters and armored batteries. In Kiel's massive fortress system, workers tore a huge breach in the escarpment and initiated the demolition of anti-aircraft batteries, shelters, and gun platforms. In addition, the work in the occupied Rhineland finally commenced, with up to 400 German laborers involved in the destruction of the system of fortifications in Mainz.[30]

In the fall the Fortifications Sub-commission witnessed a great deal of progress. Demolition of the great citadel of Wesel commenced, the concrete shelters of Istein continued to fall under the demolition teams' handiwork, and the IAMCC began efforts to destroy the forts in Cologne and Coblenz.[31] In Kiel, especially, Allied officers witnessed substantial progress as most of the concrete shelters and anti-aircraft batteries met their ignominious fate. By mid-November, the IAMCC supervised upward of 400 German laborers in the destruction of the complex of fortifications in Kiel. Allied inspectors discovered a rather spirited, but minor, attempt at deception when they found that German workers had overturned a gun platform and covered it with dirt to appear smashed; with the scheme foiled, the inspectors subsequently destroyed the platform.[32] Surprisingly, there were few attempts to obstruct or sabotage the demolition work that continued in a number of German cities and towns. Fortification demolition provided work for hundreds of Germans, offering proof that difficult financial straits in desperate times transcended political and nationalist sentiments. Any accolades for slowing down Allied efforts regarding fortifications must be given primarily to the German government. One pertinent example of government interference occurred in November when German political officials advised a local German official involved with the demolition work in Kiel to proceed as slowly as possible. The Germans hoped that delaying destruction would render a diplomatic victory as it awaited a response from the Conference of Ambassadors to one of its numerous inquiries.[33] After June 1920, however, direct efforts to impede the progress of the Fortifications Sub-commission slowed down dramatically, and the work proceeded at a steady pace.

Demolition of Germany's powerful bastions of defense experienced no respite in the cold winter months. By December, the AMCV reported that the dismantling and destruction of German fortifications was proceeding so well that it no longer posed a concern.[34] As a new year dawned, the demolition work in the mighty fortifications of Kiel, Istein, and Cologne neared completion.[35] The rapid progress dictated Allied policy changes. In April 1921, under pressure from the Conference of Ambassadors, the IAMCC began to reduce dismantling operations to diminish expenses and allowed an extension of six months for the period of dismantling the forts.[36] Progress continued through the summer to the point where the British Foreign Office expressed satisfaction with the disarmament of both land and coastal forts in Germany.[37] As the dismantling and destruction of German forts wound down, the AMCV declared that the work would be finished by the end of the year. Because Germany had reduced the armaments of its fortifications to the proper levels, the AMCV proposed an immediate 50 percent reduction in the size of the Fortifications Sub-commission and even professed a belief that the Fortifications Sub-commission could be dissolved in January 1922.[38] General Bingham concurred, hoping privately that the Allies would dissolve the Fortifications Sub-commission by the end of 1921.[39]

In February 1922, after inspectors witnessed the final dismantling and destruction of German forts in both occupied and non-occupied territory, the Allies dissolved the Fortifications Sub-commission. General Nollet reported that the Fortifications Sub-commission would be changed into an organ of liquidation to deal with any minor questions that remained. The Allies dissolved these last vestiges of the Fortification Sub-commission in February 1923.[40] One significant effect of the dissolution of the Fortifications Sub-commission that influenced the future work of the IAMCC was the decrease in the number of French on the IAMCC Council from four to three officers.[41] Surprisingly, the French agreed to this modification even though it decreased their authority and allowed the rest of the coalition (especially the British) to block French decisions more easily.

In regard to the issues surrounding the disarmament of German fortifications, the IAMCC was the force behind Allied policy. Suspicious of

German intentions, the IAMCC had refused to recognize the belated German fortification reports and demanded the right to visit, take inventories, and verify the amount of artillery contained within each eastern, southern, and coastal German fort. Yet German efforts to circumvent the enforcement of Versailles' disarmament clauses were also certainly less diligent than those schemes concocted to frustrate the execution of the armaments and effectives clauses of the treaty. In essence, the issue of fortifications for both the Allies and Germany was a less important aspect of disarmament, but the work of the Fortifications Sub-commission should not be belittled. Compared with the surrender and destruction of German armaments or the reduction in numbers of German soldiers, police, and self-defense organizations, the dismantling and destruction of German fortifications was a true Allied victory in the enforcement of the Treaty of Versailles. The work supervised by the Fortifications Sub-commission was extremely successful and must be viewed as one of the greatest accomplishments of the IAMCC. The final numbers were impressive. Overall, the Fortifications Sub-commission had seen to the destruction of twenty-six large fortresses, thirty-thee intermediate fortified works, two modern forts (Istein and Mainz), eighteen coastal batteries, 800 concrete dugouts, 300 kilometers of underground telephone cable, forty kilometers of railroad tracks, and thirty kilometers of fortress canals.[42] After a year of debates with German authorities over the interpretation of the Treaty of Versailles' fortifications clauses, the Allies had diligently enforced this area of the treaty. The Allies had rendered Germany's eastern, southern, and coastal forts harmless. Undefended and facing the tenacity of the ubiquitous inspectors, Germany's forts in the west were demolished as surely as the great fortresses of Belgium had bowed to the German victors in 1914. From the modern marvels of Istein and Mainz, to the archaic walls of Königstein and Glatz, Germany's fortresses either vanished in clouds of debris or stood as silent sentinels of yesteryear.

8 Future control

The struggle for an Allied policy

The Armaments, Effectives, and Fortifications Sub-committees had all witnessed significant progress in carrying out the military clauses of the Treaty of Versailles in the first two years of Allied disarmament operations in Germany. By the beginning of 1922, Germany had destroyed most of its armaments and the Allies had dissolved the Fortifications Sub-commission. The Allies had also witnessed progress in reducing the German army to 100,000 troops, although a number of organizational and technical concerns still presented problems. Nonetheless, the German army had witnessed a massive transformation into a relatively small army, with few artillery pieces and protected by sparsely distributed fortifications. As significant progress in the disarmament of Germany continued, an important question began to emerge: Just how long would the IAMCC remain in Germany? As the question of the duration of the IAMCC began to wax with the waning of German military strength, British and French views toward German disarmament diverged once again.

Although the peacemakers of 1919 hoped initially to disarm Germany in a matter of months, Article 203 of the Treaty of Versailles stipulated that the duration of the IAMCC depended upon the execution of the military clauses of the treaty that had specific time limits.[1] Technically, as long as these clauses remained unfulfilled, the IAMCC could remain in Germany. In addition, Article 213 gave the League of Nations the right to order investigations, presumably after the withdrawal of the IAMCC, to verify German compliance with the military aspects of the treaty. Thus, the Allies decided that after Germany had fulfilled the military clauses under the watchful eye of the IAMCC, they would transfer authority of military supervision to the Council of the League of Nations. This future transfer of power provoked British and French anxieties over the possible lack of authority of the League of Nations and potential German rearmament upon withdrawal of the IAMCC. As German disarmament progressed after a year of operations, the British began to advocate the replacement of the IAMCC with a smaller organization in an attempt to conclude the work of disarmament and normalize relations with Germany. British hopes to re-establish international stability ran up against a cornerstone of

French security policy.[2] Since the French deplored any policy other than the complete fulfillment of the Treaty of Versailles, Allied unity toward the enforcement of the military clauses of the treaty would bend, but not break, under the strain.

The British first explored the modification of the IAMCC, or the idea of future control, at the close of the first year of disarmament operations. Discussions with the French gained momentum throughout 1921 but fizzled out by the end of 1922 when serious incidents of abuse against the IAMCC suspended Allied notions of replacing the disarmament regime in Germany. The purpose of establishing a new form of military control was to maintain Allied supervision of German military strength after the IAMCC with a more efficient, less obtrusive system. In disarming Germany, Britain always placed a great deal of emphasis upon the surrender and destruction of German heavy armaments. With the bulk of German armaments destroyed in the first year of operations, British political and military leaders began to sound out ideas of replacing the IAMCC. In fact, Lloyd George's Cabinet first raised the issue in November 1920.[3] Fearing anything short of strict compliance with the military articles of the Treaty of Versailles, the French responded belatedly, and then tried to maintain Allied officers in Germany for as long as possible. The French were loath to change their original position that the IAMCC had to remain in Germany so long as the military clauses remained unfulfilled.[4] Security, measured by the physical presence of Allied troops on German soil, was paramount to French policy.

The first sign of change in Allied disarmament operations in Germany occurred with the reduction of IAMCC personnel. Due to progress in the execution of the military clauses, in December 1920, Bingham and Nollet considered gradually reducing the IAMCC by up to half its strength.[5] Even some French political authorities were impressed by the amount of destruction and reduction, pointing out in the Chamber of Deputies that Germany was experiencing gradual disarmament. Georges Leygues, whose ministry fell within a month, reveled in the gaping disparity between French and German forces, proclaiming that 800,000 French soldiers faced only 150,000 German soldiers.[6] But other French political and military officials were much more pessimistic toward the progress of disarming Germany and pointed to the myriad details of the military aspects of the treaty that had not yet been fulfilled.[7] Pressure from military authorities, including Foch and Nollet, forced Leygues to take a tougher stance on German disarmament.[8]

British authorities first considered Germany essentially disarmed after one year of disarmament operations, and henceforth initiated discussions of a change in the organization and dynamics of future Allied control. In December 1920, the British War Office claimed that Germany no longer had sufficient armaments to conduct war.[9] Particularly assured that the IAMCC had rendered Germany militarily powerless, British military authorities were generally satisfied with German fulfillment of the military clauses and claimed that Germany had "ceased to be a threat to the Allies for a considerable period of time." [10] In addition to the War Office, D'Abernon expressed exultation at the beginning of 1921 over the progress of German disarmament. D'Abernon believed that Germany would be no military threat for at least four to ten years since Germany had surrendered or destroyed its guns, airplanes, and submarines. [11] In a direct reproach of French policy toward Germany, he asserted that France had "military hegemony of the Continent" and that the issue of disarmament should be viewed according to current circumstances, not through the lenses of 1914. [12] Thus, D'Abernon had little difficulty in ignoring the provisions of the Treaty of Versailles.

British and French policies toward German disarmament were dissimilar from the inception of military control but their polarization increased over time. The crux of British policy toward German disarmament was neatly summarized by a War Office Report of January 1921: "Expert military opinion has always regarded the effective disarmament of Germany, and the destruction of all surplus war material, as the main essential in rendering Germany incapable of further aggressive action against the Allies, rather than the reduction of the German standing army." [13] There are two elements here worth noting. First, as previously discussed, the British military authorities considered the destruction of German armaments to be the key to disarming Germany. Second, and more importantly, the War Office made no reference to the fulfillment of the military clauses of the Treaty of Versailles but was satisfied that *Germany could no longer wage an aggressive war*. Thus, when most British officers saw the numbers of destroyed guns piling up, they considered Germany disarmed and the remaining fulfillment of the military clauses of the Treaty of Versailles superfluous. Many prominent British political authorities, including Lloyd George and D'Abernon, adhered to this line of policy.

This British attitude shocked French political and military authorities, most of whom advocated the complete fulfillment of *all* the clauses of the treaty that had been signed with the blood of 1.4 million Frenchmen. On 20 January 1921, newly elected French Premier Aristide Briand elicited cheers from the French Chamber of Deputies by declaring the disarmament of Germany a vital element of French security and pointing out that "the sanction of the Great War, the consecration of victory, is the execution of the treaty." [14] Although they did not consider any aspect of German disarmament inessential, French military authorities focused upon Germany's effectives strength. With the issues of police organization, paramilitary organizations, and implementation of recruiting laws far from completion at the time when Britain regarded Germany as disarmed, France had to be careful to maintain its friendship with Britain as well as the presence of the IAMCC in Germany. Consequently, most French political authorities remained silent about the idea of modifying the present system of military control, neither accepting the possibility nor rejecting it out of hand; they merely pushed for continued control and readied themselves to react when the British would inevitably demand modifications. French military authorities, especially Foch and Nollet, adamantly rejected the idea that Germany had disarmed.[15]

As the IAMCC continued to work in overseeing the execution of the military clauses of the treaty, the conflicting British and French attitudes toward German disarmament increased in intensity in the discussions over future control. Sydney Waterlow of the British Foreign Office raised the idea that Germany ("a bad-tempered, sulky and malignant child") should be awarded "good conduct prizes" for fulfilling the military clauses but believed that Britain was currently "tied to the French chariot wheels."[16] A number of British officials, led by Foreign Secretary Curzon, began to worry about the effects of Nollet's critical reports and feared that such absolute application of the treaty would do irreparable damage to their efforts to convince Germany to accept a new form of control. They demanded that Nollet send any communication with political overtones first to the Conference of Ambassadors and not directly to German officials.[17] Consequently, Bingham received a sharp rebuke from the Foreign Office, which believed that Nollet often got the better of him.[18] The French feared that taking away the initiative from the IAMCC would weaken disarmament efforts at a time when Germany had not yet fulfilled a number of military conditions of the treaty. The Allies resolved the issue on 29 January 1921 when they ruled that all political notes must be referred first to the Conference of Ambassadors.[19]

Although the Allies weakened the authority of the IAMCC with its January decision, they did nothing to muzzle Nollet in reporting detailed violations of the treaty. General Nollet persisted in sending critical reports of German non-fulfillment to Foch throughout the first half of 1921.[20] Immersed in the actual Allied execution of the disarmament clauses in Germany and a witness to the lack of German compliance with all the military clauses, Nollet was able to escape British criticism and muffle discussions of future control. Within a year, however, Nollet would recommend a future control organization stationed in Berlin.[21] If the French had to concede to a smaller control organization, they at least insisted on establishing it in the German capital. Bingham supported a smaller Allied control organization but also warned that severe reductions in IAMCC personnel could result in slackened German efforts in fulfilling the military clauses of the treaty.[22]

In the summer, the British reopened the question of future control with concrete proposals to modify the existing system. Both the War Office and the Foreign Office pushed for changes. The War Office submitted the first proposal for future control in July, after declaring that only a small "liquidating" organization would be sufficient to complete disarmament duties in 1922.[23] British military authorities questioned the authority and ability of the League of Nations to supervise remaining disarmament questions under Article 213 of the Treaty of Versailles and expressed the need for a less conspicuous form of control following the dissolution of the IAMCC. In fact, France wholeheartedly shared this lack of confidence in the ability of the League of Nations to oversee remaining disarmament questions. In July, the War Office recommended a smaller control organization of between twenty and thirty members, residing outside of Germany, to carry out investigations of military questions in Germany only when necessary.[24] Both the War Office and the Foreign Office agreed that Germany would have to accept a modified future control organization before the Allies could invest the League of Nations with supervisory power under Article 213.

As the British pressed again for future control in the summer of 1921, the French re-entered the discussions. The French ambassador in Berlin, Charles Laurent, warned that unless the Allies replaced the IAMCC with a smaller organization upon fulfillment of the May ultimatum, France would be left with nothing in Germany to ascertain its state of disarmament.[25] Thus, French motivation in replacing the IAMCC was to offset the British proposal of a watered-down control system and to prevent the possibility of permanently withdrawing all troops from German soil. Consequently, the Supreme Council met in Paris in August to discuss the reduction and possible replacement of the IAMCC but could not agree on whether a new organization would be stationed in Germany or elsewhere.[26] Nonetheless, the French agreed in principle to modify the current system of Allied disarmament operations in Germany. The one detail that obtained the consensus of Britain, France, Italy, Belgium, and Japan was Allied responsibility for the expenses of any future control organization. The AMCV refused to estimate the amount of time it would take the IAMCC to complete its task but added that it would be necessary to establish a control organization which would last "for some considerable time."[27]

The various offices of political power in London eventually formulated a plan for future military control in Germany in late October. The British government proposed a new control organization of between fifteen and twenty Allied officers, with headquarters in Berlin and larger bodies of officers stationed in Allied nations. The British insisted that investigations be carried out only when requested by Allied nations (represented by the Conference of Ambassadors) and that Germany had to accept any form of future control. The duration of the new system of control was linked to the duration of the occupation of the Cologne bridgehead by Allied troops.[28] Thus, if the treaty's clauses were "faithfully carried out," the new surveillance organization and Allied troops stationed in Cologne would withdraw from Germany. Within a month, the British added one important element to the mix. They hoped to conclude a political trade with Germany and proposed acceptance of an Allied future control organization in return for withdrawal of Allied troops from Düsseldorf, Duisburg, and Ruhrort.[29]

The War Office revised the British plan for future control in the first few months of 1922. It submitted a detailed proposal and named the anticipated control organization the "Mission of Guarantee" so as not to offend Germany with the stigma of "control." The new organization, like the IAMCC, would have a French president but would consist of only twenty officers.[30] Similar to the IAMCC, the purpose of the mission was to guarantee fulfillment of the military clauses of the treaty by giving its members the right to investigate military establishments throughout Germany. Meanwhile, Nollet's stream of negative reports continued unabated, pointing out the need to destroy excess war material, transform factories to permanent commercial facilities, and organize the *Reichswehr* according to the treaty.[31] But the IAMCC no longer had control over its own destiny.

Concerned with the British emphasis upon the necessity of imminently replacing the IAMCC, the French attempted to delay the developments concerning future control. Nollet's critical reports, in particular, had an impact upon French policy regarding the transformation of military control. As a result, the French government pointed out that the IAMCC had not yet finished its task and stressed that the time was not right to discuss a transformation of control when so many military aspects of the treaty lacked German fulfillment. The French would consider replacing the IAMCC only when Germany had satisfied Allied requirements concerning the reorganization of the police, dissolution of the paramilitary associations, transformation of factories, and the surrender of the inventory lists of 1918.[32] The French accepted the idea of replacing the IAMCC but refused to link the idea with the March 1921 military sanctions or the Rhineland occupation until the IAMCC completed its designated tasks. Although the British supported the withdrawal of occupation troops in Düsseldorf, Duisburg, and Ruhrort, the French refused to concede. To the French, military sanctions guaranteed physical security and had successfully elicited increased German fulfillment of its treaty obligations following the Allied ultimatums at Spa in July 1920 and London in May 1921. Although the French did accept the British view that the Mission of Guarantee could not be imposed upon Germany, they insisted that current discussions to replace the IAMCC with a smaller organization were still premature.[33]

The Conference of Ambassadors examined a final revision of the Mission of Guarantee, including one significant addition, on 1 March 1922. The British proposed that the Allied Council of the Mission of Guarantee reach decisions by majority vote and that it must notify the Conference of Ambassadors if it lacked a consensus of all five Allied members.[34] The British also specified that the responsibility of investigations would fall to the Conference of Ambassadors. Problems developed in the Conference of Ambassadors, however, as British and French conceptions of future control still differed. The British wanted to remove military sanctions if Germany accepted the Mission of Guarantee but the French adamantly refused to link the two issues.[35] The British government first rejected the idea of military sanctions when the Wirth government pledged itself to a policy of fulfillment. For Britain, a promise was sufficient reason to relax its attitude toward Germany. Conversely, the French demanded physical proof of fulfillment and believed that military sanctions best guaranteed German treaty compliance. French officials, however, also had to be careful not to threaten the Anglo–French relationship. The French especially feared the ramifications of the lack of British support: the dreaded possibility of dealing with Germany alone. Thus, Raymond Poincaré, the French Premier, urged his ambassadors to work in concert with their British, Italian, Belgian, and Japanese colleagues.[36] Without consensus, the Allies suspended the question of future control and asked the AMCV to examine it.[37]

With the issue of future control in the hands of the AMCV, Marshal Foch used his position and expertise to influence the subsequent discussions. He urged united Anglo–French support of prolonged military control as a guarantee of French security. Foch accepted the establishment of the Committee of Guarantee but rejected linking the duration of the proposed control system with the issue of the Rhineland. He instead pushed for a minimum five-year duration to allow for an accurate assessment of German military strength.[38] The AMCV subsequently drafted a proposal and presented it to the Conference of Ambassadors on 10 March.[39] Under the AMCV plan, the Committee of Guarantee would consist of a body of twenty Allied officers and thirty men, stationed in Berlin under a French presidency, and with the right to investigate military establishments anywhere in Germany. The committee's function would be to inform the Allied governments of the level of compliance with the military clauses, and the Conference of Ambassadors would have authority over decisions that lacked unanimity. The AMCV, influenced by Foch, now proposed an eight-year duration for the Committee of Guarantee before withdrawing it based upon treaty compliance. The British flatly rejected this plan.[40] Consequently, in another concession to the British, the French finally agreed to accept linking the duration of the Mission of Guarantee with the occupation of the Cologne bridgehead.[41] Despite the French concession, the end of military control would still be dependent upon the fulfillment of the military clauses of the treaty.

While Britain and France argued over the development of a common policy for the replacement of the IAMCC, they were also unsure of a requisite step in the implementation of their final proposal: the agreement of the German government. Sthamer, the German ambassador in London, put an end to any Allied pretenses in a letter to Curzon in April 1922.[42] Sthamer claimed that Germany had disarmed and that the Allied supervision of any remaining issues was unnecessary. Furthermore, he emphasized that any supervisory body in Germany (i.e., future control) was an infringement of the Treaty of Versailles. Thus, Sthamer attempted to use the shackles of Versailles to free Germany from eternal military control, but the French were well aware of the lack of any treaty regulations regarding the establishment of a future Allied military control body in Germany. Nollet thought that France should simply impose a surveillance organization upon Germany. Furthermore, the Foreign Ministry clearly stated French policy regarding German rejection of future control when it asserted that if Germany did not accept the Allied proposal, the Allies "will maintain the Commission of Control indefinitely."[43]

On 14 April the Conference of Ambassadors sent a proposal to Germany outlining the replacement of the Inter-Allied Aeronautical Control Commission (IAACC), which had essentially completed its task of disarming the German air force. As an integral part of its note, the Conference also proposed the replacement of the IAMCC with a small supervisory organization.[44] The anticipated Military Committee of Guarantee would consist of twenty Allied officers stationed in Berlin, with the responsibility of ensuring the fulfillment of the military clauses until the evacuation of the Cologne zone of the Rhineland occupation. Whereas the German government agreed to the replacement of the IAACC with a smaller organization, it did not respond to replacing the IAMCC. Consequently, a member of the British Foreign Office pointed out that the Allies could "not afford to leave Germany at liberty to re-arm as soon as the Commission of Control has finished its work of effective disarmament."[45] Along with the French, the British feared the disappearance of all future Allied supervision of the German military.

With Germany apparently rejecting the Mission of Guarantee and with the future course of military control and the withdrawal of the IAMCC in suspense, British policy toward the disarmament of Germany experienced a major change. In response to Nollet's report of 17 May which outlined numerous details of German non-compliance, the War Office enumerated the remaining disarmament issues according to priority. It considered the reorganization of the German police, the transformation of factories, surrender of remaining excess war material, and the surrender of the war material production lists of 1918 to be essential issues. The War Office based its support of withdrawing the IAMCC and replacing it with the Mission of Guarantee exclusively upon the fulfillment of these points. However, Germany had not yet fulfilled a number of other disarmament issues. The War Office believed that the passage of legal texts to prevent the import and export of war material, control of recruiting, and the dissolution of excess administration staff in the *Reichswehr* staff were only secondary issues. In addition, it now relegated the issues of excess staff members and NCOs in the *Reichswehr*, and the passage of legal measures to prevent mobilization to inconsequential points.[46] The Foreign Office agreed that Britain should focus only upon the remaining essential points of disarmament and that all other points would be supervised by the smaller Mission of Guarantee. The French, however, considered all of these issues to be crucial to their security policy of enforcing the Treaty of Versailles and disarming Germany.

Similar to Germany using the treaty as a defense to protect its interests, British military and political officials began to interpret and enforce the military articles of the Treaty of Versailles selectively. Britain clearly now had little intention of supporting any strict enforcement of the treaty. In fact, the War Office had become an active advocate of appeasement in 1921. While admitting to Germany's ability to expand its military strength for war, the War Office stated that "the German government will not be in a position to use this weapon unless Allied policy makes the whole population willing to accept the risks of a new war as an alternative to despair."[47] Henceforth, the War Office would work to mollify German anger through the modification of Versailles. D'Abernon and Bingham supported a more lenient policy toward Germany while Bingham's adjutant, Lieutenant-Colonel Roddie, went so far as to say that Germany would "inevitably turn to war for relief" from the restrictions of the Treaty of Versailles.[48]

The Foreign Office concurred with the abandonment of a strict enforcement of the treaty. Wigram succinctly pointed out the future course in British policy toward disarming Germany: "The object was to disarm Germany, and not – however desirable it might be and as the French seem to think – to see that Germany remained disarmed."[49] Yet this interpretation, which British policy now embraced, was fundamentally flawed. It was true that the IAMCC did not have the task of keeping Germany disarmed after the limits of the treaty had been attained but it was certainly Britain's obligation under the Treaty of Versailles to see that Germany did not violate the treaty's clauses. Although Wigram also pointed out that the task of keeping Germany disarmed was the responsibility of the League of Nations, his Foreign Office colleagues initiated discussions concerning future control due to their lack of confidence in the League's desire to oversee German fulfillment of the military clauses.

Britain's lack of support for true enforcement of the treaty clashed directly with the French assertion that security demanded the disarmament of Germany down to the treaty's last details. The French were particularly insistent on the absolute necessity of demanding the reorganization of the *Reichswehr* along the lines of the treaty.[50] Nollet still wholeheartedly supported disarmament operations and believed them necessary to execute the military aspects of the treaty. For the rest of his tenure as President of the IAMCC, Nollet remained a passionate advocate of enforcing the military clauses of the treaty in their entirety and fought to maintain his authority in the upcoming decisions regarding Allied policies toward German disarmament. Yet he was also cognizant of the impending changes to military control and knew that it would not last forever. The French General therefore comforted himself with the notion that "the results achieved by control, even if they do not really ensure the disarmament of Germany, are nevertheless considerable," since "the train of military tradition will find itself broken" in Germany as the result of even temporary disarmament.[51]

The French successfully demanded the addition to the British list of essential points of an issue they considered essential to the disarmament of Germany: the passage of legislative and administrative measures concerning the recruitment and organization of the *Reichswehr*. The British government agreed to the addition but only under the condition that it would not result in the prolongation of the duration of the IAMCC.[52] The Allies now considered five points essential to the fulfillment of the military clauses of the Treaty of Versailles: the transformation of factories, surrender of excess war material, passage of laws prohibiting the import and export of war material and enforcing the treaty's stipulations regarding the organization and recruitment of the army, the surrender of the inventory lists of 1918, and the reorganization of the German police. Despite the enumeration of the five points, the British government continued to pay lip-service to strict adherence to the Treaty of Versailles. The British line of policy supported fulfillment of the remaining military clauses, yet also proposed withdrawing the IAMCC after fulfillment of the five essential points. The Mission of Guarantee would theoretically oversee the fulfillment of all the remaining issues. In August, the War Office drafted a memo that became the basis of future Allied disarmament operations in Germany. Reiterating its priorities of the June memo, the War Office claimed that the five points would have to be carried out by Germany in order to witness the replacement of the IAMCC. The War Office unsuccessfully pressed the French to drop their insistence upon other points, including the prevention of the possession of war material by civilians, the dismissal of excess staffs and NCOs in the *Reichswehr*, and the prohibition of mobilization measures. The British had hoped to use the abandonment of these points as a bartering chip for German acceptance of the Mission of Guarantee.[53]

On 29 September 1922 the Allied governments sent a joint note to the German government offering a disarmament *quid pro quo*.[54] The Allies agreed to withdraw the IAMCC and replace it with a smaller, less obtrusive organization if the German government fulfilled the five points. Thus, through their acceptance of the five points, the French conceded to British insistence on treaty modification but maintained their tacit alliance with Britain. By acting in concert with Britain, the French avoided the possibility of having to face the German military alone, but relinquished their insistence on strict enforcement of the treaty under the IAMCC. They still hoped that the proposed Mission of Guarantee would oversee the remaining execution of all the military aspects of the treaty despite the fact that British support of enforcement was clearly fading. However, the German chancellor, Dr. Joseph Wirth, did not reply to the Allied note until the end of October. More importantly, he only indicated Germany's willingness to open negotiations over Article 213 without any reference to the

Committee of Guarantee.[55] The Germans feared and rejected the establishment of any form of permanent Allied military control, and the Allies had no intention of negotiating what they already considered to be a significant modification of the treaty. [56] Consequently, Poincaré, as head of the Conference of Ambassadors, considered the tardiness of the German reply and lack of communication regarding the Commission of Guarantee as evidence that Germany had little intention of fulfilling its remaining military obligations.[57]

By December, the issue of future control had become bogged down in a political quagmire. The majority of British officials considered Germany to be disarmed, and the French were willing to support a new form of control if Germany fulfilled the Five Points. The Allies wanted some sort of guarantee of continued compliance with the standards set by the Treaty of Versailles and to make military control less odious to Germany. But recent German attacks against IAMCC officers, which will be examined in Chapter 9, enraged the Allied political and military leadership responsible for the disarmament of Germany. The British and French had finally come to an agreement regarding future military control but now their energy was refocused upon the confrontational behavior of Germany. As a result, the IAMCC demanded action and the British and French governments suspended all talks of future control until Germany provided compensation. On that note, the third year of disarmament operations, as well as discussions of the withdrawal of the IAMCC, came to a disheartening end.

The issue of transforming the present system of Allied control in Germany vanished quickly but would return in the near future. Nonetheless, even without implementation of a new control organization in 1922, the issue transformed British and French policies toward disarmament. Embracing the idea of lessening the Allied grip upon the German military as early as 1921 by agreeing to modifications of the Treaty of Versailles, the British initiated a confrontation between British and French conceptions of post-war security. Hoping to put an end to confrontational diplomacy with Germany, Britain instead exacerbated differences in foreign policy with its *de facto* partner, France. British acceptance of modifying the Allied policy of the Paris Peace Conference threatened the French belief that their national existence was predicated upon the peacemakers of 1919. Demanding alterations to the IAMCC questioned the enforcement of the Treaty of Versailles at a time when French political and military authorities embraced nothing less than the strict application of the treaty. The failure to agree to an Anglo–French Pact at the end of 1921 further illustrated general differences in Anglo–French conceptions of post-war foreign policy.[58] The French fear of independent diplomacy in Europe, however, led them to yield reluctantly to British insistence on treaty modification. An increase in German aggression toward Allied inspections in the latter half of 1922 subsequently helped unite, at least temporarily, British and French disarmament efforts.

9 Violations, obstruction, and abuse

Throughout the period of Allied disarmament operations in Germany, the Conference of Ambassadors, the Allied Military Committee of Versailles, and the Inter-Allied Military Control Commission faced a German strategy that embodied obstruction of Allied disarmament efforts and delay in the fulfillment of the military clauses.[1] Violations of the military articles of the Treaty of Versailles presented a constant challenge to disarmament efforts. Allied officers stationed in Germany experienced spontaneous and premeditated outbreaks of nationalist violence and frustrated abuse. The attitude of various German military and administrative officials and the treatment afforded a number of members of the IAMCC by various German soldiers and civilians were a constant reminder of the relationship between the victors and vanquished. The war had placed severe strains on all the belligerents, and its destructiveness shaped those who had witnessed the terrible events. The attitude expressed by Foch on the eve of military control, namely that the war was not over, was not unique.[2] Nollet, Morgan, Cramon, and Seeckt all conveyed similar sentiments. The mutual distrust, of course, set the stage for a continuation of conflict.[3]

Prior to the work of the IAMCC, Nollet was fully cognizant of the fact that the IAMCC would have to function in an "atmosphere of tension, hostility, and hatred."[4] German nationalists referred to the members of the Control Commissions as the "hyenas of the battlefield."[5] Conversely, the French believed that the task of General von Cramon, as head of the German Army Peace Commission, was simply to discredit the IAMCC.[6] The Allies knew they would face opposition to their disarmament efforts and considered violations of the treaty, obstruction of its enforcement, and the abuse of Allied officers serious offenses.

Without a formal policy regarding violations, the Allies meted out punishments on an *ad hoc* basis. While they usually reacted to the physical or verbal abuse of IAMCC officers with swift action, often in the form of public apologies and substantial fines, delays in fulfillment and obstruction of enforcement led merely to written demands. Thus, deadlines lost meaning. Pointing out the logic that fulfillment of the military clauses would result in the withdrawal of Allied disarmament forces from

Germany seemed to have little effect upon German compliance with the treaty. Occupation ultimatums were certainly effective but only in the case when they represented truly Allied policy. Threats of occupation, when only supported by French authorities, increased German obstruction and threatened Anglo–French relations. For instance, when the German government ordered 18,000 troops into the Rhineland to quell possible communist unrest in March 1920, a violation of the demilitarized zone established by the Versailles Treaty, the French occupied a number of Rhenish cities until German troops withdrew.[7] This independent French action damaged the fragile Anglo–French entente and gave credence to the belief that France intended to destroy Germany. The Ruhr occupation in 1923 was another such case. Yet when Britain and France collectively used the threat of occupation as a weapon in forcing Germany's hand, the results were startling.

German opposition to Allied disarmament operations from government officials, military personnel, and civilians varied in intensity. Whereas German administrative and military officials deliberately planned systematic violations of the effectives clauses of the treaty, the physical abuse of Allied officers was often the result of spontaneous outbursts of civilian anger. Nonetheless, important conclusions may be drawn. German delays in meeting Allied demands affected all aspects of disarmament and military control. The Allies faced the most extensive violations regarding the treaty's effectives clauses, where General von Seeckt attempted to maintain the framework of the Imperial army until the IAMCC withdrew from Germany. Violations of the armaments clauses, such as illegal Krupp production and hidden weapons caches, were less significant. The nature of dismantling German fortifications along with the presence of an Allied occupation army in the Rhineland prevented widespread obstruction and abuse of the Fortifications Sub-commission.

Violations

In an attempt to minimize the effects of the Treaty of Versailles upon the German army, German government and military officials embarked upon a path that maintained Allied–German conflict throughout the new decade. Furthermore, Allied reactive policies often had little effect, and at times exacerbated international tensions. But delays in meeting Allied disarmament deadlines, obstruction to the tasks of Allied control officers, violations of the restrictions of the Treaty of Versailles, and attacks upon Allied officers comprised a complex mosaic of German intentions toward disarmament. Throughout the duration of Allied disarmament operations, this German strategy had a direct impact upon Allied policy-making. The end result was a disarmament process that lasted well beyond the initial expectations of all those concerned.

Delay in the fulfillment of the treaty's military clauses plagued

Allied–German relations, frustrated Allied officials responsible for disarming Germany, and prolonged the existence of the IAMCC. German military authorities and government officials hoped to delay fulfillment of the military clauses of the treaty until the IAMCC withdrew from Germany. Furthermore, the German government looked at the reduction of the IAMCC as a precursor to withdrawal. The German strategy was to ignore deadlines and offer political excuses to offset Allied anger and negate any possible reprisals. German political authorities used Bolshevism, instability, economic duress, and inequality as justifications for refusal to meet deadlines. At times, especially in the early days of disarmament, these excuses contained a semblance of validity but they soon became cynical and cliché catchwords for a policy of non-compliance. Germany simply ignored deadlines because it did not want to disarm to the levels of the Treaty of Versailles.

In order to delay fulfillment and to drive a wedge between the different levels of Allied treaty enforcement, the German government also appealed repeatedly to the IAMCC, the Conference of Ambassadors, and the Allied governments themselves for rulings and modifications of IAMCC demands. The Germans even appealed for changes, sometimes numerous times, to questions that had already been settled in the hope of modifying the stringent military limitations of the Treaty of Versailles.[8] General Nollet also complained frequently about the flood of German letters he received, most of which criticized Allied disarmament stipulations. In order to stem the tide and divisive nature of German complaints, the Allied governments eventually decided to refer them to the IAMCC.[9] Some German military establishments tried more direct methods and simply refused to hand over certain documents to Allied officers or left the IAMCC standing for hours at the entrances to various German barracks and factories.[10]

The Allies were also partly responsible for fostering a contentious German attitude to disarmament. The disappointment of the Germans in obtaining modifications at the Spa Conference and the constant threat of a Ruhr occupation by French troops heightened tensions between the former combatants.[11] In addition, the occupation of Frankfurt and Darmstadt by a Franco-Belgian force in April 1920 in opposition to the presence of German troops in the Ruhr, and the Allied occupation of Düsseldorf, Duisburg, and Ruhrort in March 1921 helped inflame German public opinion. Complaints of non-fulfillment, especially French demands for treaty compliance, also worked against the progress of disarmament. At the end of 1920, the German government believed that the IAMCC was using German non-fulfillment of various details of the treaty's military clauses as a pretext to occupy the Ruhr.[12] Yet from the British and French perspective, the threat of occupation was an attempt to force the Germans into compliance, and the Allies believed the Germans were simply trying to place the blame of a possible international crisis on to them.

Throughout the first year of enforcement, German resistance to Allied operations yielded results below Allied expectations.[13] The French complained that the IAMCC faced obstruction from German officials on all levels, and that continual local opposition to control was slowing down Allied disarmament efforts.[14] In some cases the Germans established organized surveillance systems, where agents searched Allied hotel rooms and examined official letters and telegrams.[15] Despite reports of obstruction to disarmament and the increase in the number of violent incidents between Germans and IAMCC officers in the fall of 1920, German Foreign Minister Walter Simons denied responsibility for everything: illegal weapons caches and export of war material, failure to meet deadlines, and abuse of IAMCC officials were simply the result of current conditions in Germany.[16] The German government placed the onus of guilt upon the Allies for unemployment, food shortages, and destruction of machinery, and the sight of Allied uniforms, reparations, and inspections merely increased the residual tension of warfare and defeat.

In a common tactic of delay, the German authorities often refused permission for IAMCC officers to enter a German military establishment, claiming that no liaison officer was available to allow an inspection. Allied policy concerning the presence of German liaison officers for inspections was clear: the Allies had the right to inspect and visit any establishment in Germany without the presence of any German officer, and nothing in the Treaty of Versailles gave the Germans a right to the presence of liaison officers. In reality, the Allies chose to inspect most barracks and factories with a German officer to avoid problems but they needed the right of surprise inspections to uphold their authority and to verify treaty compliance. However, the Germans had a different view of the validity of Allied inspection policy. In East Prussia, where official communications referred to the Allies as the *Feinbund* (enemy league), German military authorities ordered the replacement of any German liaison officer who fraternized with the Allies.[17] In July, the German government demanded notification of all IAMCC visits and claimed that no Allied questions would be answered without a German liaison officer present.[18] The IAMCC also discovered orders from the German organization responsible for the destruction of excess war material, the *Reichstreuhandgesellschaft*, which declared: "in no case can Entente officers be allowed to enter the premises unaccompanied by German liaison officers."[19] The IAMCC, of course, rejected these orders and upheld the right of inspection and visitation regardless of the presence of a German liaison officer. Yet, as tensions increased toward 1923, inspections without German liaison officers present were the exception, not the rule, and had less than successful results. The Allies and Germany never attained a satisfactory settlement of the issue of surprise visits.

Armaments

In the first year of disarmament, the IAMCC discovered a substantial number of war material caches.[20] The quantity and quality of this war material varied from case to case but the overall impact of these discoveries should not be underestimated. Illegal hordes of war material provided physical proof of German non-compliance with the Treaty of Versailles and inflamed many Allied officers intent on enforcing the military clauses of the treaty. Yet Allied interpretations of the discoveries varied widely. Officers like Bingham and his replacement, General Arthur Wauchope, tended to discount any serious implications of violations of the armaments clauses while officers like Nollet, Foch, and Morgan saw the discoveries as proof of a sinister plot for future aggression.

Both Allied perspicacity and German informers helped uncover illegal stashes of war material. The first reports of inspectors' discoveries of illegal German war material stores trickled into IAMCC headquarters during the spring but quickly turned into a deluge by the summer and fall. Archival sources abound with such cases so a few examples will have to suffice. In one of the earliest of many such discoveries, Allied inspectors unearthed a large cache of war material in Swinemünde in May 1920.[21] In September, IAMCC inspection teams discovered twelve medium howitzers, 1,250 rifles and bayonets, and 5,000 grenades in Hanover and 1,300 gun breeches and spare parts in Berlin.[22] The IAMCC subsequently destroyed a store of 65,000 rifles in Magdeburg.[23] Lieutenant-Colonel Roddie, Bingham's adjutant, reported that the various political groups in Germany often divulged the location of war material caches of their political opponents.[24] However, informers also paid a price for collaboration, as the German courts convicted them for divulging information of concealed armaments to the IAMCC.[25]

The issue of illegal war material caches illustrated a general difference between British and French views of disarmament. The British tended to look at the disarmament of Germany in a comparative sense. Relative to Germany's previous military dominance and to other nations, defeat and disarmament had reduced the German military to a fraction of its former strength by fall 1920. Bingham, who believed that he had all but disarmed Germany when the Armaments Sub-commission destroyed most of Germany's heavy artillery, viewed the discoveries of war material as inevitable, but minor, indiscretions. Thus, when inspectors uncovered a clandestine store of weapons in a Königsberg barracks in August, Bingham failed to notify Nollet. On the other hand, the French saw all violations of the military clauses, regardless of scope or type of infraction, as an affront to their security. No violation could be dismissed or overlooked. As a result, Bingham's lack of disclosure enraged the French General, who subsequently demanded that Bingham inform him of all violations within a twenty-four-hour period.[26]

Despite Allied prohibition of the production and manufacture of war material in Germany, unless authorized by the IAMCC, some German factories made relatively insignificant attempts at illicit production in the first half of the 1920s. For example, one German firm, Rhein-Metall, was able to produce artillery under the guise of railway development.[27] Yet there was nothing in the Treaty of Versailles that forbade the production of war material *outside* of Germany. German manufactures realized this loophole and made strides to continue armaments production abroad. Many tried to establish connections to neutral nations, and German munitions manufacturers transported their plants and established branches in the Netherlands, Switzerland, and Sweden.[28] The AMCV proclaimed this German strategy illegal, under the rationale that Germany was exporting war material (or machinery used in its production).

Krupp was able to establish business relations and subsidiary branches abroad in an attempt to circumvent Allied disarmament restrictions. When the war came to a close, Krupp opened regional offices in the Netherlands in order to maintain production.[29] As early as March 1920, Allied intelligence uncovered illegal operations of the giant German armaments firm in the Netherlands. Bofors, the Swedish armaments firm, was a beneficiary of German treaty circumvention and increased in size due to "equipment, personnel, and capital furnished by the Krupp plant."[30] In 1921, Krupp actually gained control of Bofors and sent German engineers and directors to Sweden. In addition, a small number of German troops soon arrived in Sweden to test the variety of weapons produced. Krupp also gained control of Blessing Iron Ore, sold artillery pieces to the Dutch firm, and then renamed it Siderius A.G. As an official Dutch firm, the Allies could do nothing to stop its production of war material. By 1925, when the end of Allied disarmament operations was in sight, a German firm drafted plans for tanks and artillery.[31] After the withdrawal of the IAMCC in January 1927, Krupp increased illegal production of artillery and armor plate.

Years later, when Gustav Krupp was a prime armaments producer for the Nazi regime, he claimed that he had duped the IAMCC throughout the 1920s and prepared the German military for the future.[32] He was partly right. The IAMCC saw to the destruction of most of Krupp's heavy artillery but his inter-war activities certainly helped contribute to the massive rearmament programs implemented later by Hitler. Once again, the ability of the Allies to discover German military violations was exemplary; the failure in the 1930s lay mostly in the Allied inability to enforce disarmament policies in a completely different political climate.

Effectives

The IAMCC had particular difficulty in ascertaining infractions of the effectives clauses of the treaty. The scope of these German violations was both substantial and diverse, but the core German strategy had a singular goal: to maintain the kernel of the German army as a professional and experienced cadre for future development. German military officials were quick to attempt to avoid some of Versailles' more detailed provisions that affected the German army, such as enlistment periods, size, distribution, and composition.

One of the first examples of the violation of Versailles was the lack of German respect for the twelve-year enlistment period of the German army. The IAMCC discovered numerous instances of short-term enlistments throughout the period of 1920 to 1922. Lloyd George was keenly aware of the danger of short-term enlisted soldiers that augmented the overall number of trained men in Germany. The Allies were more concerned with the fact that the *Reichswehr* was larger than Versailles' restrictions and they focused initially on reducing the German army to 100,000 troops. But excess army personnel continued to exasperate Allied officials up through 1922. Nonetheless, by the end of the first year of operations, the German army contained twice the normal limit of NCOs, a surplus of administration officials, and an overabundance of superior officers.[33]

Brigadier-General J.H. Morgan was responsible more than any other Allied officer in the entire era of military control for uncovering German attempts to circumvent the clauses of the Versailles Treaty. As the British chief of the Effectives Sub-commission with formal legal training and expertise, Morgan perceived German treaty violations as a personal affront and worked unflinchingly to discover even the smallest of discrepancies with the military clauses. A zealot of strict enforcement, Morgan often sided with the French in his views about the disarmament of Germany. In fact, like a true Frenchman, Morgan believed European peace was dependent upon the occupation of the Rhine and its bridgeheads.[34] Conversely, Bingham believed that the German government and people truly supported the fulfillment of military clauses and blamed only the military party for the "internal chaos" that prevented complete compliance.[35] This conflict in the viewpoint of the British leadership of the IAMCC helped lead to the resignation of Morgan in December 1923 and the replacement of Bingham in May 1924. Upon leaving the IAMCC, Morgan turned down the French request to withdraw his resignation but continued "to act in an advisory capacity to the President of the Commission down to its withdrawal in January, 1927." Morgan thereby fulfilled an earlier personal pledge he had given to Nollet and Foch.[36] Furthermore, Morgan sent reports to the British War Office for two years in a "purely honorary capacity." Like the IAMCC in Germany, Morgan would not just simply disappear.

Morgan's greatest contribution was to point out that Germany, under General Hans von Seeckt, was attempting to reconstitute the Imperial army. He was convinced that Germany was preparing for a future war by maintaining conscription, short-term service, and excess staff, officers, and regiments. What Morgan found was startling. Pointing to the fact that

Germany had reduced the twenty-four army corps districts of the pre-war German army to twenty after the surrender of Alsace-Lorraine, Morgan soon discovered that the transitional German army of 200,000 (the same number of that which Germany demanded in 1920) contained brigade staffs and headquarters for twenty divisions. The German army set up brigades as small model divisions, including infantry, artillery, and cavalry, which could be easily expanded in the future.[37] Thus, the *Reichswehr* of 1920 maintained the basic organization of the massive wartime German army. General von Seeckt also retained the best officers of the Imperial army, thereby establishing the cadres of a future army that French political and military leaders especially feared.[38] The General had even made plans to confer upon the new German army the same numbers, badges, and depots as the old to prepare for its restoration.[39] By 1923, the *Reichswehr* had plans to mobilize a force of 200,000 to 300,000 troops.[40] Morgan also believed that Germany was trying to expand the size of its army through short-term enlistment of troops, and numerous Allied intelligence reports verify his suspicions. Although Morgan knew that the reduction or withdrawal of the IAMCC was inevitable, he remained an advocate of any form of Allied control. He was not, however, part of mainstream British policy.

General von Seeckt, regarded as one of the most powerful men in Germany, planned to keep the core of the army intact through subterfuge and deception.[41] Morgan and other IAMCC officers found a number of violations that indicated such a grand design, and IAMCC inspections verified their fears. In order to escape the eyes of IAMCC inspectors, the German army supplemented administrative staff with civilians or soldiers dressed as civilians and transferred army administration services to civil departments. When the IAMCC realized that the *Reichswehr* had set up liquidation offices (*Abwickelungsamter*) to demobilize the army, Allied inspectors discovered that hundreds of former German staff officers and NCOs made up the personnel of these offices.[42] Thus, a large cadre of officers for a future army remained intact. Numbers of units, which could be expanded in the future, were also greater than the treaty allowed.[43] Finally, the Germans had reconstituted the Great General Staff within the Ministry of the *Reichswehr* simply by renaming it the *Truppenamt* (Troops Office).[44] By maintaining a large cadre of officers for a future army, Germany hoped to be able to call up a substantial force of troops when needed.

Official IAMCC demands for strict German compliance with the military clauses often had little effect upon German authorities as delays continued to plague the efforts of Allied disarmament officers. In some instances, Allied demands increased German intransigence. At the start of 1921, soon after the IAMCC demanded the surrender of surplus arms, reorganization of the police, and the disarmament of German fortifications, Friedrich

Sthamer, the German ambassador in London, complained that these Allied demands signaled "a new spirit of distrust and antagonism" that threatened Germany's political stability.[45] But the continued lack of progress in many areas hardened the IAMCC's attitude toward Germany as operations entered their second year. Even General Bingham claimed that the German government was sponsoring a deliberate policy of obstruction.[46] Some blamed Severing, the Prussian Minister of the Interior, for the "stiffening" German attitude toward Allied disarmament.[47] The situation worsened when Nollet reported discoveries of over fourteen tons of artillery parts and twenty-three tanks in the area of Berlin (the Germans declared them tractors), and thirty tons of machine-gun parts and accessories in Buhl.[48] The Allies also revealed that the *Reichstreuhandgesellschaft*, the German organization responsible for the destruction of excess war material, was hiding surrendered armaments and returning it to the German army.[49]

Increased German obstruction continued through the winter of 1921. Military authorities, especially, remained averse to furnishing details regarding IAMCC questions, and German intransigence to disarmament increased.[50] In fact, the IAMCC soon found concrete evidence of a deliberate German policy of obstruction. In mid-March, Allied officers discovered a *Reichswehr* Ministry document declaring that the IAMCC was an intelligence and espionage agency that had transgressed its legal powers. The memorandum directed German liaison officers to act with reserve toward the IAMCC.[51] Refusal to divulge military information increased Allied suspicions of German rearmament and directly violated Article 206 of the Treaty of Versailles.

Spring marked a new beginning as signs of life appeared in Allied–German relations. After Germany accepted the Allied May ultimatum, the Allies witnessed improvements in the fulfillment of disarmament demands. When the Allies forged a common policy and backed it by force, or its implicit threat, they were able to induce effective disarmament results from Germany. British IAMCC officers remarked that relations with German liaison officers changed perceptibly after the Wirth government accepted the ultimatum.[52] British intelligence concurred and reported that control was proceeding more smoothly.[53] French officials also reported improvement in German fulfillment of the military clauses.[54] Within two months, the French ambassador in Berlin believed that disarmament was nearly complete, and even General Nollet reported that the IAMCC could begin to reduce its personnel at the end of the year.[55] Progress in German fulfillment of the military clauses occurred in most areas of disarmament but two notable exceptions were the reorganization of the *Reichswehr* and the continued existence of paramilitary organizations.[56] Nonetheless, the Allies had accepted the surrender of the bulk of German armaments, reduced the German army to 100,000 men, and practically completed the destruction of German fortifications.

A storm broke in September when two articles appeared in *The Times* outlining German violations of the military clauses of the treaty. The articles, based on Morgan's revelations, pointed out that Germany had personnel, clothing, and armaments for 800,000 men and was transferring army staff to civilian positions. They also warned of the danger of the military nature of the *Sicherheitspolizei* and claimed that Germany was attempting to establish an army based on the historic Krümper system. The British Foreign Office immediately accused Morgan of writing the two articles, and Wigram described Morgan as an extremist bent on keeping the IAMCC in Germany for as long as possible.[57] Bingham refuted the articles' contention that there existed "two schools of thought" in the IAMCC and shrugged them off as "ridiculous."[58] But the tension between the Morgan and Bingham camps in British policy would continue to simmer until Morgan's resignation at the end of 1923.[59]

Allied officers continued to discover hidden war material caches in the second and third year of operations. At times, IAMCC inspectors displayed great ingenuity in locating some of the illegal caches. In August, at the Rockstroh–Werke plant in Dresden, officers smashed a hole in a wall and discovered parts for hundreds of heavy artillery guns. In November, inspectors peered under the floor of a military barracks in Potsdam and unearthed dozens of cases of machine-gun and pistol ammunition. In Frankfurt, they stopped trucks stocked full of arms and munitions, along with one million rounds of small arms ammunition. German workers also took part in the disarmament drama, often depending upon the political interests of the individual. Some workers supplied the IAMCC with information concerning hidden weapons while others helped in a factory's obstruction efforts. French authorities reported widespread violations of the treaty's war material stipulations throughout 1921, and the year came to a close with Morgan's sobering report of Germany's effectives violations.[60] Although obstruction to Allied disarmament plans continued throughout 1922, reports of hidden war material began to decrease in severity. Nollet claimed rightly that the Germans were still obstructing the progress of disarmament but his objections began to focus on surplus war material such as gas masks, signaling equipment, field kitchens, small arms, and tools.[61]

The reaction of the German government to continued disarmament operations, with no apparent end, was bitter. In April 1922, Sthamer blasted the IAMCC and claimed that the disarmament of Germany was essentially complete. As evidence of fulfillment, he pointed to the amount of destroyed war material and to the fact that the discoveries of hidden war material had diminished. The continued complaints of the IAMCC of even the smallest of details of the treaty exasperated the German leader. Sthamer's impatience with the continuance of Allied operations was concomitant with the increasing impatience of the IAMCC to witness the end of disarmament. He declared that the activities of the IAMCC were "consumed in making unimportant criticisms, in verifying reports of alleged concealed arms dumps, in an ever-recurring investigation of establishments, the unimportance of which was long since established."[62] Despite the vast amount of progress in disarmament, the arguments, violations, and obstruction continued, and the IAMCC remained in Germany. Rather than significantly augmenting military strength, the real effect of German violations was to strengthen Allied resolve and to prolong disarmament operations.

Abuse

Working in small teams, Allied inspectors examined German military facilities throughout the nation, leaving no stone unturned in rooting out violations of the military clauses of the Versailles Treaty. The officers and men of the IAMCC, surrounded by angry civilians and embittered military and political authorities, operated in an atmosphere bristling with danger. Working hundreds of miles from friendly bases, Allied inspectors carried the responsibility of destroying the military dominance of a nation that had only experienced war in the hinterland of east Prussia. Resentment ran high and international tensions never abated. Overall, the task at hand was immense, matched only by the determination of the Allied inspectors. A relatively small Allied force, surrounded by a hostile populace, had the responsibility of disarming the great German army. The experience of Allied inspectors in Germany is testament to their bravery and diligence. Years after the IAMCC withdrew from Germany, French General Weygand (later to be humiliated by the German army in 1940) remarked to a member of the Commission: "We never expected any of you to come back alive."[63]

The experience of Allied inspectors varied widely as the Germans generally afforded a different standard of treatment to the diverse nationalities of IAMCC officers. Inspection teams, surrounded by a hostile populace and embittered military and political authorities, faced the constant threat of danger. In the worst cases of violence, the French suffered more than their British, Belgian, Italian, and Japanese allies. The British soldier, dressed in his khaki uniform, generally received respect but the blue coat of the *poilu* was often a magnet for derision, abuse, and assault. For instance, during an inspection in Hameln in September 1920, German workers walked out of their factory due to the presence of a French officer. When the inspection team left the premises, the British member dissuaded the workers from damaging his car by telling them that it was a British model![64] General Nollet himself received a number of menacing letters.[65] German xenophobia, partly a nationalist reaction to foreign troops on German soil and to the Treaty of Versailles, was fueled by France's aggressive actions toward Upper Silesia, the Saar, and the Rhineland. The French became a scapegoat for Germany's diplomatic and domestic failings.

Nonetheless, all Allied inspection officers faced danger from violent assaults, with some experiencing particularly harrowing escapes from vindictive mobs. As a result, the German abuse of the IAMCC was one area of disarmament that solidified the fragile Anglo–French relationship. Britain and France, as the leading members of an allied effort to disarm Germany, considered an assault on any nationality of the IAMCC to be an assault on all Allied members.

Within weeks of the start of disarmament operations in Germany, IAMCC officers suffered physical abuse. One of the first violent episodes occurred when a German policeman, apparently losing a war of words with a French officer, proceeded to cut off the little finger of the Frenchman with his saber.[66] Surprisingly, apologies provided a sufficient settlement of the matter. The first large-scale incidents of abuse, however, took place in March 1920 when the political violence sparked by the Kapp *putsch* in Berlin created ripple effects throughout Germany. During a routine inspection of a barracks in the Prussian city of Prenzlau, German soldiers, still stung by their bitter defeat in the fall of 1918, hurled bricks, stones, and glass at an IAMCC inspection team made up of two British, one Italian, and one Belgian officer. The German commanding officer was able to bring the assaults to an end but not before the Belgian officer had been struck by a brick. Other incidents in March exclusively targeted the French: German civilians hauled a French soldier out of his truck at gunpoint and arrested him, knocked down a French officer in Bremen with the help of German soldiers, and actually killed a French officer of the Inter-Allied Aeronautical Commission who was hunting with fellow Allied officers.[67] A notorious incident occurred in the Hotel Adlon itself (IAMCC headquarters), where Prince Joachim of Prussia led a group of Germans in assaulting two French officers for refusing to stand during a spontaneous outburst of "*Deutschland über Alles.*"[68]

Despite expectations of a hostile reception, the Allies had no specific policy with regard to obstruction or violence against its inspection teams. Armed with the vague language of the Treaty of Versailles that lacked punishment schemes for violations of the military clauses other than the possible extension of the Rhineland occupation, and lacking concrete plans of their own, Allied leaders reacted to German obstruction and abuse in an *ad hoc* manner. They never developed an official policy regarding the mistreatment of Allied inspection teams. Only after the attacks on its inspection officers in March 1920 did the Allies first meet to discuss how to deter the abuse of Allied soldiers in Germany. The final Allied decision amounted to nothing more than demanding a public apology from the German government and fines for those guilty of assault.[69]

Allied–German relations suffered further during the anxious days of the Kapp *putsch*. Although some *Freikorps* members, loyal to the right-wing Kapp, slaughtered a large number of civilians, their treatment of Allied officers was somewhat more circumspect. Kapp needed the recognition of

Allied governments to give his regime legitimacy and he thus tried to avoid any incidents with IAMCC officers. The IAMCC members billeted elsewhere in Germany, however, experienced some tense moments. For instance, German mobs insulted and assaulted Allied officers in Bremen and Premnitz and shot at an Allied officer near Frankfurt. Bingham demanded improvement in the treatment of Allied troops in Germany and warned that the work of the IAMCC would otherwise become impossible.[70] Consequently, the IAMCC demanded compensation for the aggressive actions taken by German soldiers against Allied officers and men during the failed coup attempt.[71] Fearful of further inflaming German public opinion, the Conference of Ambassadors did nothing, and IAMCC inspectors continued to work in dangerous conditions.

On one notorious occasion at the end of March 1920, the Allies responded to threatening German workers with unprecedented ferocity. When a demonstration broke out during an Allied inspection of a Krupp plant in Essen, Lieutenant Durieux, the French officer in charge of the inspection team, ordered his troops to fire on a threatening mob of German workers. Consequently, the Allies shot thirteen German civilians dead. After the incident, Gustav Krupp, not the French officer, was fined and sentenced to prison for inciting a riot.[72] This case was a bloody exception to the usual Allied inspection procedure, even when faced with danger. In fact, many Allied inspectors did not even carry arms.[73] With Allied officers working deep in the heart of Germany, surrounded by embittered troops and frustrated civilians, violent action was certain to create an international incident and endanger subsequent inspections. In this case, the brutal nature of the Allied response failed to deter future German attacks.

Problems continued all over Germany in the summer of 1920. In Bremen, German soldiers reacted in a hostile manner to IAMCC officers who had arrived to conduct an inspection of the barracks.[74] The acrimonious reception was due to the fact that the Allied officers wore their military uniforms, an apparent affront to the defeated nation. Consequently, many inspectors dressed in mufti. During a surprise inspection of a barracks in Munster in July, German troops fought the Allied inspectors with propaganda, pasting anti-Bolshevik posters and a description of the Battle of Jutland on the sides and rear of the inspectors' automobile. The car subsequently drove off to a boisterous rendition of *"Deutschland über Alles."*[75] In August 1920, a mob ransacked and robbed IAMCC quarters in Breslau, damaged officers' automobiles, and knocked down a Belgian officer. When the local German police took no action, Nollet demanded immediate apologies to the President and officers of the district committee of Breslau, punishment of the perpetrators, and the levy of stiff fines under threat of economic sanctions.[76] A similar incident occurred in Schneidemuhle, where a mob of almost 3,000 local Germans attacked an Allied train carrying French and British soldiers. Once again the civilians targeted mostly French soldiers, beating and robbing them before the arrival of the local police.[77] A German promise to take immediate measures to satisfy the IAMCC did little to help the Allied inspectors in the field.

Stettin, Passau, and Ingolstadt

With German weapons, artillery, and an overall state of readiness significantly dismantled by the end of 1922, the attention of the IAMCC began to focus upon diminishing the scope of disarmament operations. The Allies, especially Britain, started to discuss plans for setting up an even smaller Allied inspection force. France, however, was hesitant to reduce the scale of operations with so many violations unresolved. Before the future of disarmament in Germany could be settled, however, a number of serious violent incidents against the IAMCC interrupted the discussions and tested the fragility of post-war European diplomacy. The ramification of the assaults of Allied officers was a salve to the wounds of a united Allied disarmament policy. Instead of arguing over ways to diminish inspection efforts, the Allies spoke once again of disarming Germany.

The first of three major incidents against the IAMCC occurred in east Prussia, in the far north of Germany in July 1922. On a routine barracks inspection in Stettin on the morning of 17 July, the German authorities refused entry to three IAMCC officers to a suspiciously camouflaged room. The German liaison officer left the premises, whereupon armed police arrived and forcefully removed two IAMCC officers from the barracks. As a result, Bingham demanded apologies and punishments. Nollet angrily denounced the actions as "deliberately and seriously affecting the work of Control and the prestige of the Commission, representing the Allied Governments."[78] While the Allies and Germany soon reached a settlement, German Chancellor Wirth tried to deny responsibility by claiming that the French officer involved was thoroughly intoxicated.[79] The British War Office, advocating a *quid pro quo* policy, proposed support for French demands over the Stettin incident in order to try to elicit French support for the withdrawal of the IAMCC.[80]

The abusive behavior of the Germans to IAMCC officers and soldiers in 1922 left Nollet seething. In mid-October, he declared that control was becoming impossible and that unless the Allies took action against the German authorities to stop a recurrence of incidents, the prestige of the IAMCC would be permanently damaged and the entire Allied policy of the disarmament of Germany compromised.[81] Nollet believed that effective control was predicated upon German respect for Allied officers and troops, therefore keeping the prestige of the IAMCC intact. However, Nollet was unable to convince the Conference of the imminent danger to the IAMCC, and the Ambassadors dropped the matter with no decisive action.[82] Where Nollet failed, however, the Germans would soon succeed in forcing the Conference of Ambassadors to take action.

On 24 October a more severe incident took place in the southeastern corner of Bavaria, a hotspot for anti-Versailles activities. Two IAMCC officers, French Major Bouychou and British Captain Atkinson, arrived in Passau to conduct an inspection of a *Reichswehr* barracks. A hostile crowd, shouting threats and insults at the officers, greeted their arrival at the gate. Not allowing the hostility of the local populace to interfere with their work and despite seeing unsettling posters referring to "French dogs" posted in conspicuous locations in the barracks, the officers completed the inspection.[83] Unfortunately for the Allied officers, the time allotted for the inspection also allowed the crowd to increase its size and temper. From among the throng of several hundred locals, shouts of "To the slaughter-house" echoed off the walls of the barracks. Luckily, Major Bouychou was able to obtain police protection, which provided some safety for the officers on their hasty retreat to their waiting automobile. With two members of the local police riding on the running boards of the car, the inspection officers fled the scene in a mad dash for safety. Roaring out of the gate, the car was pelted with sticks, stones, and iron pieces, breaking the rear windows and cutting the face of Major Bouychou. On their arrival back in IAMCC district headquarters, Allied officers discovered two bullet holes in the back of the car. The IAMCC blamed the battalion commander, Captain Schuster (a member of a local nationalist organization *Bund Oberland*), for organizing and inciting the crowd.[84]

The Passau incident again revealed the different treatment of British and French officers at the hands of their German hosts. Captain Atkinson asserted that the crowd aimed most of its abusive behavior at Major Bouychou.[85] The French reacted harshly. Nollet blamed the German government for not affording proper protection and facilities to the IAMCC inspection team in Passau and declared the abuse a premeditated incident. Believing that the German government was morally responsible to comply with the Treaty of Versailles, Nollet demanded apologies and the firing of the local German battalion commander and chief of police.[86] After much debate, the Allies demanded the termination of duties of the *Reichswehr* commander and the two liaison officers, an apology from the police chief, and punishment of the police.[87] They would not, however, ever develop a clear policy of sanctions or punishment.

While the German government soon complied with the Stettin demands, and discussions concerning Passau continued, another serious incident further enraged the Allies and revealed the tenuous nature of military inspections. Once again, local German reaction to an IAMCC inspection team turned violent, victimizing the same two luckless inspectors, Major Bouychou and Captain Atkinson. An angry mob ambushed the two officers as they drove to a routine inspection of a munitions establishment near Ingolstadt (Bavaria) on 22 November. The officers escaped but not until the crowd smashed the car's windows and punctured a tire. Worse, flying glass had seriously cut Atkinson's face and a bullet had come close to killing both officers. Afterward, the IAMCC cleared the German military from any responsibility (the German liaison officer actually helped the IAMCC officers flee the scene) and placed blame entirely on local workers. The Allies believed that the attack had been premeditated, given the fact that the inspection was announced two days in advance and the mob was wielding clubs upon the officers' arrival.[88]

The Allies decided to take immediate action to punish German authorities for the Ingolstadt incident and to reiterate their unfulfilled Passau demands. The lack of protection for their officers in Ingolstadt led to Allied demands for the ouster of the local police official. For both Bavarian incidents, Passau and Ingolstadt, the Allies demanded a public apology from the mayors of the cities, as well as the Bavarian prime minister, and fined each city 500,000 marks.[89] The British Foreign Office suggested the occupation of a Bavarian city.[90] Foch, however, considered a Bavarian occupation as militarily unfeasible and the Allies instead considered a complex plan of compensation by exacting the fine from a part of Bavaria.[91]

The German government had little choice but to take responsibility for the incidents and to take action to ameliorate Allied indignation. First, it complied fully with Allied demands regarding the Stettin incident.[92] Second, with regard to the violent treatment of Allied officers in Passau and Ingolstadt, Germany paid the million gold marks and apologized for the Bavarian government. Consequently, the Allies decided not to insist upon apologies from the mayors of Passau and Ingolstadt and dropped any consideration of financial action in the Rhineland.[93] Although the Cuno government had met Allied demands concerning the three violent incidents, relations between the German and Allied governments remained tense, and it seemed as though any subsequent problem between the former combatants could have serious ramifications. When Franco-Belgian forces marched into the Ruhr in 1923, heightened tensions forced the Allies to terminate all disarmament activities. It would take a year for them to resume, and then three more years to complete their operations in Germany.

The most significant contribution of German obstruction to Allied disarmament efforts and abuse of IAMCC officers was that it effectively drove the British back into line with the French, thereby resulting in the prolongation of Allied disarmament operations in Germany. German obstruction was as pervasive and ongoing as Allied military control. The delays in fulfilling deadlines without the threat of sanctions, violations of all facets of disarmament, and the abuse of Allied officers had only a minimal effect upon augmenting the strength of the German military but greatly increased French anxiety and curtailed British intentions of withdrawing from Germany. At crucial moments of Britain distancing itself from the enforcement of the military articles of the Treaty of Versailles by demanding modifications, instances of blatant German disregard for disarmament forced the British into the waiting arms of French military and political authorities. In October 1922, German abuse of Allied officers led to the cancellation of discussions regarding the replacement of the IAMCC. The subsequent abundance of Allied discoveries of German evasions of the disarmament clauses of the Treaty of Versailles not only prevented the evacuation of Allied troops from Cologne in 1925 but also prolonged the Allied military control of Germany for years. The fear that obstruction and abuse would set a precedent for the cancellation of all Allied inspections of German military facilities led Britain and France to set aside their differences and maintain disarmament efforts well beyond everyone's expectations.

From simply ignoring Allied demands to the physical assault of Allied officers, German opposition to disarmament lasted throughout the life of the IAMCC and prolonged the existence of Allied inspectors in Germany. The overall German strategy was simple but flawed. The Germans hoped that delay in the fulfillment of the military clauses of the treaty would outlast the duration of Allied control in Germany. General Nollet believed that Germany submitted to Allied disarmament demands only after trying to gain as much time as possible and yielded "only to force."[94] Opposition to the treaty's enforcement produced a vicious cycle: the longer the IAMCC remained in Germany, the more frustrated the Germans became, and the consequent increase in obstruction merely extended the existence of the IAMCC. Another factor that certainly had an impact upon the duration of the IAMCC, the Ruhr occupation, will be discussed in Chapter 10. Regardless, Germany's violations of the military articles of the Treaty of Versailles and the obstruction to Allied disarmament efforts led to more obstinate policies of both Britain and France toward the duration of military control. In addition, the physical abuse of Allied control officers heightened international tensions that festered well after the burial of the last corpse on the battlefield. The serious incidents that occurred in the latter half of 1922 actually destroyed the ongoing Anglo–French discussions concerning the replacement of the IAMCC with a smaller, less obtrusive organization. Consequently, the anticipated yet highly unrealistic initial expectation for a three-month duration of disarmament produced disillusionment among both Allied and German political and military authorities, which helped prolong Allied disarmament operations in Germany for seven years.

Part III

The Ruhr crisis and the resumption of disarmament operations (1923–1924)

10 Uncertain Allies

On 11 January 1923, three years after the Treaty of Versailles went into effect, French and Belgian troops marched into the Ruhr Valley, the industrial heart of Germany. The Reparation Commission had just found Germany in default of coal shipments, and defaults on shipments of timber and telephone poles had given Raymond Poincaré the pretext to meet his promise to occupy the Ruhr. The French Premier, exasperated by the slew of broken German promises, hoped that a military sanction would allow France to exact coal deliveries, force the Germans into compliance with the Treaty of Versailles, and solidify France's position in Europe. The occupation fanned out over almost 1,700 square miles and encompassed the cities of Essen and Dortmund. The Ruhr occupation would be both a lengthy and costly operation.[1] French and Belgian troops roamed the streets of the cities of the Ruhr for two-and-a-half years, and the effects of the German policy of passive resistance strained the already delicate economic situations in Germany and France. German inflation sky-rocketed, and French and Belgian troops became scapegoats for all of Germany's ills. Consequently, Allied disarmament operations found themselves immersed in a state of chaos.

The Anglo–French relationship suffered as a result of the Franco-Belgian military action in Germany but once again weathered the storm. Three years of frustration over reparations payments and disarmament violations left France ripe for action in 1923. Poincaré, with Belgium at his side, wanted to exact his pound of German flesh that had been bought at the cost of a generation of young men. On the other hand, Lloyd George believed that the world economy would be strengthened with the economic resurrection of Germany and that destroying Germany would have adverse effects upon the British economy. British statesmen also advocated a lenient enforcement of the Treaty of Versailles in the hopes of normalizing relations with the Germans and hoped that Germany could recover at least some of its pre-war strength. Thus, they considered the forceful takeover of Germany's industrial center reprehensible. However, the British position regarding the Franco-Belgian occupation of the Ruhr was complex, and the British did not burn any diplomatic bridges. Although Britain opposed the occupation, the British government embarked upon a policy of benevolent neutrality, allowing the French to arrest dangerous Germans within the British occupation zone in the Rhineland and to use the major railhead of Cologne to send troops into the Ruhr.[2] Overall, Anglo–French relations, and the intention to enforce the Treaty of Versailles, remained intact.

The Ruhr occupation seriously affected the Allied organizations responsible for the disarmament and military control of Germany – the Conference of Ambassadors, AMCV, and IAMCC – but the Allies never gave any serious consideration to their dissolution. Within days of the occupation of the Ruhr, General Nollet declared that the IAMCC remained united in solidarity.[3] Although serious cracks soon appeared in this Allied unity, Anglo–French differences over the military sanctions did not hopelessly divide the Allied officers responsible for the disarmament of Germany or permanently render the tasks of military control inoperable. Allied–German relations, however, were a different matter altogether.

The Allies hoped initially that disarmament operations in Germany would simply proceed normally. In fact, in light of the consequences of the Ruhr occupation, the enormity of the situation did not initially affect Allied officials responsible for disarming Germany. Curzon, the British Foreign Secretary, seemed more anxious about the future reorganization of the German police than the possibility that operations might cease to function.[4] Furthermore, as one of its first official acts after the Ruhr occupation, the IAMCC complained about the existence of illegal military associations.[5] The IAMCC soon demanded cooperation with continued operations, however, and began to pay closer attention to a situation that could adversely affect the successful execution of the remaining disarmament provisions.[6] The initial hopes that operations could continue unabated despite German antipathy to the presence of French and Belgian troops in the Ruhr soon disappeared as Allied inspections of military establishments and industries came to a halt. By March, Allied efforts were dissolving in the face of German obstruction.

The vehement opposition and bitterness of the German people toward the French and Belgian occupation of the Ruhr spilled over into disarmament. As the occupation dragged on, German resistance increased. Consequently, Allied officers faced the hostility of the German populace, which rendered inspections all but useless.[7] Inspectors working in German facilities, especially French and Belgian soldiers, faced immediate difficulties. In fact, inspections slowed to a trickle in February and March, and practically ceased altogether by April. Only British and Italian officers carried out successful inspections.[8] The Germans refused to allow the IAMCC to inspect any army establishments and prohibited the surrender of any information regarding factories to Allied officers. In addition, German liaison officers offered little help. French and Belgian inspectors faced the brunt of German obstruction to their efforts, and on 7 March, the German government forbade their presence in any German facility.[9] As General

Nollet's frustration increased, he believed the Allies had two choices: to retire the IAMCC or take the necessary measures "to force the hand of the German government."[10] Since the French General actually had no intention of dissolving the IAMCC, he pushed for a resumption of full operations. On 10 March, in a controversial decision, Nollet angrily notified the German government that the IAMCC would resume "in all its intensity, control of the execution of the military clauses of the Treaty of Versailles and of the subsequent decisions of the Allied Governments."[11] Nollet ordered this new Allied offensive on German disarmament, a move undertaken to re-establish Allied prestige and authority in enforcing the military clauses of the treaty, to begin on 15 March.

Nollet's 10 March decision established cracks in the fragile foundation of Allied unity and eventually led to the alteration in the planning of subsequent disarmament operations. Bingham had refused to vote on the issue to resume full operations because he considered it a political decision best suited to his government or to the Conference of Ambassadors. When Nollet and the IAMCC sent the note to the German government regardless of Bingham's apprehension, the British were furious that the IAMCC had ignored them and taken the initiative regarding a "political" issue. Nollet merely considered the decision to be an "internal order."[12] He also pointed out that the French, Belgian, Italian, and Japanese delegates had voted in favor of the note and emphasized that "the disarmament of Germany is not yet complete."[13]

The following day, Nollet and Bingham met to settle their differences. In what Nollet described as a "cold" conversation, Bingham stated that ignoring his input in the previous day's decision angered him. While Nollet admitted he regretted not having Bingham's consent, he also bluntly pointed out that he was less than enthusiastic about Bingham's lack of support for French and Belgian disarmament policies.[14] Ostensibly acting as peacemaker but actually attempting to enforce French policy, the AMCV, with its British representative notably in abstention, urged all Allied governments to lend their full support to the IAMCC and the 10 March decision.[15] The tension subsided on 14 March when the Conference of Ambassadors ruled in favor of British opinion by overturning Nollet's decree and demanding the continued suspension of inspections.[16]

The fall-out from Nollet's note of 10 March was not quite over. Although proclaiming that Nollet's decision was "discourteous and improper," the British government agreed suddenly to associate itself with the infamous note for the sake of Allied unity and authority.[17] The British also reasserted the decision to refer all political questions to the Conference of Ambassadors.[18] They stipulated, however, that subsequent inspections would be conducted with reserve in order to avoid incidents with Germany. When Lloyd George stated that Britain would resume disarmament operations and that Bingham would continue to cooperate with the IAMCC, the issue appeared all but settled.[19] Consequently, the Conference of Ambassadors overturned its previous decision and decided to support the complete resumption of operations in Germany. On 21 March, Poincaré notified the German government of the Allied intention to resume full control.[20] Although the French premier was satisfied with British support for resuming operations, he also warned his ambassadors of the dangerous ramifications of Allied disunity. Poincaré feared the British would drop support of a future French position regarding German disarmament, thereby isolating France in German affairs.[21] After the Allies' declaration to resume operations, the German government professed its intention to abide by Allied decisions regarding the enforcement of the treaty but continued to claim that it was unable to afford Allied inspection teams security.[22] Thus, the fall-out of the Ruhr occupation continued to create problems for the safety of Allied officers and also gave the German government an excuse for obstruction.

The issue of the resumption of Allied disarmament operations in March 1923 emphasized the problem of the overlapping hierarchy of Allied authority, especially when the Ruhr occupation exacerbated the tense atmosphere in Germany. The split in the IAMCC between the British and French factions, represented by Bingham and Nollet, respectively, worsened with the incompatibility of each man's vision and as each faced tremendous pressure from national policy-makers. In addition, the constant referral of questions to the AMCV undermined the authority of the IAMCC, and Nollet often conspired with Foch to try to establish French principles over Allied disarmament strategy. Illustrative of the problems of developing a single Allied policy, the difficulties in resuming disarmament operations stemmed in part from the British insistence in January 1921 to refer all political questions to the Conference of Ambassadors. The British had hoped to prevent a French political *fait accompli* but Nollet's 10 March initiative proved it vulnerable. Nollet's action, however, represented the last gasp of French independent initiative in disarming Germany, and the French would no longer act without British support or leadership in the enforcement of the military clauses of the Versailles Treaty. The time for independent French action toward Germany disappeared, and London now had the diplomatic initiative.

The Allies decided to test the hostile waters by carrying out a limited number of operations at the end of March. The IAMCC ordered ten official inspections of military establishments and factories, with a brief interlude for Easter, to show Germany that Allied operations had indeed resumed.[23] Although forced to accept the resumption of control, Bingham believed privately the new inspections would inevitably fail.[24] The inspections were a disaster. Allied officers were unable to carry out eight of the ten visits, due to the refusal of both German military authorities and workers to allow Allied entry; Nollet demanded new action against the German government.[25] The only successful inspections occurred in Breslau and Stettin, where British and Italian officers were able to examine a munitions factory and police school, respectively. Although minor incidents were reported, one German nationalist newspaper demanded the arrest of Nollet and advocated violence against all French and Belgian IAMCC members on German soil.[26]

The response of British and French officials to the new wave of German obstruction varied. The British reacted tepidly, with an air of self-righteousness. Foreign Secretary Curzon used the failure of inspections as justification for the British reluctance to agree to the resumption of control and placed the onus of guilt upon the French and the IAMCC.[27] D'Abernon labeled both French policy and the resumption of inspections as "foolish."[28] French military officials viewed the increase in German obstruction as a complete abrogation of the beloved treaty. The Conference of Ambassadors hoped to mollify the German authorities by notifying Germany that the Allies wished only to execute the Five Points that had been part of the Allied note of 29 September 1922.[29]

In a meeting of the Conference of Ambassadors on 25 April, British and French viewpoints regarding the resumption of inspections reached a critical impasse that nearly destroyed the Allied structure of disarmament operations in Germany. The British, represented by Eric Phipps, wanted to affirm only the theoretical maintenance of control while the French, under Jules Cambon's leadership, wholeheartedly pushed for an immediate resumption of all operations. Cambon asserted forcefully that "the British Government signed the Treaty of Versailles and it must see to its execution."[30] However, Phipps would uphold only the right of inspections and feared that any actual disarmament operations would result in violent incidents. When Cambon threatened to take separate action to enforce the treaty, Anglo–French relations teetered precariously on the edge of disaster. Phipps's refusal to back down, however, forced Cambon to retreat. Phipps rejected a Franco-Belgian demand for the immediate cessation of all obstruction, and Nollet's frustrated outburst at his inability to conduct effective control brought a sharp rebuke from Cambon.[31] In the wake of the difficulties created by the Ruhr occupation, the French could no longer afford to act independently and had to satisfy themselves with yet another written protest to the German government. French diplomatic initiative against Germany and the use of military sanctions to enforce the treaty appeared dead. Remaining disarmament operations in Germany were at a standstill and, at that moment, few shared any illusions about the efficacy of control operations. With France hesitant to act alone, Britain now held the reins of control.

Allied disarmament operations in Germany were in dismal shape in the spring of 1923, with their maintenance in suspense and their future course unknown. In response to the French protest against obstruction, the German government claimed that the Ruhr occupation rendered all French and Belgian operations infeasible and that only British and Italian officers would be allowed in German military establishments and factories.[32]

Cambon was angry with what he considered a discriminatory German policy but was not willing to take any severe action. In subsequent conference meetings, he continued to stress the urgency of the situation and warned that Germany could be rearming during the suspension of control, but the British refused to heed French exhortations and believed that the current level of German hostility would negate the value of any resumption of inspections.[33] The British War Office thought that effective operations depended upon a satisfactory resolution, not of inspections, but of the Ruhr occupation.[34] Nonetheless, the occupation dragged on and continued to hinder effective Allied disarmament.

After the Cuno government admitted that it was afraid that ordering all citizens and military authorities to stop obstructing Allied disarmament efforts would undermine its precarious position with the people, the British government experienced a change of heart. In order to maintain solidarity and also wary of the state of German armament, the British government decided to order the Cuno government to take immediate steps to facilitate a full resumption of military control. The British also added that all inspections must be conducted with "discretion and moderation."[35] British policy was again fluctuating amidst chaotic conditions, and even though the British favored leniency in disarmament matters, they also wanted to finish the task at hand. More importantly, the British government had firmly established itself as the decisive influence in disarmament operations; the power to inspect or suspend operations rested with London. In order to placate German bitterness toward the French and Belgians, and taking no chances amidst a hostile populace, the Allies ordered IAMCC inspection teams to wear civilian clothes except on special occasions.[36] Thus, inspectors were to avoid incidents at all costs so as not to upset the delicate political atmosphere in Germany. As a result, the Conference of Ambassadors notified the German government of a renewal of inspections, and the French and British stood united in policy.[37]

After months of protracted and bitter negotiations, the Allies resumed disarmament operations in Germany on 28 June, but these inspections failed in the same disheartening proportion as the prior inspections in March, as eight out of ten visits yielded no positive results. The German authorities refused entry into any facility for every team that included either French or Belgian officers whereas the two inspection teams that consisted only of British and Italian officers were able to carry out successful operations.[38] The German army withdrew its liaison officers and abused a French captain.[39] The fact that the Germans distinguished between two camps of Allies was now obvious: those who participated in the Ruhr occupation were not allowed to carry out their duties in German installations while those who remained aloof to the occupation were received, albeit reluctantly, as a necessary obligation. Nollet was completely flustered with this state of affairs but could do little to enforce German compliance.[40]

German obstruction forced the Allies to suspend disarmament operations yet again. The German government claimed that it could not protect IAMCC officers from spontaneous attacks, and some French officers even feared for their lives.[41] The Allies made no attempt to resume inspections for the remainder of the summer. Bingham believed that the Cuno regime could do little in terms of Allied protection and pinned the future success of military control upon the successful resolution of the Ruhr crisis.[42] Propaganda continued to inflame German public opinion and added to the tense atmosphere throughout Germany. General von Cramon, who had resigned his post as head of the German Army Peace Commission over the Ruhr occupation, decried the bestial manner of the IAMCC by claiming that French soldiers hung German civilians by their feet and crushed their skulls.[43] Such claims were ludicrous, but easily galvanized those who blamed the French and Belgians for their economic plight.

As hyperinflation of the Mark caused the ruin of countless individuals, winds of change began to blow through Germany. When the German government, now headed by Gustav Stresemann, abandoned its policy of passive resistance in late September, Europe sighed in relief. The new government was also willing to comply with the Treaty of Versailles and pledged Germany to a policy of fulfillment. Stresemann, an ardent expansionist during the war who had since embraced liberal politics, marked a distinct positive change in Allied–German relations. Stresemann based his foreign policy on improving relations with France and Britain in order to obtain territorial or economic concessions in the Treaty of Versailles. This was the only course of action that could "file off the fetters" of the hated treaty.[44] Stresemann, however, was also a shrewd negotiator and looked to settle two divisive issues for many Germans: the withdrawal of the IAMCC as well as the Allied occupation forces in the Rhineland. The new Chancellor/Foreign Minister hoped to oust foreign troops from German soil and re-establish true German sovereignty.[45] General von Seeckt also pressured him to believe that the Allies wanted to destroy the German army.[46]

With the renunciation of passive resistance and the adoption of a new German attitude to comply with the Treaty of Versailles, the Allies renewed disarmament operations with eager anticipation. On 3 October, the Conference of Ambassadors asked Germany to cooperate with the IAMCC in the resumption of disarmament operations. In addition, the French government agreed not to allow French or Belgian officers to participate in any inspections until the Stresemann government replied to the Conference's note.[47] However, Allied hopes of the full resumption of control disappeared when Germany reneged on promises to take security measures to protect IAMCC inspectors. At the beginning of November, the Stresemann government replied to the Conference of Ambassadors that the resumption of inspections would only aggravate the delicate political atmosphere in Germany; it believed the moment was not yet right to resume control.[48]

The remainder of 1923 saw little progress toward normalizing relations with Germany or resuming the enforcement of the military clauses of the Treaty of Versailles. The Allies were unsure of how to proceed, and the divergence of British and French policies toward the resumption of control added to the chaotic political atmosphere in Allied–German relations. In November, in a meeting of the Conference of Ambassadors, the British advocated partial control, where the IAMCC would only inspect "safe" areas in Germany.[49] This proposal clashed with the French wish to enforce new military sanctions in the occupation of more German territory. Upset over the return of the former Crown Prince to Germany (considered a war criminal) and continued obstruction to Allied disarmament efforts, the French threatened to occupy either Hamburg or Frankfurt.[50] Cambon also pointed out that the lack of a united Allied will to enforce the Treaty of Versailles was a disastrous course to take. With the negative ramifications of the Ruhr crisis plain for all to see, the British Cabinet rejected all talk of occupation. In fact, the War Office suspected that the French drive to renew inspections was a deliberate attempt to provoke Germany into violating the treaty, thereby justifying French vigilance in the Ruhr and Rhineland.[51]

In a subsequent meeting of the Conference of Ambassadors, the British, with support from the Italian delegation, threatened to withdraw themselves from the Ambassadors' Conference and the Control Commissions if the French enforced more military sanctions against Germany.[52] France backed down, and the uncertain Allies were able to forge an agreement that influenced the future course of disarmament. In order to avoid further Allied disaccord in the execution of the military clauses of the treaty, the Allies decided to refer to the Conference of Ambassadors all subsequent IAMCC decisions that lacked unanimity.[53] The Allies also decided to take action to settle the question of German disarmament. They reaffirmed the full resumption of operations, under the threat of unspecified sanctions, but prohibited all surprise visits. By taking away both the authority to approve measures without majority voting and the right to surprise visits, the Allies had left the IAMCC a shell of its former self.

The frustration of General Nollet toward the progress of disarmament had grown dramatically with the suspension of military operations during the Ruhr occupation in 1923. The steady erosion of IAMCC authority – the supremacy of the AMCV, the referral of political issues and then all non-unanimous decisions to the Conference of Ambassadors, and finally the prohibition of surprise visits – had taken its toll on the attitude of the French General. Nollet was extremely dedicated to supervising the execution of the military clauses of the treaty and with his powers stripped to the bare minimum, he felt slighted and impotent. By the end of November, Nollet loosed a torrent of criticism upon Allied decisions when he decried the elimination of surprise visits and the abrogation of Council majority decisions. He asserted that Allied decisions had paralyzed the IAMCC, destroyed morale, rendered control operations ineffective, and reduced the IAMCC to a "powerless instrument."[54] Foch considered Nollet's remarks and lack of confidence in the ability to carry out his duties to be "deplorable," "undistinguished," and warned that the head of the French delegation of the IAMCC must be the last to speak of leaving his post.[55] General Nollet had become a disgruntled subordinate to Foch and Allied policy-makers, and the proud IAMCC President would be gone in a matter of months.

Despite their opposition to the idea of the resumption of only partial control measures, the French reluctantly accepted the idea in the face of British determination. After a discussion among the Council in mid-December, Nollet decided that disarmament first had to be re-established with a few inspections before the IAMCC resumed full operations.[56] Both Bingham and Nollet agreed that all subsequent inspections had to be carried out with tact and discretion. Alhough Nollet decided to implement partial control, he was still smarting from the rebuke he received from Foch regarding his reduced role in the disarmament of Germany, but Nollet was a true soldier of France and reported to Foch that he had accepted the watered-down control policy and his diminished authority in a "superior interest." The French General also warned Foch that disarmament policy was shifting to London and that he needed all the support his government could give him.[57] Nonetheless, Nollet fixed a date for the resumption of the first stage of military control. He scheduled the new wave of test visits for 10 and 12 January 1924, in which IAMCC officers, dressed in civilian clothes and accompanied by German liaison officers, would inspect military establishments in eight German cities.[58]

The Hennessy affair

The political atmosphere in Germany all but stifled disarmament operations for much of 1923, but British and Italian officers were able to carry out a few inspections. One such inspection, however, proved that conditions in Germany were not conducive to success and in fact were dangerous for all Allied officers. On 30 October, *Reichswehr* troops stopped British Major H.G. Hennessy of the Effectives Sub-commission near the city of Chemnitz (Saxony), threatened him at gunpoint to surrender his notebook, arrested him, and then marched the inspector into custody. While detained in a Limbach hotel for four hours prior to his release, Major Hennessy noticed that a number of Germans in civilian dress appeared to be actual officers working illegally with the German army.[59] The report of clandestine rearmament at a time when French officers were unable to conduct inspections produced an immediate response from the French government. The French proposed unspecified sanctions but the British refused any further sanctions against Germany, especially since the Ruhr occupation had already all but destroyed the prospects of full disarmament operations.[60] When the IAMCC formally protested Hennessy's treatment to the German government and demanded apologies, the British Foreign Office reacted angrily to what it considered to be another breach in protocol by the IAMCC. The effect of the Hennessy affair led Bingham to believe that effective control was a useless endeavor unless Allied soldiers protected IAMCC inspectors.[61] The Allies never gave any serious consideration though to the armed enforcement of inspections.

Like the question of when to resume military control operations in Germany, the fall-out of the Hennessy affair dragged on through the rest of the year. Britain simply wanted to avoid any incidents that gave the French new pretexts to enforce more military sanctions. The irony in the aftermath of the Hennessy affair is that the French took a hard line toward Germany for its treatment of a British officer, while the British settled for lesser apologies and punishments.[62] When a German liaison officer sent an apology to Major Hennessy, the IAMCC considered it to be insufficient.[63]

Another consequence of the Hennessey affair was the status of Major-General Bingham. Similar to Nollet's predicament, Bingham's authority had been slowly eroding since the beginning of disarmament operations. Under pressure from the Foreign Office, the rulings of the Conference of Ambassadors, and Lord D'Abernon in Berlin, Bingham could do nothing without referring all issues to higher authorities. By November 1923, Bingham had to ask permission of D'Abernon and the Foreign Office to agree to any inspections in Germany.[64] He was, however, more amenable than Nollet, and his moderate stance toward relations with Germany was compatible with the restrictions placed upon him. Whereas Nollet warned of German rearmament and disdained his loss of power, Bingham denied the reports of German violations of the military clauses during the suspension of control and, unlike Nollet or Morgan, rarely complained.[65]

Resumption reprise

The new series of Allied inspections in Germany commenced on the fourth anniversary of the implementation of the Treaty of Versailles and ended two days later. The major aim of the inspections was to ascertain the state of German disarmament; in essence, the Allies wanted to know if Germany had rearmed during the IAMCC's year-long sabbatical. Effective disarmament operations had disappeared for an entire year, and the Allies wished to determine whether the German military was in exactly the same state that had existed prior to the suspension of operations in January 1923. After making this initial determination, the Allies then expected to resume complete disarmament operations in Germany with an eye to finishing the task. One point that remained in suspense, however, was whether the Allies would insist on the complete execution of all the military clauses or content themselves with the execution of the Five Points.[66] Since Germany had never accepted the Allied proposal of the Committee of Guarantee as a bargaining chip to restrict disarmament to the Five Points, the future of disarmament was steeped in uncertainty.

Two issues at the start of 1924 created a rift in the IAMCC and emphasized the growing divergence of British and French policies toward enforcing the military clauses of the treaty. The first question, a source of interminable discussion, was whether the IAMCC should carry out surprise visits to German military establishments. Ostensibly settled by the Conference of Ambassadors in November 1923, the issue of surprise visits re-emerged under the persistence of the highest ranking French officers of the IAMCC. General Henri Walch, who would soon replace Nollet as President of the IAMCC, considered surprise visits to be indispensable to the effective control of German industrial and military facilities.[67] This French position, however, ran counter to British intentions toward Germany disarmament. The British feared that surprise inspections would inflame German hostility toward the Allies and lead to violent incidents. The ramifications of such a policy could therefore provide the French with a justification to occupy more German territory. Immediately preceding the 10 and 12 January inspections, Bingham, without hesitation, told Nollet that he considered any surprise visits to be "out of the question."[68] The British and French were in agreement over the basic concept of resuming disarmament operations in Germany, and when the German government contended that the Allies had no need to make actual contact with German authorities in all subsequent inspections, the Allies held their ground. On the eve of the renewal of visits, the IAMCC upheld its right to visit any establishment in Germany whatsoever.[69]

The second issue was the assessment of the results of the January inspections concerning the state of German disarmament. After reviewing the reports of the inspection teams, the majority of the IAMCC interpreted the results of the inspections in a negative light. Nollet reported that Germany was rearming and once again posed a military threat to the Allies.[70] There was also a difference of opinion toward German behavior in the two days of inspections. British officers had no complaints but Nollet reported that the German military authorities had acted offensively toward some IAMCC officers.[71] Consequently, Generals Walch and Guffroy, members of the French and Belgian delegations of the IAMCC, respectively, proposed sanctions against Germany.[72] Only Bingham took a rosy view of the situation, denying reports of widespread German violations of the military clauses of the treaty or the blatant misbehavior of German officials.[73] With Bingham preventing IAMCC action with his refusal to support sanctions, Walch rightfully claimed that the decision to enforce unanimity of opinion in the IAMCC was destroying its ability to act.

The status of the Allied disarmament of Germany had not changed substantively a year after the Ruhr occupation uprooted Allied efforts to enforce the military clauses of the treaty. The results of the January inspections gave the Allies initial insight into potential German violations of the treaty's disarmament clauses and illustrated the continued divergence of Anglo-French opinion toward the resumption of operations. After these inspections, the German government continued to claim that it could not adequately ensure the safety of Allied control officers and the British were hesitant to push for full resumption. In addition, the *Reichswehr* Ministry opposed further inspections and any Allied notions to set up a new control organization.[74] In the face of bitter opposition from Foch, who believed that the interruption of the work of the IAMCC was destroying it, the British government pushed initially for the suspension of all inspections.[75] As the month came to a close, the British proposed instead the carrying out of "stock-taking" inspections to determine whether the state of German disarmament had changed since the suspension of operations.[76] This proposal would remain the cornerstone of Allied policy toward the disarmament of Germany for the remainder of the year.

In March 1924, Nollet tried to re-establish the authority of the IAMCC in Germany by proposing renewed inspections of German factories, depots, and barracks. No longer satisfied with the mere fulfillment of the Five Points, Nollet informed the German government on 5 March that the IAMCC intended first to verify whether Germany had rearmed during the suspension of control before continuing with the execution of the Five Points.[77] Thus, stock-taking visits would be only the first step in resuming disarmament operations in Germany. The Allies estimated that these inventory inspections would take two or three months to complete.[78] In addition, restricting the remaining disarmament obligations to the Five Points was still contingent upon German acceptance of a smaller control organization. The German government, however, soon rejected the establishment of a smaller control organization and instead supported the completion of disarmament under the League of Nations.[79]

In determining the state of German disarmament, the Allies hoped to set a course for future control and the subsequent completion of the tasks of the IAMCC. Bingham opposed such a wide array of inspections and believed they would prolong the duration of disarmament operations in Germany for up to two years. The British War Office advocated the resumption of operations, but only if they were limited to a small number of inventory inspections.[80] The key to British policy was to avoid any possibility of abusive incidents with Germany.[81] Conversely, the French were extremely suspicious of German intentions and pointed out that the true completion of the tasks of the IAMCC went beyond the execution of the Five Points; they continued to uphold the full mission of the IAMCC.[82]

The issue of stock-taking visits continued throughout the spring without any apparent hope of a conclusive settlement. Meanwhile, for those who supported the resumption of full control, anxieties increased regarding the state of German military strength. Had German officials and workers remained as passive as the IAMCC officers and men who stewed in their

German hotels during the suspension of operations? British Lieutenant-Colonel Heywood, a compatriot of Morgan, warned that Germany could rearm and replenish its military machine within six months of the withdrawal of the IAMCC.[83] Since the IAMCC had been in a state of limbo for seventeen months, this alleged German military potential certainly pointed to the need for a settlement of the resumption issue. French worries were more intense than those of their British colleagues and focused on possible increases in German military personnel. A major reason Nollet pushed for carrying out the stock-taking inspections was to assess the reported augmentation of paramilitary organizations in Germany.[84] On 28 May, the Conference of Ambassadors attempted to alleviate such fears by presenting the German government with an ultimatum. Either Germany had to accept the stock-taking visits and, contingent upon satisfactory results, the institution of a new form of control organization, or the Allies would support strict compliance of all of the military clauses of the Treaty of Versailles.[85]

Another factor in the disarmament equation was the first major changes that occurred in the leadership of the British and French governments during the occupation of the Ruhr. In January 1924, Britain elected its first Labour government, under Ramsay MacDonald, who also took the position of Foreign Minister. In the June elections in France, Edouard Herriot of the Radical Party replaced Poincaré, the zealot of enforcement. The two leftist leaders, who would last only about one year in office, took moderate stands toward Germany and were open to conciliation concerning the remaining disarmament of Germany. MacDonald and Herriot met in June 1924 at Chequers to attempt to settle ongoing problems with Germany. In addition to discussing the implementation of the Dawes Plan, MacDonald and Herriot drafted a joint note to the German government urging German cooperation in disarmament operations and professing an inclination to withdraw the IAMCC with the fulfillment of the remaining major points.[86] With such short tenures in office, however, their impact upon operations was minimal, and the Allied disarmament of Germany continued to muddle along.

Anglo–French policy differences over German disarmament in the wake of the Ruhr occupation was a step toward the eventual termination of Allied disarmament operations. After the decision to enforce Allied unanimity upon the IAMCC, the split between Nollet and Bingham helped aid the paralysis of Allied disarmament policy. Repercussions soon followed that changed the future course of the IAMCC. Fueled by the mounting criticism of Bingham, Major-General Arthur Wauchope replaced Bingham as head of the British delegation of the IAMCC in May.[87] The Foreign Office was Bingham's most persistent critic, believing that he was incapable of standing up to Nollet. Hoping to replace him, Foreign Office officials severely castigated Bingham for failing to notify the Foreign Office of incidents the IAMCC experienced during the January inspections.[88] Bingham had become the Foreign Office's scapegoat for the paralysis of

IAMCC operations and for the failure to convince the French that resumption of control was inopportune.

The debilitation of control operations and the inability of the French to coerce the British to meet France's security concerns also had an impact upon the French delegation of the IAMCC. General Henri Walch replaced Nollet, the consummate French officer who had been largely responsible for the success the IAMCC had experienced and who had been a constant voice of frustration during the absence of disarmament progress over the past two years.[89] In addition, General Royé replaced the President of the Effectives Sub-committee, General Barthélemy.[90] Nollet's support of the strict enforcement of the military clauses of the treaty clashed repeatedly with Bingham's moderate approach and, when his authority disappeared, along with the ability of the IAMCC to conduct operations, he decided his position was untenable. Nollet, however, would not be simply shunted aside as he soon became France's new Minister of War under Premier Edouard Herriot.[91] In the wake of the Ruhr occupation, the personnel of the IAMCC had witnessed a transformation. The troublemakers – Nollet, Barthélemy, Bingham, and Morgan – had all disappeared, and both Britain and France hoped that the IAMCC could now settle its internal differences and complete the work it had started four-and-a-half years earlier. Regardless, the basic question of the compatibility of British and French policy toward German disarmament, as well as the enforcement of the treaty, remained.

The General Inspection

After months of vague answers, claims of inadequate authority to protect Allied officers, and a diplomatic atmosphere filled with tension, indecision, and general chaos, the German government finally gave the Allies a positive response to the issue of the continued execution of the military clauses of the Treaty of Versailles. Formerly in opposition to the resumption of control, the German government agreed on 30 June 1924 to the Allied proposal for carrying out the General Inspection of the state of the German military.[92] Stresemann had implemented his plan to trade the fulfillment of Allied demands for treaty modifications. Above all, he wanted all Allied occupation forces out of Germany. The Marx government accepted the Allied General Inspection on condition that it would lead to the end of military control and asked for the cessation of all inspections by the end of September. The Allies were relieved that control was to resume shortly but refused to fix a specific date for the end of the inspections.[93] The inspections began in early September.

Britain and France were quite receptive to German acquiescence to the resumption of control but still had to settle the differences between them as to how to proceed. Nonetheless, they drew up detailed plans for the General Inspection.[94] Drafted by the IAMCC and approved by the AMCV and the Conference of Ambassadors, the proposal specified that the IAMCC would carry out inspections to verify whether the state of German armament – war material amounts, *Reichswehr* and police organization, factory transformation and production, and so on – had changed during the suspension of control. The IAMCC stipulated that the duration of the General Inspection would be three to four months, each inspection team would consist of two officers dressed in civilian clothes, every inspection would have a German liaison officer present, and any surprise visits had to have clear military objectives and importance. To appease German apprehension of the resumption of control after the Ruhr occupation, the Allies delayed inspecting *Reichswehr* establishments for almost two weeks, and the first surprise visits did not take place until two months into the General Inspection.[95]

Although the personnel of the IAMCC experienced great changes in 1924 with the introduction of Wauchope and Walch, the authority of the organization remained stable. Major-General Arthur Wauchope, a career infantry officer who had been severely wounded in action in both the Boer War and World War I, had spent his career in the Black Watch. His gallant service during World War I helped lead to his appointment as the new head of the British section of the IAMCC. Wauchope's role in the IAMCC was to act as a moderating influence upon French policy toward German disarmament while simultaneously mending the shaky Anglo–French relationship in the IAMCC. General Walch was similar to Nollet in his approach to French demands in the disarmament of Germany. Like his predecessor, Walch resented the diminishment of the decision-making power of the IAMCC and pushed for the execution of the military articles of the treaty. For instance, Walch advocated surprise visits and opposed the ruling of the Conference of Ambassadors to enforce unanimity of all IAMCC decisions.[96]

The Allied General Inspection of Germany finally began on 8 September 1924 and lasted for just over four months. These stock-taking visits attempted to reassess the state of German armament with an abbreviated schedule of inspections. The work for both Allied and German officers was strenuous. Initially, assessments of the new wave of visits were generally positive and, after the first week of inspections, Major-General Wauchope commented favorably upon the tasks underway. He reported that German political and military authorities, as well as liaison officers and factory directors, were cooperating with the IAMCC and believed that his opposition to some French demands had helped increase German cooperation.[97] As time wore on, and the inspections numbered into the hundreds, ominous signs began to appear that pointed to recent German violations of the military aspects of the treaty. In October, Wauchope's initial positive opinion of the state of German armament started to waver. German cooperation was waning and a number of factories that had not yet been transformed to peaceful endeavors were actually manufacturing war material once again.[98]

As the fifth anniversary of the effective date of the Treaty of Versailles approached, another aspect of the treaty emerged within the context of disarmament and became intertwined with the Allied enforcement of the military clauses. Under the terms of the Versailles Treaty, the Rhineland had been divided into three zones – Cologne, Coblenz, and Mainz – and occupied by the armies of Britain, France, Belgium, and the United States.[99] At the Paris Peace Conference, the Allies agreed to withdraw their armies from the three zones at five-year intervals if Germany fulfilled the clauses of the treaty. Thus, German compliance with the treaty would lead to the evacuation of Cologne in January 1925, Coblenz in 1930, and Mainz in 1935. If Germany did not comply with Allied decisions concerning the treaty's provisions, the French, British, Belgian, and American troops could extend the duration of the occupation. The Allies could also choose to withdraw their forces at an earlier date (American forces withdrew in 1923). Since the Dawes Plan had settled the reparations issue at least temporarily, the fulfillment of the military clauses of the treaty became the basis for the withdrawal of Allied troops from Cologne.[100] Nonetheless, January 1925 marked the first actual test of enforcement stipulated specifically by the treaty. The final report of the General Inspection would be the ultimate Allied evaluation of the state of German armament and, since it dealt with the fulfillment of the treaty, the report also had implications concerning the withdrawal of Allied troops from the Rhineland.

By the fourth and final month of the General Inspection, the French and British began to question the state of German armament. Allied officers discovered that Germany had not remained quiet during the suspension of control, let alone fulfilled the remaining disarmament provisions. At the end of November, the British War Office reported a general augmentation of German military capacity. The numerous inspections revealed significant violations of the armaments and effectives clauses of the treaty. The Armaments Sub-commission inspected 232 factories and found that twenty had not been converted into peace production and nineteen were actually producing war material. The Effectives Sub-commission discovered the existence of the core of the General Staff, short-term enlistment, trained volunteers, excess officers, as well as a centralized organization of the police. This was not passive resistance but active evasion. The War Office, however, while expressing dissatisfaction with the various violations, believed that Germany had not *substantially* increased her military capacity.[101] The Foreign Office agreed. Similar to its proclamations in 1922, the Foreign Office declared that the Allies had disarmed Germany relative to the strength of the other powers, even though Germany had not yet fulfilled the military clauses of the treaty.[102] The French perspective on the state of German armament was less forgiving, and continued uncertainty about the direction of Allied military control abounded.

In December, after three months of renewed inspections, the issue of the Rhineland reappeared in earnest in Anglo–French discussions about the military clauses of the treaty. The British War Office wanted to make the withdrawal of Allied troops contingent upon the "actual process of completion" of the Five Points.[103] In mid-December, Foch reported that the Germans had not yet even started work on the transformation of some factories and the reorganization of the police. He was certain that Germany could not fulfill the military clauses by 10 January 1925, the date of the expected withdrawal of Allied forces from Cologne.[104] Furthermore, the conclusion of the British Cabinet pointed to a future crisis with Germany. The Cabinet declared that minor violations of the military clauses would have no effect upon Allied policy but, if Germany did not fulfill major portions of the remaining disarmament issues, British soldiers would remain in Cologne.[105] Both MacDonald and Herriot agreed that the withdrawal of their troops from Cologne had to be preceded by German fulfillment of the military clauses of the treaty.

At the end of December, the AMCV produced a scathing report on the results of the General Inspection. It pointed out that Germany had not executed a number of military clauses and that there had actually been an increase in German military strength since the suspension of disarmament operations. Most importantly, Germany had made no progress on the Five Points. Consequently, the Conference of Ambassadors decided to keep Allied occupation forces in Cologne after January 1925.[106] Without waiting for the final report of the General Inspection, the Allies worked for the remainder of December drafting an appropriate note to the Marx government.[107] By the end of the month, the only issue the Allies were debating was the date in which to inform the German government of their decision to maintain their contingency of troops in Cologne. Trouble loomed ahead.

The Franco-Belgian occupation of the Ruhr had an impact upon international relations between Britain, France, and Germany, as well as the domestic affairs of France and Germany. One of the repercussions of the Ruhr crisis that historians have often ignored was the disintegrating effect it had upon the execution of the military clauses of the Treaty of Versailles. From January 1923 until the autumn of 1924, the Allied disarmament of Germany faced serious challenges to its future existence. As the German government obstructed Allied disarmament efforts, and economic destabilization fanned the flames of passionate revulsion toward Allied soldiers on German soil, Allied efforts themselves began to unravel. The British often adopted a wait-and-see approach and advocated leniency toward Germany, while their French colleagues demanded action and a return to the status quo ante Ruhr, but uncertainty was in the air. The fact that the IAMCC had increased its size to near peak strength in September 1924 is evidence of the serious nature of the disarmament of Germany during the Ruhr crisis.[108] During the suspension of disarmament operations, neither Britain nor France held steadfastly to concrete policies toward normalizing military control in Germany as both were subject to fluctuating proposals and methods. Negotiations were difficult and subject to the atmosphere of unrest and uncertainty. Anglo–French relations survived a true test when the Allies reached a compromise in the fall of 1924, but the chaotic interlude had appreciably altered their methods and attitudes toward the enforcement of the military clauses of the treaty.

A major effect of the Ruhr occupation was its impact upon Allied relations in disarming Germany. Although Britain and France feared the diminishing hold of the treaty over Germany, France's obsession with security in the 1920s rendered her policy-makers often incapable of flexibility. The chaotic political atmosphere of 1923 and 1924 precluded normal disarmament operations in Germany, and the French demand (and right) to resume full disarmament operations during the Ruhr crisis ended in failure. The more France pursued aggressive policies to enforce disarmament, the more Britain withdrew from its treaty commitments. The prolongation of disarmament, one of the direct consequences of the Ruhr occupation, allowed the French an insight into German military affairs for years to come, but such an outcome was not a conscious effort. The constant pleas to resume operations, and the frustration of Nollet and Foch prove otherwise. Witness to Britain's moderate approach to treaty enforcement, the French political and military leadership feared facing German *révanche* alone and would no longer take action against Germany without British consent. Simply put, France needed Britain more than Britain needed France, and the power of treaty enforcement, and its reciprocal, treaty modification, had shifted decisively to London. The future course of German disarmament would take a similar path.

Part IV
A new era (1925–1927)

11 Transformation

After the virtual suspension of disarmament operations for twenty months, Allied inspections resumed in earnest in September 1924 with the General Inspection of the state of German armaments. The issues of disarming Germany and withdrawing Allied troops from the Cologne zone of the Rhineland occupation had become enmeshed; the latter became dependent upon the former, with the results of the General Inspection being the decisive factor. Although the General Inspection lasted from 8 September 1924 to 25 January 1925, evidence of violations of the disarmament clauses led the Allies to inform the German government prior to the end of the inspections that they would not withdraw their troops from Cologne in January 1925. This decision bitterly disappointed Germany but the Allies remained solidly unified and intransigent to German protests of the *Allied* violation of the treaty. As the disarmament of Germany entered its sixth year, the same basic questions remained. Was Germany disarmed according to the treaty? If not, had Germany at least complied with the Five Points? Initial results of the General Inspection led the Allies to believe that the answer to both questions was resoundingly negative, and the subsequent General Report would leave no doubts.

Two major elements of the fulfillment of the military clauses of the Treaty of Versailles affected Allied disarmament operations for the remainder of the next two years. The first and most pressing concern was the evacuation of Allied troops from the Cologne zone of the Rhineland occupation. The Allies would have to address German violations of the military clauses of the treaty, and only inspections could verify compliance. The second concern, closely related to the first, was German fulfillment of those provisions of the treaty that the Allies considered essential to German disarmament: the Five Points. In order for the Allies to withdraw the IAMCC from German soil, the German government would have to redress violations of the treaty and then complete the transformation of factories, surrender all excess war material as well as the 1918 inventories, pass laws prohibiting the import and export of war material and binding the organization and recruitment of the army to the treaty, and reorganize the German police. Thus, even as the IAMCC entered its sixth year of existence, only a substantial effort from both the Allies and Germany would resolve the tasks of disarmament.

Cologne and the General Report

The report of the AMCV of December 1924, based on the inspections carried out by the IAMCC, led the Allied governments to inform Germany that their occupation troops stationed in Cologne would not withdraw on 10 January 1925.[1] In predictable fashion, Herriot insisted that the Rhineland was the key to French security while the German government, now led by Chancellor Hans Luther and Foreign Minister Stresemann, denied the validity of reported violations of the military clauses of the treaty.[2] Stresemann, a great advocate of German sovereignty, was outraged, and insisted that the German government had undertaken "considerable efforts" in meeting Allied demands of the Treaty of Versailles.[3] Claiming that the Allied memo of 5 January was "sadistic," Stresemann declared his intention to push energetically for the evacuation of Allied troops from Cologne by 10 January.[4] He believed that Germany had already disarmed and declared the findings of the General Inspection to be trivial. Nonetheless, Allied troops remained on the Rhine, their presence legally justified by German violations of the military clauses of the treaty. For the remainder of the year, Stresemann would negotiate with the Allied governments to remove all Allied soldiers from the Cologne zone of occupation.

The outcome of the General Report of the IAMCC, completed on 15 February 1925, was a foregone conclusion. The report assessed the existing state of the German military from the perspective of armaments, effectives, and fortifications and gave the Allies little indication that the disarmament of Germany would soon come to an end. Allied inspection teams discovered illegal war material (rifles, mortars, explosives, machineguns, and assorted equipment), 30,000 surplus police, and illegal machinery in the plants of Krupp and Deutsche Werke.[5] The Effectives Sub-commission, which uncovered the most egregious treaty infractions in the General Inspection, reported that Germany was preparing cadres of officers and NCOs, enlisting short-term volunteers, training youth in military instruction, recruiting soldiers illegally, and organizing its railways for war. Furthermore, Germany still maintained a General Staff, and many questions remained concerning the existence of illegal paramilitary associations. Inspectors also found violations in Germany's system of fortifications, where the Germans had modified some of their eastern forts and actually constructed new forts on their coastal waters. In addition, Germany had not yet passed any legal measures to prohibit the import or export of war material. The Allies concluded that only strenuous efforts would see to the proper execution of each of the Five Points.[6]

The final conclusion of the IAMCC in the General Report was that

German military power in terms of armaments had experienced some relatively minor increases, but the augmentation of German effectives strength was substantial. This latter increase was especially alarming to the French but Wauchope actually softened Walch's language in the final report and complained that the French were concentrating on rather minor infractions.[7] Nonetheless, the recommendations of the IAMCC left no stone unturned. The IAMCC pointed out that Germany had to reorganize and reduce its police forces, transform all unauthorized factories to peace production, surrender remaining excess war material and the inventories of 1918, pass laws to prohibit the import and export of war material and to reorganize the army according to the treaty, suppress all paramilitary formations, and restore all forts to their previous state. Essentially, the Germans still had to fulfill their obligations to the Five Points as well as address the additional infractions found concerning modifications in the system of fortifications.[8] Overall, the Allies declared that disarmament remained incomplete and that they would continue to occupy Cologne and maintain the IAMCC until Germany met their demands. The fact that German violations increased in the absence of the IAMCC and inspections also did not bode well for enforcing German disarmament in the post-IAMCC era.

Two important diplomatic events also influenced Allied policy toward German disarmament: the twin failures of the Geneva Protocol and the Anglo–French Alliance. In the fall of 1924, Prime Minister MacDonald had attempted to strengthen the League of Nations by proposing an international agreement (the Geneva Protocol) to make war an international crime, uphold the demilitarized Rhineland through the threat of League sanctions, and most importantly, give authority to the League of Nations to settle all future disputes and oversee the reduction of armaments throughout Europe.[9] However, when MacDonald's government fell in November 1924 to Stanley Baldwin and the Conservatives, British policy toward the Geneva Protocol changed dramatically; the Conservatives adamantly opposed the Geneva Protocol on the grounds that it would lead to Britain becoming the "world's policeman."[10] The Foreign Office feared that the impending rejection of the Geneva Protocol would harden French resolve in maintaining Allied troops in Cologne and increasing disarmament demands.[11] In addition, the new British Foreign Secretary, Austen Chamberlain, was anxious to allay French security fears and he lent his support to the creation of an Anglo–French alliance.[12] The Conservatives, however, rejected the Anglo–French alliance and the Geneva Protocol in March 1925. They believed that an Anglo–French alliance would only incense Germany and force her into the hands of the Soviets.[13] Without these new guarantees to their security, the French intensified their insistence on retaining troops in the Rhineland.

For the remainder of 1925, the Allies worked to see that Germany fulfilled its obligations toward the remaining points of disarmament (especially the Five Points) while the Germans worked to oust Allied troops from the Rhineland and the IAMCC from Germany. The IAMCC continued to carry out inspections of German military facilities but they were few and far between.[14] Anglo–French discussions on German rectification of treaty infractions and remaining disarmament tasks proceeded well into the spring. Some British authorities believed that Herriot was attempting to prolong the Cologne occupation to meet French security needs regardless of treaty fulfillment.[15] While Foreign Secretary Chamberlain viewed the Treaty of Versailles from a pragmatic perspective and believed that German defaults of fulfillment of the military clauses justified the prolongation of the Cologne occupation, he also pointed out that the treaty should not be used as a weapon to justify political ends.[16] Although the French were certainly content with maintaining Allied troops in the Rhineland for as long as possible, violations of the military clauses did exist and there had been little, if any, progress toward fulfillment of the Five Points since their enumeration back in the summer of 1922.

In early April 1925, the AMCV drafted a note to the German government listing the points outlined in the General Report.[17] The Allies were no longer content with fulfillment of the Five Points but demanded additional compliance with the infractions discovered by the General Inspection. On 4 June, the Conference of Ambassadors demanded that Germany fulfill the Five Points, rectify various war material issues, and dismantle all modifications to its system of fortifications before the Allies would withdraw their troops from Cologne and consider terminating the responsibilities of the IAMCC.[18] This note formed the new basis of Allied disarmament policy, and the Allies measured subsequent German fulfillment against it. The German government responded initially with exasperation and anger. Chancellor Luther declared that the current state of disarmament already outweighed the importance of fulfilling the remaining Allied demands and did not justify Allied troops remaining in Cologne.[19]

Although Stresemann considered the Allied demands "sadistic," his insatiable desire to effect the withdrawal of Allied troops from Cologne forced the hand of German policy. The German government, believing that the end of disarmament was in sight, made strides to meet Allied demands.[20] When the Germans established the Pawlesz Commission (named after its chief, Major-General Pawlesz) to work in conjunction with the IAMCC in seeing to the execution of Allied demands, the Allies overcame their initial skepticism. This new-found cooperation soon raised hopes of finishing the remaining tasks of disarmament. Despite the slow start and the multitude of tasks to complete, by October, Wauchope was reporting that the IAMCC was actually experiencing steady progress in its operations.[21] The Allied position toward the withdrawal of its occupation soldiers and inspectors remained unchanged for the remainder of 1925 as the Allied governments placed responsibility for the execution of the remaining disarmament points squarely in the hands of the German government. In the fall, Chamberlain emphasized that the evacuation of Cologne depended "solely on the fulfillment of Germany's disarmament obligations."[22] The fact that Germany now cooperated with the IAMCC, after spurning most inspections for the previous two years, filled the Allies, especially Britain, with a sense of accomplishment. In fact, Wauchope claimed that the Germans were cooperating with the IAMCC in an unprecedented fashion. Nonetheless, he still believed that the Allied disarmament of Germany would most likely not be finished before the spring of the following year.[23]

Locarno

Negotiations for a settlement of the issue of disarmament and for a new Western European peace pact had started in the summer and picked up intensity in the fall of 1925. When progress in the fulfillment of the remaining German disarmament obligations resumed in the latter half of the year, a renewed sense of optimism in Allied–German relations took shape. Personal discussions among British, French, and German foreign ministers increased in number and scope, and the bitterness of the past began to recede. Austen Chamberlain, often suspicious of German intentions, brimmed with hope and claimed that disarmament operations were proceeding with great satisfaction.[24] Two reasons account for the visible improvement in Allied–German relations. First, German entreaties in January 1925 for peaceful relations sparked interest in a new settlement in the West. Second, the emergence of the three statesmen – Stresemann, Chamberlain, and Aristide Briand – breathed life into moribund post-war Allied–German relations. Stresemann supported improving relations with the West while turning his eyes toward redressing grievances in the East, and Chamberlain was open to settling remaining issues of the treaty that continued to endanger peaceful relations. Briand, who became France's Foreign Minister in April, supported reconciliation with Germany but not at a price that would sacrifice the security of France. By October, this renewed sense of positivism culminated in the Locarno Conference, where Britain, France, and Germany addressed their post-war concerns and established a new peace settlement in the West. The "spirit of Locarno" had embraced Europe.

The negotiations that took place in Locarno in October 1925 had a significant impact upon the future of the IAMCC and general Allied disarmament operations in Germany. The background to the Locarno Conference had its roots in January 1925, when Germany faced the rumors of an impending Anglo–French alliance, the possible ratification of the Geneva Protocol, and the prolongation of the occupation of the Cologne zone. In order to offset Allied threats to German security and sovereignty, Stresemann proposed a European peace pact.[25] The security pact consisted of a non-aggression agreement between the nations of Germany, France, and

Belgium (with the United States as a hopeful trustee), arbitration treaties between Germany and Western and Eastern European nations, guarantees of the territorial status quo of Germany's western boundaries, and the maintenance of the demilitarized zone of the Rhineland.[26] After the rejection of both the Geneva Protocol and the Anglo–French alliance in March, Chamberlain, hoping to alleviate Herriot's fear of lack of French security and anxious that France might interminably delay evacuation of the Rhineland, suggested to Herriot that they consider Stresemann's peace proposal.[27] Consequently, negotiations between Britain, France, and Germany continued throughout the summer and up until the opening of the conference in October. With the withdrawal of French and Belgian troops from the Ruhr Valley on 31 July, the Allies inaugurated this conciliatory period with the resolution of a divisive issue.[28]

Delegates from the Western European powers arrived in Locarno, Switzerland, in October 1925 with hopes of ensuring international security. The Locarno Conference opened on 5 October, with Germany, France, Britain, Belgium, and Italy in attendance. Locarno, located on the shores of Lake Maggiore in Switzerland, was the ideal setting for the peaceful interludes of the negotiations. Embracing feelings of goodwill, Stresemann, Briand, and Chamberlain developed great admiration for each other. They discussed a number of issues, including disarmament and the Rhineland, and forged a common policy toward Europe with hotel room diplomacy.[29] The atmosphere of the conference, characterized by dinner parties, wine, and cruises on Lake Maggiore, was conducive to the friendly relations that generally persisted throughout the negotiations between the former enemies.

During the second week of the conference, when the agenda focused upon disarmament, Briand and Chamberlain asserted that they would not allow any evacuation of the Rhineland until they witnessed more progress in German fulfillment of the military clauses of the Versailles Treaty. In a meeting on 12 October, both Chamberlain and Briand emphasized that the evacuation of Cologne depended upon fulfillment of Germany's military obligations, not upon the signature of a new pact.[30] Against a united Anglo–French stance, Stresemann was therefore unable to make any progress toward a Cologne evacuation while trying to obviate Germany's numerous military obligations. Stresemann considered Germany to be not just disarmed, but unable to defend itself.[31] While Chamberlain and Briand worked together to rebuff German efforts to modify their disarmament demands, Allied policy toward the disarmament of Germany would never regain the level of unity evident in Locarno.

On 16 October 1925, amidst much pomp and international acclaim, the Allies and Germany signed the Treaties of Locarno, which consisted of four arbitration treaties between Germany and France, Belgium, Poland, and Czechoslovakia as well as the crux of the settlement, a Western security pact. The latter established a reciprocal treaty of non-aggression between the Rhine nations of Germany, France, and Belgium and upheld the demilitarization of the Rhineland under British and Italian guarantees. Although loopholes in the language, combined with future interpretation of the pact, would lead to a paralysis of Allied policy when Hitler re-militarized the Rhineland in 1936, in 1925 the world embraced the Locarno treaties as a major step toward preventing future war in Europe.

Days after the conclusion of the Locarno Conference, the German government produced a report on the status of its fulfillment of Allied disarmament demands. The Germans outlined four major categories of issues, all in various stages of fulfillment.[32] The first three lists were lengthy but included such issues as the transformation of factories to commercial production, surrender of various amounts of war material, prohibition of illegal instruction of reserves, and the organization of railways. The Allies were satisfied with the progress of these relatively minor points, and the Germans assured them that all would be fulfilled by mid-November. The Allies were distressed, however, that Germany considered the police and paramilitary associations to be problematic. The French particularly feared that without a settlement of these two questions, Germany would have the means to re-establish a substantial military force.[33] The Five Points, the tenets of Allied disarmament policy that Germany had to fulfill in order to initiate the withdrawal of Allied disarmament operations from its soil, still remained in suspense.

The Locarno Conference dramatically changed the final course of German disarmament. By allowing the British to use the new era of goodwill as a pretext to abandon overseeing the execution of the military articles of the Treaty of Versailles, the Locarno proceedings had a direct effect upon the subsequent dissolution of the IAMCC. After the conference, Chamberlain asserted in private that the peace of Europe could be guaranteed more effectively through an atmosphere of understanding than by the strict execution of the Treaty of Versailles. This attitude was the antithesis of French policy. Furthermore, Chamberlain pointed out that disarmament had been "fundamentally modified by the initialing of the Locarno treaties" and advocated concessions regarding German police forces and the fortress guns at Königsberg. Years before his brother would establish "appeasement" as a household name, Austen Chamberlain hoped that minor discrepancies between the IAMCC and German authorities "would not be allowed to interfere with the work of appeasement."[34] The Anglo–French effort that had refused concessions to Luther and Stresemann at the Conference now evaporated under "Locarno sunshine."[35]

Within weeks of the conference, Allied disarmament policy toward Germany experienced a great change. The British government, basking in the glow of Locarno, claimed that the new spirit of conciliation that grew out of the conference surpassed the need for strict enforcement of the Treaty of Versailles. The slow but steady erosion of the tenets of Versailles finally gave way to intense hunger for reconciliation with Germany. While

Locarno was initially sweet to the British and French palate, it would eventually leave a bitter aftertaste. Focusing upon the conversion of German war production as the one issue it deemed essential to disarmament, the British government proposed 1 December as the starting date for the withdrawal of Allied troops from Cologne, provided that Germany showed itself willing to comply with the other Allied demands.[36] After the German government stated its *intention* to cooperate, Jules Laroche, the political director of the French Foreign Ministry, and Marshal Foch agreed with the British to begin the evacuation of Cologne. On 14 November, the Conference of Ambassadors officially ruled that the evacuation of Cologne would begin on 1 December.[37] The French had agreed to evacuate Cologne but continued to assert that the IAMCC would continue operations until Germany fulfilled its treaty obligations.[38] However, the physical proof of disarmament was already adrift in the sea of Locarno tranquility.

The Locarno Conference was truly a turning point in the disarmament of Germany. Although the British had been moving steadily toward withdrawing the IAMCC from Germany and were able to coerce the French to accept a number of concessions in the strict enforcement of the Treaty of Versailles, the Conference of Locarno had convinced Austen Chamberlain that the Germans could be trusted after all. Consequently, the intimate gatherings in Chamberlain's hotel suite on the shores of Lake Maggiore that fostered the promise of Germany's good intentions pushed British policy over the hump of appeasement. Chamberlain, the Foreign Office, and the War Office began to preach the same line of policy in unison: Locarno had dramatically changed the political atmosphere in Western Europe and justified granting concessions to Germany at the expense of the Treaty of Versailles.[39] This modified line of British policy would shape all subsequent negotiations and resolutions of the disarmament issues. Following the abandonment of independent action after the Ruhr crisis, the French would be swept along with the British tide.

Sunset of the IAMCC

As the last British, French, and Belgian troops marched out of Cologne and its environs on 31 January 1926, the Allies disassociated the disarmament of Germany from the issue of the occupation of the Rhineland.[40] Despite the prognostication of Allied leaders in Paris in 1919 for a three-month disarmament and fifteen-year Rhineland occupation, the final remnants of military control in Germany would actually outlast Allied troops on the Rhine. At the start of the seventh year of disarmament operations, the Allies and Germany turned their attention exclusively to the remaining points of contention in the hope of terminating disarmament operations. All efforts focused upon the final points of disarmament that continued to elude settlement. The Five Points remained unfulfilled, and a number of other minor infractions continued to pester the French. This final full year of operations would experience painstaking Allied–German negotiations, filled with Allied concessions and German promises. Yet the same issues – the detailed organization of the *Reichswehr* and police, the existence of paramilitary associations and new fortifications, and the passage of legal measures to prohibit the import and export of war material – would outlast the negotiations. The conversion by German factories to commercial production had made huge strides in the past seven years, and without further inspections, the Allies quietly put to rest this particular issue in the aftermath of Locarno.

With the issue of the Cologne evacuation over and the inevitable withdrawal of the IAMCC appearing over the horizon, the French focused upon two major threats to their security. First, despite months of negotiations and the glow of Locarno, the lack of German compliance with questions concerning effectives issues (especially the reorganization of the police and the existence of paramilitary associations) continued to gnaw at the French. Second, the dreadful possibility that the IAMCC would cease operations before the League of Nations acquired the right to investigate Germany's military affairs led the French to believe that the entire work of the IAMCC could be wiped out relatively quickly.[41] The French strategy, therefore, focused on working to ensure German compliance with the remaining points of disarmament (contained in the June 1925 Note). If this effort failed, then they could point out that the lack of fulfillment with Allied demands must preclude the withdrawal of the IAMCC.

One other glaring problem was, of course, convincing the British that the state of Germany's military did not warrant the end of military control. Here the French faced an uphill battle. The German government noticed that the British were attempting to soften French rhetoric and policy.[42] When the Germans blamed the French for delays in settling the disarmament question, the British agreed. Orme Sargent of the British Foreign Office summarized the changing British attitude toward France, Germany, and disarmament succinctly when he asked Wauchope "to prevent disarmament negotiations from being artificially spun out by the ex-allied governments contrary to the wishes of the German government, for the express purpose of creating a pretext for the continued existence of the (Control) Commission."[43] As Allied unity diverged, chances of German fulfillment of the remaining clauses diminished.

While the first three months of disarmament operations in 1926 remained fairly quiet, in April, the police question re-emerged and dominated Allied–German disarmament discussions. The Germans were determined to take advantage of the peaceful interlude after Locarno. Despite the failure to acquire increases in the police force in 1920 and the subsequent Allied allowance for greater numbers of police in the Rhineland (but not overall numbers), Germany requested an increase of 10,000 state police. The British thought the relatively small increase would not disrupt completion of the remaining tasks but Briand stated that the 150,000 authorized police was already a formidable force. The French President and Foreign Minister also feared that another concession would open the floodgates to further German demands for modifications.[44] The general German reaction after the Locarno concessions had already been marked by avarice and raised expectations for more handouts.[45] This was the fatal flaw of appeasement, and Briand refused steadfastly to continue to disfigure the Treaty of Versailles beyond its current transformation. The Allies made no further concessions at this time but the police question, of course, remained unsettled.

In the spring and summer, the Germans continued to exploit the new political atmosphere left in the wake of Locarno. Awaiting word on whether they had been admitted to the League of Nations, the Germans continued to delay any fulfillment of the remaining disarmament issues.[46] The German government believed that admission to the League would force the Allies to replace the IAMCC with League control. Without a backbone for dealing with major diplomatic issues and lacking any post-IAMCC plans to investigate German compliance with the military measures of Versailles, the League of Nations could be swept aside by verbal acquiescence alone. The irony is that both Germany and France supported German admission to the League; Germany hoped membership would eradicate disarmament and occupation, while France saw membership as a means to secure the remaining disarmament of Germany within the League context.

Two battles continued for the remainder of disarmament operations in Germany: the Franco–German fight over fulfillment and the Franco–British struggle over the enforcement of the remaining military shreds of Versailles. The British delegation of the IAMCC, led by General Wauchope, began to appear as an apathetic bystander to the former fight, but as an active participant in the latter, seeking more substantial concessions in the future.[47] Inspections of German facilities by officers of the IAMCC had slowed considerably as the British opposed any visits unrelated to those of the prior General Inspection. The Allies would soon resolve the two conflicts but, with the French hesitant to act independently, the ultimate power of decision was in the hands of the British political and military authorities.[48] The British, however, were still not willing to concede the remaining points of disarmament to the Germans as the presence of a General Staff, excess police, paramilitary associations, illegal enlistment, and the lack of a law to prevent the import and export of war material still raised concerns for some Foreign Office members.[49]

Germany's entry as a full member to the League of Nations in September 1926 had an immediate impact upon disarmament. After Locarno, British attitudes took a prominent turn against France in support of Germany's cries for disarmament modifications. With German admission to the League, however, the British dropped any pretense in supporting the execution of the remaining disarmament issues. To the British, the new

Locarno-induced atmosphere superseded the demands of 4 June 1925 that had replaced the Five Points. The French merely saw written demands replaced by rhetoric. In September, Chamberlain mimicked Stresemann's criticism of disarmament by labeling the IAMCC a "continual source of friction and an obstacle to the policy of mutual reconciliation instituted at Locarno" and he demanded the replacement of the IAMCC with an unspecified system of control under the League of Nations.[50] The Allied effort to disarm Germany was all but finished as Chamberlain now asked whether the remaining points of disarmament that lacked fulfillment constituted a danger to *British* security. The Foreign Office suggested the imminent withdrawal of the IAMCC, and any subsequent disarmament discussions the French wished to continue could be taken up with Germany under the purview of the AMCV.

Briand attempted diligently to offset the lack of British concern toward German militarism in the last few months of 1926. First, he tried to settle Franco–German questions in mid-September by meeting secretly with Stresemann near Geneva in Thoiry. The two heroes of Locarno worked out a political deal to eradicate the Allied occupation of the Rhineland as well as the IAMCC in turn for German economic assistance of France.[51] The French and German governments, however, summarily rejected these grandiose plans. In addition, Briand pushed for the realization of the traditional French policy of security through physical guarantees. In meetings of the League of Nations in December, Briand advocated the institution of a permanent Allied inspection regime in the Rhineland. Despite the guarantee of the Locarno Treaty but under pressure from Stresemann to put an end to the Allied occupation of Germany, Briand hoped to place an Allied civilian body on the Rhine to inspect the state of the German military in the Rhineland and elsewhere in Germany.[52] Stresemann absolutely rejected any notion of permanent inspection in Germany and, without British support, Briand's plans had no chance of success.

When Britain embraced the policy of appeasement after the Locarno Conference, Major-General Wauchope became its prime instrument concerning the disarmament of Germany. Wauchope now urged concessions of all remaining points and worked to bring home the Allied troops as soon as possible. While Wauchope's attitude toward Germany and disarmament in general was similar to Bingham's, the major difference between the two was that Wauchope had the desire, demeanor, and support needed to become a forceful tool of British policy. The new appeaser sought concessions on many points dear to the French, including the police and paramilitary associations.[53] While the French worked to disarm Germany, Wauchope's skills in diplomacy disarmed the French. The British General also had the full support of the Foreign Secretary and, unlike Bingham, the Foreign Office.[54] Chamberlain continued to point out that the peace of Europe depended upon conciliatory relations and not the strict enforcement of Versailles.

French hopes of ensuring the final execution of the remaining disarmament clauses in the fall of 1926 were dimming, as the French faced the two
insurmountable obstacles of German intransigence and British appeasement. The German government paid lip-service to fulfillment while placing
the blame for lack of progress upon the Allies themselves.[55] When Philippe
Berthelot, Secretary of the French Foreign Ministry, admitted that he supported the withdrawal of the IAMCC if Germany fulfilled the remaining
disarmament points, a member of the British Foreign Office insisted that
the very points France considered crucial to security concerns were
"trivial, valueless, and unjustifiable."[56] The Foreign Office, however,
admitted that four major points remained unsettled – illegal enlistment
practices, police organization, laws for prohibiting the import and export
of war material, and paramilitary associations – but even these seemed to
change with the whims and moods of its officials.[57]

Still insisting on the execution of the military clauses of the treaty, the
French refused to agree that only four points remained. The existence of
the General Staff, new forts in Königsberg, and illegal military training
continued to raise the ire of French officials who would not part with the
Versailles Treaty. Briand was unwilling to transfer any military control to
the League of Nations with so many points unsettled.[58] French pleas did
not move the British, who used Locarno and German admission to the
League of Nations as a pretext to support their six-year contention that
Germany was essentially disarmed. Only the question of war material truly
concerned British policy-makers now.[59] The key British officials responsible for German disarmament believed the IAMCC had worn out its
welcome. As far as they were concerned, any points that bothered the
French could be worked out between France and Germany.

In December 1926, the Locarno powers gathered in Geneva to make
one last major effort to settle the remaining points of disarmament.[60]
Chamberlain, Briand, and Stresemann intimately reunited in the hope of
re-creating their success of the previous year. In an attempt to generate the
goodwill of Locarno, Chamberlain held meetings in his room at the Beau
Rivage Hotel.[61] The Allies and Germany hoped to settle the numerous
questions that had been in suspense for some time but there was no real
mystery as to the positions of all those concerned. The British wanted to
pull the IAMCC out of Germany so that the League of Nations, even
without any detailed plans, could take over any investigations of the state
of German military strength. The French still urged Germany to comply
with the litany of Allied demands that stemmed from the military clauses
of the Treaty of Versailles. Germany dug into a policy of delay, hoping
that the Allies would just walk away and allow the League of Nations to
take over an ephemeral form of military control. Many of the points left
over from June 1925, however, were working their way toward resolution.
The Allies had attained some degree of success immediately prior to the
Geneva meetings, and the Conference of Ambassadors relegated a number

of points to secondary importance only. Subsequently, they dropped the issues of the German High Command, coastal defenses, and railway organization.[62]

In Geneva, Europe's leaders focused upon two points: the import and export of war material and the construction of new fortifications in Königsberg. Without hopes of an imminent settlement on the baffling question of war material – officially defining war material and seeing to the German passage of a law to prevent its import and export – the Allies bypassed the issue in order to look at the question of German construction of eastern fortifications. The forts in question were no trivial matter, especially to Foch and Walch, who had previously reported that the Germans had built numerous concrete reinforced forts in eastern Germany.[63] The German government justified the new construction (which continued during the negotiations) on the grounds that the forts were for defensive purposes only and that German forts must be allowed to maintain modern standards.[64] The French, armed with the Treaty of Versailles, opposed any new construction while the British saw no reason to delay the withdrawal of the IAMCC. Briand, however, insisted on some sort of agreement on the final two disarmament issues before allowing the IAMCC to cease functioning in Germany.

On 12 December 1926, the final day of the meetings, a breakthrough produced a settlement that would have far-reaching effects upon the last vestiges of the disarmament and military control of Germany.[65] The Allies and Germany agreed to allow the Conference of Ambassadors to continue to discuss the war material and fortifications issues, and prohibited the construction of all fortifications in Germany until both parties reached a final settlement. More importantly, the Allies ordered the withdrawal of the IAMCC on 31 January 1927, whereupon the Council of the League of Nations would have the authority to resolve any remaining issues of German disarmament. The League had already appointed a Commission of Investigation for German military affairs that could carry out investigations of German establishments in the future but had worked out few details concerning any actual operations.[66] Not yet willing to bestow the League with absolute independent authority in Germany's military affairs, the Allies also decided to attach military experts to their Berlin embassies to help resolve the remaining disarmament issues. The French viewed the possibility of the League of Nations overseeing the state of German military affairs with skepticism and considered the IAMCC and the Conference of Ambassadors to be better suited to the task.[67] However, the pressure from Britain and Germany had been too great to be able to retain the IAMCC any longer. To some degree, the French hoped the experts would try to pick up where the IAMCC left off. Although the experts immediately replaced the IAMCC, their investigative powers and authority were still unknown.

After the December agreement, the IAMCC had six weeks left to try to complete the task of disarmament. The French and British officers of the IAMCC refused simply to relax and enjoy their last few weeks in Berlin. Up until the end, the British emphasis upon eradicating Germany's potential to either produce or import weapons of war was evident as Wauchope wondered whether the League of Nations had enough strength to prevent the German war industry from rising from the ashes. Three important questions remained under the guise of the IAMCC for the final month: the police, war material, and eastern fortifications. The Conference of Ambassadors settled the issue of the size of the German police when Germany signed an accord on 21 December 1926, restricting the overall number of police to 140,000 but conceding the exclusion of forest guards in the overall figure.[68] The other two issues, war material and eastern fortifications, remained unchanged.

The majority of French military officials were horrified at the possibility that Germany might soon be free from Allied military control. They launched futile last-ditch efforts to persuade the decision-makers to change their minds. General Barthélemy, the former French President of the Effectives Sub-commission, complained to a British officer in the Rhineland that Germany was not disarmed and that the progress of the IAMCC had been illusory.[69] At the end of the year, the French Ministry of War produced a dire Morganesque warning of German military prowess that made the work of the IAMCC appear useless. In addition to evidence of hidden stockpiles of war material and the maintenance of experienced cadres, the War Ministry estimated that Germany had upward of six million men and almost half a million officers and NCOs that could be called up, and could easily raise 120 to 150 divisions of shock troops.[70] If such a claim were true, then the seven years of disarmament had failed. However, the numbers were undoubtedly an exaggerated and desperate attempt to keep the IAMCC in Germany, and the French Foreign Ministry considered the report to be inaccurate.[71]

With the wheels in motion to bring the inspectors home, the Allies needed to agree upon a final date of withdrawal. Similar to the task of drafting the General Report in February 1925, the Allied governments had ordered the IAMCC to produce a final report of the state of German disarmament before departing. After realizing the task was complex and extensive, the Conference of Ambassadors allowed the last remnants of the IAMCC to remain in Germany until the end of February 1927.[72] The month-long reprieve would allow the IAMCC time to finish the lengthy assessment of German military strength, which was to be a primer for the incoming experts. Revealingly, Foch indicated that the Final Report would help the Allied military experts whereas Wauchope saw the report as an aid to the League of Nations in its alleged investigative role.[73] The future of German disarmament thus involved three levels: the authority of the Conference of Ambassadors to discuss and rule on the remaining military issues (in consultation with the AMCV), the unspecified role of the experts to enter discussions with the Germans in order to effect a final settlement of Allied disarmament demands, and the investigative power of the League of Nations.

The final weeks of the IAMCC produced no progress toward the settlement of any remaining issues. Discussions on police organization, illegal paramilitary associations, the lack of a law to prohibit the import and export of war material, and the existence of new fortifications in eastern Germany proved futile. The German government hoped the Allied decision to withdraw the IAMCC would lead to a settlement of all issues by the end of January 1927.[74] However, Germany would not comply with Allied demands, and the question of disarmament survived. The inability to resolve the remaining issues even dismayed the optimistic Chamberlain, who could not understand German attitudes following Locarno. Chamberlain took verbal agreements and good intentions at face value, and the inherent defect of appeasement was that it held no place for dishonor and specious motives. Chamberlain admitted privately in mid-January 1927 that Allied concessions to Germany had led merely to more German demands.[75] Just over a decade later, his brother Neville would fail to learn the same lesson. Yet Austen Chamberlain's anger over the lack of progress over the final details of war material and fortifications, or his belief that Germany hoped to reconstitute the *Reichswehr* along nefarious designs, did not allow him to fight the imminent withdrawal of the IAMCC. With regard to the German promises of complete fulfillment of the remaining military clauses of the Versailles Treaty, Chamberlain had gambled on the spirit of Locarno and lost. The disarmament of Germany was in its twilight, and the nurturing rays of "Locarno sunshine" that had given life to a new era of diplomatic trust and friendship faded away as the IAMCC vanished into the shadows.

Part V
Goodbye to all that
(1927–1931)

12 Superficial control

On 31 January 1927, the officers and men of the Inter-Allied Military Control Commission left Germany, seven years after the start of disarmament operations. Thrown into the cauldron of post-war chaos with a complex mission to disarm a twentieth-century power, the IAMCC experienced mixed results, with periods of incredible progress toward the degradation of German military strength intertwined with longer periods of frustrating inactivity. Although the IAMCC did not disarm Germany to all the levels stipulated by the Treaty of Versailles, it successfully accomplished its major tasks of eradicating German armaments, reducing the *Reichswehr* to 100,000 men, and destroying the bulk of German fortifications. The officers responsible for disarmament operations – Nollet, Bingham, Barthélemy, Morgan, Wauchope, and Walch – disappeared from Germany along with the organization that had consumed them over the last number of years.[1] The only task that remained was the production of the final report of the IAMCC. Yet one factor common to both the initiation and withdrawal of the IAMCC was the element of uncertainty over the future course of German disarmament. In fact, in 1927 the Allies faced some of the same problems that the IAMCC faced in 1920. The organization of the German police and existence of paramilitary organizations remained in suspense while new problems, such as the construction of forts in eastern Germany and the continued use of military establishments, were now the responsibility of the untested League of Nations and the embryonic Allied technical experts. The Allies had passed on the torch of disarmament but it was evident to all that the flickering flame was burning out.

Concomitant with the withdrawal of the IAMCC, the Allies and Germany worked out an accord concerning Germany's eastern fortifications, one of the more contentious remaining points of disarmament. Since 1920 Germany had constructed eighty-eight forts, and the British and French had declared any new construction illegal under the Treaty of Versailles. Unable to conduct extensive inspections since the General Inspection, and under British pressure to finalize the work of the IAMCC, the Allies made some significant compromises in the final agreement. The January Accord reiterated the original intentions of the peacemakers of

Versailles by stipulating that Germany maintain the forts on its eastern and southern frontiers in their existing state. Germany could not increase the number or dimensions of the forts and could only carry out simple maintenance and basic upkeep of the structures. The final element of the Accord, which amounted to a significant Allied concession to Germany, allowed Germany to keep fifty-four forts that they had built since the start of disarmament operations.[2] The AMCV worked out the details of the agreement, which represented the last tangible effort produced with the assistance of the IAMCC.

The experts

When the IAMCC withdrew from Germany at the end of January 1927, the question of the role of the League of Nations reappeared even as the Allies still maintained a theoretical form of military control in Germany. In their Geneva meeting of 12 December 1926 the Locarno powers had declared that the League of Nations would assume the responsibility of German disarmament upon the withdrawal of the IAMCC under Article 213 of the Treaty of Versailles. The Council of the League of Nations, however, which assumed the authority to ensure German compliance with Allied disarmament demands and which could order investigations of German violations, did not become involved with German disarmament following the withdrawal of the IAMCC. In fact, following German entrance into the League in September 1926, League control over German armaments was stillborn.[3] Despite continued reports of armaments violations following the withdrawal of the IAMCC, the League never voted to carry out any investigations. The Allied disarmament of Germany remained completely in the hands of the Conference of Ambassadors, AMCV, and the experts, and then disappeared altogether along with these organizations by January 1931.

Despite the intentions of the peacemakers of 1919 to involve the League of Nations in disarmament, the actions of League members in both German and general disarmament never amounted to anything more than speeches, proposals, reports, committees, and commissions. In addition, the seeds planted by the Allies in the Treaty of Versailles and League Covenant in 1919 for a general disarmament of the League's members never bore much fruit. Throughout the 1920s and into the 1930s, the idea that German disarmament would be a prelude to a general disarmament of the League's members found itself adrift in nationalist and security-minded politics. France, in particular, was hesitant to reduce its military capacity and consistently allocated the highest percentage of its gross national product of the Western powers to the military.[4] Instead, the dream of general disarmament was never able to free itself successfully from the multitude of disarmament committees and commissions that dominated the League's agenda.[5]

Although the Allies had decided to transfer authority over German disarmament to the League of Nations upon the withdrawal of the IAMCC,
they had also established the right to station Allied technical military personnel in Berlin to resolve the remaining disarmament issues. Consequently, the Allies created a body of four experts and ordered them to
resolve the problems associated with the Allied demands of 4 June 1925.[6]
The Conference of Ambassadors would be responsible for settling any
decision of the experts that lacked unanimity. After deciding to pay for
their expenses, the Allied governments appointed French Commandant
Durand (Effectives), British Colonel Gosset (Armaments), Italian Colonel
Azzariti (Fortifications), and Belgium Major Pulinx as the experts in
Germany (Japan, never a strong partner in the IAMCC, no longer associated itself with the disarmament of Germany). These four Allied officers
represented the final attempt to enforce the modified military clauses of the
Treaty of Versailles upon Germany, and similar to the IAMCC, their pres-
ence in Germany would be measured not in months, but in years.

The creation of the experts addressed two crucial concerns for the
British and French. First, the need to establish a new body of military
control illustrated the lack of trust and respect that Britain and France had
for the ability of the League of Nations to oversee German disarmament.
While the French were advocates of the League of Nations as one element
of their quest for post-war security, they pushed for the physical presence
of Allied troops that could verify German compliance with disarmament as
another security guarantee. Second, the experts appeared to be the most
expedient solution to continue disarmament efforts through bodies controlled by Britain and France (the Conference of Ambassadors, AMCV, as
well as the experts) without the numbers of Allied inspectors that
affronted German sovereignty. The Allies insisted that the experts were not
a replacement for the IAMCC despite the fact that their organization and
goals were almost identical.[7] For instance, the experts were an Allied body
responsible to the Conference of Ambassadors (often through the AMCV)
for continuing discussions over the former issues of the IAMCC. Allied
leaders hoped that these four officers could negotiate with German officials
and hammer out final settlements of the remaining points. One important
obstacle, though, was whether the experts had the right to carry out
inspections to determine German compliance with Allied demands. The
British, French, and Germans would debate the idea of verification
throughout the period of the experts. In essence, the experts were the
belated implementation of the idea of the Committee of Guarantee that
dominated Anglo–French disarmament discussions in 1922. Yet how could
four officers resolve the same remaining issues where dozens had failed?

The IAMCC completed its Final Report on 28 February 1927 and
entrusted it to the experts as a blueprint for continued disarmament
efforts. The report comprised a comprehensive study of the numerous
accomplishments of the IAMCC. From 1920 to 1927, the Allies had

reduced the German army from about 400,000 to 100,000 men, destroyed huge stocks of war material, abolished compulsory service, converted hundreds of factories from war to commercial production, destroyed a vast network of fortifications, and stopped the import and export of war material. Inspections, especially when supported by the threat of military sanctions, had disarmed Germany. Germany's intent to increase its military strength was obvious, but so was the fact that German military capabilities of conducting modern war had disappeared. The report also added, however, that problems remained, and that Germany continued to violate certain military articles of the Versailles Treaty. These issues included the organization of the German police, use of military establishments, existence of the High Command and paramilitary associations, illegal recruitment and training of the *Reichswehr* and volunteers, and passage of legislation to prohibit the import and export of war material.[8] Given the past history of failed negotiations of the IAMCC over settlements of these same questions, the four Allied technical experts in Berlin assumed complex tasks without the necessary means (the right of comprehensive inspections) of accomplishing them.

After the experts received the litany of mission requirements, the four Allied officers finally met as a group in Berlin on 10 March. Instead of examining one of the problems enumerated by the IAMCC, the experts discussed whether they had any right to visit German establishments to verify compliance with Allied disarmament demands. The Allies wanted specifically to be able to determine whether Germany was fulfilling its promises under the accord reached on 31 January regarding the destruction of a number of eastern fortifications. The German government opposed any inspections of the forts in question and considered its word to be sufficient verification.[9] Within a month, the British Foreign Office refuted the legal right of visitation of the experts and went so far as to oppose any future inspections of the League of Nations.[10] Although the Germans adamantly opposed any inspections by the experts, they did suggest that inspections of fortification destruction in eastern Germany be carried out by an American military attaché; Briand, however, rejected this plan.[11] The French pushed for verification of German compliance but Briand failed to convince Chamberlain or Stresemann of the necessity of inspections. In June, before seeing any progress toward the remaining disarmament issues, the War Office pointed out that the British government supported the withdrawal of the experts as soon as possible but needed at least German verbal acquiescence in fulfillment of the issues that had been outlined in the Final Report of the IAMCC.[12] The major difference between British and French policies toward German disarmament in early 1927 and throughout the era of the experts was that while the former supported verbal promises of German fulfillment, the latter demanded physical evidence.

Allied disarmament efforts first focused upon the issue of whether

Germany had honored its obligations in destroying surplus fortifications under the January Accord. The Accord, a written agreement with specific instructions, could be easily assessed by a few inspections of the forts in question. In May, the Conference of Ambassadors interceded in the ongoing discussions of the right of investigation by insisting on fort inspections. In addition, the Conference added that unless Germany allowed investigations, it would request the League of Nations to carry out necessary inspections.[13] Although Germany professed its support for the transfer of disarmament questions to the League, the German government opposed all future inspections on German soil and hoped that German membership in the League would prevent any talk of investigations. Consequently, the German government began to seek a solution to Allied verification of the fortifications issue.

As Britain's expert, Colonel Gosset sought resolutely to resolve the questions left to him and his colleagues by the IAMCC. Gosset, appointed by Major-General Wauchope for his armaments expertise, was a former IAMCC member. At odds with the Foreign Office, Gosset intended to carry out his duties as prescribed by Marshal Foch's instructions of January 1927. Consequently, in June, Gosset reported that four major disarmament issues remained – Germany's eastern fortifications (verification of the January Accord), police organization (passage of administrative measures by the German states to comply with the stipulations of Versailles), a law to prohibit the import and export of war material, and the illegal use of former *Reichswehr* establishments by the police. He pointed out that the Allies and Germany would soon settle the former three issues but believed that only direct inspections could resolve the fortifications question.[14]

On 16 June, Stresemann informed Chamberlain and Briand that he had decided to allow one or two Allied experts to inspect the fortifications in question to determine whether they had been demolished under the January Accord.[15] Although Stresemann added that this special verification was not to set a precedent for future Allied inspections in Germany, the British and French statesmen agreed with his proposal. Consequently, Commandant Durand and Major Pulinx, the French and Belgian experts respectively, carried out inspections from 4 to 8 July of Germany's eastern forts in Königsberg, Küstrin, and Glogau.[16] These inspections determined that the Germans had fulfilled their obligations under the January Accord, and the Allies formally concluded the issue of Germany's eastern fortifications with the stroke of a pen in July.[17] The Allies also resolved one other important issue. For years, the Allies had pressed Germany to pass legislation to prohibit the import and export of war material, and many technical omissions had delayed Allied satisfaction. However, on 7 July 1927, the Reichstag passed a law forbidding the importation and exportation of war material that satisfied Allied fears of a potential source for augmenting the state of the German military.[18]

Following the successful resolution of the issue of eastern fortifications, Britain and France began to push for the settlement of the other remaining disarmament questions. The fort inspections carried out by Durand and Pulinx illustrated the ease with which problems could be resolved when Germany fulfilled its disarmament obligations and allowed limited Allied inspections.[19] Even the British Foreign Office and Stresemann reluctantly agreed that a limited number of specific inspections could lead to further success and effect the withdrawal of the experts. As a result, in the summer the experts and their German counterparts agreed to a limited number of inspections of German military establishments (mostly barracks), police headquarters, and Rhenish forts.[20] Gosset personally inspected a number of military establishments throughout Germany, including those in Hanover, Leipzig, and Breslau.[21] For the next few months, the inspections by the experts proceeded to satisfy both the Germans and Allies, yet a final settlement of the nagging questions of disarmament remained elusive.

After the initial success of the experts in bringing to a close the fortifications issue and carrying out a small number of inspections, the remainder of Allied disarmament efforts in Germany focused on two major issues: the organization of the German police and the use of German military establishments.[22] Even as the experts entered their second year of duty in Germany, the police question contained many of the problems that had existed since 1920. The Allies still maintained that the German states had to pass laws that prohibited central or federal control of the police forces, stipulated a precise training regimen, and ensured compliance with personnel restrictions. Without a full schedule of inspections, the Allies demanded that Germany surrender budget reports on the police that indicated personnel and administrative matters.[23] In addition, the Allies claimed that Germany was maintaining a surplus of police personnel in former *Reichswehr* barracks (the Allies restricted the number to 35,000) and insisted on German compliance. The Allies also demanded that Germany purge the *Reichswehr*'s military establishments – the barracks, training grounds, administrative offices, army hospitals, weapons depots, and so on – of their military intentions and use them for peaceful purposes only. Hundreds of these establishments existed, particularly on the left bank of the Rhine. There were also minor issues – recruitment, organization of the German railways, military training of youth organizations, surplus war material, and German coastal batteries – that Britain and France continued to discuss with German authorities.[24]

Two major problems in enforcing Allied disarmament demands in the era of the experts were the shifting attitudes of the British toward terminating disarmament operations and the lack of an Allied policy in determining disarmament priorities. In 1927, the British Foreign Office opposed inspections while the War Office favored them in limited numbers. At the start of 1928, however, after witnessing success in some of the remaining points, the War Office considered the continuation of the experts to be a useless and expensive endeavor.[25] Much to the chagrin of the French Foreign Ministry, by May, Chamberlain believed the negative political impact of the experts upon relations with Germany outweighed any benefits of continuing disarmament efforts.[26] Chamberlain urged the reestablishment of normal relations with Germany. The Foreign Secretary pointed out that the British government considered only the issues of the police, military establishments, and Germany's coastal batteries to be important. Chamberlain's proclamations also shed light on the problem in determining the priorities of disarmament.

Both the British and the French believed that the reorganization of the police and the transformation of military establishments were crucial to disarming Germany. However, beyond these two issues, the various British and French departments, as well as the Allied disarmament organizations themselves (the experts, Conference of Ambassadors, and AMCV) seemed to select randomly a few of the remaining disarmament points at various times as "essential" to the completion of Allied efforts in Germany. The lack of a unified Allied policy toward resolving the remaining points led to indecision, uncertainty, and a prolongation of inefficient disarmament operations in Germany. Aside from prioritizing the issues of the German police and military establishments, the half-hearted attempts to attain results simultaneously in numerous issues did not lead to further successes.

The French wanted desperately to find a solution to the organization of the German police before the Allies withdrew the experts from Germany. In the spring and summer of 1928, the French considered withdrawing the experts but only on the condition that Germany satisfactorily resolved the police question.[27] Always concerned with matters regarding German armed personnel, the French pushed for a last set of inspections to determine compliance, but the German government refused all inspections. By July, the British government was ready to consider the immediate withdrawal of the experts from Germany. Even Cambon appeared willing to withdraw the experts in October. The Conference of Ambassadors demanded that Germany take precise measures regarding their police forces and paramilitary associations, and based withdrawal of the experts upon fulfillment.[28] However, a settlement remained elusive.[29]

Despite the Conference of Ambassadors' proposal to withdraw the experts if Germany resolved various disarmament issues, there was very little progress in fulfillment of Allied demands by the end of the year. The issues of the German police and military establishments remained in suspense, and other minor points remained unfulfilled. The Germans were also becoming more hostile to the continuance of the experts. On 20 October, the Mueller government declared that both the government and the people wanted the immediate termination of the experts and that the remaining questions of disarmament were internal issues only.[30] Within weeks, the Conference of Ambassadors renounced any ideas of withdrawing the experts upon completion of the police and military establishment issues and offered a compromise. The Allied delegates asked Germany to allow the experts to make spot inspections of the police and decided to give Germany four years to convert their military establishments into commercial uses.[31] But Foch opposed withdrawing the experts and declared that it would be impossible to inform the League of Nations that Germany was disarmed.[32] The Marshal was particularly angry that Allied concessions elicited only German refusal of inspections and denial of violations.[33] At this point, the British considered withdrawing their expert regardless of any common policy with the French.[34]

In December, the British Committee of Imperial Defense, emboldened by a recent *Times* article by Morgan and a War Office report, created a rather sensational stir in British military circles when it claimed that Germany was disarmed but would soon strive to become a European military power.[35] Winston Churchill, the current British Chancellor of the Exchequer, was unruffled by the claims and put his trust in the French army to counteract any German aggressive tendencies. Clearly, though, the British military still harbored some reservations about the state of German disarmament. Before the year was over, the Conference of Ambassadors expressed its disappointment with the German government by pointing out that the issues of the police and military establishments lacked fulfillment.[36] With numerous disarmament issues still in suspense, the four experts remained entrenched in Berlin, working feverishly with the German authorities to resolve the long-standing disarmament questions, and longing for home.

The end of the road

In the last days of winter, on 20 March 1929, while the experts pressed for the completion of the remaining points of disarmament, Marshal Ferdinand Foch passed away quietly in his house in Paris.[37] Foch had been one of the most vociferous proponents of enforcing the military clauses of Versailles, and as the feisty head of the Allied Military Committee of Versailles he had clashed with both French and British political and military authorities. While the authority and prestige of Foch could not be equaled, French General Baratier assumed his role on the AMCV. The consummate thorn in the German side, first as the glorious Commander-in-Chief of the Allied and Associated powers at the end of World War I and then as military adviser to the Conference of Ambassadors throughout the 1920s, was gone; the AMCV would soon meet the same fate.

The experts continued to discuss possible disarmament solutions with German military authorities throughout 1929. For the first half of the year, the AMCV and the Conference of Ambassadors allowed the experts to handle the difficulties alone. In fact, the Conference of Ambassadors met only twice during the entire year, and progress toward settling disarmament was disappearing altogether. To make matters worse, the French were even reporting new violations of the military clauses of the Versailles Treaty, no matter how small the infractions.[38] One particularly bold attempt by Germany to circumvent Allied demands included the use of receipts from the sale of military establishments (ostensibly to convert them into peaceful installations) to construct more modern versions.[39] Gosset considered German violations to be trivial but, despite his lack of consent, the experts reported to the AMCV that Germany possessed illegal war material and was organizing paramilitary forces on its eastern frontier.[40] All the AMCV could do was pass the information to the Conference of Ambassadors, which in turn would send a note to the German government demanding changes. The cycle was monotonous, and at this stage of disarmament, useless. Without the right of inspection, which both the British and the French agreed they lacked, and without German compliance, Allied efforts to complete the last points of disarmament were futile.

Allied enforcement of the disarmament clauses of the Treaty of Versailles was obviously winding down as governments and political conditions changed. The inauguration of a new Labour government in Britain under Ramsay MacDonald, with Arthur Henderson as Foreign Secretary, dramatically altered Britain's policy toward the Rhineland but had little effect upon German disarmament.[41] In France, governments continued to change but the Foreign Ministry remained stable under the guidance of Aristide Briand. While the four experts tried to settle the remaining disarmament issues, the political authorities began to reflect upon the history of disarmament. Harold Nicolson, a member of the Central Department of the Foreign Office, believed that true enforcement of the disarmament clauses of Versailles could be attained only through military force. Since neither Britain nor France were willing to threaten military sanctions to enforce the Versailles Treaty, Nicolson resigned himself to acquiescence.[42] Even Colonel Gosset admitted that withdrawing the IAMCC had deprived the Allies of the only truly effective means of supervising the state of the German military. Like Nicolson, he questioned whether the Allies had the gumption to enforce sanctions against German violations.[43] General Baratier simply indicated that the withdrawal of the experts would leave the job of disarmament incomplete.[44]

By the fall, the presence of the experts was becoming difficult to justify. The British and French had previously agreed that they had no legal right to investigate German military affairs, and negotiations were making little headway. The British were pushing for the withdrawal of the experts, but after threatening to pull Gosset out regardless of any agreement with the French, the MacDonald government agreed to maintain their expert with the others. The Foreign Office resigned itself to a pessimistic outcome and believed that France would find excuses for retaining its expert in Germany interminably; it came to the realization that the entire disarmament question would never be settled satisfactorily.[45] Publicly, the Allies did not give up hope, and they sent a joint note to the German government in November requesting negotiations to settle all outstanding military questions.[46] But the outcome of the note was obvious. Almost a decade after the Treaty of Versailles had come into effect, enforcement had become a mere shadow of its former self. With no authority behind Allied demands, and without the slightest chance of sanctions, the incentive for German fulfillment had disappeared altogether. The hope that the good-will of Locarno would spill over in the following years of European diplomacy had been naive. The Allies instead began to discuss a withdrawal date for the experts.

French and German representatives made one final attempt at the start of the new decade to settle the police and military establishment questions. The intense discussions bore fruit. On 10 January 1930, exactly one decade after the Allies officially embarked upon a crusade to disarm the German military, the Allies signed an agreement with Germany to terminate the mission of the experts. Given the struggle over negotiations regarding the outstanding final points of disarmament, the settlement came suddenly. The German government agreed to organize all state police forces according to the Prussian model (Prussia had the largest force and had been the first to organize its police along the lines of Article 162 of the Versailles Treaty) and promised either to destroy all excess military establishments or convert them to peaceful purposes by the end of May 1930.[47] Acting as an observer, the British government supported the accord and agreed to uphold its principles. The lack of a British signature, however, would later have an impact upon the French attempt to resolve the remaining issues of disarmament in concert.

Nine days after the signing of the January agreement, the Allies decided to withdraw the experts. Briand informed the German government that the Allies would terminate the mission of the experts on 31 January, whereupon they would hand over all further disarmament discussions to the Conference of Ambassadors.[48] Thus, disarmament was not yet complete, but the Allies had resolved the two issues that had frustrated the experts – the German police and military establishments. The experts remained in Germany for a few months to draw up a final report but their official capacity was over.[49] Unlike most decisions made by the Conference of Ambassadors, AMCV, or the IAMCC, the Allies negotiated with the German government to sign the January agreement. The agreement theoretically resolved the two major remaining issues and was the last success the Allies could hope to achieve. The problem that remained, of course, was Germany's willingness to comply with the agreement without any Allied will to enforce it.

The activities of the Conference of Ambassadors and its loyal advisory body, the AMCV, had diminished significantly in the early months of 1930. The AMCV, created to deal with military questions only, became expendable with the termination of the experts. In January, the Conference of Ambassadors decided to terminate the AMCV when the experts handed their Final Report to the League of Nations.[50] Yet the AMCV did not spend its remaining time quietly awaiting its departure. Dominated by French policy under Foch's replacement, General Baratier, the AMCV attempted to reintroduce the issue of inspections to verify German compliance with the 10 January Accord. Although the effort failed, the AMCV, and even Briand, continued to point out that police reorganization and the transformation of military establishments remained unfulfilled.[51] The question that remained was how the Allies intended to enforce the final vestiges of the disarmament clauses of Versailles.

In May 1930, the British put an end to all French hopes of maintaining an Allied nature to the completion of German disarmament. The British government severed its relationship to German disarmament in any official capacity by no longer recognizing the authority of the Conference of Ambassadors or the AMCV.[52] The Conference of Ambassadors had met only irregularly over the last two years and by 1930 was no longer involved substantially with German disarmament. The AMCV, on the other hand, continued to find German violations of previous Allied disarmament demands. The MacDonald government justified its disassociation with these formerly Allied bodies by claiming that Britain did not sign the agreement of 10 January and that it was strictly a Franco–German affair. Thus, Britain believed that any disarmament problems which concerned the French should be worked out between the French and German governments. The British still maintained representatives on the AMCV and the Conference of Ambassadors but their roles were not constructive. In fact, the British government instructed its representative on the AMCV not to sign reports critical of Germany.[53] Allied enforcement of the remaining elements of the disarmament clauses of the Treaty of Versailles was dead, although the British government did point out that it would honor previous agreements.[54] Ironically, Britain had to indicate its willingness to honor agreements on the anniversary of the signing of the Treaty of Versailles, an agreement that Britain did not honor in its entirety.

French military and political authorities refused to give up on the execution of German disarmament. Under British pressure to dissolve the AMCV, the French sought to exert their influence over any future international efforts needed to observe German compliance with the disarmament clauses of the Treaty of Versailles. Fears of German rearmament, fueled by years of violations of the military clauses of the Treaty of Versailles, continued to shape French foreign policy.[55] In December 1930, the French War Ministry introduced a proposal to create a substitute for the French section of the AMCV.[56] With the imminent dissolution of the AMCV, the French hoped to maintain a grasp on the outstanding military clauses of Versailles. The original proposal included the creation of a French military advisory body to the Conference of Ambassadors that precluded any Allied nature. Since the Conference of Ambassadors was still officially an Allied body, the French hoped to influence German disarmament through collective action. Thus, the goal of the new organization was to exert French authority over possible international action against Germany. The French General Staff feared that the lack of a military advisory body to the Conference of Ambassadors would leave the remaining disarmament points permanently unsettled and could lead to more German military violations in the future. However, the French did not have an abundance of time to plug the gap that would soon be left by the AMCV's departure. On 4 December, after adding its own observations, the AMCV sent the Final Report of the experts to the Conference of Ambassadors.[57]

By the end of the year, the French Foreign Ministry was convinced that the existence of the AMCV could not be prolonged. Without support from the other member nations, especially Britain, the Quai d'Orsay agreed with the Ministry of War to establish a French substitute for the AMCV.[58] The Foreign Ministry pointed out that a new military advisory body, working in conjunction with the Conference of Ambassadors, would allow at least a minimum of inter-Allied collaboration. In addition, the advisory role of the new organization would facilitate any potential future inspections of the state of the German military ordered by the Council of the League of Nations. Throughout the winter of 1931, the French ministries discussed the new organization and modified its title and overall mission.[59] Briand insisted on the confidentiality of the new organization after the British responded to its creation with distaste.[60] Both the British War Office and Foreign Office were afraid that the French would establish a monopoly of authority concerning German disarmament.[61] The British agreed that some points of disarmament remained, such as police organization, military establishments, and paramilitary associations, but were not willing to take any steps to settle them. In fact, the British hoped to reduce the critical aspects of the Conference of Ambassadors' final note to the League of Nations. Although Britain no longer enforced the military clauses of Versailles they continued to exert their influence to reduce the severity of French actions.

In March 1931, the French reached a final agreement on their new military advisory organization when the new Minister of War, General André Maginot, established the *Section Militaire d'étude des Traités* under General Baratier. The *Section Militaire* was to resolve all unsettled points of disarmament, act as technical adviser to the Conference of Ambassadors, maintain the archives of the IAMCC and AMCV, study German breaches of the military clauses of the post-war treaties (with an emphasis on Versailles), work with the military representatives of the other member nations of the Conference of Ambassadors, and prepare reports for possible investigations of the state of Germany's military.[62] Essentially, the new organization was another AMCV, without the bothersome opposition of Allied representatives but lacking international credibility.

The meetings of the Conference of Ambassadors had become all too infrequent in 1929 and 1930, and failed to produce any positive results concerning German fulfillment of the military clauses of the Treaty of Versailles. With the desire of the British government to transfer all authority to the Council of the League of Nations, the Conference was nearing the end. The withdrawal of the IAMCC, the experts, and the imminent disbanding of the AMCV clearly marked the inevitable path toward the dissolution of the Conference of Ambassadors. The Conference maintained that Germany had not yet fulfilled certain military clauses – the distribution, training, and housing of police, transformation of military establishments, illegal *Reichswehr* enlistment, and the existence of paramilitary associations – but took no action to rectify the ongoing situation.[63] The once powerful and authoritative voice of the war's victors was now but a hoarse whisper.

On 16 March 1931, after the Conference of Ambassadors sent the Final Report of the experts to the League of Nations and adjourned for one final meeting, the Allies dissolved the AMCV.[64] As its final act, the Conference of Ambassadors attached a note to the Final Report illustrating the lack of German compliance with the remaining points of disarmament but pointing out that it no longer had authority to preside over such matters.[65] These points, debated with little progress over the last few years of Allied disarmament efforts, included the organization of the German police, the transformation of military establishments, illegal recruitment practices of the *Reichswehr*, and the existence of paramilitary associations. The same old issues were now officially in the hands of the League of Nations. With this transference of authority, the Conference of Ambassadors disappeared along with any further enforcement of disarmament. Eleven years after the Treaty of Versailles went into effect, the Allied organizations responsible for the disarmament of Germany were gone, but the problems concerning the lack of German compliance with certain points of disarmament were not. As the Conference of Ambassadors faded away in obsolescence, reports of German disarmament violations continued to clutter the desks of both British and French military officials.[66] The quest for world disarmament lay ahead. The Allied disarmament of Germany was over.

13 Conclusion

Similar to calculations for a brief period of fighting in World War I, Allied expectations for a short period of disarmament became mired in a diplomatic version of trench warfare. While the combatants of August 1914 thought they would celebrate victory by Christmas, Britain and France originally hoped that they could withdraw the IAMCC after a few months of inspections. The complexity of the Allied disarmament of Germany, however, went far beyond the original expectations of Britain or France. Disarmament on such a massive scale was unprecedented. Given the scope and logistics of Allied operations, as well as the plethora of international issues at the end of the war, the Allied notion to complete the demilitarization of Germany in a matter of months was unrealistic. The destruction of armaments and fortifications, as well as the definition of war material, the transformation of industries to commercial production, and the passage of laws to prohibit the import and export of war material and to reorganize the *Reichswehr*, were just a few of the numerous points of disarmament that required clarification, discussion, and enforcement. Consequently, the Allies developed disarmament strategies and operations within the context of emerging difficulties, and the resulting Anglo–French decisions ultimately disarmed Germany without the strict enforcement of the Treaty of Versailles.

The disarmament of Germany arose in the aftermath of World War I and remained a focal point in Anglo–French relations for over a decade. Despite differences, Britain and France agreed initially that disarming Germany was a priority in the search for peace and stability. They disagreed, however, on how best to disarm Germany and to what extent. Drafting a peace settlement was difficult enough, but enforcing the treaty after such a devastating war presented the Allies with an enormous challenge. Post-war tensions and bitterness, fueled by the loss of a generation of young men, created an environment hostile to success. Disparate British and French conceptions of a post-war Europe (the balance of power versus European hegemony and security) exacerbated the difficulties of enforcing the military articles of the treaty. Yet Allied disarmament operations, though far from perfect, were able to survive for eleven years to destroy the capabilities of the powerful German military. In assessing the British and French roles in the disarmament of Germany, three major conclusions may be drawn: divergent disarmament priorities dramatically influenced overall operations, Britain was the dominant partner in determining the direction of Allied policy, and the Allies successfully destroyed German military strength, most effectively through a united policy backed by military sanctions.

Divergent Anglo–French policies

The divergence of British and French opinion over the most effective means of disarming Germany influenced the development and enforcement of Allied disarmament policy. Britain defined disarmament as the destruction of German armaments whereas the French definition encompassed the fulfillment of all the military clauses but centered upon the effectives question. From the inception of the military elements of the treaty at the Paris Peace Conference until the final withdrawal of Allied soldiers, Britain focused upon the destruction of German armaments and munitions, as well as the demilitarization of German industry, as the most effective means to disarm the most powerful industrial military complex in the world. As early as 1919, Lloyd George emerged as a decisive influence in pushing for the destruction of German armaments and industrial capability to manufacture war material. His forceful and successful personal intervention was not just evident at the Paris Peace Conference (where the Allies also appointed a British general as President of the Armaments Sub-commission), but at the Spa Conference in July 1920 when the Prime Minister demanded a report on German armaments from General von Seeckt and then severely chastised the German government for the amount of remaining war material in the country. At the London Conference in August 1922, Lloyd George further pointed out that the destruction of armaments had left Germany militarily prostrate.

Most British military and political authorities placed a priority upon the destruction of German armaments. The British Secretary of War in Lloyd George's Cabinet, Winston Churchill, agreed wholeheartedly that the destruction of German machines and factories was the best guarantee of disarmament. As a former officer in the Ministry of Munitions, Major-General Bingham based effective disarmament upon the eradication of German war material and the demilitarization of her armaments factories. From the beginning of Allied operations, Bingham considered the destruction of German artillery to be a "matter of urgency."[1] Bingham supported treaty modification through concessions but was responsible for the work of the Armaments Sub-commission when the Allies witnessed the destruction of massive amounts of German war material. As early as July 1920, Bingham reported that the IAMCC had eradicated most of Germany's guns, and within months the British government entertained ideas about replacing the IAMCC. But British interest in the armaments question did not disappear. The presence of an essentially British group of officers in the giant complex of Krupp from 1920 to 1926, and General Wauchope's emphasis upon the need to prohibit the import and export of German war material from 1923 to 1926, lend credence to the continued priority the British placed on controlling German armaments.

With the armaments question essentially settled by 1921, Britain became more aloof to enforcement and considered many of the remaining military articles of the treaty irrelevant to successful disarmament. Hoping to withdraw the IAMCC from Germany in turn for the fulfillment of the Five Points, the British alienated themselves from the French insistence upon fulfillment of all the disarmament demands and began to advocate general leniency in enforcing the remainder of the military clauses. Only serious German evasions of the military clauses of the treaty, most notably in May 1921 and January 1925, re-established at least temporary Anglo–French unity. By the end of 1925, however, Austen Chamberlain, the Foreign Office, and the War Office considered the disarmament section of the Treaty of Versailles to be an anachronism.

French political and military authorities looked to the enforcement of the entire treaty to ensure security. They considered every article of the Treaty of Versailles, but especially the disarmament of Germany, to be crucial to the safety of French sovereignty. Throughout the work of the IAMCC and into the era of the experts, Marshal Foch and Generals Nollet and Walch insisted that Germany fulfill its military obligations before they would consider the withdrawal of Allied disarmament organizations from Germany. Although by 1922 the French had relinquished any effective means to enforce all the military clauses of the treaty by accepting the British conception that only the Five Points remained, they never abandoned the hope to enforce all the Allied military demands upon Germany. As long as Allied troops remained in Germany, the French authorities believed that complete German disarmament was possible.

Within the context of the total enforcement of the Versailles Treaty, the French were particularly intent upon German fulfillment of the effectives clauses of the treaty. The fact that France had recently suffered the highest proportional losses of any of the great powers in the war and had a significantly smaller population than Germany led French political and military leaders to emphasize German military potential in terms of the superior manpower that Germany possessed. General Nollet hoped the demilitarization of Germany would morally disarm the population and, when it failed to do so, the French demanded physical disarmament. Thus, the French consistently advocated the reduction of the *Reichswehr* and police, and the eradication of the paramilitary associations as necessary steps in the Allied effort to demilitarize the most urgent German threat of military force. However, the British, never as concerned about the effectives question as the French, considered doubling the size of the German army to combat Bolshevism in February 1920, increasing the size of the German urban police in July 1922, and were often soft on the existence of German paramilitary organizations.

The French emphasis on the effectives question was apparent throughout German disarmament. As early as March 1919, at the Paris Peace Conference, Clemenceau and Foch effectively negated Germany's manpower potential by demanding that the German army be limited to only 100,000 troops. A single line in the Versailles Treaty therefore reduced the powerful German army proportionally to one of the smallest military forces in Europe. Five months after the German government failed to convince the Allies to double the size of its army at the Spa Conference in July 1920, Allied inspectors reported that the *Reichswehr* numbered about 100,000 troops. Similar to the enforcement of the major armaments clauses, a year of Allied disarmament efforts had crippled the German army, but a significant difference appeared between British and French reactions to such progress. Whereas the British considered the issues of armaments and the reduction of the *Reichswehr* finished by the end of 1920 and started to withdraw from their treaty commitments, the French insisted upon the complete compliance with the treaty and emphasized the reduction of the police, eradication of paramilitary associations, and reorganization of the 100,000-man *Reichswehr*. British evaluations of disarmament, with the exception of Morgan, often pointed to past successes of the IAMCC while the French, especially Foch and Nollet, instead looked ahead to the points of disarmament that remained unfulfilled. The French remained highly sensitive to effectives issues, especially the organization of the *Reichswehr* and police and the existence of paramilitary organizations, until the end of Allied disarmament operations.

British dominance

Since Britain and France had done most of the fighting on the Western Front and emerged from the war as Europe's predominant powers, they eagerly inherited the responsibility and authority to determine the shape of a new Europe. The development and course of German disarmament was essentially an Anglo–French affair, with Britain becoming the dominant partner. Although Italy, Belgium, and Japan had representatives on the Conference of Ambassadors, the Allied Military Committee of Versailles, and the Inter-Allied Military Control Commission, they rarely played any decisive role in disarmament affairs except to side with either Britain or France. The United States, a crucial player in the drafting of the peace settlement, had only a temporary advisory role.

Modifications to the military clauses of the Treaty of Versailles as early as 1920 established a crack in the rigid foundations of the French policy of total enforcement, and from 1925 onward the British policy of appeasement turned the crack into a fatal fissure. Abandoning the complete enforcement of the military clauses of the treaty undermined the original French position and allowed for the successful implementation of the British concept of a disarmed Germany. The formal signing of the treaty justified strict enforcement but French misgivings to act independently proved too strong. France never recovered from its terrible ordeal in the war when only Britain, Russia, and the United States allowed it to remain free from German domination. Consequently, French political and military leadership decided that acquiescence to British disarmament schemes and the consequent maintenance of the tacit Anglo–French alliance addressed the issue of security more than the complete execution of the Treaty of Versailles and the loss of support against possible German aggression. Instead of establishing itself as the pre-eminent European power after the defeat of Germany, France sanctioned British modification to the Treaty of Versailles and thus resigned itself to a future of diplomatic acquiescence that lasted until the eruption of hostilities in 1939.

French submission to British policy allowed the seeds of appeasement to take root in 1920 and bloom in the fertile ground of Locarno. Although the first modifications of the disarmament clauses of the treaty were Anglo–French decisions in face of German non-fulfillment, specifically the decision to extend the period of reducing the *Reichswehr* to 100,000 soldiers in July 1920 at the Spa Conference, Britain soon followed an independent course. The first signs of Britain's willingness to modify the military clauses of the treaty without regard to French wishes occurred a year after Spa, when British military and political authorities believed they had disarmed Germany and advocated replacing the IAMCC with a smaller Allied organization. In January 1921, Lloyd George agreed with his close adviser, Philip Kerr, that disarmament was open to modification. Although the French continued to demand German fulfillment of all the disarmament clauses of the treaty, they accepted the British conception of the Five Points and the Committee of Guarantee in 1922. This change of heart abandoned the complete enforcement of the treaty to modification and weakened German motivation in fulfilling other disarmament aspects of the treaty. The French had sacrificed the policy of strict enforcement on the altar of Allied unity.

The French desire for British support to meet their quest for security against Germany was not reciprocal. The enforcement of disarmament shifted decisively to London during the Ruhr occupation and remained dominated by British policy until the termination of operations. As early as March 1922, after the British rejected the French hope to apply military sanctions against Germany for lack of treaty fulfillment, Raymond Poincaré urged his ambassadors to work with the British regarding disarmament operations. This need for common action subordinated the French to British policy. For example, in April 1923, when the French tried to force the resumption of Allied inspections and threatened to take independent action, British insistence in suspending all Allied inspections forced the

French to back down, thereby revealing the emptiness of the French threat and the fear of acting without British support. In November, the French threat to occupy Hamburg or Frankfurt if Germany refused to allow inspections and the return of the ex-Crown Prince to Germany resulted in Britain threatening to withdraw from the Conference of Ambassadors and the Control Commissions; consequently, France dropped the idea of any additional independent occupation of German territory. By December 1923, the French accepted the British idea of partial control and agreed reluctantly that all inspections had to be made with discretion. General Bingham's rejection of French wishes to enforce sanctions in case of German evasion of the military clauses in January 1924 rendered the IAMCC powerless to act without British support. This is precisely what Britain foresaw when it insisted in November 1923 that the IAMCC could act only through the unanimous consent of all its members. France, punished for its Ruhr indiscretion, subsequently had to witness almost two years of negligible disarmament results.

British policy toward German disarmament vacillated in response to serious German treaty evasions but continued to determine the direction of the Allied disarmament of Germany from 1921 until the end of operations. Britain advocated moderation after the first year of disarmament operations but the Locarno treaties and German membership in the League of Nations justified appeasement. After all, since the crux of the Locarno treaties pledged Britain to support France in case of German aggression, why should the Allies need to continue to disarm Germany so strictly? Only weeks after Chamberlain and Briand stood their ground against Stresemann's attempts to obtain evacuation of Cologne without fulfillment of the military clauses in October 1925, Chamberlain accepted German promises of fulfillment as actual compliance. The French buckled under the loss of support for treaty enforcement and assented to British demands.

When Germany joined the League of Nations in September 1926, the British Foreign Office referred to the remaining points of German disarmament as "trivial, valueless, and unjustifiable."[2] Chamberlain now openly doubted their relevance to British security. After the withdrawal of the IAMCC, the experts were able to attain some degree of progress toward the issues of fortifications and police despite the fact that the British government had withdrawn its active and effective participation with disarmament operations, and even obstructed progress by denying the validity of inspections. In mid-July 1928, Chamberlain claimed that the existence of the experts prevented the establishment of normal diplomatic relations with Germany and pushed for their withdrawal. After the dissolution of the experts in May 1930, Britain severed official ties with the Conference of Ambassadors and the AMCV, effectively terminating the Allied disarmament of Germany. As the experts, Conference of Ambassadors, and Allied Military Committee of Versailles faded quietly away by January 1931, any hopes of disarming Germany strictly under the Treaty of Versailles died with them. The French had traded the enforcement of the Treaty of Versailles for the maintenance of a semblance of the Anglo–French entente of 1914 to 1918. As a result, Allied disarmament operations disappeared before the complete enforcement of the military clauses of the Versailles Treaty, and the Allies ultimately disarmed Germany under British conditions.

Assessing Allied disarmament operations

Despite the scope and complexity involved in enforcing the military clauses of the Treaty of Versailles, the Allies were able to disarm Germany with a great amount of success. The size and offensive capability of the German army in 1918 presented formidable challenges to Allied disarmament efforts, yet the final results of the work of the IAMCC were impressive. At the start of disarmament operations, Germany had an army of approximately 400,000 men, huge stocks of war material, thousands of factories involved in military production, and an extensive fortress system. By 1927, when the IAMCC ceased to function, Allied inspections had verified the destruction of the stockpiles of armaments, the reduction of the German army to 100,000 troops, the transformation of German military production, and the dismantling of the German system of fortifications. Allied disarmament operations had eradicated Germany's modern military strength by destroying thousands of artillery pieces and mortars, tens of thousands of machine-guns, and millions of rifles, small arms, and rounds of ammunition. General von Seeckt, the mastermind of effectives violations, knew that Germany could never survive an Allied attack without an army equipped with a modern arsenal of weapons.[3] The German army had become a small defensive force, lacking the size and armaments to fight its former adversaries and new neighbors. The Allies had also forced Germany to retool her war industries and left her borders without a significant network of fortresses and defensive works. Although Britain and France never enforced all the military clauses of the treaty – especially those concerning the German police and other organizational manpower issues – the IAMCC and its inspectors from 1920 to 1927 had destroyed Germany's ability to wage a modern war.

With a team of four experts, the Allies successfully resolved some of the less pressing issues of disarmament from 1927 to 1931. In this final period of Allied disarmament operations, the Allies forced Germany to pass a law forbidding the importation and exportation of war material, dismantle a number of illegal eastern forts, and agree to reorganize its state police forces. Only minor problems, such as the use of military establishments and the existence of some paramilitary units, remained when the Allies finally disbanded the Conference of Ambassadors, AMCV, and experts in 1931.

The IAMCC experienced its greatest period of success from the start of operations in 1920 to the beginning of 1921, after the progress exacted by the Spa Protocol. During this period, the IAMCC witnessed the surrender or destruction of over 80 percent of the total armaments that Germany would ultimately surrender or destroy.[4] In addition, inspectors ascertained that Germany had reduced the *Reichswehr* to approximately 100,000 troops and dismantled most of its fortifications network. The remaining years of Allied disarmament efforts essentially focused on verifying that Germany remained at these levels and enforcing the less important remaining points of disarmament that Germany steadfastly refused to fulfill. The British assessment in 1922 that the Allies had disarmed Germany, therefore, was accurate to a point: Germany had no real offensive capability but still had not complied with the details of the Treaty of Versailles.

The Allied enforcement of all three elements of disarmament – armaments, effectives, and fortifications – experienced varying degrees of success. Both the British and French agreed that Allied inspections verified almost complete German compliance with the armaments clauses of the treaty. The IAMCC in its Final Report in 1927 considered the armaments question resolved. In essence, the destruction of war material ceased to be a major Allied concern following eighteen months of IAMCC operations. But the illegal production and export of war material and discoveries of weapons caches continued the need for Allied vigilance and indicated that German fulfillment of the armaments clauses was never completely satisfactory. Allied prognostications regarding the impact of the enforcement of the armaments clauses were also never wholly reassuring. Because the Germans refused to turn over an accurate inventory of war material at the beginning of disarmament operations, the Allies had to rely on the best assessments of IAMCC and intelligence officers stationed in Germany. Nonetheless, two of the biggest skeptics involved in disarming Germany – Nollet and Morgan – believed that the Allies had all but destroyed Germany's armaments, particularly her heavy artillery.[5]

The multifaceted nature of the effectives question made it the most difficult to enforce. Unlike the armaments question, the French were never satisfied with Allied progress in reducing German armed personnel. General Nollet, Marshal Foch, and French military intelligence, along with Brigadier-General Morgan, uncovered many surplus German military formations, reserves, and associations. Inspectors could easily verify the destruction of guns, shells, and fortified works but, short of constant surveillance or even armed conflict, there was no similar method that could be used to assess the potential threat of German military personnel. The Allies placed severe restrictions upon the size and organization of the German army and police forces, and hoped to dissolve the paramilitary organizations altogether. Enforcing the effectives clauses was thus a lengthy and arduous process. Despite German obstruction and General von Seeckt's attempts to establish German cadres for the future, the pervasive character of the work of Allied inspections rendered the German army little more than a domestic police force. By the beginning of 1921, after Britain and France strengthened treaty enforcement through the threat of military sanctions, the IAMCC had reduced the German army to 100,000 troops, though the excess numbers of officers and the existence of a High Command continued to plague Allied efforts until the end of operations. By the time the Allies withdrew from Germany in 1931, they had also reduced and reorganized the German police forces and eradicated most of the organized paramilitary forces in Germany.

Allied disarmament operations concerning the destruction of German fortifications were initially a complete success. Progress in dismantling the massive German network of fortifications, from the concrete bunkers in the Rhineland to the coastal forts around Königsberg, led to the dissolution of the Fortifications Sub-commission in February 1922. When the British and French later discovered the construction of illegal German forts in East Prussia, however, they allowed Germany to retain a number of them simply because the Allies never viewed German defenses, especially those in the east, as a serious threat to their security. Instead the Allies wished to settle the remaining armaments and effectives questions, which raised the more important possibility of offensive German operations.

Much of the credit for successfully disarming Germany belongs to the Inter-Allied Military Control Commission and especially its teams of inspectors, who worked feverishly to disarm Germany in an atmosphere fraught with obstruction and danger. A rather modest force of inspectors of the Armaments and Effectives Sub-commissions successfully supervised the destruction of tons of war material, dismantled thousands of German war production facilities, and presided over the reduction and reorganization of the *Reichswehr*. They also worked assiduously to discover numerous treaty violations, as Germany attempted to increase its military strength beyond the scope of the Treaty of Versailles. Despite facing obstruction at every turn and experiencing violent reactions from a frustrated populace, from 1920 to 1923 Allied inspectors all but destroyed the military power that had recently threatened to dominate Europe.

The German strategy to circumvent disarmament was largely futile as the Allies consistently rejected German attempts to modify the enforcement of the military clauses of the Versailles Treaty. Time and again the Allies foiled German efforts to modify disarmament demands, most importantly when they rejected the German request for the establishment of a 200,000-man *Reichswehr* at the Spa Conference in July 1920. Other German attempts to increase their military strength above the restrictions of the Treaty of Versailles that the Allies rejected included the conservation of artillery and light arms in fortifications in 1920, maintenance of the *Sicherheitspolizei*, modification of the definition of war material, increase in the number of authorized war production factories, insistence on the presence of a German liaison officer for all inspections, and demands to evacuate Cologne in January 1925. Nonetheless, the Germans were able to achieve one significant success in modifying Allied disarmament demands. After the German government successfully petitioned the Allies for police increases, the Allies obliged them at Boulogne in June 1920 by granting an increase in the German police to 150,000 men. This Allied modification was an Anglo–French policy undertaken to combat the possible rise of Bolshevism at a time when the Weimar Republic was fighting for its political livelihood.

Although the Germans were able to increase their military strength beyond the restrictions of Allied demands through a strategy of obstruction and delay, these increases were trivial. By refusing to fulfill Allied disarmament demands, obstructing Allied inspections, and repeatedly petitioning the IAMCC and the Conference of Ambassadors with requests for disarmament modifications, the German government was able to eschew its military obligations under the Treaty of Versailles. Consequently, Allied deadlines for various facets of disarmament often became meaningless, and some details of the military clauses of the treaty remained without resolution for years. But German military violations did not equal the success that Allied modifications of the military clauses of the Treaty of Versailles provided.

The fact that the British and French remained in Germany until Germany fulfilled the most significant military demands negated the value of obstruction and delay. This German strategy allowed Germany to violate some of the military clauses of the treaty but it also provided the Allies with a justification to remain in Germany for eleven years. Other than reinforcing the Anglo–French entente, the overall impact of German treaty evasions was negligible when compared to the overall Allied demilitarization of Germany. Illicit production and stores of war material, excess police and *Reichswehr* officers and soldiers, and the maintenance of paramilitary organizations added little weight to the state of the German military in the 1920s. When measured against the quantitative and qualitative strength of the French army alone, the German army was a second-rate defensive force. Germany had the intent to violate Versailles and increase its military strength but certainly never had the capability to threaten any of its neighbors. Hitler's remilitarization of Germany started in 1935 on an unprecedented scale because nothing impeded it – no longer did Allied inspectors, supported by the threat of an Anglo–French policy of military sanctions, have a presence on German soil.

The effectiveness of Allied sanctions

The disarmament section of the Treaty of Versailles was extensive but the peacemakers did not give the same level of detail or foresight to the efficacy of enforcing the military clauses. As difficulties emerged, for instance, the passing of the initial deadline without progress, defining war material, or authorizing the number of German armaments factories, the Allies had to develop disarmament policies that the peacemakers of 1919 did not address. This flexibility fit the British mold of post-war diplomacy but often created problems for the rigidity of French security policy. The most egregious mistake of the Paris peacemakers was not to include specific plans in the treaty to induce German fulfillment of the military clauses through sanctions. Without the benefit of experience, Britain, France, and their smaller partners had to develop spontaneous policies regarding the detailed operations of disarmament while ensuring German fulfillment of the treaty. The Allied coalition often formulated disarmament strategies in Germany on an *ad hoc* basis, and this reactive and uncertain policy-making facilitated the widening of Anglo–French differences and allowed Germany to attempt to weaken Allied resolve. Yet when the coalition worked together and formulated disarmament demands supported by military sanctions, the IAMCC experienced tremendous progress.

The most important factor in assessing the progress and success of the Allied disarmament of Germany was the level of Anglo–French unity involved in the development of policies and the enforcement of the military clauses of the Treaty of Versailles. When Britain and France formulated common disarmament strategies and enforced them under the threat of military sanctions, Allied disarmament policy was markedly more success-ful in eliciting German compliance than when Britain or France felt coerced into a decision or when they refused to threaten Germany with sanctions. Three major events in the first five years of disarmament illus-trate that common Allied policy supported by the possibility of sanctions resulted in remarkable progress in the execution of the military clauses of the treaty and accounted for the preponderance of the overall success of disarmament. At the Spa Conference in July 1920, the May ultimatum in 1921, and in discussions regarding Cologne in January 1925, Britain and France developed policies in concert that led to immediate increases in the amount of German fulfillment and prevented any substantial successes for German aspirations of disarmament evasions.

The first year of Allied disarmament operations in Germany experi-enced the greatest amount of fulfillment of the disarmament clauses of the Treaty of Versailles, and the preponderance of success occurred as a result of the proclamation of the Spa Protocol in July 1920.[6] After demanding fulfillment of the disarmament clauses at the Boulogne Conference in June with no visible results, at the Spa Conference Britain and France reiterated their demands for compliance with the military clauses of the treaty. Most importantly, they backed their demands with an occupation ultimatum. The threat of French and British troops in the Ruhr set an Allied precedent for the use of military sanctions as a political weapon and had a startling effect upon German disarmament. For the remainder of the year, the success of the IAMCC was unparalleled as the Allies witnessed an increase in the amount of armaments that Germany surrendered and destroyed, and Germany reduced the *Reichswehr* to 100,000 troops by the revised deadline of 1 January 1921. The key to success was the strength of Anglo–French unity at the Spa Conference in July 1920 where Britain especially demonstrated conviction in enforcing disarmament upon Germany. The effectiveness of the use of sanctions in the Spa Protocol influenced subsequent Allied decisions when the rate of disarmament progress once again diminished.

After a successful period of disarmament, by 1921 German fulfillment of the military clauses began to wane, so the Allies took steps once again to enforce compliance. In the Paris meetings of January 1921, Britain and France threatened to increase the extent of the Rhineland occupation unless Germany continued to comply with disarmament. This ultimatum failed to elicit any further progress in disarmament, and the Allies subsequently occupied Duisburg, Ruhrort, and Düsseldorf for the next four years. Although the Paris ultimatum marked the sole occurrence where the threat of military sanctions failed to force the hand of Germany in the fulfillment of the disarmament clauses of the treaty, it illustrated Allied convictions in resolutely carrying out the decision to use force. Therefore, when Britain and France decided to apply an even more forceful policy in London in the spring, the newly formed Wirth government pledged itself to a policy of fulfillment. The London ultimatum of May 1921, in which the Allies threatened to occupy the Ruhr if Germany did not comply with new Allied disarmament demands, consequently resulted in further progress in the reduction and organization of the *Reichswehr* and the destruction of armaments. In fact, disarmament operations, buoyed by the Spa Protocol and London ultimatum, convinced the British that the disarmament of Germany was nearing completion by July 1921. The Allied attempt to elicit final German compliance through the replacement of the IAMCC with a smaller control organization (the Committee of Guarantee) in September 1922, however, resulted in no progress. The threat of sanctions was simply a more effective means of enforcing disarmament than the positive reinforcement of German fulfillment.

The third test of Allied willpower in the enforcement of the disarmament clauses of the Treaty of Versailles occurred at the beginning of January 1925. In a show of united strength and determination, Britain and France informed the German government that Allied troops would not evacuate Cologne due to the discovery of widespread evasions of the military clauses of the treaty that occurred during the suspension of inspections. Unlike the previous Spa and London ultimatums, the decision to maintain an Allied military presence in Cologne was legally justified by the Treaty of Versailles. After the initial outrage of Luther and Stresemann had abated, the German government decided to cooperate with the Allies with alacrity, and the resumption of progress toward disarmament carried into the Locarno Conference. Even at Locarno in October 1925, Chamberlain and Briand stood united against Stresemann's insistence upon the evacuation of Cologne before the fulfillment of disarmament when the

British and French statesmen refused jointly to withdraw Allied troops from Cologne until Germany complied with the military clauses. The Locarno Conference was the swan-song of Allied efforts toward the enforcement of disarmament. Soon afterward, Chamberlain wavered and accepted German promises instead of actual proof of compliance. Self-serving policies inflamed by the conflict of appeasement versus security put an effective end to truly Allied policy toward the disarmament of Germany. Any subsequent German compliance occurred sporadically and was never close to the extent of progress that occurred under united Allied policy supported by military sanctions.

Making and maintaining peace, especially after one of the most catas-trophic conflicts in human history, was a monumental challenge to the peacemakers in 1919 and beyond. A successful peace depended upon the effective disarmament of Germany, one of the foremost military powers in the world. While largely successful in destroying German military power, the Allies did not always overcome such difficulties as the concealment of war material and surplus troops; nor did they prevent obstruction, treaty violations, and abuse. Consequently, some lessons may be learned from the Allied disarmament experience in Germany. First, despite the strength of the German army and industrial capacity at the end of the war, the size of the IAMCC peaked at only about 1,200 soldiers, with even fewer inspectors. An increased number of inspectors and surprise inspections would have strengthened Allied assessments of German military capability and led to a more effective means of disarming Germany. Second, the lack of contingency plans for German opposition, even when most IAMCC officers expected difficulties, diminished the otherwise solid record of Allied disarmament. A firm Allied policy of sanctions, developed before the start of disarmament operations, might have avoided the endless delays and debates that followed discoveries of German violations or reports of attacks on inspection teams. With a typical *ad hoc* Allied response often bereft of stringent punitive schemes, military violations continued, and the IAMCC, dissatisfied with the lack of compliance and fearful of German intentions, remained in Germany well after disarmament deadlines had passed. Third, if the Allies had continued periodic inspections of the German military establishment after the departure of the IAMCC and the experts, or had at least strengthened the initial plan for the League of Nations to conduct and support subsequent inspections with possible sanc-tions, German rearmament in the 1930s may have taken a different path.

The experience of Allied inspectors in the disarmament of Germany after World War I should not be cast aside as obsolete or obscured by the shadow of Hitler's rearmament. With diligence, ingenuity, and the support of an international coalition, IAMCC inspectors roamed the German countryside in the early 1920s and stripped the German military of its prowess. Only in their absence, and in a radically altered political and diplomatic climate, was Germany truly able to rearm itself for war. As disarmament and inspections continue to capture the attention of the international community in the twenty-first century, especially in places such as Iraq, Iran, and Libya, Allied disarmament efforts from 1920 to 1931 should not be dismissed out of hand. Although this study does not provide a blueprint for the policy-makers of today, it does shed light on the experiences, successes, and failures that international weapons inspectors faced in disarming a powerful and embittered nation. Such lessons continue to be valuable today.

When the Allied disarmament of Germany came to a close in 1931, Britain, France, and Germany were all left with questions. Britain had imprinted Allied disarmament policy with its own stamp but had to face the fact that operations had been prolonged for eleven years. France emerged from the end of disarmament operations with the same amount of national insecurity as at the end of the war. Germany was left with a small defensive military and remained embittered toward Allied infringement of its sovereignty. Overall, Allied disarmament from 1920 to 1931 had been too long for Britain, too little for France, and too much for Germany. Nonetheless, Allied disarmament operations proved to be a successful but transitory endeavor to secure peace. The inherent industrial and military potential of Germany proved too much for Britain, France, and the League of Nations in the aftermath of the Great Depression, and Hitler transformed the nation into the foremost military power in the world. Without the presence of Allied inspectors, Germany resurrected the piles of gun barrels, masses of discharged soldiers, and the dusty debris of fortifications that Allied disarmament had left in its wake. The hinge of Anglo–French relations in the 1920s had been the disarmament of Germany, and the bolt in the hinge was the Allied enforcement of the Treaty of Versailles. Without that bolt, the door to the future security of Europe fell open, and Europe soon shuddered once again under the impact of war.

Notes

1 Introduction

1 Martin Gilbert, *The First World War, A Complete History* (New York: Henry Holt, 1994), p. 541. This figure does not include civilian deaths.
2 For sake of convenience, the terms "Allies" and "Allied" will refer to Britain and France, or the disarmament coalition for the entire study.
3 Philip Towle, *Enforced Disarmament: From the Napoleonic Campaigns to the Gulf War* (Oxford: Clarendon Press, 1997), pp. 17–50.
4 See Michael Dockrill and Brian McKercher (eds), *Diplomacy and World Power* (Cambridge: Cambridge University Press, 1996), pp. 83–103 and pp. 122–7 for a discussion of Britain's adherence to the balance of power stratagem.
5 Towle, *Enforced Disarmament*, p. 11.
6 David Williamson, *The British in Germany, 1918–1930: The Reluctant Occupiers* (New York and Oxford: Berg Publishers, 1991), pp. 1–2, n. 1. Dr Williamson was kind enough to lend me the proofs of John Hartman Morgan's unpublished second volume of *Assize of Arms*, an invaluable asset to my study.
7 Michael Salewski, *Entwaffnung und Militärkontrolle in Deutschland, 1919–1927* (Munich: R. Oldenbourg Verlag, 1966), pp. 392–4.
8 Francis Ludwig Carsten, *The Reichswehr and Politics: 1918–1933* (Berkeley, CA: University of California Press, 1966), pp. 200–34.
9 Barton Whaley, *Covert German Rearmament 1919–1939* (Frederick, Maryland: University Publications of America, 1984).
10 Arnold Wolfers, *Britain and France Between Two Wars* (New York: Harcourt, Brace, 1940); William M. Jordan, *Great Britain, France and the German Problem, 1918–1939* (London, New York and Toronto: Oxford University Press, 1943).
11 William Laird Kleine-Ahlbrandt, *The Burden of Victory: France, Britain and the Enforcement of the Versailles Peace, 1919–1925* (Lanham, New York, and London: University Press of America, 1995).
12 Sara Moore, *Peace Without Victory for the Allies 1918–1932* (Oxford and Providence: Berg Publishers, 1994).
13 Manfred Boemeke, *et al.* (eds) *The Treaty of Versailles: A Reassessment After 75 Years* (Cambridge: Cambridge University Press, 1998). There are only vague references to German disarmament in the essays by David French and Stephen Schuker.

2 Allied demands at the Paris Peace Conference

1 David French, *The Strategy of the Lloyd George Coalition 1916–1918* (Oxford: Clarendon Press, 1995), pp. 272–3.

2 Lloyd George's Trade Unions speech on 5 January 1918 and Woodrow Wilson's Fourteen Points speech on 8 January 1918 both vaguely demanded a general reduction in armaments.

3 The following figures are conservative estimates of manpower losses in World War I of only those nations that concern this study: Germany 1.8 million; Britain 743,000; France 1,384,000; United States 48,000. See Gilbert, *The First World War*, p. 541.

4 Arno J. Mayer, *Politics and Diplomacy of Peacemaking, 1918–1919* (New York: Alfred A. Knopf, 1967), pp. 647–8.

5 The Supreme War Council was formed in November 1917 and consisted of the Prime Minister, a chosen member, and an appointed military representative of each fighting nation. National Archives, College Park, Maryland, Records of the American Commission to Negotiate the Peace (1918–1931), Record Group 256, 180.0401/1. Hereafter cited as NA, RG 256.

6 Ferdinand Foch, *The Memoirs of Marshal Foch*, trans. by T. Bentley Mott (Garden City, NY: Doubleday, Doran and Company, 1931), pp. 451–2; Bullitt Lowry, *Armistice 1918* (London and Kent: The Kent State University Press, 1996), pp. 20–2.

7 David Stevenson, *French War Aims Against Germany, 1914–1919* (Oxford: Clarendon Press, 1982), pp. 119–20.

8 Tasker H. Bliss, "The Armistices," *American Journal of International Law*, October 1922, 16 (4), pp. 520–1.

9 Gerda Richards Crosby, *Disarmament and Peace in British Politics 1914–1919* (Cambridge, MA: Harvard University Press, 1957), p. 83; Stevenson, *French War Aims*, p. 117; Lowry, *Armistice 1918*, p. 72.

10 United States Department of State, *Papers Relating to the Foreign Relations of the United States: The Paris Peace Conference, 1919–1920* (Washington, 1947), Vol. II, p. 2 (hereafter cited as *FRUS, PPC*); Military Conditions of an Armistice with Germany, 2 November 1918 and SWC 357, 11 November 1918, Container 308, Tasker Bliss Papers, Library of Congress (LC), Washington, DC; Foch, *Memoirs*, pp. 478–80; Harold W.V. Temperley, *A History of the Peace Conference*, Vol. II (London: Oxford University Press, 1920), p. 124; Harry Rudin, *Armistice 1918* (New Haven, CT: Yale University Press, 1944), Appendix G, p. 426. The French were centered in Mainz, the British in Cologne, the Belgians on the northern Rhine and the Americans in Coblenz.

11 Samuel G. Shartle, *Spa, Versailles, Munich: An Account of the Armistice Commission* (Philadelphia, PA: Dorrance Publishers, 1941), pp. 51–2.

12 Lorna S. Jaffe, *The Decision to Disarm Germany* (Boston, MA: Allen & Unwin, 1985), p. 41. See also V.H. Rothwell, *British War Aims and Peace Diplomacy, 1914–1918* (Oxford: Clarendon Press, 1971) for the uncertainty over British aims during the war.

13 Gordon A. Craig and Felix Gilbert, *The Diplomats*, Vol. I (Princeton, NJ: Princeton University Press, 1953), pp. 16–25, and Alan J. Sharp, "The Foreign Office in Eclipse 1919–22," *History*, 1976, 61, pp. 198–218; C.J. Lowe and M.L. Dockrill, *The Mirage of Power: British Foreign Policy, 1914–1922*, Vol. 2 (London and Boston, MA: Routledge & Kegan Paul, 1972), pp. 335–6; Paul W. Doerr, *British Foreign Policy 1919–1939* (Manchester and New York: Manchester University Press, 1998), pp. 29–30. Lloyd George also relied on his personal advisers Maurice Hankey and Phillip Kerr. See London, House of Lords Record Office, David Lloyd George Papers, F/89/2/14 and F/89/2/38 (hereafter cited as LG Papers).

14 Jaffe, *The Decision to Disarm Germany*, pp. 141–71; Robin Higham, *Armed Forces in Peacetime: Britain, 1918–1940, A Case Study* (Hamden, CT: 1962),

p. 10. Jaffe argues that British policy toward the disarmament of Germany at the Paris Peace Conference was more a matter of public opinion and general disarmament than British fear of future German military aggression.

15 For the issue of demobilization at the war's end in Britain, see Stephen Richards Graubard, "Military Demobilization in Great Britain Following the First World War," *The Journal of Modern History*, December 1947, volume 19 (4), pp. 297–311.

16 Jere Clemens King, *Foch Versus Clemenceau: France and German Dismemberment, 1918–1919*, (Cambridge, MA: Harvard University Press, 1960), pp. 1–31; McDougall, *France's Rhineland Diplomacy*, pp. 37–44; Stevenson, *French War Aims*, p. 141; Sir George Aston, *The Biography of the Late Marshal Foch* (New York: Macmillan, 1929), p. 403; B.H. Liddell Hart, *Foch The Man of Orleans* (Boston, MA: Little, Brown, 1932), p. 412; Judith M. Hughes, *To the Maginot Line: The Politics of French Military Preparedness in the 1920s* (Cambridge, MA: Harvard University Press, 1971), p. 82.

17 Stevenson, *French War Aims*, p. 169; Pierre Renouvin, "Les buts de guerre du gouvernement français, 1914–1918," *Revue historique*, 1966, 235, pp. 1–38; P.E. Tournoux, "Si l'On Avait Ecouté Foch," *Revue des Deux Mondes*, 1959, 17, pp. 84–7; F. Tuohy, "France's Rhineland Adventure," *Contemporary Review*, 1930, 138, p. 30.

18 Georges Clemenceau, *Grandeur and Misery of Victory*, trans. F.M. Atkinson (New York: Harcourt, Brace, 1930), pp. 345–9.

19 Arthur Walworth, *Wilson and his Peacemakers: American Diplomacy at the Paris Peace Conference, 1919* (New York and London: W.W. Norton and Company, 1986), p. 12; Robert Lansing, *The Peace Negotiations: A Personal Narrative* (Boston, MA, and New York: Houghton Mifflin, 1921), p. 4.

20 Lloyd E. Ambrosius, *Woodrow Wilson and the American Diplomatic Tradition* (Cambridge, MA: Harvard University Press, 1987), pp. 57–8; Tasker Bliss essay, "The Problem of Disarmament," in *What Really Happened at Paris: The Story of the Peace Conference, 1918–1919*, ed. by Edward M. House and Charles Seymour (New York: Scribner's, 1921), p. 373.

21 Klaus Schwabe, *Woodrow Wilson, Revolutionary Germany, and Peacemaking, 1918–1919* (Chapel Hill and London: The University of North Carolina Press, 1985), p. 89.

22 Arno J. Mayer, *Politics and Diplomacy of Peacemaking, 1918–1919* (New York: Alfred A. Knopf, 1967), pp. 10–11.

23 David Lloyd George, *The Truth About the Peace Treaties*, Vol. 1 (London: Victor Gollancz, 1938), pp. 407–8; Antony Lentin, *Lloyd George and the Lost Peace: From Versailles to Hitler, 1919–1940* (Basingstoke: Palgrave, 2001), pp. 10–11.

24 John M. Thompson, *Russia, Bolshevism, and the Versailles Peace* (Princeton, NJ: Princeton University Press, 1966), p. 21.

25 Inga Floto, *Colonel House in Paris: A Study of American Policy at the Paris Peace Conference 1919* (Princeton, NJ: Princeton University Press, 1973), pp. 117–18.

26 Supreme Council Minutes, 24 January 1919, LG Papers, F/121/3.

27 Foch, *Memoirs*, pp. 470–4; Thompson, *Russia, Bolshevism and the Versailles Peace*, pp. 22–3.

28 Ralph James Q. Adams, *Arms and the Wizard, Lloyd George and the Ministry of Munitions 1915–1916* (College Station: Texas A&M University Press, 1978), pp. 181–2; Chris Wrigley, *Lloyd George* (Oxford: Blackwell, 1992), pp. 72–3.

29 Lloyd George's preoccupation with disarming Germany through the destruc-

tion of German armaments may also be seen throughout the Allied conferences of Hythe, Boulogne and Spa. See *DBFP*, 8, pp. 257, 308–9, 321, 340–2,436, 457–60, 471, 482–3.

30 Supreme Council Minutes, 24 January 1919, LG Papers, F/121/3; *FRUS, PPC*, III, p. 711.

31 SWC Meeting, 23 January 1919, NA, RG 256, 185.1161/7; *FRUS, PPC*, III, p. 707.

32 Supreme Council Minutes, 24 January 1919, LG Papers, F/121/3; King, *Foch Versus Clemenceau*, pp. 22–3.

33 This was subsequently known as the Loucheur Committee, made up of Louis Loucheur (a French delegate at the Conference), American General Bliss, Marshal Foch, Winston Churchill (Minister of War), and Italian General Diaz.

34 Supreme Council on Limitation of German Arms, 1 February 1919, LG Papers, F/121/2. At this point, excess material were dependent upon the number of troops the German army was allowed to maintain.

35 LG to Kerr, 12 February 1919, LG Papers, F/89/2/8.

36 CIGS British Delegation Meeting, 5 February 1919, LG Papers, F/121/2.

37 David Hunter Miller, *My Diary of the Conference*, XIV, Minutes of the Supreme War Council, 7 February 1919, pp. 258–9; Meeting, NA, RG 256, 185.1161/9. The Loucheur Committee proposed to limit the Germans to 1,000 heavy guns, 1,575 field guns, 3,825 machine-guns, 1,400 trench mortars, 4,500 automatic rifles and 412,500 rifles. Thirty divisions were roughly equivalent to 450,000 to 500,000 troops.

38 Miller, *Diary*, XIV, p. 257.

39 SWC Meeting, 7 February 1919, LG Papers, F/121/2.

40 Miller, *Diary*, XIV, 14, p. 242.

41 Meeting of the Supreme War Council, 8 February 1919, *FRUS, PPC*, III, 929; Bureau of the Conference Meeting, 8 February 1919, NA, RG 256, 185.1161/9.

42 John Hartman Morgan, galley slips of the unpublished second volume of *Assize of Arms*, Appendix 1, p. 78 (hereafter cited as *Assize of Arms*, II). These were kindly lent to me by David G. Williamson, Highgate School, London.

43 Morgan, *Assize of Arms*, II, Appendix 1, p. 79. This figure included a temporary number of troops (80,000) to protect German borders against Bolshevism (see below).

44 Ibid., Appendix 1, pp. 78–9.

45 Morgan, *Assize of Arms*, II, Appendix I, p. 78.

46 SWC Meeting, 12 February 1919, LG Papers, F/121/2.

47 Bliss Memo, 2 March 1919, NA, RG 256, 185.1161/18.

48 SWC Meeting, 3 March 1919, LG Papers, F/121/2; Supreme Council Meeting, Report of Foch's committee, 3 March 1919, *FRUS, PPC*, IV, pp. 183–5.

49 SWC Meeting, 3 March 1919, LG Papers, F/121/2.

50 Bureau of the Conference Meeting, 6 March 1919, NA, RG 256, 185.1161/24.

51 Morgan, *Assize of Arms*, II, Appendix 1, p. 79.

52 SWC Meeting, 7 March 1919, LG Papers, F/121/2; Bureau of the Conference Meeting, 7 March 1919, NA, RG 256, 185.1161/27.

53 After the defeat of Prussian forces by Napoleon in 1806, Napoleon placed strict limits on the size of the Prussian army. To counteract a ceiling on the size of the Prussian army, Krümper, a Prussian officer, devised a system of short-term training to increase the overall number of trained soldiers. See Walter Goerlitz, *History of the German General Staff* (New York: Praeger, 1953).

54 Bureau of the Conference Meeting, 7 March 1919, NA, RG 256, 185.1161/27.

55 Clemenceau, *Grandeur and Misery*, p. 126; King, *Foch Versus Clemenceau*, p. 49.
56 Supreme War Council Minutes, 10 March 1919, *FRUS, PPC*, IV, pp. 296–7.
57 SWC Meeting, 10 March 1919, LG Papers, F/121/2.
58 Supreme War Council Minutes, 17 March 1919, *FRUS, PPC*, IV, pp. 400–1. The Allies also established the Inter-Allied Naval Control Commission and the Inter-Allied Aeronautical Control Commission to supervise the disarmament of the German navy and air force, respectively.
59 Supreme War Council Minutes, 17 March 1919, *FRUS, PPC*, IV, pp. 358–60. See Bliss, Analysis of the Military Terms with Germany, 14 March 1919 and Memo for Wilson, 17 March 1919, Container 308, Bliss Papers, LC.
60 *FRUS, PPC*, IV, pp. 375–6.
61 The interpretation of the phrase "existing state" regarding fortresses, the number of factories authorized by the Allies to produce war materials and the definition of war materials were just a few of the most persistent problems.
62 IC 176I (CF 124), 26 April 1919, NA, RG 256; William Jordan, *Great Britain, France, and the German Problem 1918–1939*, p. 134. This formed the basis for the brief introduction to Part V of the Versailles Treaty.
63 Dick Richardson, *The Evolution of British Disarmament Policy in the 1920s* (London: Pinter Publishers, 1989), pp. 7–8.
64 The issue was finally settled by Adolf Hitler when the German delegation walked out of the Disarmament Conference in 1933 and Germany proceeded with full-scale rearmament in 1935.

3 The organization and hierarchy of Allied disarmament and military control

1 Paul Roques, *Le Contrôle Militaire Interallié en Allemagne* (Paris: Berger-Levrault, 1927), pp. 7–10; Morgan, *Assize of Arms*, p. 37.
2 Council of Four Minutes, 26 June 1919, CF 93, NA, RG 256; Notes of a Meeting Held at President Wilson's House, 26 June 1919, *FRUS, PPC*, VI, p. 14.
3 Heads of Delegation Meeting, 9 July 1919, HD 3, NA RG 256; Heads of Delegation Meeting, 9 July 1919, *FRUS, 1919*, VII, pp. 76–80; Great Britain, Her Majesty's Printing Office, *Documents on British Foreign Policy 1919–1939*, Series I (London, 1947), I, pp. 52–5. Hereafter cited as *DBFP*.
4 These appointments were not yet official.
5 Heads of Delegation Meeting, 2 August 1919, *FRUS, 1919*, VII. The Allies linked pay to the standard of living in Germany. Due to the constant fluctuations of German currency in the early 1920s, the pay and allowances of the members of the IAMCC changed frequently.
6 In 1920, the IAMCC numbered about 1,200 soldiers, whereas the IANCC comprised only about 200 officers and the IAACC included approximately 450 soldiers.
7 Conference of Ambassadors, Note, "Commissions de Contrôle en Allemagne," 24 December 1920, Ministère des Affaires Étrangères, Archives Diplomatiques, Serie Z, Europe 1918–1929, Allemagne, Vol. 223. Hereafter cited as MAE; NA, RG 256, HD3, 9 July 1919; *FRUS, PPC*, VII, Heads of Delegation Meeting, 9 July 1919, pp. 76–80; *DBFP*, I, 52–5; Michael Salewski, *Entwaffnung und Militärkontrolle in Deutschland 1919–1927* (München: R. Oldenbourg Verlag, 1966), p. 43.
8 Gerhard Weinberg, *A World At Arms* (Cambridge: Cambridge University Press, 1994), p. 18.

9 Heads of Delegation Meeting, 8 August 1919, HD 27, NA, RG 256; *FRUS, PPC*, VII, pp. 632–3. The size of the IAMCC fluctuated throughout its existence.

10 United States Delegation Dispatch, 23 July 1919, 185.11641/3A, NA, RG 256.

11 *Le Matin*, 15 June 1924, p. 3; Boyle, *France, Great Britain, and German Disarmament 1919–1927*, p. 19; Salewski, *Entwaffnung und Militärkontrolle*, p. 44.

12 Roques, *Le Contrôle Militaire*, pp. 16–19.

13 IAMCC Tables and Composition, 29 July 1919, Container 308, Bliss Papers, LC; Nollet to Clemenceau, 30 September 1919, 185.11641/6, NA, RG 256.

14 Charles Nollet, *Une Expérience de Désarmement* (Paris: L'Imprimerie Moderne, 1932), pp. 12–13.

15 The French officers were Nollet, his adjutant General Walch, Barthélemy and Bizouard. The British officers were Bingham and Brigadier-General John Morgan while the Belgian, Italian and Japanese delegations were represented by de Guyffroy, Calcagno and Furriya, respectively. See Morgan, *Assize of Arms*, II, p. 286; Roques, *Le Contrôle Militaire*, p. 14; Nollet, *Une Expérience*, pp. 14–15, 50–4; Salewski, *Entwaffnung und Militärkontrolle*, p. 49.

16 IAMCC Tables and Composition, 29 July 1919, Container 308, Bliss Papers, LC; Salewski, *Entwaffnung und Militärkontrolle*, p. 51; Nollet, *Une Expérience*, p. 19. These district committees were located in Berlin (AE), Munster (A), Hanover (AE), Cologne (A), Stettin (AE), Königsberg (AE), Coblenz (F), Kiel (F), Frankfurt (AE), Munich (AE), Dresden (AE), Stuttgart (AEF) and Breslau (AE).

17 IAMCC Tables and Composition, 22 October 1919, Container 308, Bliss Papers, LC. The new figures for total personnel of the IAMCC were 292 officers, 91 interpreters, 622 troops, and 157 automobiles.

18 Minutes of the Conference of Ambassadors (hereafter cited as CA), CA 75, 11 August 1919, NA, RG 256; Heads of Delegation Meeting, 11 August 1919, 185.1164/11, NA, RG 256. The first official Anglo–German diplomatic ties were established in the spring of 1919, when the Military Mission in Berlin was set up under Major-General Neil Malcolm. See WO to General Haking, 8 April 1919, PRO, WO 32/5377; House of Commons, 17 March 1920, *The Parliamentary Debates: Official Report*, House of Commons, 1920, volume 126, 5th series, p. 2217.

19 Weygand to Clemenceau, 17 August 1919, 185.1164/13, NA, RG 256; *FRUS, PPC*, VII, pp. 806–7.

20 Foch (Desticker) to Clemenceau, 3 September 1919, 185.1164/17, NA RG 256.

21 Report of Captaine Laperche, 3 September 1919, Appendix A to HD 47, NA, RG 256; *FRUS, PPC*, VIII, pp. 107–8.

22 Heads of Delegation Meeting (HD 47), 4 September 1919, NA, RG 256; *DBFP*, I, 619–620; *FRUS, PPC*, VIII, pp. 96–7.

23 Heads of Delegation Meeting, 9 September 1919, NA, RG 256; Clemenceau to Lersner, 11 September 1919, 185.1164/20, NA, RG 256; *FRUS, PPC*, VIII, pp. 128–9.

24 Heads of Delegation Meeting, 15 October 1919, HD 70, NA, RG 256; German Delegation Request, 14 October 1919, *DBFP*, I, p. 964.

25 Stewart Roddie, *Peace Patrol* (New York: G.P. Putnam's Sons, 1933), p. 76.

26 Bingham Diary, 20 September 1919, Ball Papers, Imperial War Museum (Hereafter cited as IWM), London.

27 Bingham Diary, Ball Papers, IWM; John Hartman Morgan, *Assize of Arms* (New York: Oxford University Press, 1946), pp. 32–5.

28 Minutes of the IAMCC Council, 23 April 1920, CA 45, NA, RG 256.

29 Bingham Diary, Ball Papers, IWM; Morgan, *Assize of Arms*, II, 298. Morgan claimed that Germany produced about 1,100 guns per month from the date of the Armistice up until 10 January 1920.
30 Williamson, *The British in Germany*, p. 72; Nollet, *Une Expérience*, pp. 21–2.
31 Nollet, *Une Expérience*, p. 21; Morgan, *Assize of Arms*, p. 60.
32 General von Cramon detested Allied disarmament efforts and, similar to Nollet and Foch, believed that the war had not come to an end in 1918. See Salewski, *Entwaffnung und Militärkontrolle*, p. 60.
33 Williamson, *The British in Germany*, p. 73.
34 The German government used a strict interpretation of the Treaty of Versailles to try to protect its war material stored on Dutch territory in 1920, to oppose the Allied occupation of Düsseldorf, Duisburg and Ruhrort in 1921 and the establishment of a new form of military control in 1922, and to prevent any organization except the League of Nations from assuming authority over disarmament when Allied discussions focused on establishing modified control after Locarno.
35 *DBFP*, I, pp. 1–2.
36 HD 17, 28 July 1919, NA, RG 256; *DBFP*, I, pp. 225–32.
37 Dresel to Polk, 18 October 1919, 180.033/3, NA, RG 256.
38 *FRUS*, 1919, I, pp. 16–17.
39 Allied Meeting, 18 October 1919, 180.033/3, NA, RG 256.
40 The first representatives of the Conference of Ambassadors were: Britain – Lord Derby, France – Alexandre Millerand, United States – Hugh Wallace, Italy – Bonin Longare.
41 Jacquemyns to Clemenceau, 23 November 1919, 180.033/5, NA, RG 256.
42 CA Minutes, 2 February 1920, CA 8, 180.033/8, NA, RG 256.
43 Gerhard P. Pink, *The Conference of Ambassadors*, Geneva Studies, Vol. 12 (Geneva: Geneva Research Center, 1942), pp. 43–4.
44 Allied Meeting, 21 January 1920, 180.033/7, NA, RG 256.
45 Heads of Delegation Meeting, 28 October 1919, HD 77, NA, RG 256; Foch to Clemenceau, 28 October 1919, *FRUS, PPC*, VIII, Appendix A, pp. 795–6.
46 Heads of Delegations Meeting, 28 October 1919, HD 77, NA, RG 256; *FRUS, PPC*, VIII, p. 786; *DBFP*, II, p. 84.
47 Anglo–French Conference, 12 December 1919, *DBFP*, II, p. 738.
48 Anglo–French Conference, 13 December 1919, *DBFP*, II, p. 755; Davis to Lansing, 13 December 1919, *FRUS*, 1919, I, p. 29. See also Cyril Falls, *Marshal Foch* (London: Blackie and Sons, 1939), p. 174.
49 The Italians feared that the need for Foch to preside over the AMCV would imply that the treaty itself did not have sufficient force to insure peace. See *DBFP*, V, Note from the Italian Ambassador in London, 29 December 1919, pp. 939–942.
50 Foch to Conference of Ambassadors, 19 March 1920, MAE, Europe 1918–1940, Allemagne, Vol. 58; Ministers of Foreign Affairs Meeting, 10 January 1920, 180.03501, NA, RG 256; CA Minutes, 3 March 1920, CA 23, 180.033/23, NA, RG 256; CA Minutes, 23 March 1920, CA 24, 180.033/24, NA, RG 256; *DBFP*, II, pp. 724–5; *FRUS, PPC*, IX, p. 858.
51 AMCV, Report of the Work of the British Section During 1920, PRO, FO 371/58444, C4674/4674/62.

4 Armaments: the Allied offensive on war materials

1 Under Table III of Article 166, Germany was allowed to maintain 84,000 rifles, 50,000 short pistols, 18,000 carbines, 792 heavy machine-guns, 1,134 light

machine-guns, sixty-three medium trench mortars, 189 light trench mortars, 204 field guns of 77 mm caliber, and eighty-four field guns of 105 mm caliber. The IAMCC also fixed the total number of hand and rifle grenades at three million for the *Reichswehr* and police combined. See Washington, *Treaty of Peace With Germany* (Government Printing Office, 1919), p. 78 and CA Minutes, CA 91, Appendix F, NA, RG 256; Nollet to Foch, Report #30, 18 January 1921, PRO, FO 371/5981, C2544/461/18.

2 Britain (and the United States) significantly reduced the size of its army in the 1920s. The difference was that it did so to satisfy its own interests, not as an obligation under the treaty. France, on the other hand, did not disarm. However, both nations retained the freedom to produce any type of weapon.

3 There was some discrepancy in the military clauses regarding the time Germany was given to fulfil them. While Germany had two months to surrender all excess war material, she was given until 31 March not to exceed prescribed amounts of war material. This covered the contingency of delayed ratification.

4 *Treaty of Peace With Germany*, p. 73.

5 Hotels for officers included the Hotel Adlon, Bristol, Continental, Furstenhof, Kaiserhof, Excelsior, Eden, Hessler, Am zoo, Brek, and Esplanade, while the men were billeted in the Saxonia, Bremerhof, and Stadt Hanover. See Nollet to Foch, 17 August 1920, PRO, FO 371/4795, C5347/700/18 and CA Minutes CA 75, 180.03301/75, NA, RG 256.

6 IAMCC, Table and Composition, 29 July 1919, Container 308, Bliss Papers, LC.

7 Nollet, *Une Expérience*, p. 49.

8 Williamson, *The British in Germany*, p. 70; Memorandum by the Secretary of State For War, 28 June 1920, PRO, CAB 24/108, CP 1550.

9 See, e.g. Bingham Diary, 3 October 1919, IWM, Ball Papers, Derby to Curzon, 27 July 1920, British Museum, D'Abernon Papers, 48923, and Roddie Report, 23 April 1920, LG Papers, F/199/8/4.

10 Nollet, *Une Expérience*, p. 19. The Armament District Committees were located in Stuttgart, Königsberg, Breslau, Cologne, Munster, Stettin, Dresden, Hanover, Frankfurt, Berlin and Munich.

11 Foch to Conference of Ambassadors, 19 March 1920, MAE, Europe 1918–1940, Allemagne, Vol. 58.

12 Morgan, *Assize of Arms*, p. 37; Morgan, *Assize of Arms*, II, Proofs "Materiel de Guerre"; Williamson, *The British in Germany*, p. 135.

13 Nollet, *Une Expérience*, p. 169; Salewski, *Entwaffnung und Militärkontrolle*, p. 99.

14 Nollet to Foch, Report 24, 17 October 1920, MAE, Europe 1918–1940, Allemagne, Vol. 61.

15 CA Minutes, 21 May 1920, CA 43, 180.033/43, NA, RG 256. See also Dodds Memorandum, 1 November 1922, *DBFP*, XX, pp. 570–1.

16 Derby Telegram to FO, 6 November 1920, PRO, FO 371/4751, C10566/59/18; *DBFP*, X, pp. 106–8.

17 CA Minutes, 26 May 1920, CA 45, 188.03301/45, NA, RG 256.

18 Nollet to Foch, Report #30, 18 January 1921, PRO, FO 371/5981, C2544/461/18. The Conference of Ambassadors first rejected German appeals for gas masks on 20 May 1921. See CA Minutes, 20 May 1921, CA 121, 180.03301/121, NA, RG 256.

19 CA Minutes, 25 March 1922, CA 171, 180.03301/171, NA, RG 256.

20 CA Minutes, 10 February 1920, CA 10, 180.033/10, NA, RG 256.

21 CA Minutes, 2 February 1921, CA 105, 180.03301/105, NA, RG 256.

22 Foch to CA, 19 March 1920, MAE, Europe 1918–1940, Allemagne, Vol. 58. See also Derby to Curzon, 6 June 1920, *DBFP*, X, pp. 131–2 and Curzon to Derby, 10 June 1920, *DBFP*, X, p. 133.
23 CA Minutes, 21 May 1920, CA 43, 180.03301/43, NA, RG 256.
24 D'Abernon to Curzon, July 1921, PRO, FO 371/5878, C16345; Bingham to D'Abernon, 15 July 1921, PRO, FO 371/5878.
25 CA Minutes, 24 November 1920, CA 94, 180.03301/94, NA, RG 256.
26 Morgan, *Assize of Arms*, II, pp. 290–6; Nollet to Foch, Report #37, 8 February 1922, PRO, FO 371/7449.
27 Intelligence Summary, 20 October 1920, PRO, FO 371/4794, C11382; Nollet, *Une Expérience*, p. 170. This replaced the *Reichsverwertungs-Amt* which had been involved in the liquidation, surrender, and destruction of German war material before Allied control.
28 Nollet, *Une Expérience*, p. 170.
29 Report of the Inter-Allied Military Commission of Versailles, 13 August 1921, PRO, FO 371/5878, C16555/47/18. See also Morgan, *Assize of Arms*, II, p. 308.
30 Bingham Diary, 23 January 1920 and 11 May 1920, Ball Papers, IWM, London; Roddie, *Peace Patrol*, p. 316.
31 Morgan, *Assize of Arms*, II, p. 329; Nollet, *Une Expérience*, pp. 170–1; Major-General Francis R. Bingham, "Work With the Allied Commission of Control in Germany, 1919–1924," *Journal of the Royal United Services Institution*, 1924, 69, p. 755.
32 Foch to Conference of Ambassadors, 19 March 1920, MAE, Europe 1918–1929, Allemagne, Vol. 58.
33 General Staff Memo, 7 April 1920, PRO, CAB 24/103.
34 *DBFP*, X, pp. 23–4, 127.
35 CA Minutes, 20 March 1920, CA 23, 180.033/23, NA, RG 256.
36 Memorandum by the Secretary of State For War, 28 June 1920, PRO, CAB 24/108, CP 1550.
37 Cambon to Hankey, 1 June 1920, *DBFP*, X, pp. 119–20.
38 Echéances du Désarmement du 13 Mai au 1 Juillet, 1920, MAE, Europe 1918–1940, Allemagne, Vol. 59.
39 Morgan, *Assize of Arms*, II, p. 178.
40 Nollet to Foch, Report 15, 12 June 1920, MAE, Europe 1918–1940, Allemagne, Vol. 59; Nollet to Foch, Report #16, 9 July 1920, PRO, FO 371/4792, C1029; War Office Memo, 14 August 1920, Lloyd George Papers, F/148/7/8.
41 The Germans reported to have destroyed some 17,500 guns and barrels, 21,000 machine-guns, and over 1,000,000 rifles. See Allied Military Committee of Versailles (AMCV), Execution des Clauses Militaires, 17 June 1920, MAE, Allemagne, Europe 1918–1940, Vol. 59. Non-German war material included French, British, Italian, Belgian, and Russian weapons of which approximately 3,000 guns and barrels, 1,700,000 shells, and 750,000 rifles and machine-guns had been destroyed by mid-June. See Nollet to Foch, Report 15, 12 June 1920, MAE, Allied Military Committee of Versailles (AMCV), Execution des Clauses Militaires, 17 June 1920, Allemagne, Vol. 59.
42 For Allied discussions concerning German military disarmament at the Conference of San Remo and the Conferences of Hythe, see *DBFP*, VIII, pp. 144–5, 153–6, 199–204, 209–10, 229, 231–2, 257–8, 308–9, 311–12, 320–2.
43 Boulogne Dispatch to German government, 22 June 1920, PRO, FO 371/4756, C857/113/18; Statement of Military Experts, 21 June 1920, *DBFP*, VIII, pp. 357–8, 371–3.

44 Dispatch to the German government on the Subject of Disarmament, 22 June 1920, PRO, FO 371/4756, C857/113/18, Appendix I.

45 Derby to Curzon, 3 May 1920, Oriental and India Office, Curzon Papers, MssEur 112/197.

46 Seeckt claimed that out of this number, 1.5 million rifles were destroyed, 117,000 were given to police, and 600,000 were given to the *Einwohnerwehr*. See Spa Conference, 6 July 1920, 180.0801/2, NA, RG 256. Major-General Bingham privately supported German insistence for a 200,000-man army but the instability of the spring led ironically to a change of heart. Henceforth, Bingham advocated restricting the *Reichswehr* to its treaty limitations. See Bingham Diary, May 1920, IWM, Ball Papers.

47 Carsten, *The Reichswehr and Politics*, pp. 167–82. This topic is discussed in Chapter 9.

48 Spa Conference, 7 July 1920, 180.0801/3, NA, RG 256. See also André François-Poncet, *De Versailles à Potsdam: La France et la problème allemande contemporain* (Paris: Flammarion, 1948), 88 and Salewski, *Entwaffnung und Militärkontrolle*, pp. 135–7.

49 Spa Conference, 8 July 1920, Lloyd George Papers, F/148/7/4; Spa Conference, 8 July 1920 (afternoon), 180.0801/5, NA, RG 256; Note Sur L'État d'Execution du Traité de Versailles, 12 November 1920, MAE, Europe 1918–1940, Allemagne, Vol. 62; Protocol de la Conférence de Spa, 16 July 1920, *Documents Relatifs aux Réparations*, Vol. I (Paris: Imprimerie Nationale, 1922), pp. 50–2.

50 Spa Conference, 98 July 1920, 180.0801/6, NA, RG 256; *Manchester Guardian*, 17 July 1920, p. 9.

51 Intelligence summaries From IAMCC, 11 August 1920, PRO, FO 371/4793, C3619/676/18.

52 Intelligence summaries From IAMCC, 28 July 1920, PRO, FO 371/4792, C2382/676/18. See also Carsten, *The Reichswehr and Politics* for a look into Seeckt's political ambitions and intelligence summaries from IAMCC, 17 September 1920, PRO, FO 371/4793, C6543/676/18 for the extent of monarchism in the *Reichswehr*.

53 General Staff Memo, 14 August 1920, Lloyd George Papers, F/148/7/8.

54 Army Headquarters, Paris, 27 August 1920, MAE, Europe 1918–1940, Allemagne, Vol. 60.

55 Operations of the IAMCC, 17 September 1920, PRO, FO 371/4793, C6541/676/18.

56 Intelligence summaries from IAMCC, 10 September 1920, PRO, FO 371/4793, C6026/676/18. In the first ten days after the Peters Proclamation, 122,000 rifles, 913 machine guns, eleven trench mortars, eleven guns and thirteen flamethrowers were surrendered as well as other arms. See William Seeds to Lord Curzon, 7 October 1920, PRO, FO 371/4757, C8448/113/18.

57 General Staff Memorandum on the Execution By Germany of the Military Articles of the Peace Treaty of Versailles, 15 January 1921, PRO, FO 371/5854, C1271/13/18.

58 Intelligence summaries from IAMCC, 6 October 1920, PRO, FO 371/4794, C8021/676/18. At the end of October, British intelligence estimated the number of illegal rifles in German hands to be between 200,000 and one million. See Intelligence summary from IAMCC, 17 November 1920, PRO, FO 371/4794, C11382/676/18.

59 Nollet to Foch, Report #23, 3 October 1920, PRO, FO 371/4794, C9200/676/18.

60 CA Minutes, 24 July 1920, CA 66, 180.03301/66, NA, RG 256.

61 Nollet to Foch, Report #23, 3 October 1920, PRO, FO 371/4794, C9100/676/18.
62 Nollet to Foch, Report 24, 17 October 1920, MAE, Europe 1918–1940, Allemagne, Vol. 61.
63 D'Abernon to Curzon, 6 November 1920, *DBFP*, X, 427–8; *DBFP*, X, p. 28.
64 Nollet to Foch, Report #27, 30 November 1920, PRO, FO 371/4795, C12720/676/18.
65 General Staff Memorandum on the Execution By Germany of the Military Articles of the Peace Treaty of Versailles, 15 January 1921, PRO, FO 371/5854, C1271/13/18. See also General de la Panouse, Memoire, 21 January 1921, MAE, Europe 1918–1929, Allemagne, Vol. 65.
66 Figures based on German amounts surrendered in 1920 to 1924. Nollet to Foch, Report #28, 29 November 1920, PRO, FO 371/4795, C13847/676/18; FO Minute, The Disarmament of Germany, 7 August 1922, PRO, FO 371/7451, C11164/6/18; FO Memo, 23 June 1924, PRO, FO 371/9725, C9665/9/18.
67 AMCV Report on Execution of Military Clauses, 30 December 1920, PRO, FO 371/5853.
68 Allied Conference in Paris, 24 January 1921, *DBFP*, XV, pp. 4–5. For a list of Allied decisions in Paris, see Paris Decisions, 29 January 1921, PRO, FO 371/5961, C2317/386/18.
69 Philip Kerr to Lloyd George, 2 September 1920, LG Papers, F/90/1/18.
70 President of the Inter-Allied Conference in Paris to President of the German Delegation, 29 January 1921, MAE, Europe 1918–1929, Allemagne, Vol. 65; Désarmement de l'Allemagne en 1921, 1 December 1921, MAE, Europe 1918–1929, Allemagne, Vol. 72; Conseil Suprême du 29 Janvier 1921, Documents *Relatifs aux Réparations*, Vol. I, pp. 115–19.
71 House of Lords, 11 May 1921, *The Parliamentary Debates, Official Report*, House of Lords, 5th series, Vol. 45, p. 291.
72 Allied Conference in Paris, 24–29 January 1921, *DBFP*, XV, pp. 110–18 and Allied Conference in London, 1–7 March, *DBFP*, XV, pp. 216–32. For occupation operations, see Memo for Colonel P. Bagby, 9 March 1921, Library of Congress, U.S. Military Intelligence Reports; J.E. Edmonds, *The Occupation of the Rhineland* (London: His Majesty's Stationery Office, 1944, reprint 1987), p. 221.
73 Nollet to Foch, Report #32, 24 March 1921, PRO, FO 371/5982, C7081/461/18.
74 Nollet to Foch, Report #33, 11 April 1921, PRO, FO 371/5982, C8137/461/18.
75 Supreme Council of London, Décision des Gouvernements, 5 May 1921, *Documents Relatifs aux Réparations*, Vol. I, pp. 154–5; British Section of AMCV, 1921 Report of AMCV, 20 February 1922, PRO, FO 371/7441, C2626/2626/62.
76 Sthamer to Prime Minister, 11 May 1921, MAE, Europe 1918–1929, Allemagne, Vol. 67.
77 Gessler to Foreign Office, 3 June 1921, ADAP, Series A, V, pp. 74–6.
78 Intelligence notes from IAMCC, 24 June 1921, PRO, FO 371/5983, C13628/461/18. See also Jacques Néré, *The Foreign Policy of France From 1914–1945* (London and Boston, MA: Routledge & Kegan Paul, 1975), p. 32.
79 Foreign Office Memorandum (Wigram), 13 August 1921, PRO, FO 371/5864, C18725/37/18; Foreign Office Memorandum, 28 July 1921, PRO, FO 371/6010. Wigram would later become an anti-appeasement advocate in opposing Hitler's rearmament.

80 General Staff Memo on the Progress in the Disarmament of Germany Subsequent to the Allied Ultimatum, Command Paper 3198, PRO, CAB 24/126.
81 Nollet to Foch, 1 July 1921, PRO, FO 371/5878, C15043/47/18.
82 Nollet to Foch, Report 29, 30 November 1920, MAE, Europe 1918–1940, Allemagne, Vol. 62.
83 Nollet to Foch, Report #30, 18 January 1921, PRO, FO 371/5981, C2544/461/18.
84 Intelligence summary, 8 September 1920, PRO, FO 371/4793, 6026/676218.
85 Nollet to Foch, Report 26, 30 October 1920, MAE, Europe 1918–1940, Allemagne, Vol. 61. See also Nollet to Foch, Report 27, 15 November 1920 and Nollet to Foch, Report 29, 30 November 1920, MAE, Europe 1918–1940, Allemagne, Vol. 62.
86 Report of the AMCV, 13 August 1921, PRO, FO 371/5875, C16555/47/18.
87 For example, inspectors discovered machine-guns, small arms, and munitions in a school in Frankfurt and other war material caches in Heidenau, Düsseldorf, Potsdam, Kalthof and other cities. See CA Minutes, 29 November 1921, CA157, 180.03301/157, NA, RG 256.
88 British Section of AMCV, 1921 Report of AMCV, 20 February 1922, PRO, FO 371/7441, C2626/2626/62.
89 Nollet to Foch, Report #37, 8 February 1922, PRO, FO 371/7449 and *BDFA*, Series F, Europe, 1919–1939, Vol. 33, Germany, 1922, pp. 55–64.
90 Sthamer to Curzon, 8 April 1922, PRO, FO 371/7450, C5463/6/18.
91 CA Minutes, 5 April 1922, CA 172, Annex C, 180.03301/172, NA, RG 256.
92 Nollet to Foch, Report #40, 11 July 1922, PRO, FO 371/7451, C10661/6218.
93 War Office (Cubitt) to Foreign Office, 11 July 1922, PRO, FO 371/7532, C9942/592/18; *DBFP*, XX, pp. 497–8.
94 Notes of an Allied Conference, 7 August 1922, PRO, FO 371/7481, C11243/99/18.
95 Foreign Office Summary, 2 November 1922, PRO, FO 371/7452, C15081/6/18; Note des Alliés, 29 September 1922, MAE, Europe 1918–1940, Allemagne, Vol. 81; German Foreign Office, 5 December 1922, National Archives, Records of the German Foreign Office, Record Group 242, Serial 3170 (D677023–5). Hereafter cited as NA, RG 242.
96 Wirth Note, 27 October 1922, *BDFA*, Series F, Europe, 1919–1939, Vol. 33, Germany, 1922, p. 327; CA Minutes, 10 November 1922, CA 193, 180.033/193, NA, RG 256.
97 Two authors who point out that the Allies had reduced the German military to a defensive force early in the era of disarmament are Chantal Metzger, "L'Allemagne: Un Danger Pour la France en 1920?," *Guerres Mondiales et Conflits Contemporains*, Revue d'Histoire, September 1999, #193, p. 22, and Bernice A. Carroll, "Germany Disarmed and Rearming, 1925–1935," *Journal of Peace Research*, 1966, 3 (2), p. 114.

5 Armaments: the Allied offensive on war production

1 Article 170, *Treaty of Peace With Germany*, p. 174.
2 This was justified under Article 211, which stipulated that Germany must pass legal and administrative measures to conform to the treaty.
3 Morgan, *Assize of Arms*, II, p. 344.
4 The number of countries involved in the import of war material from Germany was substantial: the Netherlands, Russia, Czechoslovakia, Finland, Persia, Argentina, Sweden, Lithuania, Norway, Ireland, Switzerland, and Spain.

5 W.J. Hee Skerk Memo, 28 January 1920, MAE, Europe 1918-1940, Allemagne, Vol. 58.

6 Foch to Conference of Ambassadors, 19 March 1920, MAE, Europe 1918-1940, Allemagne, Vol. 58; CA Minutes, 18 March 1920, CA 22, 180.033/22, NA, RG 256.

7 Derby to Curzon, 4 March 1920, *DBFP*, X, p. 29.

8 R. Graham to Curzon, 28 May 1920, *DBFP*, X, p. 109, n. 2.

9 R. Graham to Curzon, 4 May 1920, *DBFP*, X, pp. 76-8.

10 CA Minutes, 18 March 1920, CA 22, 180.03301/22, NA, RG 256.

11 CA Minutes, 21 April 1920, CA 33, 180.03301/33, NA, RG 256.

12 AMCV Report, 30 April 1920, CA Minutes, CA 39, 180.03301/39, NA, RG 256.

13 CA Minutes, 30 June 1920, CA 55, 180.03301/55, NA, RG 256.

14 CA Minutes, 8 November 1920, CA 91, 180.03301/91, NA, RG 256.

15 CA Minutes, 24 July 1920, CA 66, 180.03301/66, and 8 November 1920, CA 91, 180.03301/91, NA, RG 256.

16 CA Minutes, 24 November 1920, CA 94, 180.03301/94, NA, RG 256.

17 CA Minutes, 27 December 1920, CA 99, 180.03301/99, NA, RG 256.

18 CA Minutes, 8 May 1920, CA 39, 180.03301/39, NA, RG 256.

19 CA Minutes, 2 October 1920, CA 76, 180.03301/76, NA, RG 256.

20 CA Minutes, 20 October CA 84, 180.03301/84, NA, RG 256. This war material included 46,509 rifles, 11,932 carbines, 61,200 bayonets, 1,036 machine-guns, sixty-six trench mortars and fourteen artillery pieces.

21 CA Minutes, 2 February 1921, CA 104, 180.03301/104, NA, RG 256.

22 CA Minutes, 27 April 1921, CA 117, 180.03301/87, NA, RG 256. Germany said that Finland, Czechoslovakia and Paraguay were potential buyers. See CA Minutes, 15 June 1921, CA 126, 180.03301/126, NA, RG 256. Later, Spain was added to the list. See CA Minutes, 23 November 1921, CA 153, 180.03301/153, NA, RG 256.

23 CA Minutes, 17 August 1921, CA 138, 180.03301/138, NA, RG 256; Hardinge to Curzon, 2 February 1921, *DBFP*, XVI, p. 630.

24 CA Minutes, 11 October 1922, CA 189, 180.033/189, NA, RG 256.

25 Gustav Hilger, *The Incompatible Allies* (New York: Macmillan., 1953), p. 194.

26 R. Lindsay to Chamberlain, 22 February 1927, *DBFP*, Series Ia, III, pp. 42-4.

27 Leslie to Porter, 16 July 1920, *DBFP*, X, p. 360.

28 Intelligence summary, 1 September 1920, PRO, FO 371/4793, C5359/676/18.

29 Intelligence summary, 13 October 1920, PRO, FO 371/4794, 8746/676/18; CA Minutes, 11 January 1922, NA, RG 256, CA 161, 180.03301/161.

30 CA Minutes, 14 February 1920, CA 11, 180.03301/11, NA, RG 256; CA Minutes, 4 March 1920, CA 16, 180.03301/16, NA, RG 256.

31 Derby to Curzon, 4 March 1920, *DBFP*, X, pp. 28-9.

32 CA Minutes, 5 August 1921, CA 136, 180.03301/136, NA, RG 256; CA Minutes, 23 November 1921, CA 153, 180.03301/153, NA, RG 256.

33 CA Minutes, 16 February 1922, CA 166, 180.03301/166, NA, RG 256.

34 Sthamer to Curzon, 8 April 1922, PRO, FO 371/7450, C5463/6/18.

35 IAMCC to the Director of Foreign Affairs of the German Empire (*sic*), 12 May 1921, *DBFP*, XVI, p. 876.

36 See William Henderson, *The Rise of German Industrial Power* (London: Temple Smith, 1975); Helmut Bohme, *An Introduction to the Social and Economic History of Germany* (New York: St. Martin's Press, 1978); David S. Landes, *The Unbound Prometheus: Technological Change and Industrial Development in Western Europe From 1750 to the Present* (Cambridge: Cambridge University Press, 1969), pp. 263-73.

37 Conference between Winston Churchill and André Lefevre, 30 April 1920, *DBFP*, X, p. 62. Churchill was skeptical, however, about the idea of maintaining the disarmament of Germany. See Donald G. Boadle, *Winston Churchill and the German Question in British Foreign Policy, 1918–1922* (The Hague: Martinus Nijhoff, 1973), p. 25.

38 *Treaty of Peace With Germany*, p. 74.

39 CA Minutes, 10 February 1920, CA 10, 180.03301/10, NA, RG 256; G. Grahame to Curzon, 10 February 1920, *DBFP*, X, pp. 18–19, and Derby to Curzon, 22 May 1920, *DBFP*, X, pp. 105–6.

40 AMCV, Execution des Clauses Militaires et Aeriennes du Traité de Paix, 6 June 1920, MAE, Europe 1918–1940, Allemagne, Vol. 59; Memorandum by the Secretary of State for War, 28 June 1920, CAB 24/108, CP 1550. The Allies authorized two factories for artillery, two factories for machine-guns and rifles, and two factories for ammunition.

41 Oertzen to Reparations Commission, CA Minutes, 29 September 1922, CA 195, NA, RG 256.

42 Nollet to Foch, Report #37, 8 February 1922, PRO, FO 371/7449 and *BDFA*, Series F, Europe, 1919–1939, Vol. 33, Germany, 1922, pp. 55–64; Morgan Report, 15 December 1921, FO 371/6076, C23963/23963/18; Morgan, *Assize of Arms*, II, p. 179. In Morgan's second volume, he claims that upwards of fifteen German factories were authorized to produce war material.

43 Morgan, *Assize of Arms*, II, p. 313.

44 Report of the AMCV to the Supreme Council, 13 August 1921, PRO, FO 371/5878, C16555/47/18; Nollet, *Une Expérience*, p. 178; Morgan, *Assize of Arms*, II, p. 290. Morgan states that the Germans claimed only 3,400 factories. The AMCV earlier reported that Germany claimed 2,400 state factories. See AMCV, Execution des Clauses, 6 June 1920, MAE, Europe 1918–1940, Allemagne, Vol. 59. French Army Headquarters reported that Germany had about 3,500 factories and stated that Germany claimed only about 1,500. The discrepancies in these numbers are most likely due to the distinction between state and private factories and the fact that as control wore on more factories were discovered. Regardless, Germany claimed far fewer factories than the Allies discovered. See also Army Headquarters, 27 August 1920, MAE, Europe 1918–1940, Allemagne, Vol. 60.

45 Morgan, *Assize of Arms*, II, p. 343. German factories were given a *Quitus*, or a clearance certificate.

46 Salewski, *Entwaffnung und Militärkontrolle*, p. 101.

47 WO Memo, 3 March 1924, PRO, FO 371/9724.

48 Nollet, *Une Expérience*, pp. 21–2. This subject will be subsequently examined.

49 AMCV, Report on the Work of the British Section During 1920, PRO, FO 371/5844, C4674/4674/62; Air Commodore Masterman to Herr Mertens, 22 March 1920, *DBFP*, X, pp. 53–4.

50 Nollet to Foch, Report #30, 18 January 1921, PRO, FO 371/5981, C2544/461/18.

51 Question of the "Deutsche Werke," CA Minutes, 12 December 1921, CA 159, 180.03301/159, NA, RG 256; Opinion of the IAMCC, CA Minutes, 20 June 1921, CA 130, 180.03301/130, NA, RG 256.

52 Minutes of the IAMCC Council, 23 April 1920, CA Minutes, CA 45, 180.03301/45, NA, RG 256. In a rare state of mutual agreement, General Morgan supported Bingham and believed that the IAMCC had no legal right to destroy machinery intended for general use.

53 AMCV Report of 7 May 1920, CA Minutes, 26 May 1920, CA 45, 180.03301/45, NA, RG 256; Morgan, *Assize of Arms*, II, pp. 318–19. Morgan

points out that 90 percent of German machinery that had been employed in war production was left intact, 5 percent dispersed, and only 5 percent destroyed.

54 Morgan, *Assize of Arms*, II, pp. 321–5; Williamson, *The British in Germany*, p. 189; Opinion of the IAMCC, CA Minutes, 20 June 1921, CA 130, 180.03301/130, NA, RG 256.
55 CA Minutes, 4 March 1920, CA 16, 180.03301/16, NA, RG 256.
56 Salewski, *Entwaffnung und Militärkontrolle*, pp. 104–5.
57 Bingham to Lloyd George, 19 April 1920, Lloyd George Papers, F/9/2/26.
58 AMCV, Execution des Clauses Militaires et Aeriennes du Traité de Paix, 6 June 1920, MAE, Europe 1918–1940, Allemagne, Vol. 59.
59 Morgan, *Assize of Arms*, II, p. 343.
60 Morgan Report, 21 December 1921, PRO, FO 371/ 6076, C23963.
61 Nollet, *Une Expérience*, pp. 183–4; Benoist-Méchin, *Histoire de L'Armée Allemande*, 1918–1946, I, p. 341.
62 Bingham to Director of Military Intelligence, 30 August 1920, PRO, FO 371/4810, C6170/1196/18.
63 Simons to Nollet, 14 October 1920, PRO, FO 371/4844, C8801/8801/18; Nollet to Foch, Report 27, 15 November 1920, MAE, Europe 1918–1940, Allemagne, Vol. 62.
64 Bingham to D'Abernon, 15 July 1921, PRO, FO 371/5878, C16345.
65 Salewski, *Entwaffnung und Militärkontrolle*, pp. 102–3.
66 Nollet to Foch, Report #30, 18 January 1921, PRO, FO 371/5981, C2544/461/18.
67 Nollet to Foch, Report #31, 24 February 1921, PRO, FO 371/5982, C4694/461/18.
68 Nollet to Foch, Report #32, 24 March 1921, PRO, FO 371/5982, C7081/461/18.
69 WO to FO, 13 July 1921, PRO, FO 371/5858, C14312/13/18.
70 Morgan, *Assize of Arms*, II, p. 326; Gordon Young, *The Fall and Rise of Alfried Krupp* (London: Cassell, 1960), pp. 13–21; Peter Batty, *The House of Krupp* (New York: Stein & Day, 1966), pp. 41–114.
71 Oertzen to Reparations Commission, CA Minutes, 29 September 1922, CA 195, 180.03301/195, NA, RG 256.
72 Bernhard Menne, *Krupp: The Lords of Essen* (London: William Hodge, 1937), p. 347; Gert von Klass (trans. James Cleugh), *Krupp: The Story of an Industrial Empire* (London: Sidgwick & Jackson, 1954), p. 328; William Manchester, *The Arms of Krupp 1587–1968* (Boston, MA, and Toronto: Little, Brown, 1968), p. 324.
73 Cambon to Hankey, 1 June 1920, *DBFP*, X, p. 121.
74 Morgan, *Assize of Arms*, II, p. 328; Salewski, *Entwaffnung und Militärkontrolle*, p. 102; Nollet, *Une Expérience*, p. 179. Five or six British officers and two French officers lived in Essen with full access to the plant.
75 Bingham, "Work With the Allied Commission of Control in Germany, 1919–1924," p. 755; Manchester, *The Arms of Krupp 1587–1968*, pp. 323–4.
76 Morgan, *Assize of Arms*, II, p. 330; Williamson, *The British in Germany*, p. 189.
77 Werner Hänsel, "Historische Aspekte der Abrüstung in Deutschland und die Rüstungskonversion in der DDR," *Militärgeschichte*, 1990, 29 (4), p. 381; Barton Whaley, "Covert Rearmament in Germany 1919–1939: Deception and Misperception," *File Journal of Strategic Studies*, 1982, 5 (1), p. 4; Manchester, *The Arms of Krupp*, p. 305.
78 Opinion of the IAMCC, CA Minutes, 20 June 1921, CA 130, 180.03301/130, NA, RG 256; Morgan, *Assize of Arms*, II, pp. 334–5.

79 Williamson, *The British in Germany*, p. 189.
80 D'Abernon Annual Report, 2 February 1922, PRO, FO 371/7556, C2067/2067/18.
81 War Office to Curzon, 5 December 1921, PRO, FO 371/5865, C22955/37/18; Dr. Lucien-Graux, *Histoire des violations du traité de paix*, III (Paris: Les Éditions G. Crès, 1921–27), p. 246.
82 Smallbones to Curzon, 8 November 1921, PRO, FO 371/5879, C21610/47/18.
83 Hardinge to Curzon, 29 November 1922, *DBFP*, XX, p. 612.
84 Waterlow Conversation with German Ambassador, 12 December 1921, *DBFP*, XVI, p. 991; Seeds to Curzon, Memorandum of the Bavarian Minister of Commerce, 24 November 1921, PRO, FO 371/5880, C22648/47/18.
85 Question of the "Deutsche Werke," CA Minutes, 12 December 1921, CA 159, 180.03301/159, NA, RG 256.
86 Salewski, *Entwaffnung und Militärkontrolle*, p. 103; Nollet, *Une Expérience*, p. 182. Deutsche Werke no longer existed in its original state but was renamed *Vereinigte Industrie-Unternehmungen*.
87 Nollet to Foch, Report #37, 8 February 1922, PRO, FO 371/7449. See also *DBFP*, XX, p. 430.
88 Hoesch to Poincaré, 16 August 1922, PRO, FO 371/7452, C14535/6/18.
89 FO Summary, 2 November 1922, PRO, FO 371/7452, C15081/6/18. Four of the five demands concerned armaments: the transformation of factories, surrender of excess war material, surrender of 1918 armament registers, passage of legislation forbidding the import and export of war material, as well as reorganizing the German army.

6 Effectives: the reduction of German military forces

1 For the development and training of the *Reichswehr*, see David N. Spires, *Image and Reality: The Making of the German Officer, 1921–1933* (Westport, CT, and London: Greenwood Press, 1984).
2 Nollet Memoire, 15 May 1920, MAE, Europe 1918–1929, Allemagne, Vol. 59.
3 See Nollet, *Une Expérience*, pp. 233–6, 246–7.
4 Army Headquarters, Le Désarmement de l'Allemagne, 27 August 1920, MAE, Europe 1918–1929, Allemagne, Vol. 60.
5 Nollet to the President of the Council, 4 October 1920, MAE, Europe 1918–1929, Allemagne, Vol. 61. See also Roques, *Le Contrôle Militaire Interallié en Allemagne*, p. 5.
6 Nollet to the President of the Council, 18 March 1922, MAE, Europe 1918–1929, Allemagne, Vol. 224.
7 Nollet, *Une Expérience*, p. 35.
8 IAMCC, Tables and Composition, 29 July 1919, Container 308, Bliss Papers, LC.
9 Nollet, *Une Expérience*, p. 19. The Effectives District Committees were located in Berlin, Breslau, Dresden, Königsberg, Munich, Munster, Stettin, and Stuttgart.
10 Nollet, *Une Expérience*, p. 50.
11 John Hartman Morgan, *German Atrocities: An Official Investigation* (New York: E.P. Dutton, 1916), pp. 35–57. The German press reacted violently to Morgan's claims. See von Este article from *Berliner Lokal Anzeiger*, 28 January 1925, Library of Congress, U.S. Military Intelligence Reports (translation).

12 CA Minutes, 17 February 1920, CA12, 180.03301/12, NA, RG 256; Kilmarnock to Curzon, 23 January 1920, *DBFP*, X, pp. 1–2.
13 General Staff Memorandum, 29 December 1919, PRO, CAB 24/96, Command Paper 428; Edmonds, *The Occupation of the Rhineland*, p. 213.
14 General Staff Memorandum, 5 February 1920, PRO, CAB 24/98, Command Paper, 632; Curzon to Kilmarnock, 11 March 1920, *DBFP*, X, pp. 34–5; Hardinge to Curzon, 22 April 1920, *DBFP*, X, p. 70.
15 CA Minutes, 17 February 1920, CA 12, 180.03301/12, NA, RG 256; Derby to Curzon, 18 February 1920, *DBFP*, X, p. 20.
16 Army Headquarters, Le Désarmement de l'Allemagne, 27 August 1920, MAE, Europe 1918–1940, Allemagne, Vol. 60; Lloyd George to Sthamer, 18 February 1920, *DBFP*, X, p. 21.
17 Foch to Conference of Ambassadors, 19 March 1920, MAE, Europe 1918–1940, Allemagne, Vol. 58 and *DBFP*, X, pp. 51–2.
18 Nollet to Foch, Report 9, 24 April 1920, MAE, Europe 1918–1940, Allemagne, Vol. 58.
19 Nollet to Foch, Report 10, 1 May 1920, MAE, Europe 1918–1940, Allemagne, Vol. 59. The German government reported in June that the *Freikorps* had been disbanded, with some of the units incorporated into the *Reichswehr*. See IAMCC Intelligence summaries, 6 July 1920, PRO, FO 371/4792, C676/676/18.
20 CA Minutes, 21 April 1920, CA 33, 180.033/33, NA, RG 256.
21 Morgan, *Assize of Arms*, II, p. 183; AMCV Note, 1 June 1920, MAE, Europe 1918–1940, Allemagne, Vol. 59; AMCV Draft Report, 19 May 1920, *DBFP*, X, pp. 113–17; G. Grahame to Curzon, 1 June 1920, *DBFP*, X, pp. 112–13.
22 Kerr to Lloyd George, 12 May 1920, LG Papers, F/90/1/8; Göppert to Foreign Office, 12 April 1920, ADAP, Serie A, III, pp. 191–2.
23 CA Minutes, 20 June 1920, CA 52, 180.033/52, NA, RG 256.
24 AMCV, Execution des Clauses Militaires du Traité de Paix, 17 June 1920, MAE, Allemagne, Europe 1918–1940, Vol. 59; Morgan, *Assize of Arms*, II, pp. 190–4.
25 Notes of a Conservation, San Remo Conference, 24 April 1920, *DBFP*, VIII, p. 144.
26 Allied Declaration, 26 April 1920, *DBFP*, VIII, pp. 209–10.
27 Statement of the Military Experts, 21 June 1920, *DBFP*, VIII, pp. 357–8.
28 Spa Conference, 6 July 1920, 180.0801/2, NA, RG 256. See also *DBFP*, VIII, pp. 433–4. Seeckt insisted that a 200,000-man army was a necessity for Germany. See Seeckt to Simons, 27 June 1920, ADAP, Serie A, III, pp. 302–6.
29 Seeckt proposed a gradual reduction of the *Reichswehr* in steps: 190,000 by 10 October 1920, 180,000 by 10 January 1921, 160,000 by 10 April 1921, 130,000 by 10 July 1921, and 100,000 by 10 October 1921. See Spa Conference, 7 July 1920, 180.0801/3, NA, RG 256; *DBFP*, VIII, p. 466; and Walter Goerlitz, *History of the German General Staff* (New York: Prager, 1953), p. 216.
30 Spa Conference, 8 July 1920, LG Papers, F/148/7/4.
31 Spa Conference, 8 July 1920, 180.0801/5, NA, RG 256; *DBFP*, VIII, p. 481; ADAP, Serie A, III, pp. 353–8. Lloyd George was influenced by both General Bingham and his adjutant, Lt.-Colonel Roddie, in modifying the effectives clauses to allow Germany more troops to quell any popular unrest. See Roddie, *Peace Patrol*, pp. 162–5.
32 Spa Conference, 8 and 9 July 1920, 180.0801/5 and 180.0801/6, NA, RG 256.

33 IAMCC Intelligence summaries, 2 August 1920, PRO, FO 371/4793, C3619/676/18.
34 For Seeckt's plans to reduce the *Reichswehr* to 100,000 men, see Seeckt to the Inter Allied Military Control Commission, 27 August 1920, ADAP, Series A, III, pp. 525–6.
35 Nollet to Foch, Report #26, 17 November 1920, PRO, FO 371/4794, C11538/676/18.
36 IAMCC Intelligence summaries, 12 November 1920, PRO, FO 371/4795, C11789/676/18; Nollet to Foch, Report #28, 29 November 1920, PRO, FO 371/4795, C13847/676/18; Foch to the President of the Conference of Ambassadors, 28 December 1920, FO 371/5853.
37 IAMCC Intelligence summaries, 26 November 1920, PRO, FO 371/4795, C13152/676/18.
38 Annual Report 1920, FO 371/6060, C9605/9605/18.
39 War Office Memo, 15 January 1921, Command Paper 2472, PRO, FO 371/5854, C1271/13/18.
40 Kilmarnock to Curzon, 7 May 1921, PRO, FO 371/6060, C9605/9605/18.
41 Nollet to Foch, Report #30, 18 January 1921, PRO, FO 371/5981, C2544,/461/18; Nollet to Foch, Report #31, 24 February 1921, PRO, FO 371/5982, C4694/461/18; Briand to President of German Delegation, 29 January 1921, LG Papers, F/113.
42 Nollet to Foch, Report #32, 24 March 1921, PRO, FO 371/5982, C7081/461/18; War Office Memo, 19 April 1921, *DBFP*, XVI, p. 650.
43 Nollet to Foch, Report #33, 11 April 1921, PRO, FO 371/5982, C8137/461/18; War Office Memo, 5 August 1921, PRO, CAB 24/126, CP 3198. See also Nollet to Foch, Report #32, 24 March 1921, FO 371/5982, C7081.
44 AMCV Report, 13 August 1921, PRO, FO 371/5878 and CAB 24/127, CP 3233.
45 See Morgan's three reports of 12 March, 12 May, and 10 June 1920 in *DBFP*, X, pp. 36–42, 86–104, and 134–7, respectively. These reports led to a clash between Morgan and Bingham which will be examined below in Chapter 8.
46 Morgan Memo, 20 June 1921, PRO, FO 371/6076 and *DBFP*, XVI, pp. 905–15.
47 Nollet to Foch, Report #37, 8 February 1922, PRO, FO 371/7449 and *BDFA*, Series F, Europe, 1919–1939, Vol. 33, Germany, 1922, pp. 55–64.
48 Milne Cheetham to Balfour, 24 July 1922, PRO, FO 371/7451, C10566/6/18.
49 General Nollet to German government, 11 July 1922, PRO, FO 371/7451, C10566/6/18; Nollet to Foch, Report #40, 25 July 1922, PRO, FO 371/7451, C10661/6/18. This issue will be discussed below in Chapter 8.
50 FO Minutes, 30 June 1922, PRO, FO 371/7451, C9663/6/18. See also Morgan to Tyrrell, 28 November 1922, *DBFP*, XX, p. 609, n. 1.
51 FO Minutes, 23 December 1922, PRO, FO 371/ 7561, C17141/3589/18.
52 CA Minutes, 5 April 1922, CA 172, 180.033/172, NA, RG 256.
53 The attacks upon IAMCC officers in Passau and Ingolstadt will be addressed below in Chapter 9.
54 General Staff Memorandum, 1 November 1921, *DBFP*, XVI, pp. 970–1.
55 Nollet Memoire, 15 May 1920, MAE, Europe 1918–1940, Allemagne, Vol. 59.
56 IAMCC Intelligence notes, 24 June 1921, PRO, FO 371/5983, C13628/461/18. Armaments for the police were designated as follows: one sword/dagger per man, one short pistol per man, one rifle or carbine with bayonet per three men, one machine pistol per twenty men (300 for the entire force), and 150 armored cars for the entire force.

57 Foch to Conference of Ambassadors, 19 March 1920, MAE, Europe 1918–1940, Allemagne, Vol. 58; Nollet Memoire, 15 May 1920, MAE, Europe 1918–1940, Allemagne, Vol. 59; Lucien-Graux, *Histoire des Violations du Traité de Paix*, I, p. 136, n.1; General Staff Memorandum, 1 November 1921, *DBFP*, XVI, pp. 970–2. For the creation of the *Sipo*, see Salewski, *Entwaffnung und Militärkontrolle*, p. 82.

58 General Staff Memorandum, 29 December 1919, PRO, CAB 24/96, CP 428.

59 War Office Memo, 5 February 1920, *DBFP*, IX, p. 42; Morgan Report, 12 March 1920, *DBFP*, X, pp. 37–8; AMCV Report, 19 May 1920, *DBFP*, X, p. 115; AMCV Report, 26 May 1920, *DBFP*, X, p. 122; Foch to CoA Pres., 19 March 1920, *DBFP*, X, p. 52.

60 Memorandum by the Secretary of State for War, 28 June 1920, PRO, CAB 24/108, CP 1550.

61 IAMCC Intelligence summaries, 5 July 1920, FO 371/4792, C1314/676/18.

62 Echéances du Désarmement du 13 Mai au 1er Juillet 1920, MAE, Europe 1918–1940, Allemagne, Vol. 59.

63 AMCV Report, 1 June 1920, MAE, Europe 1918–1940, Allemagne, Vol. 59; AMCV Report, 19 May 1920, *DBFP*, X, pp. 115–17.

64 See also AMCV Report, 26 May 1920, *DBFP*, X, p. 118.

65 Nollet to Foch, Report 22, 18 September 1920, MAE, Europe 1918–1940, Allemagne, Vol. 61; CA Minutes, 20 June 1920, CA 52, NA, RG 256; General Staff Memorandum, 1 November 1921, *DBFP*, XVI, pp. 970–4; Foreign Office Memo, 19 June 1922, *DBFP*, XX, p. 487.

66 Army Headquarters, Le Désarmement de L'Allemagne, 27 August 1920, MAE, Europe 1918–1940, Allemagne, Vol. 60.

67 Nollet, *Une Expérience*, p. 208.

68 Nollet to Foch, Report 26, 30 October 1920 and Nollet to Foch, Report 27, 15 November 1920, MAE, Europe 1918–1940, Allemagne, Vol. 61. The other German states were Württemberg, Baden, Hesse, Lübeck, Saxony, Brunswick, and Hamburg, though Baden and Hesse omitted clauses that forbade heavy armament of its police. See also IAMCC Intelligence summaries, 14 October 1920 and 17 October 1920, PRO, FO 371/4794, C9099/676/18 and C10309/676/18, respectively.

69 LG Papers, Agreement Between the Allied Powers, 29 January 1921, F/113, CP 2572; War Office Memorandum, 15 January 1921, CP 2472, PRO, FO 371/5854, C1271/13/18.

70 IAMCC Intelligence summaries, 12 November 1920, PRO, FO 371/4795, C11789/676/18; General Staff Memorandum, 1 November 1921, *DBFP*, XVI, p. 973.

71 IAMCC Intelligence summaries, 17 December 1920, PRO, FO 371/4795, C15050/676/18.

72 Berlin Note, 27 December 1920, PRO, FO 371/5853, C267/13/18.

73 General Staff Memorandum, 1 November 1921, *DBFP*, XVI, p. 974.

74 Kilmarnock to Curzon, 25 January 1921, *DBFP*, X, p. 624, n. 4.

75 Sthamer to Curzon, 3 January 1921, PRO, FO 371/5853, C352/13/18.

76 Kilmarnock to Foreign Office, 28 December 1920, PRO, FO 371/4759, C14887/113/18.

77 General Staff Memorandum, 19 April 1921, *DBFP*, XVI, p. 651; AMCV Report, 13 August 1921, PRO, FO 371/5878.

78 General Staff Memo, 31 March 1922, *DBFP*, XX, p. 431 and Orme Sargent to Lampson, 10 June 1922, *DBFP*, XX, p. 471; Foreign Office Memo, 19 June 1922, *DBFP*, XX, p. 487.

79 Nollet to Foch, Report, 8 February 1922, PRO, FO 371/7449 and *BDFA*,

Series F, Europe, 1919–1939, Vol. 33, Germany, 1922, pp. 55–64; Nollet to Rathenau, 23 March 1922, ADAP, Series A, VI, pp. 56–7.

80 Foreign Office Memo, 19 June 1922, *DBFP*, XX, p. 487.

81 The German term for paramilitary organizations was *Selbstschutz*: self-defense or self-protection forces.

82 James M. Diehl, *Paramilitary Politics in Weimar Germany* (Bloomington and London: Indiana University Press, 1977), p. 28.

83 Foch to Conference of Ambassadors, 19 March 1920, MAE, Europe 1918–1940, Allemagne, Vol. 58; David Clay Large, "The Politics of Law and Order: A History of the Bavarian Einwohnerwehr, 1981–1921," *Transactions of the American Philosophical Society*, 1980, 70 (2), p. 66.

84 General Staff Memorandum, 7 April 1920, PRO, CAB 24/103, CP 1030.

85 Diehl, *Paramilitary Politics in Germany*, pp. 28–36. British intelligence included the *Zeitfreiwillige* as a subsidiary organization of the *Einwohnerwehr*. See General Staff Memorandum, 29 December 1919, PRO, CAB 24/96, CP 428.

86 Morgan Report, 12 May 1920, *DBFP*, X, p. 89 and Nollet to Foch, Report 9, 24 April 1920, MAE, Europe 1918–1940, Allemagne, Vol. 58; Robert G. L. Waite, *Vanguard of Nazism: the Free-Corps Movement in Postwar Germany 1918–1923* (Cambridge, MA: Harvard University Press, 1952), p. 40; Craig, *The Politics of the Prussian Army, 1640–1945* (New York: Oxford University Press, 1964, first published 1955), p. 360; Diehl, *Paramilitary Politics in Weimar Germany*, p. 29.

87 Nollet to Foch, Report 9, 24 April 1920, MAE, Europe 1918–1940, Allemagne, Vol. 58.

88 Nollet to Foch, Report #37, 8 February 1922, PRO, FO 371/7449 and *BDFA*, Series F, Europe, 1919–1939, Vol. 33, Germany, 1922, pp. 55–64.

89 General Staff Memorandum, 29 December 1919, PRO, CAB24/96, CP 428.

90 Nollet Memoire, 15 May 1920, MAE, Europe 1918–1940, Allemagne, Vol. 59.

91 War Office Memo, 5 February 1920, *DBFP*, IX, p. 42.

92 Morgan Report, 12 May 1920, *DBFP*, X, p. 90.

93 Nollet to Foch, Report 15, 12 June 1920 and AMCV Observations, 16 June 1920 and AMCV, Execution des Clauses Militaires, 17 June 1920, MAE, Europe 1918–1940, Allemagne, Vol. 59; Memorandum by the Secretary of State for War, 28 June 1920, PRO, CAB 24/108, CP 1550.

94 Salewski, *Entwaffnung und Militärkontrolle*, p. 91.

95 General Staff Memorandum, 29 December 1919 and 5 February 1920, PRO, CAB24/96, CP 428 and CAB 24/98, CP 632 respectively; Nollet Memoire, 15 May 1920, MAE, Europe 1918–1940, Allemagne, Vol. 59.

96 Bingham Diary, 21 October 1919, Ball Papers, IWM; Seeds to Curzon, 14 April 1921, *DBFP*, XVI, pp. 649–50.

97 Nollet Memoire, 15 May 1920, MAE, Europe 1918–1940, Allemagne, Vol. 59; War Office Memo, 5 February 1920, *DBFP*, IX, p. 42; Malcolm Notes, 2 December 1920, *DBFP*, X, p. 452. The actual strength of the *Einwohnerwehr* was in constant flux and hard to determine at any particular time. Morgan estimated their strength to be about 500,000. See Morgan Report, 12 May 1920, *DBFP*, X, p. 100.

98 IAMCC Intelligence summaries, 3 August 1920, PRO, FO 371/4792, C3029/676/18; see Large, "The Politics of Law and Order," for a detailed look at the politics of the *Einwohnerwehr*.

99 Morgan Report, 12 March 1920, *DBFP*, X, p. 39; Curzon to Smallbones, 20 September 1920, *DBFP*, X, pp. 389–90.

100 AMCV, Execution des Clauses Militaires, 17 June 1920, MAE, Europe 1918–1940, Allemagne, Vol. 59; Cambon to Hankey, 1 June 1920, *DBFP*, X, p. 122.
101 Nollet to Foch, Report 19, 21 August 1920, MAE, Europe 1918–1940, Allemagne, Vol. 60.
102 Echéances du Désarmement du 13 Mai au 1er Juillet 1920, MAE, Europe 1918–1940, Allemagne, Vol. 59.
103 Smallbones to Curzon, 14 April 1920, *DBFP*, X, p. 63.
104 German government to Nollet, 12 March 1920, CAB 24/108, CP 1550.
105 Nollet to Foch, Report #16, 24 June 1920, PRO, FO 371/4792, C1029/676/18.
106 Army Headquarters, 27 August 1920, MAE, Europe 1918–1940, Allemagne, Vol. 60. See also CA Minutes, 5 June 1920, CA 47, 180.03301/47, NA, RG 256. The overall numbers are difficult to evaluate precisely but the French tended to consolidate all the self-defense organizations under the *Einwohnerwehr*.
107 Nollet to Foch, Report 19, 21 August 1920 and Report 20, 4 September 1920, MAE, Allemagne, Europe 1918–1940, Vol. 60 and Report 24, 17 October 1920, Report 25, 18 October 1920, MAE, Europe 1918–1940, Allemagne, Vol. 61.
108 War Office to Curzon, 28 August 1920, PRO, FO 371/4784, C5130/484/18. See also Robert Kelley to Director of Military Intelligence, 4 November 1920, Illegal Military Organizations in Germany, U.S. Military Intelligence Reports: Germany, 1919–1941, University Publications of America, 1983, Library of Congress (taken from Record Group 165, Records of the War Department General and Special Staffs, Military Intelligence Division, National Archives, Washington, D.C.). Hereafter cited as U.S. Military Intelligence Reports.
109 IAMCC Intelligence summaries, September 1920, PRO, FO 371/4794; Kilmarnock to Curzon, 13 August 1920, *DBFP*, X, pp. 373–5.
110 IAMCC Intelligence summaries, 16 August 1920, PRO, FO 371/4793, C5359/676/18: Intelligence summaries, 12 November 1920, PRO, FO 371/4795, C11789/676/18; Nollet to Foch, Report 19, 21 August 1920, MAE, Allemagne, Vol. 60, Europe 1918–1940. See also Note sur la Question des Einwohnerwehren, 16 January 1921, MAE, Europe 1918–1929, Allemagne, Vol. 65.
111 Nollet to Foch, Report #27, 15 November 1920, PRO, FO 371/4795, C12720/676/18.
112 Memorandum by Captain P.G.E. Warburton, 10 November 1920, *DBFP*, X, pp. 435–8.
113 Nollet to German government, 11 December 1920, PRO, FO 371/4758, C14196/113/18. See also CA Minutes, 27 December 1920, CA 99, 180.03301/99, NA, RG 256.
114 Foreign Office Minutes, 28 December 1920, PRO, FO 371/4759, C14811/113/18.
115 War Office, Memorandum on the Execution by Germany of the Military Articles of the Peace Treaty of Versailles, 15 January 1921, PRO, FO 371/5854, C1271/13/18; Williamson, *The British in Germany*, pp. 143–5; WO to FO, 24 December 1920, PRO, FO 371/ 4758, C14711/113/18; D'Abernon to Curzon, 22 October 1920 and 23 November 1920, British Museum, D'Abernon Papers, 48924A; Viscount Edgar Vincent D'Abernon, *An Ambassador of Peace*, Vol. I (London: Hodder & Stoughton, 1929), pp. 20–4, 87.
116 Seeds to Curzon, 8 April 1921, *DBFP*, XVI, p. 644.
117 Simons to Ritter von Kahr, 7 January 1921, and Ritter von Kahr to the Foreign Office, 10 January 1921, ADAP, Series A, IV, pp. 230–1 and 239–44.

118 Large, "The Politics of Law and Order," pp. 73–4.
119 IAMCC Intelligence summaries, 4 June 1921, PRO, FO 371/5983, C13628/461/18. The Einwohnerwehr reportedly still possessed approximately 250,000 rifles. See Seeds to Curzon, 14 April 1921, and Kilmarnock to Curzon, 9 May 1921, *DBFP*, XVI, pp. 649 and 871, respectively.
120 Nollet to Foch, Report #37, 8 February 1922, PRO, FO 371/7449 and *BDFA*, Series F, Europe, 1919–1939, Vol. 33, Germany, 1922, pp. 55–64.
121 D'Abernon to Curzon, 10 July 1921, D'Abernon Papers, 48924A.
122 The *Einwohnerwehr* became the *Bund Bayern und Reich* in 1922, and lasted for seven years until it merged with the Stahlhelm. See Diehl, *Paramilitary Politics in Weimar Germany*, pp. 102–3. Other paramilitary organizations in Germany that existed under Allied control were the *Stahlhelm*, *Sturmabteilung* (SA), *Deutscher Notbann*, and *Reichsbanner*. Yet these organizations never threatened Allied disarmament efforts as had the *Einwohnerwehr* from 1920 to 1921. Infighting and the golden years of the Weimar kept them largely in check.
123 AMCV Report, 13 August 1921, FO 371/5878.
124 CA Minutes, 5 April 1922, CA 172, 180.03301/172, NA, RG 256.
125 Nollet to Foch, Report #40, 11 July 1922, PRO, FO 371/7451, C10661/6/18.

7 Fortifications: the destruction of German defenses

1 Among others, there were German fortifications located in Cologne, Mainz, Coblenz, Istein, Kiel, Königsberg, Elten, Wesel, Germersheim, Rastaat, Bruckenkopf, Robsdorf, Pillau, Swinemünde, Küstrin, and Ulm. For example, See Nollet to Foch, Report #31, 24 February 1921, PRO, FO 371/5982, C4694/461/18.
2 Article 167 allowed 1,500 rounds for each gun 105 mm and smaller and only 500 rounds for guns above this caliber.
3 CA Minutes, 22 May 1920, CA 44, 180.03301/44, NA, RG 256.
4 IAMCC, Tables and Composition, 29 July 1919, Container 308, Bliss Papers, LC.
5 Nollet, *Une Expérience*, p. 19.
6 Bingham to Lloyd George, 19 April 1920, Lloyd George Papers, HLRO, F/9/2/26; Bingham Diary, 15 March 1920, Ball Papers, IWM; IAMCC Opinion, CA Minutes, 16 October 1920, CA 91, 180.03301/91, NA, RG 256; Morgan, *Assize of Arms*, II, p. 205. The number included 2,034 heavy guns, 1,491 light guns, and 510 anti-aircraft guns. See Morgan, *Assize of Arms*, II, p. 208, note 2.
7 Foch to Conference of Ambassadors, 19 March 1920, MAE, Europe 1918–1940, Allemagne, Vol. 58.
8 Nollet to Cramon, 9 February 1920 and Nollet to Foch, 26 February 1920, MAE, Europe 1918–1940, Allemagne, Vol. 58.
9 Cramon to Nollet, 21 February 1920, MAE, Allemagne, Europe 1918–1940, Vol. 58.
10 CA Minutes, 11 March 1920, CA 18, 180.033/18, NA, RG 256; Foch to Conference of Ambassadors, 19 March 1920, MAE, Europe 1918–1940, Allemagne, Vol. 58; Memorandum of the Secretary of State for War, 28 June 1920, PRO, CAB 24/108, CP 1550; AMCV, Report on the Work of the British Section During 1920, PRO, FO 371/5844, C4674/4674/62.
11 Nollet to Cramon, CA Minutes, 13 March 1920, CA 91 and IAMCC Opinion, CA Minutes, 16 October 1920, CA 91, 180.03301/91, NA, RG 256. These

forts were located in Breslau, Neisse, Glatz, Glogau, Spandau, Boyen, Marienburg, Ingolstadt, and Königstein.

12 AMCV, Observations Concernant l'Execution des Clauses Militaries du Traité
de Paix, 16 June 1920, MAE, Europe 1918–1940, Allemagne, Vol. 59.
13 Nollet to Foch, 1 May 1920, Report 10, MAE, Europe 1918–1940, Allemagne,
Vol. 59.
14 AMCV, Observations Concernant l'Execution des Clauses Militaries du Traité
de Paix, 16 June 1920, MAE, Europe 1918–1940, Allemagne, Vol. 59.
15 Memorandum by the Secretary of State for War, 28 June 1920, CAB 24/108,
CP 1550.
16 Bingham to Nollet, 10 June 1920, MAE, Europe 1918–1940, Allemagne, Vol.
59.
17 Nollet to Foch, Report #16, 24 June 1920, PRO, FO 371/4792, C1029/676/18
and Nollet to Foch, Report 17, 4 July 1920, MAE, Europe 1918–1940, Allemagne, Vol. 59. Inventories were made for Küstrin, Königsberg, Marienburg,
Memel, Ulm, Cuxhaven, Brusbuttel, Pillau, Ingolstadt, and only the forts of
Königstein, Neisse, and Glatz remained.
18 Nollet to Cramon, 23 July 1920, MAE, Europe 1918–1940, Allemagne, Vol.
59.
19 Morgan, *Assize of Arms*, II, p. 211.
20 Morgan, *Assize of Arms*, II, pp. 205–10; Bingham Diary, 15 March 1920, Ball
Papers, IWM.
21 Morgan, *Assize of Arms*, II, pp. 205–10.
22 Nollet to Foch, Report 22, 18 September 1920, MAE, Europe 1918–1940,
Allemagne, Vol. 61.
23 Nollet to Foch, Reports #23 and #24, 23 and 24 October 1920, and Bingham
to Foch, Report #26, 30 October 1920, PRO, FO 371/4794, C9100/676/18,
C10309/676/18, and C11538/676/18, respectively.
24 Nollet to Foch, Report 29, 30 November 1920, MAE, Europe 1918–1940,
Allemagne, Vol. 62.
25 Agreement Between the Allied Powers for the Settlement of Certain Questions
Relating to the Execution of the Treaty of Versailles, January 1921, HLRO,
Lloyd George Papers, F/113; Echéances du Désarmement du 13 Mai au 1er
Juillet 1920, MAE, Europe 1918–1940, Allemagne, Vol. 59; Désarmement de
l'Allemagne en 1921, 1 December 1921, MAE, Europe 1918–1929, Allemagne,
Vol. 72. The former French document lists the number of guns incorrectly as
1,986, not 1,086.
26 Morgan, *Assize of Arms*, II, p. 211.
27 Memorandum by the Secretary of State for War, 28 June 1920, CAB 24/108,
CP 1550.
28 Nollet to Foch, Report #16, 24 June 1920, PRO, FO 371/4792,
C1029/676/18.
29 Ibid.
30 Nollet to Foch, Report #20, 4 September 1920, PRO, FO 371/4793,
C6541/676/18.
31 Nollet to Foch, Report #23, 3 October 1920, PRO, FO 371/4794,
C9100/676/18.
32 Nollet to Foch, Report #24, 17 October 1920, PRO, FO 371/4794,
C10309/676/18.
33 Nollet to Foch, Report 28, 29 November 1920, MAE, Europe 1918–1940,
Allemagne, Vol. 62.
34 AMCV Report, 30 December 1920, PRO, FO 371/5853.
35 Nollet to Foch, Report # 30, 8 January 1921, PRO, FO 371/5981,

C2544/461/18; Nollet to Foch, Report #32, 24 March 1921, PRO, FO 371/5982, C7081/461/18.
36 CA Minutes, 1 April 1921, CA 112, 180.03301/112, NA, RG 256.
37 Wigram Memo, 28 July 1921, PRO, FO 371/6010, C15452/2262/18.
38 AMCV Report, 13 August 1921, PRO, FO 371/5878, C16555/47/18.
39 Bingham to D'Abernon, 18 October 1921, PRO, FO 371/5865, C20375/37/18.
40 IAMCC Council Minutes, 20 February 1923, MAE, Europe 1918–1929, Allemagne, Vol. 82.
41 Paul Roques, *Le Contrôle Militaire Interallié en Allemagne* (Paris: Berger-Levrault, 1927), p. 15.
42 Nollet, *Une Expérience*, p. 160.

8 Future control: the struggle for an Allied policy

1 Most of the military clauses included specific time limits but others, like the prohibition of the import and export of war material, tanks, and poison gas, as well as the abolition of short-term enlistments, compulsory military service, and the Great General Staff, did not.
2 John P. Fox, "Britain and the Inter-Allied Military Commission of Control, 1925–26," *Journal of Contemporary History*, 1969, 4 (2), p. 145.
3 Conclusions of the Cabinet, 11 November 1920, PRO, CAB 23/23, Cabinet 60 (20). See also Jürgen Heideking, "Vom Versailler Vertrag zur Genfer Abrüstungskonferenz: Das Scheitern der Alliierten Militärkontrollpolitik gegenüber Deutschland nach dem Ersten Weltkrieg," *Militärgeschichtliche Mitteilungen*, 1980 (2), p. 46.
4 Tardieu Questionnaire, 1920, MAE, Europe 1918–1929, Allemagne, Vol. 59.
5 Bingham to War Office, December 1920, PRO, FO 371/5864, C37/37/18.
6 Sackville-West to British Ambassador, Paris, 18 December 1920, PRO, FO 371/5462, W3494/254/17.
7 Note sur L'État d'Execution du Traité de Versailles, 12 November 1920, MAE, Europe 1918–1929, Allemagne, Vol. 62.
8 Mayer to Foreign Office, 6 January 1921, ADAP, Series A, IV, pp. 228–9.
9 WO to FO, 24 December 1920, PRO, FO 371/4758, C14711/113/18.
10 WO to Lloyd George, 12 January 1921, LG Papers, F/9/2/54; WO Report, 15 January 1921, PRO, FO 371/5854, C1274/13/18.
11 D'Abernon to Curzon, 28 December 1920, PRO, FO 371/4730, C14940/8/18.
12 D'Abernon to FO, 6 November 1921, British Museum, D'Abernon Papers, 48924A. See also D'Abernon to Curzon, 30 September 1921, *DBFP*, XVI, pp. 946–7 for D'Abernon's views toward the success of disarmament in Germany.
13 WO Report, 15 January 1921, PRO, FO 371/5854, C1274/13/18 and *DBFP*, XVI, n. 1, pp. 611–13.
14 Annales de la Chambre des Députés, 20 January 1921, Vol. 113.1, *Débats Parlementaires*, 12me Législature, pp. 13–14.
15 Foch to President of Conference of Ambassadors, 28 December 1920, PRO, FO 371/5853, C90/13/18.
16 Waterlow Memo, 20 January 1921, PRO, FO 371/5854, C1805/13/18 and *DBFP*, XVI, pp. 620–1; Williamson, *The British in Germany*, p. 145.
17 Curzon to Buchanan and Curzon to Hardinge, 31 December 1920, PRO, FO 371/4759, C14811/113/18; Curzon to Kilmarnock, 3 January 1921, Oriental and India Library, Curzon Papers, MssEur 112/240; Leygues and Berthelot to Foch, 3 January 1921, MAE, Europe 1918–1929, Allemagne, Vol. 223.
18 Waterlow Minute, 29 December 1920, PRO, FO 371/4759, C14888/113/18.

19 Roques, *Le Contrôle Militaire en Allemagne*, p. 26. See also Cabinet Decision, 12 January 1921, PRO, FO 371/5854, C854/13/18.
20 See Nollet to Foch, Report #30, 18 January 1921, PRO, FO 371/5981, C2544/461/18; Nollet to Foch, Report #32, 24 March 1921, PRO, FO 371/5982, C7081/461/18; Nollet to Foch, Report #33, 11 April 1921, PRO, FO 371/5982, C8137/461/18.
21 AMCV Report, British Section, 20 February 1922, PRO, FO 371/7441, C2626/2626/62.
22 Bingham to WO, 20 July 1921, PRO, FO 371/5864, C15301/37/18.
23 Army Council to Bingham, 1 July 1921, PRO, FO 371/5864.
24 WO to FO, 13 July 1921, PRO, FO 371/5858, C14312/13/18, Curzon Papers, MssEur 112/240, *DBFP*, XVI, pp. 927–8.
25 French Ambassador (Berlin) to Foreign Minister, 9 July 1921, MAE, Europe 1918–1929, Allemagne, Vol. 223.
26 Hardinge to FO, 13 August 1921, PRO, FO 371/5864, C16356/37/18; FO Memo, 30 August 1921, PRO, FO 371/5864, C18725/37/18; CA Minutes, 8 October 1921, CA 141, 180.03301/141, NA, RG 256.
27 AMCV Report, 13 August 1921, PRO, FO 371/5878, C16555/47/18 and CAB 24/127, C.P. 3233.
28 AMCV Report, British Section, 20 February 1922, PRO, FO 371/7441, C2626/2626/62; WO Report, 1 November 1921, PRO, FO 371/5858.
29 Wigram Minute, 30 December 1921, PRO, FO 371/5865, C24133/37/18, *DBFP*, XVI, pp. 1000–3.
30 War Office Proposal, 11 February 1922, PRO, FO 371/7448, C2427/6/18.
31 Nollet to German Foreign Minister, 10 February 1922, MAE, Europe 1918–1929, Allemagne, Vol. 224.
32 Note of the French Delegation to the Conference of Ambassadors, 14 February 1922, MAE, Europe 1918–1929, Allemagne, Vol. 74.
33 Hardinge to Curzon, 18 February 1922, PRO, FO 371/7448, C2460/6/18; Hardinge to Curzon, 4 March 1922, PRO, FO 371/7479, C9521/99/18. Hardinge's sympathies were pro-German, as he insinuated during these discussions that the French air force was a threat to Britain. See Hardinge to Curzon, 23 February 1922, Oriental and India Library, Curzon Papers, MssEur, 112/200B.
34 British Embassy Proposal, 1 March 1922, PRO, FO 371/7448, C3079/6/18. The five members were Britain, France, Italy, Belgium, and Japan.
35 CA Minutes, 4 March 1922, CA 169, 180.03301/169, NA, RG 256; Hardinge to Curzon, 4 March 1922, *DBFP*, XX, pp. 396–8.
36 Poincaré telegram, 5 March 1922, MAE, Europe 1918–1929, Allemagne, Vol. 224.
37 Conference of Ambassadors Resolution, CA 168, 1 March 1922, MAE, Europe 1918–1929, Allemagne, Vol. 224; CA Minutes, 4 March 1922, CA 169, 180.03301/169, NA, RG 256.
38 Foch to the President of the Council, MAE, 2 March 1922, MAE, Europe 1918–1929, Allemagne, Vol. 224.
39 Foch to the President of the Conference of Ambassadors, 10 March 1922, MAE, Europe 1918–1929, Allemagne, Vol. 74, 224. See also Hardinge to Curzon, 15 March 1922, *DBFP*, XX, pp. 405–6.
40 CA Minutes, 15 March 1922, CA 170, 180.03301/170, NA, RG 256.
41 CA Minutes, 5 April 1922, CA 172, 180.03301/172, NA, RG 256; Hardinge to Curzon, 1 April 1922, *DBFP*, XX, pp. 422–3.
42 Sthamer to Curzon, 8 April 1922, PRO, FO 371/7450, C5463/6/18.
43 Note pour le Président du Conseil, 21 March 1922, MAE, Europe 1918–1929,

Allemagne, Vol. 224. See also Note du General Weygand, 11 March 1922, MAE, Europe 1918–1929, Allemagne, Vol. 224.

44 Poincaré to Mayer, 14 April 1922, *DBFP*, XX, pp. 438–45; Hoesch to Poincaré, 16 August 1922, PRO, FO 371/7452, C14535/6/18.
45 Lampson Minute, 21 April 1922, PRO, FO 371/7450, C5463/6/18.
46 WO to FO, 13 June 1922, PRO, FO 371/7450, C8493/6/18.
47 General Staff Memorandum, 1 November 1921, *DBFP*, XVI, p. 964.
48 Roddie, *Peace Patrol*, p. 265.
49 Wigram Minute, 5 July 1922, PRO, FO 371/7450, C8493/6/18; Balfour to Hardinge, 7 July 1922, *DBFP*, XX, p. 483.
50 FO Minutes, 28 July 1922, PRO, FO 371/7451, C10566/6/18.
51 Nollet to Foch, 9 July 1922, PRO, FO 371/7451, C10661/6/18, C10278/6/18.
52 Balfour to Cheetham, 1 August 1922, PRO, FO 371/7451, C10566/6/18.
53 FO Memo, 7 August 1922, PRO, FO 371/7451, C11164/6/18, *DBFP*, XX, pp. 532–4.
54 Allied Ambassador (Berlin) to German Chancellor, 29 September 1922, PRO, FO 371/10711, C13952/6/18; Foreign Minister to Foch, 7 November 1922, MAE, Europe 1918–1929, Allemagne, Vol. 225; FO Memo, 2 November 1922, PRO, FO 371/7452, C15081/6/18; Germany Annual Report, 1922, PRO, FO 371/8807, C2758/2758/18; Note, 29 September 1922, Library of Congress, U.S. Military Intelligence Reports; Hardinge to Curzon, 28 August 1922, *DBFP*, XX, p. 542, note 5; Salewski, *Entwaffnung und Militärkontrolle*, p. 197.
55 Wirth to Conference of Ambassadors, 27 October 1922, CA Minutes, CA 193, 180.03301/193, NA, RG 256.
56 Gessler to Foreign Minister, 23 October 1923, ADAP, Series A, VI, p. 459.
57 Poincaré to Mayer, 17 November 1922, CA Minutes, CA 193, 180.03301/193, NA, RG 256. D'Abernon considered the German reply to be proof of German acceptance of the Allied 29 September 1922 memo. See D'Abernon telegram, 30 October 1922, PRO, FO 371/7452, C14925/6/18; D'Abernon to Curzon, 31 October and 1 November 1922, *DBFP*, XX, pp. 568 and 569.
58 Discussions of the Anglo–French Pact may be found in Curzon to Hardinge, 5 December 1921, and Eyre Crowe Memo, 29 December 1921, PRO, FO 371/7000, as well as Curzon Memo, 28 December 1921, PRO, FO 371/7000, C13355/12716/16. Lloyd George would simply not consider violation of the military clauses of the Treaty of Versailles a *casus foederis*. See Hughes, *To the Maginot Line*, p. 95, and Lowe and Dockrill, *The Mirage of Power: British Foreign Policy, 1902–1922*, Vol. III, pp. 738–40.

9 Violations, obstruction, and abuse

1 A number of German violations of the military articles of the Treaty of Versailles have already been addressed. This chapter will focus on the overall German strategy, schemes to circumvent Allied disarmament demands, and Allied reaction.
2 Williamson, *The British in Germany*, p. 69.
3 General von Cramon resigned in the fall of 1921 after claiming that Nollet was simply paid to disarm Germany and was one of the nation's worst enemies. He considered it an honor to frustrate Nollet. See Nollet to Foch, 27 September 1921, MAE, Europe 1918–1929, Allemagne, Vol. 223. Cramon's opinion of Bingham was much more conciliatory. See Roddie, *Peace Patrol*, p. 314.
4 Nollet, *Une Expérience*, p. 33. Overall, Cramon believed the IAMCC poisoned German–Allied relations. See August Frederick von Cramon, *Fort mit den Interalliierten Kontrollkommissionen* (Berlin: Scherl, 1922), p. 27.

5 IAMCC Intelligence summary, 28 October 1920, PRO, FO 371/4794, C10419/676/18. For a diatribe accusing the IAMCC of espionage, see Vivian Stranders, *Die Wirtschaftsspionage der Entente* (Berlin: E. S. Mittler and Sohn), 1929.

6 Consul (Nuremburg) au President du Conseil, MAE, 19 January 1922, MAE, Europe 1918–1929, Allemagne, Vol. 224.

7 See Tardieu Questionnaire, 1920, MAE, Europe 1918–1929, Allemagne, 59; CA Minutes, 18 March 1920, CA 22, 180.033/22, NA, RG 256; Akten Zur Deutschen Auswartigen Politik 1918–1945, Series A, Band III, Nummern 70–104 (hereafter cited as ADAP); Kleine-Ahlbrandt, *The Burden of Victory*, pp. 61–2.

8 Nollet to Foch, Report #30, 18 January 1921, PRO, FO 371/5981, C2544/461/18.

9 Conference of Ambassadors to German Ambassador, 15 November 1922, *DBFP*, XX, p. 585; Hardinge to Curzon, 10 November 1922, *DBFP*, XX, pp. 577–9.

10 IAMCC Intelligence notes, 8 May 1921, PRO, FO 371/10007/461/18.

11 IAMCC Intelligence summary, 16 August 1920, PRO, FO 371/4793, C5359/676/18.

12 Kilmarnock to Curzon, 28 December 1920, *DBFP*, X, p. 343.

13 Nollet to Foch, Report 9, 24 April 1920, MAE, Europe 1918–1929, Allemagne, Vol. 58.

14 Army Headquarters, Paris, 27 August 1920, MAE, Europe 1918–1940, Allemagne, Vol. 60.

15 IAMCC Intelligence summary, 5 July 1920, PRO, FO 371/4792, C1314/676/18.

16 Simons to Nollet, 14 October 1920, PRO, FO 371/4844, C8801/8801/18.

17 IAMCC Intelligence summary, 16 August 1920, PRO, FO 371/4793, C5359/676/18. See also Morgan, *Assize of Arms*, pp. 64–7.

18 Nollet to Foch, Report 23, 3 October 1920, MAE, Europe 1918–1929, Allemagne, 61; Roques, *Le Contrôle Militaire Interallié en Allemagne*, pp. 38–9.

19 Memorandum from the *Reichstreuhandgesellschaft* to its Branch Offices, 8 October 1920, *DBFP*, X, p. 397; Derby to Curzon, 30 October 1920, *DBFP*, X, p. 311.

20 See Lucien-Graux, *Histoire des Violations du Traité de Paix*, Vol. III, pp. 247–8.

21 Nollet to Foch, Report 13, 15 May 1920, MAE, Europe 1918–1929, Allemagne, Vol. 59.

22 Nollet to Foch, Report #20, 4 September 1920, MAE, Allemagne, Vol. 60; Nollet to Foch, Report #22, 18 September 1920, MAE, Allemagne, Vol. 61. A list of numerous war material caches uncovered by the Allies may be found in Dr. Lucien-Graux, *Histoire des Violations du Traité de Paix* (Paris: Les Éditions G. Crès and Librairie Ancienne Honoré Champion, 1921–27), Vol. III, pp. 247–8.

23 Nollet to Foch, Report #24, 17 October 1920, PRO, FO 371/4794, C10309/676/18.

24 Roddie, *Peace Patrol*, pp. 83–4. Roddie discounted the importance of the discoveries of war material caches.

25 Morgan, *Assize of Arms*, II, p. 293.

26 Nollet to Bingham, 10 August 1920, MAE, Europe 1918–1929, Allemagne, Vol. 60.

27 Goerlitz, *History of the German General Staff*, p. 246.

28 AMCV Report, 2 December 1921, CA 161, NA, RG 256.

29 Foch to Conference of Ambassadors, 19 March 1920, MAE, Europe 1918–1929, Allemagne, Vol. 58.
30 AMCV Report, 2 December 1921, CA 161, NA, RG 256. See also Goerlitz, *History of the German General Staff*, p. 247.
31 Whaley, *Covert German Rearmament, 1919–1939*, pp. 10–11; Manchester, *The Arms of Krupp*, pp. 332–6; Batty, *The House of Krupp*, pp. 147–52; Menne, *Krupp or the Lords of Essen*, pp. 365–7.
32 Young, *The Fall and Rise of Alfried Krupp*, pp. 41–3; Batty, *The House of Krupp*, pp. 144–6.
33 Nollet to Foch, Report 29, 30 November 1920, MAE, Europe 1918–1929, Allemagne, Vol. 62.
34 Morgan, "The Disarmament of Germany and After," *Quarterly Review*, October 1924, 242, p. 451.
35 Memorandum by the Secretary of State for War, 28 June 1920, CAB 24/108, CP 1550; H. Rumbold to Curzon, 27 July 1920, *DBFP*, X, p. 363.
36 Morgan letter, 13 February 1925, FO 371/10711; Morgan letter, *The Times*, 15 November 1928, MAE, Europe 1918–1929, Allemagne, Vol. 137.
37 Morgan, *Assize of Arms*, II, pp. 196–200 and "The Disarmament of Germany and After," *Quarterly Review*, October 1924, 242, pp. 432–5; Carsten, *The Reichswehr and Politics*, pp. 200–20 and *Britain and the Weimar Republic*, pp. 47–8; Arthur L. Smith, Jr., "Le désarmement de l'Allemagne en 1919: Les vues du général von Seeckt," *Revue historique*, 1962, 228, pp. 19–21; Jean-Paul Péron, "Le Réarmement de l'Allemagne Entre les Deux Guerres Mondiales," *Information Historique*, 1974, 36 (5): p. 244.
38 S.J. Lewis, *Forgotten Legions: German Army Infantry Policy, 1918–1941* (New York: Praeger, 1985), p. 15.
39 Morgan, *Assize of Arms*, II, p. 236.
40 Bernice A. Carroll, "Germany Disarmed and Rearming, 1925–1935," *Journal of Peace Research*, 1966, 3 (2), p. 115.
41 Carsten, *The Reichswehr and Politics*, pp. 153–4.
42 Williamson, *The British in Germany*, p. 140; Morgan, *Assize of Arms*, II, p. 191.
43 Nollet to Foch, Report #24, 17 October 1920, PRO, FO 371/4794, C10309/676/18.
44 Nollet to Foch, Report #37, 8 February 1922, PRO, FO 371/7449 and *BDFA*, Series F, Europe, 1919–1939, Vol. 33, Germany, 1922, pp. 55–64. This has been documented in a number of published studies.
45 Curzon to Kilmarnock, 3 January 1921, Curzon Papers, MssEur 112/240 and *DBFP*, XVI, pp. 600–2.
46 Kilmarnock to Curzon, 29 December 1920, PRO, FO 371/5853, C267/13/18.
47 Kilmarnock, Annual Report 1920, 7 May 1921, PRO, FO 371/6060, C9605/9605/18.
48 Kilmarnock to Curzon, 25 January 1921, PRO, FO 371/5855, C2153/13/18.
49 Nollet to Foch, Report #30, 18 January 1921, PRO, FO 371/5981, C2544/461/18; Nollet, *Une Expérience*, p. 171.
50 IAMCC Intelligence summary, 18 February 1921, PRO, FO 371/5981, C4212/461/18.
51 IAMCC Intelligence summary, 4 March 1921, PRO, FO 371/5982, C5337/461/18.
52 Kilmarnock to Curzon, 11 August 1921, PRO, FO 371/5974, C1649/416/18. In *Entwaffnung und Militärkontrolle*, pp. 173–4, Salewski points out that the German government had no choice but to accede to the London ultimatum, when the authority of the IAMCC was at its zenith.

53 IAMCC Intelligence summary, 17 June 1921, PRO, FO 371/5983, C13113/461/18; WO Report, 5 August 1921, CAB 24/126, C.P. 3198; D'Abernon to Curzon, 20 May 1921, *DBFP*, XVI, p. 879.
54 Désarmement de l'Allemagne en 1921, MAE, Europe 1918–1929, Allemagne, Vol. 72. The major exception to improved compliance was the maintenance of paramilitary organizations, especially in southern Germany.
55 French ambassador to the French Foreign Ministry, 9 July 1921, Nollet to Foch, 27 September 1921, MAE, Europe 1918–1929, Allemagne, Vol. 223.
56 Désarmement de l'Allemagne en 1921, 1 December 1921, MAE, Europe 1918–1929, Allemagne, Vol. 72.
57 War Office Memo, 26 September 1921, PRO, FO 371/5858, C18716/13/18.
58 Bingham to D'Abernon, 29 September 1921, PRO, FO 371/5858, C19191/13/18.
59 Williamson, *The British in Germany*, p. 195.
60 AMCV (French Section) Note, 29 November 1921, CA 157, NA, RG 256.
61 Nollet to Foch, 19 May 1922, MAE, Europe 1918–1929, Allemagne, Vol. 225.
62 Sthamer to Curzon, 8 April 1922, PRO, FO 371/7450, C5463/6/18.
63 Morgan, *Assize of Arms*, p. 29.
64 IAMCC Intelligence summary, 16 September 1920, PRO, FO 371/C7099/676/18.
65 Nollet, *Une Expérience*, pp. 83–5.
66 Bingham Diary, 21 February 1920, IWM, Ball Papers.
67 Foch to Conference of Ambassadors, 12 March 1920, CA 19, NA, RG 256. See also Roques, *Le Contrôle Militaire Interallié en Allemagne*, pp. 33–4.
68 Foch to Conference of Ambassadors, 12 March 1920, NA, RG 256, CA 19; Kilmarnock to Curzon, 10 March 1920, *DBFP*, X, p. 32, n. 1.
69 Foch to CA, 12 March 1920, NA, RG 256, CA 19; Derby to Curzon, 13 March 1920, *DBFP*, X, pp. 42–6; Paul Cambon Note, 15 March 1920, *DBFP*, X, pp. 46–7.
70 Bingham Diary, 18 and 19 March 1920, IWM, Ball Papers; Williamson, *The British in Germany*, p. 138.
71 CA Minutes, 16 March 1920, CA 21, 180.033/21, NA, RG 256.
72 William Manchester, *The Arms of Krupp 1587–1968* (Boston, MA, and Toronto: Little, Brown, 1968), pp. 315–21. Krupp was sentenced to fifteen years in prison but was released after seven months.
73 Morgan, *Assize of Arms*, p. 21.
74 IAMCC Intelligence summary, 5 July 1920, PRO, FO 371/4792, C1314/676/18; Kilmarnock to Curzon, 10 March 1920, *DBFP*, X, p. 32.
75 IAMCC Intelligence summary, 12 July 1920, PRO, FO 371/4792, C1987/676/18.
76 Nollet to Goeppert, 2 September 1920, MAE, Allemagne, 60 and PRO, FO 371/4793, C6541/676/18.
77 CA Minutes, 10 September 1920, NA, RG 256, CA 72, 180.03301/72.
78 Nollet to Foch, 1 August 1922 and AMCV (French Section), Draft Note, 4 August 1922, PRO, FO 371/7451, C11260/6/18.
79 D'Abernon, *An Ambassador of Peace*, II, pp. 73–4.
80 Milne Cheetham to Balfour, 8 August 1922, PRO, FO 371/7451, C11260/6/18.
81 CA Minutes, 20 October 1922, CA 190, 180.03301/190, NA, RG 256.
82 Hardinge to Curzon, 20 October 1922, *DBFP*, XX, pp. 559–60.
83 Captain Atkinson Report, 25 October 1922, PRO, FO 371/7453, C15239/6/18.
84 William Seeds to Curzon, 26 October 1922, PRO, FO 371/7453, C15089/6/18.

85 Captain Atkinson Report, 25 October 1922, PRO, FO 371/7453, C15239/6/18.
86 CA Minutes, 10 November 1922, NA, RG 256, CA 192, 180.03301/192; Mayer Telegram, 13 November 1922, NA, RG 242, Serial 3170 (D677009–10); AMCV to Conference of Ambassadors, 3 November 1922, *DBFP*, XX, p. 572, n. 1.
87 CA Minutes, 10 November 1922 NA, RG 256, CA 192, 180.03301/192; Curzon to Cheetham, 14 August 1922, *DBFP*, XX, pp. 538–9; Poincaré to Mayer, 13 November 1922, *DBFP*, XX, pp. 582–3; Wirth to D'Abernon, 16 November 1922, *DBFP*, XX, pp. 592–3.
88 Atkinson and Bouychou Report, 22 November 1922, NA, RG 256, CA 195, 180.03301/195; Nollet to Foch, 23 November 1922, NBA, RG 256, CA 195, 180.03301/195; Mayer Telegram, 30 November 1922, NA, RG 242, Serial 3170 (D677012–16).
89 CA Minutes, 6 December 1922, NA, RG 256, CA 196, 180.03301/196.
90 Eyre Crowe to Curzon, 27 November 1922, *DBFP*, XX, pp. 605–6.
91 Hardinge to Curzon, 29 November 1922, *DBFP*, XX, pp. 610–11.
92 Dr. Mayer to CA, 25 November 1922, NA, RG 256, CA 194.
93 Dr. Mayer to CA, 10 December 1922, NA, RG 256, CA 197; Hardinge to Curzon, 15 December 1922, *DBFP*, XX, pp. 630–3. The Allies decided to divide the million-mark payment equally among Britain, France, Italy, Belgium, and Japan and to use part of the proceeds to pay for IAMCC expenses in drafting their final report in the future. See CA Minutes, 24 January 1923, NA, RG 256, CA 201, 180.03301/021.
94 Nollet to Foch, Report #30, 18 January 1921, PRO, FO 371/5981, C2544/461/18.

10 Uncertain Allies

1 For studies concerning the Ruhr occupation, see Royal J. Schmidt, *Versailles and the Ruhr: Seedbed of World War II* (The Hague: Martinus Nijhoff, 1968); Denise Artaud, "A Propos de l'Occupation de la Ruhr," *Revue d'Histoire Moderne et Contemporaine*, January March 1970, Vol. XVII, pp. 1–21; Jacques Chastenet, *Raymond Poincaré* (Paris: Julliard, 1948); Paul Guinn, "On Throwing Ballast in Foreign Policy: Poincaré, the Entente and the Ruhr Occupation," *European History Quarterly*, 1988, Vol. 18, pp. 427–37.
2 Foreign Office Memorandum, 8 January 1923, *British Documents on Foreign Affairs*, ed. Christopher Seton-Watson, Series F, Europe 1919–1939, Vol. 34, Germany, 1923 (Frederick, MD: University Publications of America, 1990), pp. 4–5, (hereafter cited as *BDFA*); David Williamson, "Great Britain and the Ruhr Crisis, 1923–24," *British Journal of International Studies*, 1977, 3, p. 74. Elspeth Y. O'Riordan, in *Britain and the Ruhr Crisis* (Basingstoke: Palgrave, 2001), argues that British policy, reactive and weak, vacillated from benevolent neutrality to "tentative intervention."
3 Nollet to Foch, 19 January 1923, MAE, Europe 1918–1929, Allemagne, Vol. 225.
4 Curzon to Crewe, 2 February 1923, *DBFP*, XXI, pp. 748–9; Crewe to Curzon, 5 March 1923, *DBFP*, XXI, pp. 759–60.
5 CA Minutes, 14 March 1923, CA 209, 180.03301/209, NA, RG 256.
6 Nollet to Moraht, 10 March 1923, MAE, Europe 1918–1929, Allemagne, Volume 82; NA, RG 242, Serial 3170 (D677178).
7 Désarmement de l'Allemagne en 1922, 26 February 1923, MAE, Europe 1918–1929, Allemagne, Vol. 82.
8 Joseph Addison to Curzon, 27 June 1923, PRO, FO 371/8780,

C11556/1083/18. An attached table provides excellent details of evaluations of all inspections from January to May 1923. This table also appears in *BDFA*, Series F, Europe, 1919–1939, Vol. 34, Germany, 1923, p. 218. See also D'Abernon to Curzon, 11 March 1923, *DBFP*, XXI, pp. 764–5.

9 Nollet to Foch, 10 March 1923, MAE, Europe 1918–1923, Allemagne, Vol. 83; CA Minutes, CA 209, 180.03301/209, NA, RG 256; Roddie, *Peace Patrol*, pp. 313–15.

10 Nollet to the President of the Council, 24 February 1923, MAE, Europe 1918–1929, Allemagne, Vol. 82.

11 Nollet to Moraht, 10 March 1923, MAE, Europe 1918–1929, Allemagne, Vol. 83; IAMCC Council, 9 March 1923, PRO, FO 371/8777, C5044/1083/18.

12 Nollet to the President of the Council, MAE, 10 March 1923, MAE, Europe 1918–1929, Allemagne, Vol. 83.

13 Nollet to Foch, 10 March 1923, MAE, Europe 1918–1929, Allemagne, Vol. 83; CA Minutes, CA 209, 180.03301/209, NA, RG 256.

14 Nollet to Walch, 11 March 1923, MAE, Europe 1918–1929, Allemagne, Vol. 225.

15 AMCV Opinion, 13 March 1923, MAE, Europe 1918–1929, Allemagne, Vol. 83; Phipps Telegram, 14 March 1923, PRO, FO 371/8777, C4796/1083/18; Phipps to Curzon, 14 March 1923, *DBFP*, XXI, pp. 765–6.

16 Resolution of the Conference of Ambassadors, CA 209, 14 March 1923, MAE, Europe 1918–1929, Allemagne, Vol. 83; CA Minutes, CA 209, 180.03301/209, NA, RG 256.

17 Eyre Crowe Minute, 15 March 1923, PRO, FO 371/8777, C4527/1083/18; British Embassy to French government, 16 March 1923, MAE, Europe 1918–1929, Allemagne, Vol. 83; HMG Memo, 19 March 1923, CA Minutes, CA 210, 180.03301/210, NA, RG 256.

18 HMG Memo, 26 March 1923, CA Minutes, CA 211, 180.03301/211, NA, RG 256; Curzon to D'Abernon, 15 March 1923, *DBFP*, XXI, pp. 767–8; Curzon to Phipps, 17 March 1923, *DBFP*, XXI, p. 771; Crewe to Curzon, 28 March 1923, *DBFP*, XXI, p. 781.

19 Colonel Wedgwood Memo, 24 March 1923, PRO, FO 371/8778, C5740/1083/18.

20 Conference of Ambassadors Resolution, CA 210, 21 March 1923, Poincaré to Hoesch, 21 March 1923, MAE, Europe 1918–1929, Allemagne, Vol. 83.

21 Poincaré to Berlin and London ambassadors, 29 March 1923, MAE, Europe 1918–1929, Allemagne, Vol. 225.

22 Lampson Memo, 19 March 1923, *DBFP*, XXI, pp. 776–7.

23 Nollet to Foch, 22 March 1923, *DBFP*, XXI, p. 778, no. 1.

24 Bingham to WO, 20 March 1923, PRO, FO 371/8778, C5770/1083/18.

25 Nollet to Foch, 28 March 1923, FO 317/8778, C6203/1083/18. Allied inspectors visited sites in Breslau, Stettin, Berlin, Frankfurt, Hamburg, Königsberg, Dresden, Munster, Stuttgart, and Munich. See also Phipps to Curzon, 3 April 1923, *DBFP*, XXI, pp. 782–3.

26 Excerpt from Lokal-Anzeiger, 31 March 1923, PRO, FO 371/8778, C5770/1083/18.

27 Curzon to Phipps, 6 April 1923, *DBFP*, XXI, pp. 786–8.

28 Wigram Minute, 6 April 1923, PRO, FO 371/8778, C6111/1083/18.

29 Poincaré to German Embassy, 18 April 1923, *DBFP*, XXI, pp. 792–3.

30 CA Minutes, 25 April 1923, CA 213, 180.03301/213, NA, RG 256.

31 Phipps to Curzon, 25 April 1923, *DBFP*, XXI, p. 795.

32 CA Minutes, 2 May 1923, CA 214, 180.03301/214, NA, RG 256.

33 CA Minutes, 16 May 1923, CA 216, 180.03301/216, NA, RG 256; Curzon to Crewe, 15 May 1923, *DBFP*, XXI, pp. 805–6.
34 WO to FO, 14 May 1923, PRO, FO 371/8779; Crewe to Curzon, 16 May 1923, *DBFP*, XXI, pp. 808–11.
35 British Charge d'Affaires to the Conference of Ambassadors, 1 June 1923, MAE, Europe 1918–1929, Allemagne, Vol. 85; CA Minutes, 1 June 1923, CA 217, 180.03301/217, NA, RG 256; Crewe to Curzon, 1 June 1923 and 5 June 1923, *DBFP*, XXI, pp. 822–4 and 826–7, no. 3.
36 Conference of Ambassadors to the German Charge d'Affaires, 6 June 1923, MAE, Europe 1918–1929, Allemagne, Vol. 85; CA Minutes, 7 June 1923, CA 218, 180.03301/218, NA, RG 256.
37 Conference of Ambassadors Resolution, CA 217, 1 June 1923, MAE, Europe 1918–1929, Allemagne, Vol. 85.
38 Nollet to Foch, 5 July 1923, MAE, Europe 1918–1929, Allemagne, Vol. 85; CA Minutes, 27 June 1923, CA 223, 180.03301/223, NA, RG 256; Addison to Curzon, 29 June 1923, *DBFP*, XXI, p. 846. There was one small exception where a Belgian member of the IAMCC was allowed entry due to the presence of a British officer.
39 WO Memo, 1 June 1923, PRO, FO 371/8779.
40 Nollet to the President of the Council, 6 July 1923, MAE, Europe 1918–1929, Allemagne, Vol. 85.
41 Bingham to Director of Military Operations and Intelligence, 19 June 1923, PRO, FO 371/8780, C11093/1083/18.
42 Bingham to Director of Military Operations and Intelligence, 3 July 1923, PRO, FO 371/8780.
43 Translation of article from *Neue Preussische Zeitung*, 13 June 1923, PRO, FO 371/8780, C11093/1083/18.
44 Robert Grathwol, "Gustav Stresemann: Reflections on His Foreign Policy," *Journal of Modern History*, 1973, 45(1), p. 68.
45 Jon Jacobson, *Locarno Diplomacy, Germany and the West, 1925–1929* (Princeton, NJ: Princeton University Press, 1972), pp. 5–12; Manfred J. Enssle, "Stresemann's Diplomacy Fifty Years After Locarno: Some Recent Perspectives," *Historical Journal*, 1977, 20(4), p. 941.
46 General von Seeckt to Stresemann, 15 September 1923, ADAP, Series A, VIII, pp. 380–1.
47 Alexander Cadogan to Secretary to the Army Council, 16 October 1923, PRO, FO 371/8781, C17551/1083/18; Crewe to Curzon, 5 October 1923, *DBFP*, XXI, pp. 867–8.
48 CA Minutes, 12 November 1923, CA 235, 180.03301/235, NA, RG 256.
49 CA Minutes, 15 November 1923, CA 237, 180.03301/237, NA, RG 256. See also D'Abernon Telegram, 16 November 1923, PRO, FO 371/8782, C19950/1083/18. The IAMCC ruled out traditionally hostile areas of Germany, particularly Bavaria.
50 Cabinet Conclusions, 14 November 1923, PRO, CAB 23/46. The threat of the former Crown Prince, considered to be a war criminal, returning to Germany, inflamed French opinion.
51 WO to FO, 13 November 1923, FO 371/8782.
52 D'Abernon, *An Ambassador of Peace*, II, p. 277; Williamson, *The British in Germany*, p. 256.
53 Conference of Ambassadors Resolution, CA 238, 19 November 1923, MAE, Europe 1918–1929, Allemagne, Vol. 87; CA Minutes, 19 November 1923, CA 238, 180.03301/238, NA, RG 256; Poincaré to Hoesch, 21 November 1923, MAE, Europe 1918–1929, Allemagne, Vol. 87; FO Memo, 21

November 1923, PRO, FO 371/9726, C10534/9/18; Roques, *Le Contrôle Militaire Interallié en Allemagne*, p. 15.

54 Nollet, Note sur la situation du Contrôle, 26 November 1923, MAE, Europe 1918–1929, Allemagne, Vol. 87.

55 Foch to Nollet, 4 December 1923, MAE, Europe 1918–1929, Allemagne, Vol. 87.

56 IAMCC Council, Minutes #245, 15 December 1923, MAE, Europe 1918–1929, Allemagne, Vol. 87.

57 Nollet to Foch, 19 December 1923, MAE, Europe 1918–1929, Allemagne, Vol. 87.

58 Nollet to Moraht, 30 December 1923, MAE, Europe 1918–1929, Allemagne, Vol. 88. The IAMCC planned inspections for Berlin, Rostock, Dresden, Stuttgart, Munich, Paderborn, Frankfurt, and Breslau.

59 Major H.G. Hennessy Report, 31 October 1923, PRO, FO 371/8781, C19237/1083/18.

60 Crewe Telegram, 12 November 1923, PRO, FO 371/8781, C19569/1083/18.

61 Lampson Minute, 13 November 1923, PRO, FO 371/8782, C19737/1083/18; *DBFP*, XXI, pp. 895–6.

62 FO Minutes, 22 November 1923, PRO, FO 371/8783, C20230/1083/18; Bingham to WO, 12 December 1923, PRO, FO 371/8785, C21547/1083/18.

63 FO to WO, 24 November 1923, FO 371/8783, C20308/1083/18.

64 WO to Control Commission, 26 November 1923, PRO, FO 371/8784, C20536; Morgan, *Assize of Arms*, II, Galley Slips III.

65 Bingham Observations, 30 November 1923, PRO, FO 371/8785; Bingham to WO, 11 July 1923, *DBFP*, XXI, p. 853. Morgan believed the suspension of inspections in 1923 marked the effective end of control operations. See Morgan, *Assize of Arms*, p. 268.

66 WO to FO, 31 January 1924, PRO, FO 371/9723, C1725/9/18.

67 Walch Opinion, 16 January 1924, MAE, Europe 1918–1929, Allemagne, Vol. 88.

68 Bingham to Nollet, 9 January 1924, MAE, Europe 1918–1929, Allemagne, Vol. 88.

69 FO Memo, 1 February 1924, PRO, FO 371/9723, C1804/9/18.

70 Nollet to Foch, 16 January 1924, PRO, FO 371/9723.

71 FO Memo, 30 January 1924, PRO, FO 371/9723, C1704/9/18; D'Abernon to Curzon, 10 January 1924, *DBFP*, XXVII, pp. 983–4, no. 3.

72 IAMCC Council Minutes, 15 January 1924, MAE, Europe 1918–1929, Allemagne, Vol. 88.

73 Bingham to Nollet, 16 January 1924, PRO, FO 371/9723; AMCV Opinion, 26 and 30 January 1924, MAE, Europe 1918–1929, Allemagne, Vol. 88; Bingham to WO, 10 and 15 January 1924, *DBFP*, XXVII, pp. 982–3 and 985, respectively.

74 Gessler to the Foreign Office, 14 January 1924, ADAP, Series A, pp. 240–1.

75 CA Minutes, 13 February 1924, CA 246, 180.03301/246 and 20 February 1924, CA 247, 180.03301/247, NA, RG 256; MacDonald to Crewe, 15 February 1924, *DBFP*, XXVII, pp. 994–5.

76 British Embassy to Conference of Ambassadors, 25 February 1924, CA Minutes, CA 248, 180.03301/248, NA, RG 256; CA Minutes, 5 March 1924, CA 249, 180.03301/249, NA, RG 256.

77 FO Minutes, 4–7 April 1924, PRO, FO 371/9724, C5508/9/18; FO Minutes, 6 April 1924, PRO, FO 371/9724, C5719/9/18; FO to WO, 14 April 1924, PRO, FO 371/9724, C5508/9/18; CA Minutes, 19 June 1924, CA 258, 180.03301/258, NA, RG 256; Pink, *The Conference of Ambassadors*, p. 153.

78 FO Memo, 31 May 1924, PRO, FO 371/9725, C5981/9/18; CA Minutes, 28 May 1924, CA 256, 180.03301/256, NA, RG 256.

79 Hoesch to Conference of Ambassadors, 31 March 1924, CA Minutes, CA 252, 180.03301/252, NA, RG 256. See also Note, 5 April 1924, Military Control in Germany, G-2 Report, Library of Congress, US Military Intelligence Reports.

80 Nollet to Foch, 22 March 1924, PRO, FO 371/9724, C5327/9/18.

81 WO to FO, 27 March 1924, PRO, FO 371/9724, C5186/9/18.

82 French Observations, CA Minutes, 25 April 1924, CA 252, 180.03301/252, Appendix B, NA, RG 256.

83 Lt.-Colonel Heywood Memo, 8 May 1924, PRO, WO 155/4. Morgan estimated a rebirth of German strength a year after the end of Allied operations in Germany. See Morgan, "The Dismemberment of Germany and After," p. 457. The Paris newspapers constantly issued warnings of German rearmament. See e.g. *Le Matin*, 15 June 1924, p.1, and *Le Temps*, 2 July 1924, p. 1.

84 Stuart Memo, 13 May 1924, PRO, WO 155/4.

85 Poincaré to Hoesch, 28 May 1924, CA Minutes, CA 256, Appendix D, 180.03301/256, NA, RG 256; Conference of Ambassadors to German Ambassador, 28 May 1924, PRO, FO 371/9726, C8683/9/18 and *DBFP*, XXVII, pp. 1061–5.

86 Ramsay MacDonald and Edouard Herriot to German government, 22 June 1924, PRO, FO 371/9726, *DBFP*, XXVII, pp. 1072–4, and *BDFA*, Series F, Europe, 1919–1939, Vol. 35, Germany, 1924, pp. 251–2.

87 Note of the British Ambassador, 31 March 1924, MAE, Europe 1918–1929, Allemagne, Vol. 226; Roques, *Le Contrôle Militaire Interallié en Allemagne*, pp. 21–2; *The Times* (London), 5 April 1924, p. 12. The IAMCC allowed Bingham to remain in Berlin for a few weeks to enable Wauchope to familiarize himself with control work.

88 FO Minutes, 5 February 1924, PRO, FO 371/9723, C2044/9/18; Eyre Crowe Minute, 6 February 1924, PRO, FO 371/9723.

89 Foch to the President of the Council, MAE, 27 June 1924, Note of the French Delegation, 28 June 1924, Foch to the President of the Council, MAE, 3 July 1924, MAE, Europe 1918–1929, Allemagne, Vol. 226; Phipps Memo, 16 June 1924, PRO, FO 371/9831, C9616/9/18. For Nollet's resignation, see also Lampson Report, 23 June 1924, PRO, FO 371/9726, C10116/9/18. Nollet, a good soldier until the end, adds nothing to the details of his resignation in his IAMCC memoir, *Une Expérience de Désarmement*. Walch had been Nollet's adjutant.

90 Roques, *Le Contrôle Militaire Interallié en Allemagne*, p. 23.

91 *Le Matin*, 15 June 1924, p. 1; Jules Laroche, *Au Quai d'Orsay avec Briand et Poincaré, 1913–1926* (Paris: Hachette, 1957), pp. 194–5.

92 Hoesch to Conference of Ambassadors, 30 June 1924, PRO, FO 371/9726, C10438/9/18; CA Minutes, 12 July 1924, CA 261, Annex C, 180.03301/261, NA, RG 256.

93 Conference of Ambassadors to Hoesch, 8 July 1924, PRO, FO 371/9726, C11044/9/18.

94 Response of the President of the IAMCC, Appendix A, Instructions Générales Relatives à la Reprise des Operations de Contrôle, 9 July 1924, Appendix B, CA Minutes, CA 261, NA, RG 256. See also AMCV, Instruction a la CMIC, 21 June 1924, *DBFP*, XXVII, pp. 1075–7.

95 Walch to Foch, Report 46, 15 February 1925, "Rapport d'Ensemble sur l'Inspection Générale (8 Septembre 1924–25 Janvier 1925)," MAE, Europe 1918–1929, Allemagne, Vol. 104.

96 Walch to Foch, 7 July 1924, CA 261, NA, RG 256.
97 Wauchope to WO, 13 September 1924, PRO, FO 371/9728.
98 Wauchope to Director of Military Operations and Intelligence, 22 October 1924, PRO, FO 371/9728, C16631/9/18.
99 See Walter McDougall, *France's Rhineland Diplomacy* (Princeton, NJ: Princeton University Press, 1978); Ernst Fraenkel, *Military Occupation and the Rule of Law* (London, New York, and Toronto: Oxford University Press, 1944); William Jordan, *Great Britain, France, and the German Problem 1918–1939*, and Wolfers, *Britain and France Between Two Wars*.
100 A. Chamberlain to Crewe, 20 December 1924, *DBFP*, XXVII, p. 1124.
101 Wauchope to WO, 30 November 1924, PRO, FO 371/9729, C18122/9/18.
102 FO Memo, 12 December 1924, PRO, FO 371/9804, C18884/737/18.
103 WO Memo, 3 December 1924, *DBFP*, XXVII, pp. 1117–18.
104 CA Minutes, 17 December 1924, CA 268, 180.03301/268, NA, RG 256.
105 Cabinet Conclusions, 17 December 1924, FO 371/9833, CAB 67 (24).
106 CA Minutes, 27 December 1924, CA 269, 180.03301/269, NA, RG 256. See also Jacques Bainville, *Journal 1919–1926* (Paris: Librairie Plon, 1949), p. 218.
107 CA Minutes, 31 December 1924, CA 270, 180.03301/270, NA, RG 256.
108 AMCV Report, CA Minutes, 29 April 1925, CA 278, 180.03301/278, NA, RG 256. The IAMCC numbered 388 officers and 743 men on 8 September 1924 but only 110 officers and 301 men by 1 March 1925.

11 Transformation

1 Allied Ambassadors to German government, 5 January 1925, NA, RG 242, Serial 3170; Wadsworth Garfield, *German Disarmament* (Paris: The Reference Service on International Affairs, 1926), pp. 7–8.
2 FO Memo, 2 February 1925, PRO, FO 371/10707, C1571/21/18; Stresemann Note, 3 January 1925, *Gustav Stresemann*, Vol. II, pp. 16–17.
3 CA Minutes, 15 January 1925, CA 271, 180.03301/271, NA, RG 256. In December 1924, Stresemann pointed out Germany's military prostration in a letter to the League of Nations. See Stresemann to Eric Drummond, 12 December 1924, pp. 4–5, Library of Congress, U.S. Military Intelligence Reports.
4 Gatzke, *Stresemann and the Rearmament of Germany* (Baltimore, MD: Johns Hopkins University Press, 1954), pp. 29–36; Heideking, "Vom Versailler Vertrag zur Genfer Abrüstungskonferenz: Das Scheitern der Alliierten Militärkontrollpolitik gegenüber Deutschland nach dem Ersten Weltkrieg," p. 54.
5 Walch to Foch, Report 46, 15 February 1925, "Rapport d'Ensemble sur l'Inspection Générale (8 Septembre 1924–25 Janvier 1925)," MAE, Europe 1918–1929, Allemagne, Vol. 104; PRO, FO 371/10709, C7703/21/18; PRO, FO 371/10708, C3052/21/18. See summary of report in *DBFP*, XXVII, pp. 958–65.
6 Walch to Foch, Report 46, 15 February 1925, "Rapport d'Ensemble sur l'Inspection Générale (8 Septembre 1924–25 Janvier 1925)," MAE, Europe 1918–1929, Allemagne, Vol. 104; PRO, FO 371/10709, C7703/21/18; PRO, FO 371/10708, C3052/21/18.
7 Wauchope's Notes, 16 February 1925, PRO, FO 371/10708, C2407/21/18.
8 Walch to Foch, Report 46, 15 February 1925, "Rapport d'Ensemble sur l'Inspection Générale (8 Septembre 1924–25 Janvier 1925)," MAE, Europe 1918–1929, Allemagne, Vol. 104; PRO, FO 371/10709, C7703/21/18; PRO, FO 371/10708, C3052/21/18.
9 Wolfers, *Britain and France Between Two Wars*, p. 345.

10 David Dutton, *Austen Chamberlain: Gentleman in Politics* (Bolton, Lancs: Ross Anderson Publications, 1985), p. 238.
11 Lampson Minute, 2 February 1925, PRO, FO 371/10707, C1552/21/18.
12 Douglas Johnson, "Austen Chamberlain and the Locarno Agreements," *University of Birmingham Historical Journal*, 1961, 8, p. 71; Arthur Turner, "Austen Chamberlain, *The Times* and the Question of Revision of the Treaty of Versailles in 1933," *European History Quarterly*, 1988, 18 (1), pp. 55–6; Robert Self (ed.), *The Austen Chamberlain Diary Letters: The Correspondence of Sir Austen Chamberlain With His Sisters Hilda and Ida, 1916–1937* (Cambridge: Cambridge University Press, 1995), pp. 265–6. Chamberlain was convinced that the stability of Europe depended upon an entente between Britain and France. See N.H. Waites, *Troubled Neighbors: Franco–British Relations in the Twentieth Century* (London: Weidenfeld, 1971), p. 109. Chamberlain, however, was particularly tough on France concerning the withdrawal of the IAMCC. See Fox, "Britain and the Inter-Allied Commission of Control," p. 164.
13 Richard Grayson, *Austen Chamberlain and the Commitment to Europe: British Foreign Policy, 1924–1929* (London and Portland, OR: Frank Cass, 1997), p. 49; F. G. Stambrook, " 'Das Kind' – Lord D'Abernon and the Origins of the Locarno Pact," *Central European History*, 1968, 1, p. 245.
14 Crewe to A. Chamberlain, 29 January 1925, *DBFP*, XXVII, pp. 924–5.
15 Crewe to A. Chamberlain, 23 January 1925, *DBFP*, XXVII, pp. 921–2.
16 A. Chamberlain to Crewe, 2 January 1925, *DBFP*, XXVII, pp. 931–2.
17 AMCV Report, CA Minutes, 29 April 1925, 180.03301/278, CA 278, NA, RG 256. There were now officially thirteen points: the Five Points as well as fortification and other war material infractions. The IAMCC soon dropped one of the Five Points, the surrender of the 1918 production dossiers.
18 FO Memo, 16 June 1925, PRO, FO 371/10709, C8109/21/18. The Allies published this as *Note presented to the German government by the British, French, Italian, Japanese and Belgian Ambassadors at Berlin, 4 June 1925*, Command 2429 (HMSO, 1925). See also Mildred S. Wertheimer, "The Evacuation of the Rhineland," *Foreign Policy Association Information Service*, V (1), 20 March 1929, pp. 10–11, and Salewski, *Entwaffnung und Militärkontrolle*, pp. 300–7.
19 FO Memo, 30 November 1925, PRO, FO 371/10711, C15299/21/18.
20 Forster Minute, 24 July 1925, ADAP, Series A, XIII, pp. 622–4; Eric Sutton (ed.), *Gustav Stresemann: His Diaries, Letters, and Papers*, II (New York: Macmillan), p. 249.
21 FO Memo, 30 November 1925, PRO, FO 371/10711, C15299/21/18. For initial progress, see Wauchope Notes #36, 19 September 1925, *DBFP*, XXVII, pp. 1061–74.
22 Austen Chamberlain to Sthamer, 29 September 1925, Austen Chamberlain Papers, 38/1/1, University of Birmingham Library.
23 FO Memo, 30 November 1925, PRO, FO 371/10711, C15299/21/18.
24 A. Chamberlain to W. Tyrrell, 8 October 1925, Austen Chamberlain Papers, 38/1/1, University of Birmingham Library.
25 Manfred Enssle, "Stresemann's Diplomacy Fifty Years After Locarno: Some Recent Perspectives," *Historical Journal*, 1977, 20 (4), p. 942.
26 D'Abernon, *The Diary of an Ambassador*, Vol. 3 (Garden City, NY: Doubleday, Doran, and Company, 1931), p. 276.
27 F.G. Stambrook, "The Foreign Secretary and Foreign Policy: The Experiences of Austen Chamberlain in 1925 and 1927," *International Review of History and Political Science*, 1969, 6, p. 118.

28 The Allies evacuated the cities of Düsseldorf, Duisburg, and Ruhrort on 25 August 1925.

29 McKercher, "Austen Chamberlain's Control of British Foreign Policy, 1924–1929," *International History Review*, 1984, 6 (4), p. 586.

30 Locarno Meeting, 12 October 1925, Austen Chamberlain Papers, 38/1/1, University of Birmingham Library.

31 British Secretary's Notes of Locarno Meeting, 8 October 1925, *DBFP*, Series I, XXVII, Appendix, p. 1111.

32 Hoesch to Conference of Ambassadors, 23 October 1925, *Correspondence Between the Ambassadors' Conference and the German Ambassador at Paris Respecting German Disarmament, Evacuation of Cologne Zone and Modifications in the Rhineland Régime, Paris, October–November 1925* (London: HMSO, 1925); *British and Foreign State Papers*, 1925, part I, CXXI (London: HMSO, 1929), pp. 866–9; CA Minutes, 27 October 1925, CA 286, 180.03301/286, NA, RG 256. The complete lists may be found in *DBFP*, Series Ia, I, 307–10.

33 AMCV Report, 6 November 1925, CA Minutes, CA 287, Appendix A, 180.03301/287, NA, RG 256; FO Memo, 30 November 1925, PRO, FO 371/10711, C15299/21/18.

34 Austen Chamberlain to Crewe, 3 November 1925, PRO, FO 371/10710, C14018/21/18; *DBFP*, Series Ia, I, pp. 82–6. The British government had embraced the policy of appeasement by this time. See Memorandum on the Foreign Policy of His Majesty's Government, *DBFP*, Series Ia, I, p. 857.

35 Chamberlain used this term to refer to the feelings of international goodwill that Locarno produced in him *after* the Conference. See Chamberlain to Addison, 20 January 1927, *DBFP*, Series Ia, II, pp. 744–5. He also referred to the Conference as the "wonderful week." See C. Petrie, *The Life and Letters of the Right Honourable Sir Austen Chamberlain*, Vol. II (London: Cassell and Company, 1940), p. 287.

36 Hoesch to the Foreign Office, 6 November 1925, ADAP, Series A, XIV, pp. 556–7; FO Memo, 30 November 1925, PRO, FO 371/10711, C15299/21/18.

37 CA Minutes, 14 November 1925, CA 288, 180.03301/288, NA, RG 256; Jacobson, *Locarno Diplomacy*, pp. 63–4.

38 Crewe to Chamberlain, 15 November 1925, *DBFP*, Series Ia, I, pp. 151–4.

39 See WO Memo, 12 January 1926, PRO, FO 371/11286; Wauchope to D'Abernon, 20 January 1926, PRO, FO 371/11286.

40 The Conference of Ambassadors fixed midnight on 31 January as the official deadline of the Cologne withdrawal. See CA Minutes, 27 January 1926, CA 293, 180.03301/293, NA, RG 256.

41 President of the Council to Fleuriau, 11 January 1926, PRO, FO 371/11286, C522/436/18; IAMCC Council Minutes #340, 4 December 1925, MAE, Europe 1918–1929, Allemagne, Vol. 114.

42 Pawlesz Minute, 22 January 1926, ADAP, Series B, I, 1, pp. 146–8; Kopke to the Ambassador in Paris, 13 February 1926, Series B, I, 1, pp. 235–6.

43 Orme Sargent to WO, 13 April 1926, PRO, FO 371/11287, C4104/436/18.

44 FO Memo, 10 April 1926, FO 371/11287, C4658/436/18; FO Memo, 27 August 1926, PRO, FO 371/11290, C9512/436/18. The Conference of Ambassadors, with Britain in abstention, decided to allow no increase in the German police force in May 1926. See CA Minutes, 27 May 1926, CA 299, 180.03301/299, NA, RG 256.

45 Chamberlain to D'Abernon, 1 and 7 February 1926, *DBFP*, Series Ia, I, pp. 380–2 and 404–5. Chamberlain was perplexed by Germany's attitude after promises given in the intimate setting of Locarno.

46 Wauchope Notes, #53, 19 May 1926, PRO, FO 371/11287, C6113/436/18.

47 Wauchope Notes, #59, 17 July 1926, PRO, FO 371/11289, C8239/436/18.

48 John P. Fox claims that the initiative of disarmament in 1926 lay with the French but British modifications to the treaty precluded any real hope of executing the disarmament clauses. Fox, "Britain and the Inter-Allied Commission of Control, 1925-26," p. 155.

49 M. Lampson Report, 26 July 1926, PRO, FO 371/11289, C8453/436/18; FO Memo, 27 August 1926, PRO, FO 371/11290, C9512/436/18.

50 FO to WO, 21 September 1926, PRO, FO 371/11290, C9950/436/18; *DBFP*, Series Ia, II, no. 1, pp. 351–70.

51 Gustav Stresemann, *Vermachtnis; der Nachlass in Drei Banden*, III (Berlin: 1932–33), pp. 17–23; Sutton (ed.), *Gustav Stresemann*, III, pp. 17–26; Jacobson, *Locarno Diplomacy*, pp. 84–90; Robert Grathwol, *Stresemann and the DNVP* (Lawrence, KA: The Regents Press of Kansas, 1980), p. 183; Vincent Pitts, *France and the German Problem: Politics and Economics in the Locarno Period 1924–1929* (New York and London: Garland Publishing, 1987), pp. 150–5; Jon Jacobson and John Walker, "The Impulse for a Franco–German Entente: The Origins of the Thoiry Conference, 1926," *Journal of Contemporary History*, 1975, 10 (1), pp. 157–81.

52 Jacobson, *Locarno Diplomacy*, pp. 93–8. Stresemann warned that he would be forced to resign under popular antagonism if Allied troops did not withdraw from the Rhineland. The use of instability as a political weapon successfully influenced Allied policy, which generally did not promote replacing Stresemann. See Salewski, *Entwaffnung und Militärkontrolle*, pp. 341–50.

53 Wauchope Report #66, 29 September 1926, PRO, FO 371/11290; Wauchope Notes #71, 2 November 1926 and Wauchope Notes #72, 3 November 1926, PRO, FO 371/11292, C11795/436/18.

54 While the FO criticized Bingham repeatedly for being bested by the French, it lauded Wauchope upon his departure from Germany for his "tact, good judgement, and resourcefulness." See FO Memo, January 1927, PRO, FO 371/12117.

55 Rieth to Conference of Ambassadors, 6 September 1926, *DBFP*, Series Ia, I, pp. 347–8.

56 Phipps to W. Tyrrell, 22 November 1926, PRO, FO 371/11292, C12317/436/18.

57 FO Memo, 29 November 1926, PRO, FO 371/11293, C12572/436/18.

58 Briand to Crewe, 16 November 1926, *DBFP*, Series Ia, II, pp. 512–13; French Foreign Ministry to British Embassy, 25 November 1926, *DBFP*, Series Ia, II, pp. 526–30.

59 Chamberlain to Crewe, 27 November 1926, *DBFP*, Series Ia, II, pp. 532–4.

60 The nations were represented by Chamberlain, Briand, Stresemann, Vandervelde (Belgium), Scialoja (Italy), and Ishii (Japan), and met from 10–12 December.

61 Chamberlain to Tyrrell, 12 December 1926, PRO, FO 371/11295, C13219/436/18.

62 CA Minutes, 9 December 1926, CA 307, Appendix D, 180.03301/307, NA, RG 256. The Allies had been upset about the centralized control over the army that von Seeckt maintained as *Chef der Heeresleitung*. See German High Command Memo, 9 November 1925, *DBFP*, Series Ia, I, p. 118–20.

63 Foch reported fifty-three new forts in Königsberg, fifteen in Lotzen, fourteen in Glogau, and five in Küstrin. See Foch to Walch, 12 October 1926, *DBFP*, Series Ia, II, pp. 448–9; CA Minutes, 13 November 1926, CA 304, 180.03301/304, NA, RG 256.

234 Notes

64 Notes of Geneva Meetings, 10 and 11 December 1926, DBFP, Series Ia, II, p. 616 and p. 631.
65 Geneva Arrangement, 12 December 1926, PRO, FO 371/11295, C13219/436/18, 13188/436/18; DBFP, Series Ia, II, p. 650; BDFA, Series F, Europe 1919–1939, Vol. 37, Germany 1926, p. 369.
66 Benes Report, League of Nations, 11 December 1926, PRO, FO 371/11295, C13219/436/18; Note, 16 December 1926, MAE, Europe 1918–1929, Allemagne, Vol. 127. The League of Nations established the right of investigative bodies in September 1924 for Germany, Austria, Hungary, and Bulgaria.
67 Note, 16 December 1926, MAE, Europe 1918–1929, Allemagne, Vol. 127.
68 Conference of Ambassadors to Hoesch, 21 December 1926, DBFP, Series Ia, II, pp. 672–3.
69 Ryan Memorandum, 3 January 1927, PRO, FO 371/12131, C304/304/18; DBFP, Series Ia, II, pp. 701–3.
70 Minister of War, Note sur les Possibilités de l'Allemagne, 28 December 1926, MAE, Europe 1918–1929, Allemagne, Vol. 27.
71 Foreign Minister to Minister of War, 6 January 1927, MAE, Europe 1918–1929, Allemagne, Vol. 127.
72 Conference of Ambassadors Resolution, CA 309, 29 December 1926, MAE, Europe 1918–1929, Allemagne, Vol. 227; CA Minutes, 29 December 1926, CA 309, 180.03301/309, NA, RG 256; Le Temps, 21 February 1927, p. 1.
73 Foch to Walch, 5 January 1927, PRO, FO 371/12116; Wauchope Notes #79, 9 January 1927, PRO, FO 371/12115, C342/11/18.
74 Hoesch to Foreign Office, 11 January 1927, ADAP, Series B, IV, pp. 43–4.
75 Chamberlain to Lindsay, 12 January 1927, PRO, FO 371/12115, C180/11/18.

12 Superficial control

1 The Conference of Ambassadors bid adieu to the IAMCC after thanking its officers "for the devotion, conscience, and success with which they carried out their mission." See CA Minutes, 27 January 1927, CA 310, 180.03301/310, NA, RG 256. These officers disappeared from Germany but not from continued military or civilian activities. General Nollet was the French Minister of War under Herriot; Bingham became Lieutenant-Governor of Jersey until 1929; Morgan returned to teaching constitutional law and later served as a legal adviser to the American War Crimes Commission at the Nuremburg War Trials; Wauchope later served in England and Northern Ireland before becoming the High Commissioner of Palestine and Trans-Jordan from 1931 to 1938; Walch became Commander of the 12th Army Corps at Limoges and later became a member of the Conseil superieur de la Guerre (Army Council) and the Military Governor of Strasbourg in 1932.
2 Pawlesz and Baratier, Accord realise au sujet du Systeme des Ouvrages fortifies des Frontieres Est et Sud de l'Allemagne, 31 January 1927, Service historique de l'Armée de Terre, Chateau de Vincennes, 4N95, dossier 1. Hereafter cited as Vincennes; PRO, FO 371/12118, C1084/11/18; DBFP, Series Ia, II, pp. 797–8; ADAP, Series B, IV, pp. 188–9; Troutbeck Minute, 2 February 1927, PRO, FO 371/12117, C952/11/18. CA Minutes, 1 February 1927, CA 311, 180.03301/311, NA, RG 256. After the start of disarmament operations, the Germans constructed forts in Königsberg (53), Lotzen (15), Glogau (15), and Küstrin (5) but the Accord allowed the following numbers: Königsberg (31), Lotzen (15), and Glogau (8). In Königsberg, the Allies allowed the Germans to choose seventeen of the twenty-two forts they had to destroy.
3 Alfred Zimmern, The League of Nations and the Rule of Law, 1918–1935

(London: Macmillan 1936), p. 355. The League Council had ruled in December 1926 that a majority vote could request an investigation of German armaments under Article 213 of the Versailles Treaty.

4 Robert Doughty, "The French Armed Forces, 1918–1940," *Military Effectiveness, Volume II: The Interwar Period*, p. 43; Anthony Adamthwaite, *Grandeur and Misery: France's Bid For Power in Europe, 1914–1940* (London and New York: Arnold, 1995), pp. 126–9. See Erich M. Marcks, "France's Security," in *The Problem of Disarmament*, ed. Richard Schmidt and Adolf Grabowsky (Berlin: Heymanns Verlag, 1933), p. 119, and Heinrich Schnee and Hans Draeger, *Zehn Jahre Versailles*, II (Berlin: Brückenverlag, 1929), p. 142 for a comparison of French and German military forces between the wars. The French army was about six times as large as its German counterpart. A pro-German account advocating general disarmament may be found in Hans Rohde, *Franco-German Factors of Power: Comparative Studies of the Problem of Disarmament* (Berlin: Berliner Borsen Zeitung, 1932).

5 See e.g., Richard Dean Burns, "International Arms Inspection Policies Between World Wars, 1919–1934," *Historian*, 1969, 31 (4), pp. 583–603; David Carlton, "The Anglo–French Compromise on Arms Limitation, 1928," *Journal of British Studies*, 1969, 8, pp. 141–62; René Albrecht-Carrié, *A Diplomatic History of Europe Since the Congress of Vienna* (New York: Harper & Brothers, 1958), p. 412; Heald, *Memorandum on the Progress of Disarmament, 1919–1932* (London: Royal Institute of International Affairs, 1932). For an apologia of Versailles regarding European military strengths, see William Harbutt Dawson, *Germany Under the Treaty* (New York: Longmans, Green & Co., 1933), pp. 390–2.

6 Foch to Conference of Ambassadors, 29 January 1927, MAE, Europe 1918–1929, Allemagne, Vol. 227; Instructions to experts, 10 February 1927, PRO, FO 371/12896, C1329/11/18; Wauchope Notes #80, 12 January 1927, PRO, FO 371/12116; Note, CMAV, 6 November 1929, Vincennes 4N95, dossier 1.

7 British Embassy, 31 January 1927, MAE, Europe 1918–1929, Allemagne, Vol. 227; Instructions to experts, 10 February 1927, PRO, FO 371/ 12896, C1329/11/18.

8 Rapport final de la Commission Militaire Interallié de Contrôle en Allemagne, 28 February 1927, WO 155/63. See also Foch to Conference of Ambassadors, 15 June 1927, CA Minutes, CA 316, 180.03301/316, NA, RG 256, and Briand to the Secretary-General of the League of Nations, 22 July 1927, *League of Nations Official Journal*, September 1927, p. 1058.

9 Schubert Minute, 24 and 26 March 1927, ADAP, Series B, V, pp. 62–3, 79–81.

10 FO Memo, 9 April 1927, PRO, FO 371/12119, C3400/11/18.

11 Forster Minute, 9 May 1927, ADAP, Series B, V, pp. 310–11; Stresemann to the Washington Ambassador, 10 May 1927, ADAP, Series B, V, pp. 317–19; Crewe to FO, 12 May 1927, PRO, FO 371/12120, C4263/11/18. For the German attitude toward inspections, see Lindsay to Chamberlain, 27 March 1927 and 5 April 1927, Gosset to WO, 25 March 1927, *DBFP*, Series Ia, III, pp. 142–6 and 189–90.

12 WO to Gosset, 3 June 1927, PRO, FO 371/12120.

13 Conference of Ambassadors Resolution, CA 315, 5 May 1927, MAE, Europe 1918–1929, Allemagne, Vol. 212; CA Minutes, 5 May 1927, CA 315, 180.03301/315, NA, RG 256.

14 Gosset to WO, 8 June 927, PRO, FO 371/12120, C5053/11/18; Gosset to WO, 15 June 1927, *DBFP*, Series Ia, III, pp. 387–9.

15 Selby Note, 16 June 1927, Stresemann to Chamberlain, 16 June 1927, and

Chamberlain to Stresemann, 18 June 1927, PRO, FO 371/12896, C5345/11/18. Consistent with Stresemann's diplomacy, he preferred to deal individually with Chamberlain than jointly with the Allies or with the Conference of Ambassadors (which, of course, included a French member).

16 Experts' Report, 13 July 1927, CA Minutes, CA 317, Appendix A, 180.03301/317, NA, RG 256; Rapport du Major Pulinx et Commandant Durand, 8 July 1927, *DBFP*, Series Ia, III, pp. 439–42.

17 Pawlesz, Durand, and Pulinx Accord, 8 July 1927, *BDFA*, Series F, Europe, 1919–1939, Vol. 38, Germany, 1927, p. 253; FO Memo, 5 December 1927, PRO, FO 371/12125, C9801/11/18.

18 AMCV Report, 1 May 1928, CA Minutes, CA 322, Appendix B, 180.03301/322, NA, RG 256. See also Gosset Report, 8 June 1927, PRO, FO 371/12120.

19 Gosset to WO, 3 September 1927, PRO, FO 371/12123, C7474/11/18; FO Memo, 27 October 1927, PRO, FO 371/12124, C8739/11/18.

20 Sargent Memo, 28 July 1927, *DBFP*, Series Ia, III, pp. 483–6; FO Memo, 5 December 1927, PRO, FO 371/12125, C9801/11/18; J. V. Perowne Memorandum, 30 November 1927 and 2 March 1928, *DBFP*, Series Ia, IV, pp. 147–51 and 288–92. The German government supported these limited inspections over the initiation of League investigations. Nonetheless, inspections all but came to an end in November 1927. Colonel Gosset raised the idea of inspections after the Durand/Pulinx visits in informal talks with General von Pawlesz in July. See Gosset to WO, 9 July 1927, *DBFP*, Series Ia, III, n. 9, p. 442.

21 CA Minutes, August 1927, CA 319, 180.03301/319, NA, RG 256.

22 Briand to Hoesch, 20 August 1928, MAE, Europe 1918–1929, Allemagne, Vol. 137; Chamberlain to Crewe, 22 May 1928, PRO, FO 371/12896, C3810/394/18; Conference of Ambassadors to the German Ambassador, 20 August 1928, Vincennes, 4N95, dossier 1.

23 AMCV, Resume du Compte-Rendu du 31 July 1929, Vincennes 4N95, dossier. 1.

24 AMCV Report, 1 May 1928, CA Minutes, CA 322, Appendix B, 180.03301/322, NA, RG 256. See also experts to Foch, 29 November 1927, *DBFP*, Series Ia, IV, pp. 144–5.

25 J.R. Perowne Minutes, 12 January 1928, PRO, FO 371/12895 and 19 April 1928, PRO, FO 371/12896, C3184/394/18; Perowne Memorandum, 2 March 1928, *DBFP*, Series Ia, IV, pp. 288–92.

26 Pierre de Margerie to Foreign Minister, 27 July 1928, MAE, Europe 1918–1929, Allemagne, Vol. 137; Chamberlain to Crewe, 29 March 1928, *DBFP*, Series Ia, IV, pp. 327–8; Chamberlain to Crewe, 22 May 1928, PRO, FO 371/12896, C3810/394/18; *DBFP*, Series Ia, V, pp. 62–5.

27 M.H. Huxley Memo, 30 June 1928, PRO, FO 371/12896, C5157/394/18; *BDFA*, Series F, Europe, 1919–1939, Vol. 39, Germany, 1928, pp. 131–9; Crewe to Chamberlain, 15 July 1928, PRO, FO 371/12897, C5555/394/18.

28 CA Minutes, 25 July 1928, CA 323, 180.03301/323, NA, RG 256.

29 Conference of Ambassadors to the British Ambassador, 20 August 1928, Vincennes 4N95, dossier 1.

30 Reith to Briand, 20 October 1928, MAE, Europe 1918–1929, Allemagne, Vol. 137; Rieth to Foreign Office, 26 October 1928, ADAP, Series B, X, pp. 221–2.

31 Note, 8 November 1928, MAE, Europe 1918–1929, Allemagne, Vol. 137; Cambon to Hoesch, 16 December 1928, MAE, Europe 1918–1929, Allemagne, Vol. 138.

32 Foch to Conférence des Ambassadeurs, 28 November 1928, MAE, Europe

1918–1929, Allemagne, Vol. 137; CA Minutes, 3 December 1928, CA 324, 180.03301/324, NA, RG 256.

33 AMCV, Résumé de la Situation à la fin de 1928, Vincennes, 4N95, dossier 1.

34 Sargent to Tyrrell, 20 November 1928, *DBFP*, Series Ia, V, pp. 472–3.

35 War Office Memorandum, Committee of Imperial Defense (CID), 6 December 1928, PRO, CAB 24/199; Cabinet Conclusions, 1 May 1929, Cabinet 19 (29), PRO, CAB 23/60; CID Minutes, 13 December 1928, PRO, CAB 24/199. Morgan, who refused to let the issue of disarmament fade away and still remained in touch with the War Office, had responded critically to Lloyd George's recent statements on the weakness of the German military. See Morgan's article in *The Times*, 15 November 1928 and MAE, Europe 1918–1929, Allemagne, Vol. 137. For fears of German military budget increases, see Note MAE, 9 January 1929, MAE, Europe 1918–1929, Allemagne, Vol. 138.

36 Cambon to Hoesch, 16 December 1928, *DBFP*, Series Ia, V, pp. 592–5.

37 For a detailed account of Foch's funeral, see Tyrrell to Chamberlain, 27 March 1929, PRO, FO 371/14077, W2897/2605/17.

38 Progress concerning the police and military establishment was scant. See AMCV, Situation au 1er Novembre, 1929, Vincennes 4N95, dossier 1; Note, MAE, March 1929 and Minister of War to AMCV President, 30 May 1929, MAE, Europe 1918–1929, Allemagne, Vol. 138.

39 AMCV, Resume du Compte-Rendu du 15 May 1929, Vincennes 4N95, dossier 1.

40 Military experts to Foch, 28 June 1929, MAE, Europe 1918–1929, Allemagne, Vol. 138. Oddly enough, the experts addressed the report to Foch, who had died three months earlier. The violations did not concern Gosset. See Gosset to WO, 24 August 1929 and Gosset Observations, 25 August 1929, PRO, FO 371/13622, C6858/49/18.

41 The Allies agreed to evacuate the second and third zones of the Rhineland occupation five years ahead of schedule: Coblenz by 30 November 1929 and Mainz by 30 June 1930. This did have one effect upon disarmament, as the experts had subsequently to inspect the destruction of the forts in the zones. See Gosset to Nugent, 11 March 1930, PRO, FO 371/14368, C2010/282/18; Cutsem to Carr, 13 March and 17 March 1930, PRO, FO 371/14368, C2010/282/18. An agreement was finally signed on 29 June 1930 settling the issue of the destruction of the Kehl forts. See Gosset to FO, PRO, FO 371/14368/C5310/282/18.

42 Harold Nicolson to A. Henderson, 9 August 1929, PRO, FO 371/13622, C6267/49/18; *BDFA*, Series F, Europe, 1919–1939, Vol. 40, Germany, 1929, pp. 247–9.

43 Gosset Reports, 9 and 12 August 1929, PRO, FO 371/13622, C6267/49/18.

44 General Baratier to the Conference of Ambassadors, 18 September 1929, MAE, Europe 1918–1929, Allemagne, Vol. 138.

45 E.H. Carr Minute, 11 October 1929, PRO, FO 371/13622, C7700/49/18.

46 Nicolson to Henderson, 16 November 1929, PRO, FO 371/13623, C8837/49/18.

47 Massigli and Forster, Allied Agreement, 10 January 1930, PRO, FO 371/14366, C611/273/18 and *BDFA*, Series F, Europe, 1919–1939, Vol. 41, Germany, 1930, pp. 8–9; Tyrrell to Henderson, 10 January 1930, PRO, FO 371/14366, C292/273/18 and *BDFA*, Series F, Europe, 1919–1939, Vol. 41, Germany, 1930, p. 1; Tyrrell to FO, 10 January 1930, PRO, FO 371/14366. The Allies soon agreed to a slight modification where Germany could station extra police in the Rhineland in emergencies. See Briand to Hoesch, 19 January 1930, PRO, FO 371/14366, C611/273/18.

48 Briand to Hoesch, 19 January 1930, PRO, FO 371/14366, C611/273/18.
49 WO Memo, 2 April 1930, and Rumbold to Henderson, 7 April 1930, PRO, FO 371/14356, C2906/273/18.
50 CA Minutes, 12 January 1931, CA 327, 180.03301/327, NA, RG 256; Resolution, Conference of Ambassadors, CA 327, 12 January 1931, MAE, Europe 1930–1940, Allemagne, Vol. 652; PRO, FO 371/15206, C997/997/62; Vincennes, 4N95, dossier 1.
51 AMCV to Conference of Ambassadors, 17 and 27 March 1930, MAE, Europe 1930–1940, Allemagne, Vol. 652; Briand to Hoesch, 22 July 1930, MAE, Europe 1930–1940, Allemagne, Vol. 652.
52 Tyrrell to Henderson, 10 May 1930, PRO, FO 371/14367, C3605/273/18; Major-General Charles to Sir Robert Vansittart, 14 May 1930, PRO, FO 371/14345, C3761/283/62. The first report of severing ties occurred in January when Tyrrell claimed he no longer recognized the Conference of Ambassadors or the AMCV. See Tyrrell to Henderson, 10 January 1930, PRO, FO 371/14345, C283/283/62.
53 Tyrrell to Henderson, 10 May 1930 and 29 October 1920, PRO, FO 371/14367, C3605 and C8044/273/18.
54 Orme Sargent to Lord Tyrrell, 28 June 1930, PRO, FO 371/14367, C5156/273/18.
55 See Paul Tirard, *La France sur le Rhin: Douze années d'occupation rhénane* (Paris: Librairie Plon, 1930), pp. 170–5 for a contemporary warning.
56 Army Headquarters, 2eme Bureau, Note au Sujet du CMAV, 20 December 1930, Vincennes 4N95, dossier 1.
57 Foreign Minister to Louis Barthou (Minister of War), 26 December 1930, Vincennes, 4N95, dossier 1.
58 Ibid.
59 Barthou to Foreign Minister, 6 January 1931, Vincennes, 4N95, dossier 1; Army Headquarters, 2eme Bureau, 11 February 1931, Remarque au Sujet du Projet du General Baratier; Projet, 11 February 1931; Projet, 6 March 1931; Note, 20 March 1931, Vincennes, 4N95, dossier 2.
60 Briand to Maginot, 31 March 1931, Vincennes 4N95, dossier 2; Orme Sargent to Lord Tyrrell, 19 February 1931, PRO, FO 371/15206, C1102/997/62.
61 War Office Minutes, 28 January 1931, PRO, FO 371/15220, C581/136/18; Orme Sargent to Lord Tyrrell, 19 February 1931, PRO, FO 371/15206, C1102/997/62.
62 Maginot to Foreign Minister, 20 March 1931, Vincennes 4N95, dossier 2.
63 Conference of Ambassadors, Observations, 1 March 1931, PRO, FO 371/15220, C2590/136/18.
64 Conference of Ambassadors Resolution, CA 327, 30 March 1931, Vincennes 4N95, dossier 2.
65 Briand to the Secretary General of the League of Nations, 16 March 1931, *League of Nations Official Journal*, March 1931, p. 783; CA Minutes, CA 327, 180.03301/327, NA, RG 256; PRO, FO 371/15220, C2590/136/18, and C2030/136/18; *DBFP*, Second Series, I, pp. 585–7; Pink, *The Conference of Ambassadors*, p. 160.
66 For British examples see Colonel J.H. Marshall-Cornwall to Sir Horace Rumbold, 9 December 1931, PRO, FO 371/15221, C9316/136/18 and FO 371/15225, C9523/84518. The French examples are quite numerous. See MAE, Europe 1918–1940, Allemagne, Vol. 652 onward.

13 Conclusion

1 Memorandum by the Secretary of State For War, 28 June 1920, PRO, CAB 24/108, CP 1550.
2 Phipps to W. Tyrrell, 22 November 1926, PRO, FO 371/11292, C12317/436/18.
3 Metzger, "L' Allemagne: Un Danger Pour la France en 1920?," p. 9.
4 Artillery pieces surrendered – 30,511 (November 1920); 33,452 (August 1922); 33,552 (June 1924); trench mortars surrendered – 10,099; 11,596; 11,616; machine guns surrendered – 63,151; 87,076; 87,950. The figures are taken from Nollet to Foch, Report #28, 29 November 1920, PRO, FO 371/4795, C13847/676/18; FO Minute, The Disarmament of Germany, 7 August 1922, PRO, FO 371/7451, C11164/6/18; FO Memo, 23 June 1924, PRO, FO 371/9725, C9665/9/18.
5 Nollet, *Une Expérience*, p. 175; Morgan, *Assize of Arms*, II, pp. 285–306.
6 The amount of war material destroyed from the Spa Ultimatum until November 1920 is far greater than that destroyed in the same amount of time beforehand. Compare IAMCC Intelligence Summary, 28 June 1920, PRO, FO 371/4792, C676/676/18 with Nollet to Foch, Report #28, 29 November 1920, PRO, FO 371/4795, C13847/676/18.

Bibliography

Unpublished sources

France

Ministère des Affaires Étrangères (Paris). Archives diplomatiques. Serie Z, Europe, 1918–1929, Allemagne.

Service historique de l'Armée de Terre, Château de Vincennes. L'Etat de Foch (Série 4N).

Germany

Records of the German Foreign Office (Record Group 242, Microfilm, National Archives, College Park, Maryland).

Great Britain

Public Record Office (Kew Gardens):
CAB 23 (Conclusions of the Cabinet)
CAB 24 (Cabinet Papers)
FO 371 (Foreign Office – General Correspondence)
FO 800
WO 32 (Registered Papers, General Series)
WO 106 (Directorate of Military Operations and Intelligence: Papers)
WO 137 (Papers of Lord Derby)
WO 155 (Allied Military Committee of Versailles)
Major C.J.P. Ball Papers (Imperial War Museum, London)
Austen Chamberlain Papers (University of Birmingham Library, Birmingham)
Lord Curzon Papers (Oriental and India Office, London)
Lord D'Abernon Papers (British Library, London)
Lloyd George Papers (House of Lords Record Office, London)
John Hartman Morgan Papers (proofs and galley slips of *Assize of Arms, II*)

United States

Papers of General Tasker Bliss, Washington, DC, Library of Congress, Manuscript Division.

Record Group 256, Records of the American Commission to Negotiate the Peace (1918–1931), Washington, DC, National Archives, College Park, MD.

U.S. Military Intelligence Reports: Germany, 1919–1941. A Microfilm Project of University Publications of America, Inc., 1983. Taken from Record Group 165, Records of the War Department General and Special Staffs, Military Intelligence Division, National Archives, Washington, DC.

Published sources

France

Ministère des Affaires Étrangères. *Documents diplomatiques: Documents relatif auz negotiations concernant des garanties de securité contre une aggression de l'Allemagne (10 janvier 1919–7 décembre 1923)*. Paris: Imprimerie nationale, 1924.

——. *Documents Diplomatiques Français*. Tome I, 1920. Paris: Imprimerie nationale, 1998.

——. *Documents relatifs aux réparations*. 2 Tomes. Paris: Imprimerie Nationale, 1922.

——. Assemblée Nationale. *Journal officiel. Débats parlementaires. Chambre des Députés*.

——. Assemblée Nationale. *Journal officiel. Débats parlementaires. Sénat*.

Germany

Auswärtiges Amt, *Akten zur Deutschen Auswaritigen Politik 1918–1945*, Series A and B, Gottingen, Vandenhoeck and Ruprecht, 1966–1995.

——. *Materialien zur Entwaffnungsnote*. Berlin: 1925.

Great Britain

British and Foreign State Papers. London: HM Stationery Office, 1919–1929.

Foreign Office. *Correspondence between the Ambassador's Conference and the German Ambassador at Paris Respecting German Disarmament, Evacuation of the Cologne Zone, and Modifications in the Rhineland Régime, Oct.–Nov. 1925*. Command Paper 2527 (1925).

——. *Collective Note of the Allied Powers Presented to the German Government on June 4, 1925, in Regard to the Fulfillment of the Obligations of the Treaty of Versailles with Regard to Disarmament*. Command 2429 (1925).

——. E.L. Woodward and Rohan Butler (eds). *Documents on British Foreign Policy 1919–1939*, Series I and Ia. London: HM Stationery Office, 1946.

Parliament. *Parliamentary Debates*. House of Commons. London: HM Stationery Office.

——. *Parliamentary Debates*, House of Lords, 5th Series, vols 31–77. London: HM Stationery Office.

Seton-Watson, Christopher (ed.). *British Documents on Foreign Affairs*. Series F, Europe, 1919–1939. Frederick, MD: University Publications of America, 1990.

United States

Department of State. *Papers Relating to the Foreign Relations of the United States: The Paris Peace Conference, 1919*, 13 Vols. Washington, DC, 1947.
——. Office of Strategic Services. *Lessons From the Disarmament of Germany After World War I*. Washington, DC, 1945.
——. Office of Public Affairs. *The Organization of Allied Control in the Rhineland, 1918–1930*. Washington, DC, 1950.
Treaty of Peace With Germany. Washington, DC: Government Printing Office, 1919.

Miscellaneous

League of Nations. Secretariat. Information Section. *An Eleven Year Review of the League of Nations*. The League of Nations Association, 1930.
——. *Arbitration, Security and Reduction of Armaments*. Pamphlet No. 8. Geneva, 1924.
——. *The League From Year to Year, 1928–1931*, Geneva, 1930–32.
——. *Official Journal*.
——. *Political Activities*. Pamphlet No. 1. Geneva, 1925.

Contemporary sources

Apex (pseud. for R.G. Coulson). *The Uneasy Triangle: Four Years of Occupation*. London: J. Murray, 1931.
Berber, Friedrich Joseph. *Locarno: A Collection of Documents*. London: W. Hodge, 1936.
Bingham, Francis R. "Work With the Allied Commission of Control in Germany, 1919–1924." *Journal of the Royal United Services Institution*, 1924, 69: 747–63.
Bliss, Tasker. "The Armistices." *American Journal of International Law*, 1922, 16: 509–22.
Cambon, Jules and Austen Chamberlain. *The Permanent Bases of Foreign Policy*. New York: Council on Foreign Relations, 1931.
Chamberlain, Austen. "Great Britain as a European Power." *International Affairs*, 1930, 9: 180–8.
——. *Peace in Our Time*. London: Philip Allan & Co., 1928.
Estienne, Jean. "Les forces materielles a la guerre." *Revue de Paris*, 1922, 29: 225–38.
Garfield, Wadsworth. *German Disarmament*. Paris: The Reference Service on International Affairs, 1926.
Lucien-Graux, Dr. *Histoire des Violations du Traité de Paix*, 4 vols. Paris: Les Éditions G. Crès and Librairie Ancienne Honoré Champion, 1921–27.
Morgan, J.H. "The Dismemberment of Germany and After." *Quarterly Review*, 1924, 242: 415–57.
Poincaré, Raymond. "Since Versailles." *Foreign Affairs*, 1929, 7: 519–31.
Poupard, Emmanuel. *L'Occupation de la Ruhr et le droit des gens*. Paris: Les Presses universitaires de France, 1925.
Spaight, James. *Pseudo-Security*. London and New York: Longmans, Green, & Co., 1928.

Stranders, Vivian. *Die Wirtschaftsspionage der Entente*. Berlin: E. S. Mittler & Sohn, 1929.

Tuohy, F. "France's Rhineland Adventure." *Contemporary Review*, 1930, 138: 29–38.

Wertheimer, Mildred S. "The Evacuation of the Rhineland." *Foreign Policy Association Information Service*, 1929, 5(1).

Memoirs

Allen, Henry. *My Rhineland Journal*. Boston, MA, and New York: Houghton Mifflin, 1923.

——. *The Rhineland Occupation*. Indianapolis: The Bobbs-Merrill Co., 1927.

Bainville, Jacques. *Journal, 1919–1926*. Paris: Plon, 1949.

Chamberlain, Austen. *Down the Years*. London: Cassell & Co., 1935.

Clemenceau, Georges. *Grandeur and Misery of Victory*, Trans. F.M. Atkinson. New York: Harcourt, Brace & Co., 1930.

Cramon, August Frederick von. *Fort mit den Interalliierten Kontrollkommissionen*. Berlin: Scherl, 1922.

D'Abernon, Edgar. *An Ambassador of Peace*, 3 vol. Garden City, NY: Doubleday, Doran, Co., 1930.

Foch, Ferdinand. *The Memoirs of Marshal Foch*, trans. T. Bentley Mott. Garden City, NY: Doubleday, Doran & Co., 1931.

Hankey, Maurice. *The Supreme Council at the Paris Peace Conference, 1919: A Commentary*. London: G. Allen & Unwin, 1963.

Headlam-Morley, James. *A Memoir of the Paris Peace Conference 1919*. London: Methuen & Co., 1972.

House, Edward and Charles Seymour, (eds). *What Really Happened at Paris: The Story of the Peace Conference, 1918–1919, By American Delegates*. New York: Charles Scribner's Sons, 1921.

Lansing, Robert. *The Peace Negotiations, A Personal Narrative*. Boston, MA, and New York: Houghton Mifflin, 1921.

Laroche, Jules. *Au Quai d'Orsay avec Briand et Poincaré, 1913–1926*. Paris: Hachette, 1926.

Lloyd George, David. *The Truth About the Peace Treaties*, 2 vols. London: Victor Gollancz, 1938.

——. *War Memoirs of David Lloyd George, 1917–1918*, 6 vols. Boston, M: Little, Brown, 1937.

Mantoux, Paul. *The Deliberations of the Council of Four (March 24–June 28, 1919)*, 2 vols. Princeton, NJ: Princeton University Press, 1992 (reprint).

Miller, David Hunter. *My Diary at the Conference of Paris*, 20 vols. New York: Appeal Printing Co., 1928.

Morgan, John Hartman. *Assize of Arms, The Disarmament of Germany and Her Rearmament (1919–1939)*, London: Oxford University Press, 1945.

——. *German Atrocities: An Official Investigation*. London: T. F. Unwin, 1916.

——. *Germany's Dishonoured Army*. London: The Parliamentary Recruiting Committee, 1915.

——. *The Present State of Germany*. London: University of London, 1924.

Nicolson, Harold. *Diaries and Letters*. New York: Atheneum, 1966–68.

——. *Peacemaking, 1919*. Boston, MA, and New York: Houghton Mifflin, 1933.

Nollet, Charles Marie. *Une Expérience de désarmament: Cinq ans de contrôle militaire en Allemagne*. Paris, 1932.

Petrie, C. *The Life and Letters of the Right Honourable Sir Austen Chamberlain*, 2 vols. London: Cassell, 1939–40.

Reynolds, Bernard. *Prelude to Hitler: A Personal Record of the Post-war Years in Germany*. London: Jonathan Cape, 1933.

Roddie, Stuart. *Peace Patrol*. New York: G. P. Putnam's Sons, 1933.

Roques, Paul. *Le Contrôle Militaire Interallié en Allemagne*. Paris: Berger-Levrault, 1927.

Self, Robert, (ed.). *The Austen Chamberlain Diary Letters: The Correspondence of Sir Austen Chamberlain With His Sisters Hilda and Ida, 1916–1937*. Cambridge: Cambridge University Press, 1995.

Seymour, Charles. *The Intimate Papers of Colonel House*, 4 vols. Boston, MA, and New York: Houghton Mifflin, The Riverside Press Cambridge, 1928.

Stresemann, Gustav. *Vermächtnis; der Nachlass in Drei Bänden*, 3 vols. Berlin, Ullstein, 1932–1933.

Sutton, Eric (ed.). *Gustav Stresemann, His Diaries, Letters and Papers*, 3 vols. New York: Macmillan, 1935.

Tardieu, Andre. *The Truth About the Treaty*. Indianapolis: Bobbs-Merrill Co., 1921.

Temperley, H.W.V. (ed.). *A History of the Peace Conference of Paris*, 6 vols. London: Institute of International Affairs, 1920.

Tirard, P. *La France sur le Rhin: Douze années d'occupation rhénane*. Paris: Librairie Plon, 1930.

Tuohy, Ferdinand. *The Cockpit of Peace*. London: John Murray, Albemarle Street West; 1926.

——. *Occupied, 1918–1930: A Postscript to the Western Front*. London: Butterworth, 1931.

Secondary sources

Adams, Ralph James Q. *Arms and the Wizard, Lloyd George and the Ministry of Munitions, 1915–1916*. College Station: Texas A&M University Press, 1978.

Adamthwaite, Anthony. *Grandeur and Misery: France's Bid For Power in Europe, 1914–1940*. London and New York: Arnold, 1995.

Albrecht-Carrié, René. *A Diplomatic History of Europe Since the Congress of Vienna*. New York: Harper & Brothers, 1958.

——. *France, Europe, and the Two World Wars*. New York: Harper, 1961.

Alexander, Fred. *From Paris to Locarno and After, The League of Nations and the Search For Security, 1919–1928*. London and Toronto: J. M. Dent & Sons, 1928.

Ambrosius, Lloyd E. *Woodrow Wilson and the American Diplomatic Tradition: The Treaty Fight in Perspective*. Cambridge: Cambridge University Press, 1987.

Angell, James W. *The Recovery of Germany*. New Haven, CT Yale University Press: 1929.

Aston, Sir George. *The Biography of the Late Marshal Foch*. New York: Macmillan, 1929.

Batty, Peter. *The House of Krupp*. New York: Stein & Day, 1966.

Bell, P.M.H. *France and Britain 1900–1940: Entente and Estrangement*. London and New York: Longman Group, 1996.

Bennett, G.H. *British Foreign Policy During the Curzon Period, 1919–1924.* London: St. Martin's Press, 1995.

Benoist-Mechin, Jacques. *Histoire de l'Armée Allemande 1918–1946,* 10 vols. Paris, 1936 (reprint A. Michel, 1964).

Berlia, Georges. *Le problème internationale de la sécurité de la France.* Cours de Grands Problèmes Politiques Contemporains. Paris: Le cours de droit, 1967.

Bessel, Richard. *Germany After the First World War.* London and New York: Oxford University Press, 1993.

Birdsall, Paul. *Versailles: Twenty Years After.* New York: Reynal and Hitchcock, 1941.

Birn, Donald S. *The League of Nations Union, 1918–1945.* Oxford: Clarendon Press, 1981.

Boadle, Donald G. *Winston Churchill and the German Question in British Foreign Policy, 1918–1922.* The Hague: Martinus Nijhoff, 1973.

Boemeke, Manfred F., Gerald D. Feldman, and Elisabeth Glaser, (ed). *The Treaty of Versailles: A Reassessment After 75 Years.* Cambridge: Cambridge University Press, 1998.

Bond, B. *British Military Policy Between the Two World Wars.* Oxford: Clarendon Press, 1980.

Bretton, Henry. *Stresemann and the Revision of Versailles: A Fight For Reason.* Stanford, CA: Stanford University Press, 1953.

Bruun, Geoffrey. *Clemenceau.* Cambridge, MA: Harvard University Press, 1943.

Carr, Edward H. *Britain, A Study of Foreign Policy From the Versailles Treaty to the Outbreak of War.* London: Longmans, Green & Co., 1939.

———. *International Relations Between the Two World Wars, 1919–1939.* London: Macmillan, 1963.

———. *The Twenty Years' Crisis, 1919–1939.* London: Macmillan, 1939.

Carsten, Francis Ludwig. *Britain and the Weimar Republic.* New York: Schocken, 1984.

———. *The Reichswehr and Politics: 1918–1933.* Berkeley: University of California Press, 1966.

Chaput, Rolland. *Disarmament in British Foreign Policy.* London: Allen & Unwin, 1935.

Chastenet, Jacques. *Raymond Poincaré.* Paris: Julliard, 1948.

———. *L'Histoire de la Troisième Republique.* Vol. 5. *Les années d'illusion, 1918–1931.* Paris: Hachette, 1960.

Connell, John (pseud. for John Robertson). *The "Office"; a Study of British Foreign Policy and its Makers, 1919–1951.* New York: St. Martin's Press, 1958.

Craig, Gordon A. *Germany, 1866–1945.* Oxford and New York: Oxford University Press, 1978.

———. *The Politics of the Prussian Army, 1640–1945.* New York: Oxford University Press, 1964. First published 1955.

Craig, Gordon A. and Felix Gilbert. *The Diplomats: 1919–1939.* Princeton, NJ: Princeton University Press, 1953 (reprint New York: Atheneum, 1965).

Czernin, Ferdinand. *Versailles, 1919, The Forces, Events, and Personalities That Shaped the Treaty.* New York: G.P. Putnam's Sons, 1964.

Dallas, Gregor. *At the Heart of the Tiger, Clemenceau and His World 1841–1929.* New York: Carroll & Graf, 1993.

Dawson, William H. *Germany Under the Treaty.* London: Allen & Unwin, 1933.

Diehl, James M. *Paramilitary Politics in Weimar Germany*. Bloomington and London: Indiana University Press, 1977.

Dockrill, Michael. *British Establishment Perspectives on France, 1936–40*. New York: St. Martin's Press, 1999.

Dockrill, Michael and John Fisher. *The Paris Peace Conference, 1919: Peace Without Victory?* New York: Palgrave, 2001.

Dockrill, Michael and Brian McKercher (ed). *Diplomacy and World Power*. Cambridge: Cambridge University Press, 1996.

Dockrill, Michael and Douglas Goold. *Peace Without Promise: Britain and the Peace Conferences, 1919–1923*. Hamden, CoT: Archon Books, 1981.

Doerr, Paul W. *British Foreign Policy 1919–1939*. Manchester and New York: Manchester University Press, 1998.

Dugdale, Blanche. *Arthur James Balfour*, 2 Vols. New York: Putnam's Sons, 1937.

Duroselle, Jean B. *La politique extérieure de la France de 1914–1945*. Paris: Centre de documentature universitaire, 1965.

Dutton, David. *Austen Chamberlain: Gentleman in Politics*. Bolton, Lancs: Ross Anderson Publications, 1985.

Dyakov, Yuri and Tatyana Bushuyeva. *The Red Army and the Wehrmacht: How the Soviets Militarized Germany, 1922–1933, and Paved the Way For Fascism*. Amherst, NY: Prometheus Books, 1995.

Edmonds, J.E. *The Occupation of the Rhineland*. London: HM Stationery Office, 1944 (reprint 1987).

Eyck, Erich. *A History of the Weimar Republic*, 2 vols, trans. Harlan P. Hanson and Robert G. L. Waite. Cambridge, MA: Harvard University Press, 1962.

Falls, Cyril. *Marshal Foch*. London: Blackie & Son, 1939.

Felix, David. *Walter Rathenau and the Weimar Republic: The Politics of Reparation*. Baltimore, MD, and London: Johns Hopkins University Press, 1971.

Ferris, John R. *Men, Money, and Diplomacy: The Evolution of British Strategic Policy, 1919–1926*. Cornell, NY: Ithaca University Press, 1989.

Fink, C. *The Genoa Conference: European Diplomacy, 1921–1922*. Chapel Hill: University of North Carolina Press, 1984.

——. *Genoa, Rapallo, and European Reconstruction in 1922*. Cambridge: Cambridge University Press, 1991.

Floto, Inga. *Colonel House in Paris: A Study of American Policy at the Paris Peace Conference 1919*. Princeton, NJ: Princeton University Press, 1973.

Fraenkel, Ernst. *Military Ocupation and the Rule of Law: Occupation Government in the Rhineland, 1918–1923*. London, New York, and Toronto: Oxford University Press, 1944.

François-Poncet, André. *De Versailles à Potsdam, la France et la Problème Allemande Contemporain, 1919–1943*. Paris: Flammarion, 1948.

French, David. *The Strategy of the Lloyd George Coalition 1916–1918*. Oxford: Clarendon Press, 1995.

Fry, Michael G. *Lloyd George and Foreign Policy*. Montreal and London: McGill-Queen's University Press, 1977.

Furnia, Arthur. *The Diplomacy of Appeasement: Anglo–French Relations and the Prelude to World War II*. The University Press of Washington, DC, 1960.

Gatzke, Hans W. *Stresemann and the Rearmament of Germany*. Baltimore, MD: Johns Hopkins University Press, 1954.

—— (ed.). *European Diplomacy Between Two Wars, 1919–1939.* Chicago: Quadrangle, 1972.

Gavin, Catherine. *Britain and France: A Study of Twentieth Century Relations.* London: Jonathan Cape, 1941.

Gilbert, Martin. *Britain and Germany Between the Wars.* London: Longmans, 1964.

——. *The First World War, A Complete History.* New York: Henry Holt, 1994.

——. (ed.). *Lloyd George.* Englewood Cliffs, NJ: Prentice Hall, 1968.

——. *The Roots of Appeasement.* New York: The New American Library, 1966.

Glasgow, George. *MacDonald as Diplomatist: The Foreign Policy of the First Labour Government in Great Britain.* London: Jonathan Cape, 1924.

Gordon, Harold. *The Reichswehr and the German Republic 1919–1926.* Princeton, NJ: Princeton University Press, 1957.

Görlitz, Walter. *History of the German General Staff.* New York: Praeger, 1953.

Grathwol, Robert. *Stresemann and the DNVP.* Lawrence: The Regents Press of Kansas, 1980.

Grayson, Richard. *Austen Chamberlain and the Commitment to Europe: British Foreign Policy, 1924–1929.* London and Portland, OR: Frank Cass, 1997.

Gudgin, Peter. *Military Intelligence, The British Story.* London: Arms and Armour Press, 1989.

Haigh, R. H. *British Politics and Society, 1918–1938: The Effect on Appeasement.* Manhattan, KA: Military Affairs/Aerospace Historian Publishers, 1980.

Hankey, Lord Maurice. *Diplomacy By Conference 1920–1941.* London: E. Benn, 1946.

——. *The Supreme Council at the Paris Peace Conference.* London: Allen & Unwin, 1963.

Headlam-Morley, James. *Studies in Diplomatic History.* New York: Alfred H. King, 1930.

Heald, Stephen A. *Memorandum on the Progress of Disarmament, 1919–1932.* London: Royal Institute of International Affairs, 1932.

Higham, Robin. *Armed Forces in Peacetime: Britain, 1918–1940, A Case Study.* Hamden, CT Orchor Books, 1962.

Hilger, Gustav. *The Incompatible Allies.* New York: Macmillan, 1953.

Holborn, Hajo. *A History of Modern Germany, 1840–1945.* Princeton, NJ: Princeton University Press, 1969.

House, Edward and Charles Seymour. *What Really Happened at Paris: The Story of the Peace Conference, 1918–1919.* New York: Charles Scribner's Sons, 1921.

Hovi, Kalervo. *Cordon Sanitaire or Barrière de l'Est? The Emergence of the New French Eastern European Alliance Policy, 1917–1919.* Turku, Finland: Turun Yliopisto, 1975.

Howard, John E. *Parliament and Foreign Policy in France, 1919–1939.* London: Cresset Press, 1948.

Hughes, Judith M. *To the Maginot Line: The Politics of French Military Preparedness in the 1920s.* Cambridge, MA: Harvard University Press, 1971.

Jacobson, Jon. *Locarno Diplomacy: Germany and the West, 1925–1929.* Princeton, NJ: Princeton University Press, 1972.

Jaffe, Lorna S. *The Decision To Disarm Germany: British Policy Towards Postwar German Disarmament, 1914–1919.* Boston, MA: Allen & Unwin, 1985.

Jenkins, Roy. *Baldwin.* London: Collins, 1987.

Johnson, Gaynor. *The Berlin Embassy of Lord D'Abernon, 1920–1926.* Basingstoke, Palgrave, 2002.

Jordan, William M. *Great Britain, France and the German Problem 1918–1939.* London: Oxford University Press, 1943.

Keeton, Edward David. *Briand's Locarno Policy: French Economics, Politics, and Diplomacy 1925–1929.* New York: Garland, 1987.

Kennedy, Paul. *Strategy and Diplomacy, 1870–1945.* London and Boston, MA: Allen & Unwin, 1983.

King, Jere Clemens. *Foch Versus Clemenceau: France and German Dismemberment, 1918–1919.* Cambridge, MA: Harvard University Press, 1960.

Kleine-Ahlbrandt, William Laird. *The Burden of Victory: France, Britain and the Enforcement of the Versailles Peace, 1919–1925.* New York, London, and Lanham: University Press of America, 1995.

Kochan, Lionel. *The Struggle for Germany, 1914–1945.* Edinburgh: Edinburgh University Press, 1963.

Kocka, Jurgen. *Facing Total War: German Society 1914–1918.* Cambridge, MA: Harvard University Press, 1984.

Lentin, Antony. *Lloyd George and the Lost Peace: From Versailles to Hitler, 1919–1940.* Basingstoke: Palgrave, 2001.

Lewis, S.J. *Forgotten Legions: German Infantry Policy, 1918–1941.* New York: Praeger, 1985.

Liang, Hsi-Huey. *The Berlin Police Force in the Weimar Republic.* Berkeley: University of California Press, 1970.

Liddell Hart, B.H. *Foch: The Man of Orleans.* Boston, MA: Little, Brown, 1932.

Lowe, C.J. and M.L. Dockrill. *The Mirage of Power: British Foreign Policy, 1902–1922,* 3 vols. London, and Boston, MA: Routledge & Kegan Paul, 1972.

Lowry, Bullitt. *Armistice 1918.* Kent, Ohio, and London UK: The Kent University Press, 1996.

Luckau, Alma. *The German Delegation at the Paris Peace Conference.* New York: Columbia University Press, 1940.

Luvaas, Jay. *The Education of an Army: British Military Thought 1915–1940.* Chicago, IL: The University of Chicago Press, 1964.

McDougall, Walter. *France's Rhineland Diplomacy.* Princeton, NJ: Princeton University Press, 1978.

McKercher, B.J.C. and D.J. Moss (eds). *Shadow and Substance in British Foreign Policy, 1895–1939.* Edmonton: The University of Alberta Press, 1984.

MacMillan, Margaret Olwen. *Paris 1919: Six Months That Changed the World.* New York: Random House, 2002.

Manchester, William. *The Arms of Krupp 1587–1968.* Boston, MA, and Toronto: Little, Brown, 1968.

Marks, Sally. *The Illusion of Peace.* New York: St. Martin's Press, 1976.

Marquand, David. *Ramsay MacDonald.* London: Jonathan Cape, 1977.

Mayer, Arno J. *Political Origins of the New Diplomacy, 1917–1918.* Hamden, CT: Yale University Press, 1959.

Medlicott, W.N. *British Foreign Policy Since Versailles.* London: Methuen, 1940.

Mee, Charles L. Jr. *The End of Order: Versailles 1919.* New York: E.P. Dutton, 1980.

Menne, Bernhard. *Krupp: The Lords of Essen.* London: William Hodge & Co., 1937.

Middlemas, Keith and John Barnes. *Baldwin, A Biography*. New York: Macmillan, 1970.

Millett, Allan R. and Williamson Murray. *Military Effectiveness, Volume II: The Interwar Period*, ed. Allan R. Millet and Williamson Murray. Boston, MA: Allen & Unwin, 1988.

Mommsen, Hans. *The Rise and Fall of Weimar Democracy*. Chapel Hill: University of North Carolina Press, 1996.

Morgan, Austen. *James Ramsay MacDonald*. Manchester: Manchester University Press, 1987.

Mowat, Charles. *Britain Between the Wars 1918–1940*. Chicago, IL: University of Chicago Press, 1955.

Mowat, R.B. *A History of European Diplomacy, 1914–1925*. London: Edward Arnold, 1927.

Nelson, Harold. *Land and Power: British and Allied Policy on the German Frontier, 1916–1919*. London: Routledge & Kegan Paul, 1963.

Nelson, Keith. *Victors Divided: America and the Allies in Germany, 1918–1923*. Berkeley, University of California Press, 1975.

Néré, Jacques. *The Foreign Policy of France from 1914 to 1945*. London and Boston, MA: Routledge & Kegan Paul, 1975.

Newman, William J. *The Balance of Power in the Interwar Years, 1919–1939*. New York: Random House, 1968.

Newton, Douglas. *British Policy and the Weimar Republic, 1918–1919*. Oxford: Clarendon Press, 1997.

Nicolson, Harold. *Curzon: The Last Phase 1919–1925*. Boston, MA, and New York: Houghton Mifflin, 1934.

Noble, G. Bernard. *Policies and Opinions at Paris, 1919, Wilsonian Diplomacy, the Versailles Peace, and French Public Opinion*. New York: Macmillan, 1935.

Northedge, F.S. *The Troubled Giant: Britain Among the Great Powers 1916–1939*. New York: Praeger, 1966.

Orde, Anne. *Great Britain and International Security, 1920–1926*. London: Royal Historical Society, 1978.

O'Riordan, Elspeth Y. *Britain and the Ruhr Crisis*. Basingstoke: Palgrave, 2001.

Ostrower, Gary B. *The League of Nations From 1919 to 1929*. Garden City, NY: Avery Publishing, 1996.

Palmer, Frederick C. *Bliss, Peacemaker: The Life and Letters of General Tasker Howard Bliss*. New York: Dodd, Mead & Co., 1934.

Pink, Gerhard. *The Conference of Ambassadors 1920–1931*. Geneva: Geneva Research Centre, 1942.

Pitts, Vincent, J. *France and the German Problem: Politics and Economics in the Locarno Period 1924–1929*. New York: Garland, 1987.

Posen, Barry R. *The Sources of Military Doctrine: France, Britain, and Germany Between the World Wars*. Ithaca, NY: Cornell University Press, 1984.

Renouvin, Pierre. *War and Aftermath, 1914–1929*, trans. Remy Hall. New York: Harper & Row, 1968.

Reynolds, Philip Alan. *British Foreign Policy in the Interwar Years*. London and New York: Longmans, 1954.

Richardson, Dick. *The Evolution of British Disarmament Policy in the 1920s*. New York: St. Martin's Press, 1989.

Riddell, Lord George. *Lord Riddell's Intimate Diary of the Peace Conference and After*. New York: Reynal & Hitchcock, 1934.

Rohde, Hans. *Franco-German Factors of Power: Comparative Studies of the Problem of Disarmament*. Berlin: Berliner Borsen Zeitung, 1932.

Rothwell, V.H. *British War Aims and Peace Diplomacy, 1914–1918*. Oxford: Clarendon Press, 1971.

Rowland, Peter. *Lloyd George*. London: Barrie & Jenkins, 1975.

Rudin, Harry R. *Armistice 1918*. New Haven, CT: Yale University Press, 1944.

Salewski, Michael. *Entwaffnung und Militärkontrolle in Deutschland, 1919–1927*. Munich: R. Oldenbourg Verlag, 1966.

Schmidt, Royal J. *Versailles and the Ruhr, Seedbed of World War II*. The Hague: Martinus Nijhogg, 1968.

Schnee, Heinrich and Hans Draeger. *Zehn Jahre Versailles, 1919–1929*. Berlin: Breckenverlag, 1929–30.

Schuker, Stephen A. *The End of French Predominance in Europe: The Financial Crisis of 1924 and the Adoption of the Dawes Plan*. Chapel Hill: University of North Carolina Press, 1976.

Schwabe, Klaus. *Woodrow Wilson, Revolutionary Germany, and Peacemaking, 1918–1919, Missionary Diplomacy and the Realities of Power*, trans. Rita and Robert Kimber. Chapel Hill and London: University of North Carolina Press, 1985.

Seymour, Charles. *Letters From the Paris Peace Conference*. Hamden, CT: Yale University Press, 1965.

Sharp, Alan. *The Versailles Treaty: Peacemaking in Paris, 1919*. New York: St. Martin's Press, 1991.

Shartle, Samuel. *Spa, Versailles, Munich: An Account of the Armistice Commission*. Philadelphia, PA: Dorrance & Co., 1941.

Shotwell, James T. *At the Paris Peace Conference*. New York: Macmillan, 1937.

Sontag, Raymond. *A Broken World, 1919–1939*. The Rise of Modern Europe. New York: Harper & Row, 1968.

——. *European Diplomatic History, 1871–1932*. New York and London: The Century Company, 1933.

Spaight, James. *Pseudo-Security*. London and New York: Longmans, Green, & Company, 1928.

Spires, David. *Image and Reality: The Making of the German Officer, 1921–1933*. Westport, CT: Greenwood, 1984.

Stevenson, David. *French War Aims Against Germany, 1914–1919*. Oxford: Clarendon Press, 1982.

Sutton, Eric (ed.). *Gustav Stresemann, His Diaries, Letters and Papers*, 2 vols. New York: Macmillan, 1935.

Temperley, Major-General A.C. *The Whispering Gallery of Europe*. London: Collins, 1938.

Thomas, Valentine. *Briand, Man of Peace*. New York: Covici-Friede, 1930.

Thompson, John M. *Russia, Bolshevism, and the Versailles Peace*. Princeton, NJ: Princeton University Press, 1966.

Tillman, Seth P. *Anglo–American Relations at the Paris Peace Conference of 1919*. Princeton, NJ: Princeton University Press, 1961.

Towle, Philip. *Enforced Disarmament: From the Napoleonic Campaigns to the Gulf War*. Oxford: Clarendon Press, 1997.

Toynbee, Arnold J. *Survey of International Affairs 1920–1923*. London: Royal Institute of International Affairs, 1925.

——. *Survey of International Affairs 1924*. London: RIIA, 1926.

——. *Survey of International Affairs 1925*. 2 Vols. London: RIIA, 1927.

——. *Survey of International Affairs 1926*.

——. *Survey of International Affairs 1927*.

Trachtenberg, Marc. *Reparation in World Politics: France and European Diplomacy, 1916–1923*. New York: Columbia University Press, 1980.

Turner, Henry. *Stresemann and the Politics of the Weimar Republic*. Princeton, NJ: Princeton University Press, 1963.

Vallentin, Antonia. *Stresemann*. New York: R.R. Smith, 1931.

von Klass, Gert. *Krupp: The Story of an Industrial Empire*, trans. James Cleugh. London: Sidgwick & Jackson, 1954.

Waite, Robert G. L. *Vanguard of Nazism: The Free-Corps Movement in Postwar Germany 1918–1923*. Cambridge, MA: Harvard University Press, 1952.

Waites, N.H. *Troubled Neighbors: Franco–British Relations in the Twentieth Century*. London: Weidenfeld, 1971.

Walworth, Arthur. *Wilson and His Peacemakers: American Diplomacy at the Paris Peace Conference, 1919*. New York: W.W. Norton, 1986.

Wandycz, Piotr. *France and Her Eastern Allies, 1919–1925: French–Czechoslovak–Polish Relations From the Paris Peace Conference to Locarno*. Minneapolis: University of Minnesota Press, 1962.

——. *The Twilight of French Eastern Alliances, 1926–1936: French-Czechoslovak–Polish Relations From the Paris Peace Conference to Locarno*. Princeton, NJ: Princeton University Press, 1988.

Watson, David K. *Clemenceau: A Political Biography*. London: Eyre-Methuen, 1974.

Weinberg, Gerhard. *A World at Arms*. Cambridge: Cambridge University Press, 1994.

Whaley, Barton. *Covert German Rearmament 1919–1939*. Frederick, MD: University Publications of America, 1984.

Wheeler-Bennett, John W. *Disarmament and Security Since Locarno 1925–1931*. London: Allen & Unwin, 1932.

——. *Germany and Disarmament*. London: Chatham House, 1933.

——. *Information on the Reduction of Armaments*. London: Alan & Unwin, 1925.

——. *The Nemesis of Power. The German Army in Politics, 1918–1945*. London: Macmillan, 1954.

Williamson, David G. *The British in Germany, 1918–1930: The Reluctant Occupiers*. New York and Oxford: Berg Publishers, 1991.

Wolfers, Arnold. *Britain and France Between Two Wars: Conflicting Strategies of Peace Since Versailles*. New York: Harcourt, Brace, 1940.

Woodward, David R. *Lloyd George and the Generals*. London and Toronto: Associated University Presses, 1983.

Wright, Gordon. *Raymond Poincaré and the French Presidency*. Stanford, CA: Stanford University Press, 1942.

Wrigley, Chris. *David Lloyd George and the British Labor Movement, Peace and War*. Hassocks, SX: The Harvester Press, 1976.

——. *Lloyd George*. Oxford, and Cambridge, MA: Blackwell, 1992.

Yates, Louis. *United States and French Security, 1917–1921*. New York: Twayne Publishers, 1957.

Young, Gordon. *The Fall and Rise of Alfried Krupp*. London: Cassell, 1960.
Zimmern, Alfred Eckhard. *British Foreign Policy Since the War*. Nottingham, University College, 1934.
——. *The League of Nations and the Rule of Law, 1918–1935*. London: Macmillan, 1936.

Periodicals

Le Matin
Le Temps
The Manchester Guardian
The Times (London)

Articles

Artaud, Denise. "À propos de l'occupation de la Ruhr." *Revue d'Histoire Moderne et Contemporaine*, 1970, 17: 1–21.
Bariety, Jacques. "La Place de la France dans la 'Westorientung.'" *Revue d'Allemagne*, 1976, 8 (1): 35–50.
Burns, Richard Dean. "International Arms Inspection Policies Between World Wars, 1919–1934." *Historian*, 1969, 31 (4): 583–603.
——. "Supervision, Control and Inspection of Armaments: 1919–1941." *Orbis*, 1971, 15 (3): 943–52.
Carley, Michael J. "Le déclin d'une grande puissance: La politique étrangère de la France en Europe, 1914–24." *Canadian Journal of History*, 1986, 21: 397–407.
Carlton, David. "The Anglo–French Compromise on Arms Limitation, 1928." *Journal of British Studies*, 1969, 8: 141–62.
Carroll, Bernice A. "Germany Disarmed and Rearming, 1925–1935." *Journal of Peace Research*, 1966, 3 (2): 114–24.
Crowe, Sybil. "Sir Eyre Crowe and the Locarno Pact." *English Historical Review*, 1972, 87: 49–74.
Crozier, Andrew. "The Colonial Question in Stresemann's Locarno Policy." *International History Review*, 1982, 4 (1): 37–54.
Dent, Philip. "The D'Abernon Papers: Origins of 'Appeasement.'" *British Museum Quarterly*, 1973, 37: 103–7.
Duroselle, Jean-Baptiste. "Reconsidering the Spirit of Locarno: Illusions of Pactomania." *Foreign Affairs*, 1972, 50: 752–64.
——. "French Diplomacy in the Postwar World." *Diplomacy in a Changing World*, pp. 204–8. Notre Dame: 1954.
Enssle, Manfred. "Stresemann's Diplomacy Fifty Years After Locarno: Some Recent Perspectives." *Historical Journal*, 1977, 20 (4): 937–48.
Fox, John P. "Britain and the Inter-Allied Military Commission of Control, 1925–26." *Journal of Contemporary History*, 1969, 4 (2): 143–64.
Grathwol, Robert. "Stresemann Revisited." *European Studies Review*, 1977, 7 (3): 341–52.
——. "Gustav Stresemann: Reflections on His Foreign Policy." *Journal of Modern History*, 1973, 45 (1), 52–70.
Graubard, Stephen R. "Military Demobilization in Great Britain Following the First World War." *Journal of Modern History*, 1947, 19: 297–311.

Guinn, Paul. "On Throwing Ballast in Foreign Policy: Poincaré, the Entente and the Ruhr Occupation." *European History Quarterly*, 1988, 18: 427–37.

Hänsel, Werner. "Historische Aspekte der Abrüstung in Deutschland und die Rüstungskonversion in der DDR." *Militärgeschichte*, 1990, 29 (4): 379–83.

Heideking, Jürgen. "Vom Versailler Vertrag zur Genfer Abrüstungskonferenz: Das Scheitern der Alliierten Militärkontrollpolitik gegenüber Deutschland nach dem Ersten Weltkrieg." *Militärgeschichtliche Mitteilungen*, 1980 (2): 45–68.

Jacobson, Jon. "Strategies of French Foreign Policy After World War I." *Journal of Modern History*, 1983, 55 (1): 78–95.

Jacobson, Jon and John T. Walker. "The Impulse For a Franco–German Entente: The Origins of the Thoiry Conference, 1926." *Journal of Contemporary History*, 1975, 10 (1): 157–81.

Johnson, Douglas. "Austen Chamberlain and the Locarno Agreements." *University of Birmingham Historical Journal*, 1961, 8: 60–91.

Large, David Clay. "The Politics of Law and Order: A History of the Bavarian Einwohnerwehr, 1981–1921." *Transactions of the American Philosophical Society*, 1980, 70 (2): pp. 1–87.

McKercher, B.J.C. "Austen Chamberlain's Control of British Policy 1924–1929." *International History Review*, 1984, 6 (4): 570–91.

Marcks, Erich. "France's Security." *The Problem of Disarmament*. English Supplement of the *Zeitschrift fur Politik*, ed. Richard Schmidt and Adolf Grabowsky. Berlin: Carl Heymanns Verlag, 1933.

Marks, Sally. "The Misery of Victory: France's Struggle for the Versailles Treaty." *Canadian Historical Journal*, 1986: 117–33.

——. "1918 and After: The Postwar Era." *The Origins of the Second World War: Reconsidered*, pp. 17–48, ed. Gordon Martel. Boston, MA: Allen & Unwin, 1986.

Péron, Jean-Paul. "Le Réarmement de l'Allemagne Entre les Deux Guerres Mondiales." *Information Historique*, 1974, 36 (5): 242–9; 1975, 37 (1): 53–7.

Renouvin, Pierre. "Les buts de guerre du gouvernement français, 1914–1918." *Revue historique*, 1966: 1–38.

Schuker, Stephen A. "The End of Versailles." *The Origins of the Second World War: Reconsidered*, pp. 49–72, ed. Gordon Martel. Boston, MA: Allen & Unwin, 1986.

Sharp, Alan J. "The Foreign Office in Eclipse, 1919–1922." *History*, 1976, 61: 198–218.

Smith, Arthur L. Jr. "Le Désarmement de l'Allemagne en 1919: Les Vues du Général von Seeckt." *Revue Historique*, 1962, 228 (1): 17–34.

Stambrook, F.G. "The Foreign Secretary and Foreign Policy: The Experiences of Austen Chamberlain in 1925 and 1927." *International Review of History and Political Science*, 1969, 6: 109–27.

——. "'Das Kind': Lord D'Abernon and the Origins of the Locarno Pact." *Central European History*, 1968, 1: 233–63.

Tournoux, P.E. "Si l'on a ecouté Foch." *Revue des Deux Mondes*, 1959, 17: 84–92.

Towle, Philip. "Realpolitik, Deceit, and Disarmament." *Army Quarterly and Defence Journal*, 1981, 111 (1): 62–72.

Trachtenberg, Marc. "Versailles after Sixty Years." *Journal of Contemporary History*, 1982, 17: 487–506.

Turner, Arthur. "Austen Chamberlain, The Times and the Question of Revision of the Treaty of Versailles in 1933." *European History Quarterly*, 1988, 18 (1): 51–70.

Whaley, Barton. "Covert Rearmament in Germany 1919–1939: Deception and Misperception." *Journal of Strategic Studies*, 1982, 5 (1): 3–39.

Williamson, David G. "Cologne and the British." *History Today*, 1977, 27: 695–702.

——. "Great Britain and the Ruhr Crisis, 1923–24." *British Journal of International Studies*, 1977, 3: 70–91.

Wright, Jonathan. "Stresemann and Weimar." *History Today*, 1989, 39: 35–41.

Dissertations and theses

Boyle, Thomas E. *France, Great Britain, and German Disarmament, 1919–1927.* Yale University, 1972.

Fike, Stephen. *Germany and the Disarmament Movement, 1919–1933.* Masters thesis, University of Maryland, 1974.

Ruine, Joan Jane. *Anglo–French Diplomatic Relations, 1923–1936.* Masters thesis, Georgetown University, 1949.

Simon, Han Paul. *The German Response to Allied Demands for Disarmament, 1918 to 1924.* University of Toronto, 1978.

Twichell, Heath Jr. *The German Army and Disarmament During the Weimar Period: A Study of the Evasion of the Disarmament Provisions of the Treaty of Versailles.* Masters thesis, The American University, 1964.

Index